THE EXPANDED FIELD OF CONSERVATION

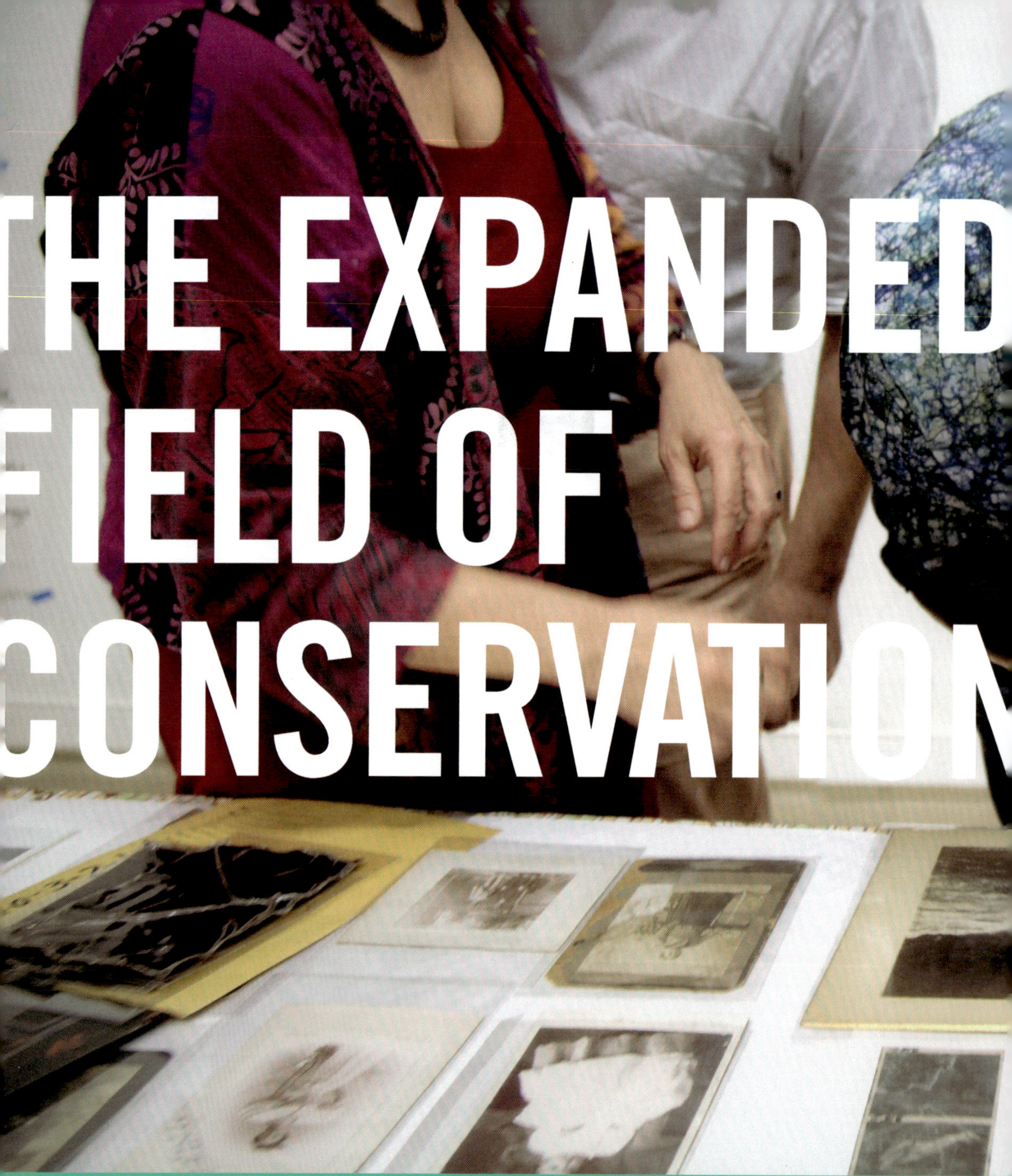

THE EXPANDED FIELD OF CONSERVATION

Clark Studies
in the Visual Arts

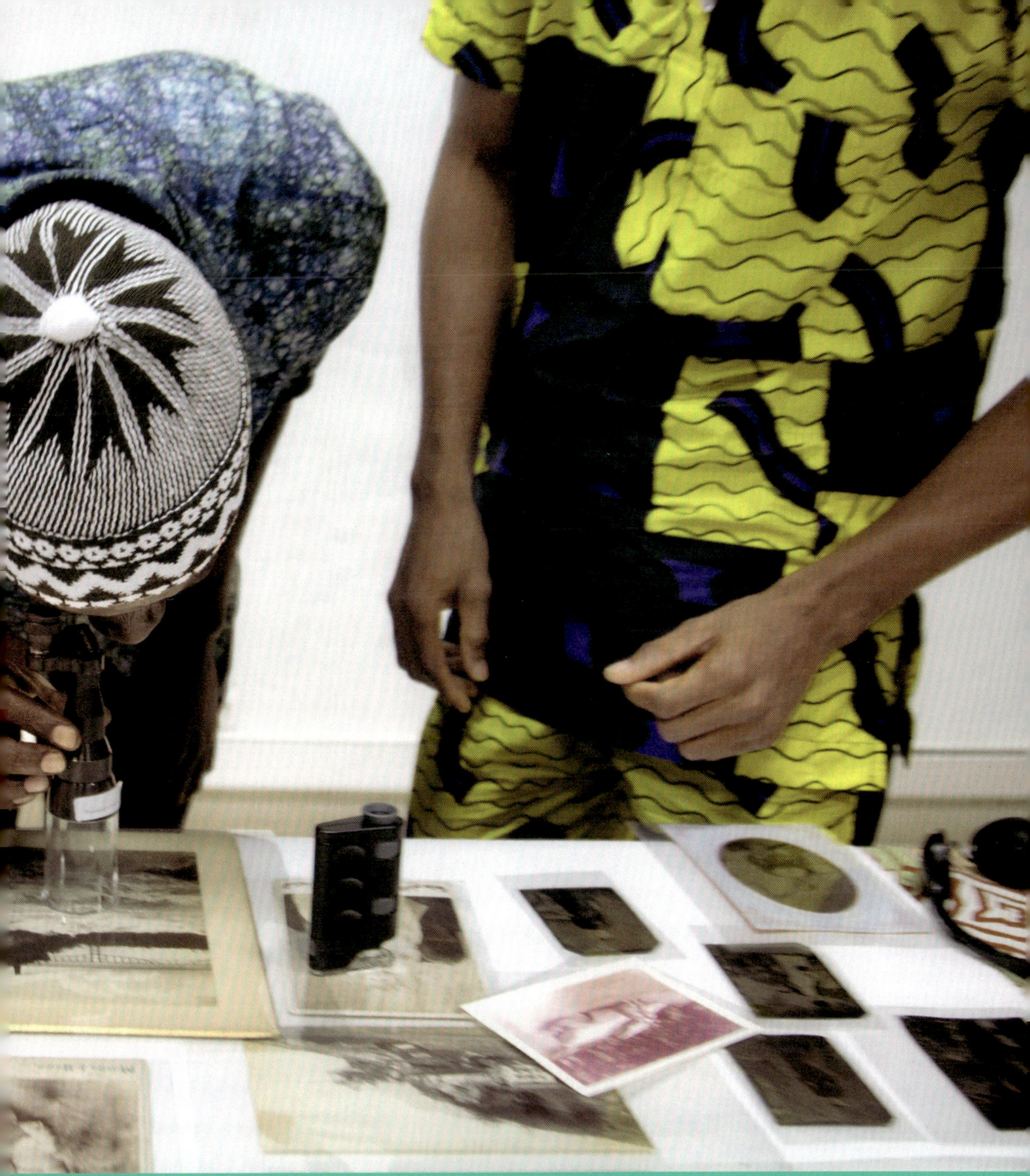

Edited by
Caroline Fowler
and Alexander Nagel

Clark Art Institute
Williamstown, Massachusetts

Distributed by Yale University Press
New Haven and London

CONTENTS

PREFACE

This volume is about how methods of conservation determine the object of art history, and about how ways of thinking about art and its history shape approaches to conservation. We originally conceived of the conference preceding this publication, titled Conservation | Making | Art | History, held at the Clark Art Institute April 8–9, 2021, as a much-needed dialogue between scholars trained in conservation and those in art history. As the conversation continued, the scope and definition of what can be called conservation expanded before our eyes, leading us to a wider engagement of disciplinary perspectives, including art history, anthropology, comparative literature, media theory, art practice, and philosophy.

All the contributors to this volume share a belief that approaches to conservation are integral to the political and institutional histories that put works of visual art on display, set them into ideological frameworks, and give them voice across space and time. To grasp these interactions is basic to understanding how communities come into definition by shaping their pasts as they are shaped by them, and also to seeing how communities disappear or are erased. For the scholars in this volume, writing about art is inseparable from thinking about how it is cared for, archived, classified, mounted, preserved, made to move, undone, and remade. The essays that follow approach works of visual art not as images but as participants within particular environments. They approach conservation not only as something that occurs in a lab but as an array of practices that respond to the work as an invitation to act on it in the present and so give it a role into a future.

Some key interlocutors from the conference chose not to contribute to the written volume, and we would like to recognize their important voices as nonetheless necessarily present within our thinking and dialogue. Thank you to Ina Archer, Chương-Đài VÕ, Fatima Fall, Erma Hermens, and Jacqueline Stewart.

Caroline Fowler
Starr Director
Research and Academic Program
Clark Art Institute

Alexander Nagel
Craig Hugh Smyth Professor of Renaissance Art
Institute of Fine Arts
New York University

INTRODUCTION
CONSERVATION AS PERFORMANCE

Alexander Nagel

For Preservation is a Creation; and more, it is a continued Creation, and a creation every moment.

—George Herbert

Biological humans existed for more than 100,000 years before they started to make works of visual art about 70,000 years ago, first abstract patterns and then figurative art. Art did not happen because we became human, but was part of the process through which we developed the capacities we have, eventually becoming part of what defines us. Visual art is not a by-product of biological humanity but an essential part of what makes us what we are.

Works of visual art are both related to and different from ephemeral modes of performance, such as the preliminary form of theater that arose when early human hunters recounted their exploits to those who had remained at the camp, or when they acted out their experiences with their hunting mates, or in those situations where rhythm keeping and singing developed their earliest forms. Works of physical art are ways of extending forms and communications beyond events and also beyond performative commemorations, propitiations, lustrations, and other organized actions. An artifact makes it possible for an expression to extend in time, sometimes far beyond the maker's life, and also in space, as objects and/or their copies travel, reaching communities far from the maker of the work or its first audience. Sometimes the intention is to make works of physical art extend in this way, and sometimes it is not, yet it happens that they extend anyway. If they are preserved by subsequent generations, it is because those later people took some responsibility for a work, either by interacting with it, ritually or more informally, or simply by housing it, by putting up some resistance to the course of entropy. And then there are the chance survivals buried in the earth or in ice, or submerged in water, or even above ground, as permitted by particular geological and atmospheric conditions.

Humans choose to preserve even as physical materials deteriorate, yielding the paradox that works have often been partially or wholly replaced in efforts to make them persist. A fundamental form of preservation is more art making. Most art in most cultures is made out of older art, either materially by reworking or repainting it, or conceptually in the sense that new works are grounded in the forms or techniques of older artworks. Works of art extend into a sort of protracted performance that creates continuity through the discontinuities of human lives and deaths and larger processes, such as displacement or migration. The protracted performance can become the work of whole societies and can, in fact, help produce societies. It seems you cannot have an imagined community without works of visual art. Ephemeral performance is essential and irrepressible, but an extended phase of community develops when communities come together to preserve and extend material memories, something they did long before the development of writing.

Modernism, in its insistence on making it new, might seem to have broken with this age-old conception of art as a process of making, maintenance, and remaking. Yet, as modernism and its aftermaths have themselves become part of art history, it has become easier to see the larger patterns running right through them. This means not only seeing Kazimir Malevich in dialogue with icons, or Marcel Duchamp in the tradition of the relic cult, or Surrealism in relation to occult traditions, or paleolithic art as a modernist discovery. In the last forty years, a retrospective cast has dominated artistic production in general. A number of years ago, the magazine *Artforum* did a roundup of all the different forms of *re-* that dominate contemporary art: *restage*, *reframe*, *remix*, *reperform*, *reinstall*, *refabricate*, etc. They even included the word *relic*—from the Latin *reliquia*, composed of *re-* ("back") + *linquere* ("to leave")—on their list, given the ubiquity of reliquary-like stagings in contemporary art.[1] Reworking older materials now seems as much a part of twentieth-century and contemporary art as of any other period's art.

This volume is an effort to bring into view the expanded field of conservation by considering its involvement with acts of making and remaking, and of making art history. The acts that have gone into the performance of the work are indeed wide ranging. They can include acts of storytelling that have accompanied or contextualized works, as well as acts of physical enshrinement, mounting, framing, and thus protection of works. And they can include ritual cleanings and or repaintings or re-coatings or wholesale replacements of works. Pretty much all the *re-*s are part of the expanded framework in which to think about conservation.

Conservation was isolated from its family of practices when the idea of the artwork as a relic found its institutional home and theoretical justification in proto-museums and then actual museums that arose in the eighteenth and nineteenth centuries in Europe, as well as in the institutions of modern Western art, such as the collection or exhibition catalogue and the mechanisms of the modern art market. The emergence of these institutions had the effect of hiving conservation off from the larger processes I have been describing, sending it out of view and eventually into the lab. And it remains largely out of view to this day, in the sense that it remains separate, specialized, and in a strangely subservient relation to the more public-facing institutions of the museum, the gallery, the auction house, and the publications they produce.

Ritual observance set in motion by and around artifacts can sometimes seem like the opposite of modern practices of conservation, especially when they expose the work to damage and degradation, as when statues are splattered with wax or ash, or works are carried in procession. From the point of view of this volume and the conference that preceded it, however, these practices are to be seen as part of the wider family of practices with which conservation is deeply affiliated. All of these and many other interventions are ways of performing the work.

It is not only the works and their users and audiences that are doing the performing, but also the museums and other art-world institutions that put them on view and give them the life-support systems provided by state-of-the-art conservation labs. All these human and institutional actors perform a constitutive role in the definition and maintenance of art—the definition and maintenance of individual works of art, and of governing ideas of what art is. Several essays in this volume, such as those by Jennifer Bajorek, Brian Michael Murphy, Fernando Domínguez Rubio, and Gabriela Siracusano, extend into areas and problems that are not usually part of the remit of art history, such as storage vaults, transportation networks and shipping containers, air conditioning systems, and the disparity of storage conditions between the global north and global south, thus expanding our understanding of artistic institutions beyond conditions of exhibition and display to a whole infrastructure of maintenance that extends into digitized archives. We go into many of these spaces as we follow Domínguez Rubio down all the paths taken by the institutional work of "mimeographic labor"—the labor of keeping works of art "the same" in the face of passing decades and centuries, as well as exhibition travel. Going down institutional-infrastructural byways also reveals new configurations, new forms of the material, and thus new historical formations. As Murphy shows, for example, the digitization of the Bettmann collection made possible an expanded conception of lynching imagery that challenges long-held categorizations and thus definitions of historical images of racial violence.

As scholars begin to focus on such invisible structures, museums are beginning to experiment with displays of institutional "transparency," such as performative exhibitions devoted to conservation, sometimes placing working conservators on display in museum galleries. As conservation goes on display, historians are getting their hands dirty with reenactments of historical techniques. Sven Dupré engages with performance theory as a means of inserting actors and bodies into narratives that have typically focused on the object as an independent unit free from human intervention in its "materiality." Reperforming the techniques that produced works of the past necessarily takes technical research out of the laboratory and opens up new "epistemologies of reconstruction research."

These recent developments can be seen as efforts to reverse or at least throw light on the cultural shift that moved conservation into the lab about 200 years ago, a development that accompanied the rise of art museums in Europe. Before that shift in the West, and still in many parts of the world, the acts that we would now call conservation practices were inextricably bound up with a host of other practices that make up the performance of the work of visual art. Taking this prehistory as a premise, the essays in this volume reframe even the recent past in taking an emphatically wide view of all those practices that have made up and continue to make up the performance of the work of art, including the interventions that fall under the banner of art conservation as now practiced.

As conservation and preservation—well-defined fields in themselves, with their own experts and historiography—are reconnected with this longer history and wider array of practices, they are not only seen anew but, in fact, change direction, as they are brought into open dialogue with ephemerality, loss, and contingency. Bajorek's essay offers an exploration of the "prospects for bringing Indigenous knowledge and practices into the conversation about conservation" under conditions where the state-of-the-art conditions and technologies described by Domínguez Rubio are not available. Siracusano's essay documents a journey into a world of fragments whose parts allow for multiple assemblies to come into being, inviting historians, curators, and conservators on an adventure for which their training may not have prepared them.

Developing an observation Alois Riegl made over 100 years ago, Noémie Étienne's essay makes clear that the formation of the nation-state and its art historical correlates are inseparable from histories of conservation. Kavita Singh, in turn, reveals how the rhetoric and procedures of monument conservation have been used as a means of advancing an ethnic-nationalist initiative of Hindu temple revival in Tamil Nadu. The aesthetic goal of such initiatives—a look of antiquity that suppresses color—itself, Singh shows, conforms to the standards of the Archaeological Survey, a legacy of colonialism that is now revived in the name of "uplifting the old." Any attempt to decolonize art history, these essays demonstrate, must deal with histories and ideologies of conservation.

Currently, we live in the era of the exhibition industry, a world that came into being in the 1970s and now seems impossible to escape. The temporary exhibition was most commonly used in earlier times to present contemporary art, such as the salons of eighteenth- and nineteenth-century Europe. Before 1970, it was very unusual for museums to host temporary exhibitions; to be a curator meant to be a keeper of a collection, and occasionally to acquire new works. But by 1990, the mode of the exhibition — blockbuster or less than blockbuster — had become the industrial norm and had already provoked hand-wringing editorials in the pages of newspapers and magazines. For the last generation at least, the job description of the curator has been redefined in such a way that the organizing of exhibitions is the curator's central activity, without which no curator can advance in the field. Most people today believe the job of the curator is to make exhibitions.

Much of the work museum conservators currently do is initiated and paid for in relation to an upcoming exhibition. Conservators are often busy preparing objects, as time allows for more intensive conservation, in an effort to ready artworks for travel to exhibitions. Upon a work's return, they inspect it and sometimes repair minor or major damage caused by the travel. As one curator (who will remain anonymous) put it, "The works never come back in better condition." Caroline Fowler's essay offers perhaps the first-ever genre analysis of a primary document resulting from these circumstances — the condition report. The condition report is the institutional response to the acceleration of entropy caused by the transport of works of art for exhibitions.

It is a strange and unsustainable cycle, where the work of conservation is pressed into service to make artworks travel, exposing them to accelerating degradation, giving conservators more work to do. Here again, the conservation work that sustains the exhibition industry, sometimes done under extreme pressure, is done out of view. Exhibition visitors mostly have no clue what efforts went into making a given object magically appear there in the company of the other objects on view. For all the fanfare surrounding the masterpieces made available by an exhibition, there is something disembodied about the assembly of works in an exhibition space. That is the logic of the spectacle — things are made highly available yet somehow unreal. Maybe the whole exhibition complex is our contemporary form of consecration or lustration ceremony.

The halt imposed by the pandemic of 2020–22 has not provoked a major rethinking of the basic protocols of exhibition practice, nor of the role conservation is made to play in those protocols. There has been even less rethinking than there was after the 2008 financial crisis, when for mostly budgetary reasons some museums shifted for a time to exhibitions that were smaller and more focused on their own collections. Yet the time is ripe and the ingredients are there for a forceful redirection. We have, on the one hand, an artistic culture that is retrospective in its orientation and has been engaged for some decades in an active and ongoing redefinition of the boundaries between artworks and exhibitions, and between curatorial and artistic activity. On the other, there is the exhibition industry, constantly sending works of art into circulation. Yet outside of contemporary art, they interact rarely. Strange! The artist as curator, like the artist as art historian and art conservator, is a familiar combination of roles in many cultures, as the essays of Annika Svendsen Finne, Murad Khan Mumtaz, Iwatarō Oka, and Yukio Lippit make clear in subtle detail. What would happen if our culture reanimated this tradition, allowing artists to do more of the managing, presenting, and curating of older art? It is impossible to predict what would happen—a good thing—yet, at the least, it seems likely that exhibitions would become more focused and would move away from the tired model of the fossil fuel–intensive shipping of art trophies around the world.

Even a brief tour through the expanded field of conservation in different cultures reveals a different understanding not only of the shape of art history but of the nature of works of art. As Mumtaz points out, the *vasli* paper used in Persian miniature painting is made by gluing together scraps of paper and then burnishing and sizing the top layer, a multiple-material support for a painting practice (*musavvari*) built out of the citation and combination of models, and for the compiling of paintings from different periods into the form of the album (*muraqqa'*), a word that means "patched" and carries "strong associations with the patched cloak worn by Sufis and dervishes as a sign of spiritual poverty." Dynamics of reuse and repair, he shows, form a pervasive model of artistic practice as well as of the teaching and conservation of art, including his own painting and pedagogy, which are a form of conservation.

Lippit and Oka trace the use, conservation, and reconstitution of mountings in the Japanese tradition of scroll paintings, an approach that encourages us to think in terms of pictorial objects rather than pictures, raising the fundamental question: Where does the artwork, with its surroundings, begin? This also prompts the related question: What is the time of the artwork? The repositories of knowledge of historical mounting practices, Lippit shows, are not art historians but those professionals who engage with traditional crafts in their own work—conservators, dealers, and artists. The extra-academic continuity means the traditions are open to change, as in the case of the photographer, designer, and collector Hiroshi Sugimoto's unprecedented use of silver foil as a mounting surface for an eighth-century sutra fragment inscribed in silver pigment, a work once owned by him and now at the Museum of Fine Arts, Boston. The partly oxidized and tarnished silver surround was, perhaps, Sugimoto's way not only of framing and setting off a venerable work of painting, but of honoring the material fate of this fragment, which had survived a fire at the monastery of Tōdaiji in Kyoto.

Finne returns us to an artistic tradition—the early history of panel painting in Italy—that involved a dynamic interaction of painting with other media, such as sculpture, glyptic, and metalwork, not only in the material embedding or combination of one with the other, but in the continual efforts especially on the part of painting to translate the effects from one medium to another. A practicing artist and conservator as well as an art historian, Finne encourages us to see repaintings of older works, traditionally seen as assertions of the ascendancy of newer styles of painting over older ones, as modes of artistic reworking in line with a skillful managing of "unlikeness" within the tradition itself. To look in this way is to see works, alone or in series, as the result of multiple making, and thus to think outside of models of single authorship that have governed Western art history (and, by extension, art conservation) in recent centuries.

These are some ways to perform the score that is art, in Alva Noë's formulation. How one inhabits these models determines how communities hold space for a past and a future.

NOTES

Epigraph: George Herbert, *Priest to the Temple, or the Country Parson: His Character and Rule of Holy Life* (London: T. Maxey for T. Garthwait, 1652), chap. XXXIV, http://anglicanhistory.org/herbert/parson.html.

1. Martha Buskirk, Amelia Jones, and Caroline A. Jones, "The Year in 'Re-,'" *Artforum* 52, no. 4 (December 2013), http://www.artforum.com/print/201310/the-year-in-re-44068.

MAKING—REMAKING

CHAPTER 1

COPY I REPEAT

CONSERVING SOUTH ASIAN PAINTING THROUGH PRACTICE

Murad Khan Mumtaz

In the spring of 2021, in collaboration with the Williams College Museum of Art (WCMA), I taught an undergraduate studio art course on the practice of traditional South Asian drawing and painting.[1] We converted one of the WCMA galleries into a studio that also acted as an exhibition space showcasing historical Indian artworks from which the students learned (fig. 1.1). The Indian drawing and painting technique itself has several names. In Persian it is called *musavvari*. In Hindi it is *chitrakala*, and since the European and colonial turn it has been known, by both contemporary practitioners and connoisseurs, as miniature painting. Teaching a course on a South Asian art form in a Western context, in a museum setting, during a pandemic that restricted normative modes of learning, forced me to rethink my practice, both as an artist and as an educator. How could I impart knowledge of a very specific art form in a meaningful way to a diverse group of students—most whom were not of South Asian heritage—in the Berkshires? In that context, so far from South Asia, could we think of pedagogy as a mode of conservation? And what does the historical practice of miniature painting tell us about conservation?

In his essay for this volume, Alva Noë discusses the roles of pedagogy and enactment as embodied means of conserving art: both help transmit the art form, thereby keeping it alive and relevant for contemporary audiences and practitioners. "It is precisely because of the ephemeral, always-only-ever-enacted character of the work that it lives not only in performance but also in its transmission, and this technology supports the teaching and training of new dancers, new casts."[2] This radical idea is in contrast to the more conservative practice of isolating an artwork to conserve it, for instance, in a museum lab. Similar to Noë's proposal, for this essay I use the term "conservation" broadly: in this instance as a concept that evokes the idea of conserving a traditional art form, a means of passing it down, a practice that is an embodied way of preserving knowledge. In particular, I will be focusing

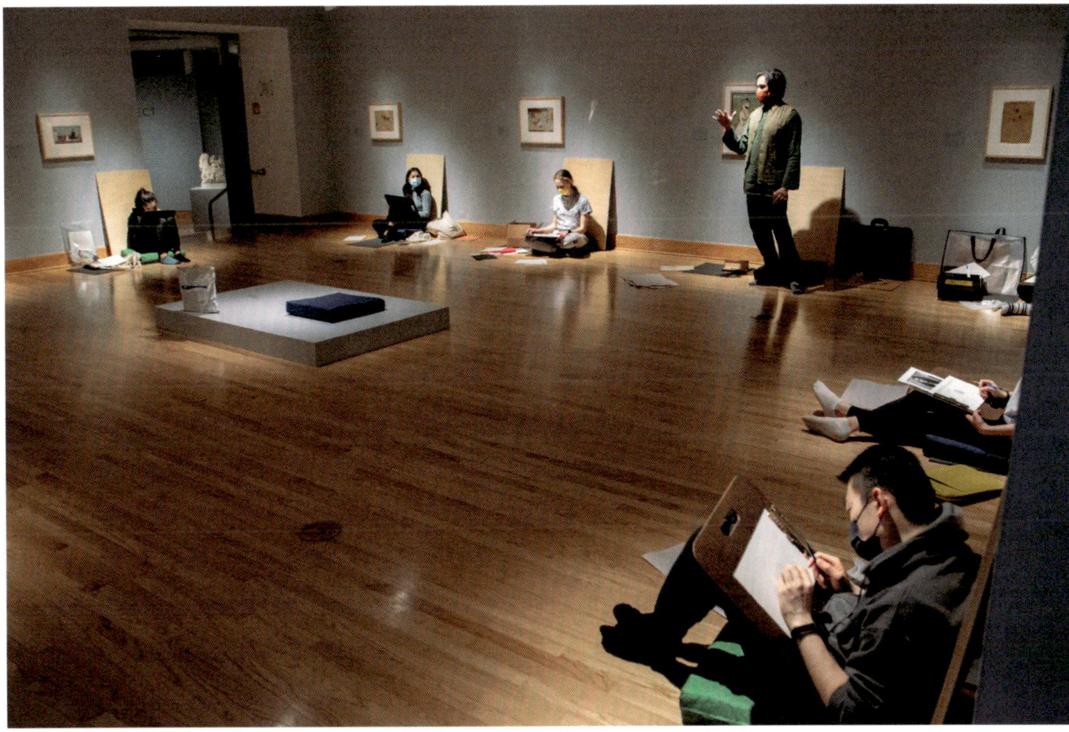

Fig. 1.1. Williams College students during a class session in the exhibition *Tasvir Khana: Practicing Indian Drawing and Painting*, Williams College Museum of Art, Williamstown, Massachusetts, spring 2021

on the Persianate, Indo-Muslim legacy of this practice, one that has a long history of patronage and production that stretches back to the twelfth century and is best remembered for the artwork produced for the Mughal courts (1526–1858) in northern South Asia.

One question that initiated this essay was to consider who is a conservator in this embodied transmission of skill and knowledge? In a premodern South Asian context, it would be the master artist and the students. But it would also be the compiler of an album, who literally patches together various loose folios and artworks to form new meanings. In a contemporary context, the teacher is not a conservator as such, but someone who is a channel of transmission. Conservation happens in the classroom through the actions and mark making of the students, and through this enactment the tradition is kept alive and relevant within its own modern or contemporary context.

PART 1: GOING BACK IN HISTORY, FROM THE TWENTY-FIRST CENTURY TO THE COLONIAL PERIOD

In order to find answers to some of the questions posed above, I will journey back, beginning with my own education and its connection to a larger history of *musavvari* in South Asia. I learned miniature painting practice in Lahore, at the National College of Arts (NCA). Until recently, the NCA was the only undergraduate college in the world that gave a BFA degree in this art form. Initially known as the Mayo School of Art, the NCA was established by the British in the late nineteenth century with a goal to stimulate the production of local crafts for the purpose of international trade.[3] A few years after the partition of the Indian Subcontinent in 1947, the Mayo School was reorganized as the NCA and remodeled as a modern art school. Miniature painting was one of the few local art forms that survived this transition, although until 1980 it was offered only as a minor subject. My own teacher, *Ustad*[4] Bashir Ahmad, was the only trained miniaturist of note to emerge from the school during this period.[5] Once he became the instructor in 1980, he successfully campaigned for the art form's introduction into the undergraduate curriculum, and within two decades the program had become the most popular in the school, leading to international recognition and a new genre known as "contemporary miniature."[6]

Bashir Ahmad's own *ustad* was Sheikh Shujaullah, a master *musavvir* who came from a family of traditional practitioners from Amber, near Jaipur in Rajasthan, and who taught for twelve years at the college. The other instructor, Haji Muhammad Sharif, was trained in Punjabi schools of painting. Both learned their trade in the first half of the twentieth century during the British colonial period, a time when Indigenous systems of learning and local patterns of patronage were either collapsing or transitioning at a rapid pace. At a time when elite local patronage shifted to photography as the main mode of representation and began privileging European aesthetics, artists such as Muhammad Sharif and Shujaullah found sustenance producing pastiches of precolonial, Persian, Pahari, and Mughal-era artworks. Much of their work represents a popular, very-late-Mughal idiom that was circulating widely during the colonial period. In terms of quality and inspiration, a lot of the work is quite removed from its Mughal and Rajput predecessors and has undergone serious alterations. Its partial dialogue with its own tradition is often sustained through colonial-period modifications. And yet, despite the fact that Indian painting has a history of change, renewal, and transition—made even more rapid in the colonial and postcolonial periods—there are certain core practices that have remained constant, which I briefly outline in this essay.

PART 2: COPY AND REPEAT: MAINTAINING A DIALOGUE WITH HISTORY

A central habit that miniature-painting students internalize from day one of their learning is to engage in a meaningful dialogue with the practice's own history. It

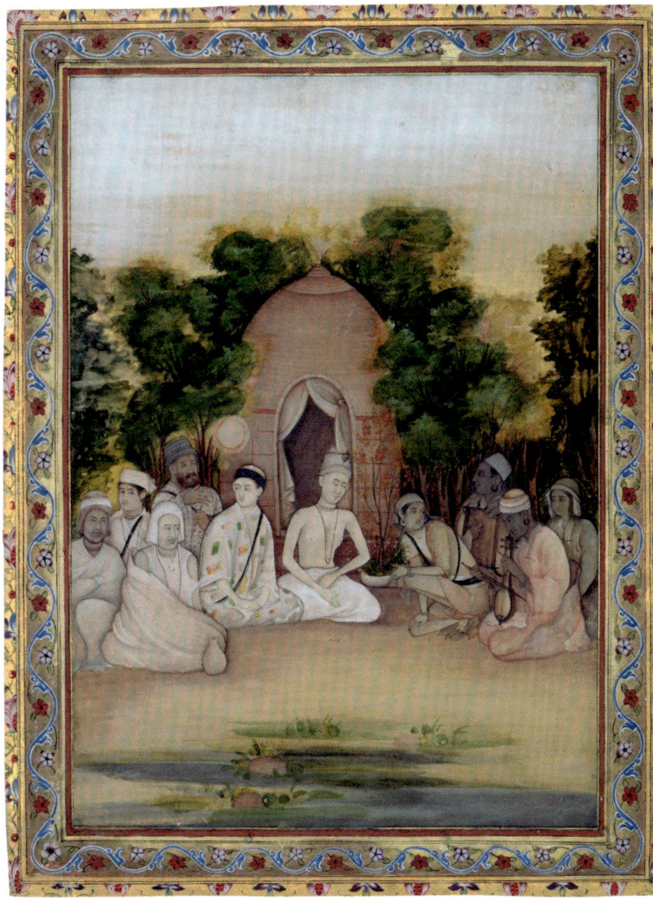

Fig. 1.2. Mir Kalan Khan (South Asian, active 18th century), *A Gathering of Holy Men of Different Faiths*, c. 1770. Opaque watercolor and gold on paper, 10½ × 7½ in. (26.7 × 19.1 cm). Metropolitan Museum of Art, New York. Purchase, Friends of Islamic Art Gifts, 2009, 2009.318

is most effectively maintained through the act of copying, and this mode of imitation or historical reflection is never considered to be a derogatory act. Throughout the history of *musavvari*, artists have acknowledged the perfection of skill and expression achieved by past masters, and this recognition—built into the very practice—links modern and contemporary iterations of miniature painting with its precolonial, traditional forebears. This practice of copying is evident not just in preliminary exercises but also in completed artworks. One painting from around 1770 (fig. 1.2), made by the court artist Mir Kalan Khan for the Nawab of Lucknow, for instance, repurposes a section of a well-known Mughal painting made for Prince Dara Shikoh in the 1650s. The original composition consists of an odd patchwork of scenes stitched together into a single large painting showing a gathering—or gatherings—of ascetics.[7] While Sufi saints dominate the central composition, Indic saints occupy the lowest register. Mir Kalan Khan's painting, made more than a century later, repurposes the saints from the lower register of the Dara Shikoh painting to create a completely new composition that specifically highlights two figures: the fifteenth-century *bhakti* saint Kabir and his son Kamal. While the figures are all faithful copies from the Mughal painting, the technique gives the composition a new meaning. Rather than using the opaque watercolor technique of the original, Kalan Khan uses thinner tints of transparent washes, closer to a technique known as *nim qalam*. While acknowledging the creative debt he owes to the original source material, the artist's use of thin layers of paint aids in blending the figures with the surroundings, rather than making them appear as staged. Compared to the original, Kalan Khan's artwork is less an odd patchwork of figures and more a seamless composition. The overall muted, ochre tones evoke a devotional gathering at dusk, in a painting in which the ascetic figures appear ghostlike. This conscious artistic choice of technique helps in creating a timeless, contemplative artwork, unlike the original, which is a pseudo-historical composition.

In a somewhat similar pattern, contemporary miniaturists working in a global context continue to reference historical works. Simultaneously, however—akin to Kalan Khan and his patron from Lucknow—contemporary artists are also acutely aware of their own position in a particular space and time. Imran Qureshi's 2013 rooftop garden commission at the Metropolitan Museum of Art in New York, for example, is a visceral response to the violence that Pakistan was embroiled in at the time, represented through large blood splatters (fig. 1.3). The red acrylic that symbolizes blood also evokes one of the most familiar hues used in Rajasthani and Punjabi miniature painting. Upon closer inspection, the red stains covering the Met's roof reveal a repeating pattern of tiny blooming flowers taken from Mughal and Rajput paintings. Qureshi's work, like the work of most other contemporary miniaturists, is engaged in a two-way, multilingual dialogue: one with a local, South Asian past and the other with a global present. The mania for conversing with history concurrently keeps the present moment front and center, allowing for the artform to participate in changing contexts while still rooted in its own history.

Another principle that is connected to the act of copying, and one that is a key ingredient for the practice of *musavvari*, is repetition; this is evident in every aspect of the art form, from repeating patterns on clothes, drapery, and borders, to the accumulation of hair or jewelry in a portrait, to the repetitive blades of grass and leaves in the foliage, down to the very process of rendering—known as *pardakht*. *Pardakht* is the gradual, uniform accumulation of dots and dash-like strokes used to render a surface.[8] One large drawing from Jaipur, measuring more than two feet high, made by the artist Sahib Ram in around 1800, is an excellent example, as it contains all the core techniques of Indian painting but on a large scale, thereby making the marks on the paper—the intentionality of the artist's hand—clearly visible (fig. 1.4). I also use this example since my own teacher's *ustad*, Sheikh

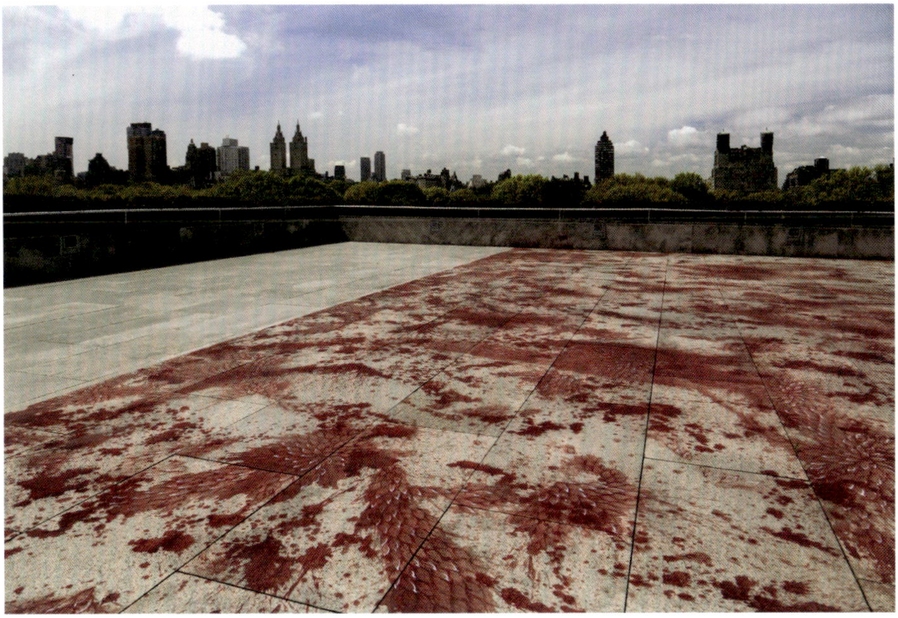

Fig. 1.3. Imran Qureshi (Pakistani, b. 1972), *And How Many Rains Must Fall before the Stains Are Washed Clean*, 2013. Acrylic, 30 × 24 in. (76.2 × 61 cm). Installed in the Metropolitan Museum of Art's Iris and B. Gerald Cantor Roof Garden, New York, 2013

Shujaullah, came from the same region. An artwork such as this contains several technical and stylistic elements that were shared across northern South Asia and have been passed down through generations into the present day. Believed to be a preparatory study for a large wall painting, the drawing shows Krishna, the eighth avatar of Lord Vishnu. Originally, it was made as a line drawing in black ink, and the outlines were all perforated in order to transfer the drawing onto a wall. Sometime later, the artist reworked it into a completed drawing by redoing the outlines and adding color and details into the portrait and headgear. A close analysis of the artwork reveals repeating strokes across the composition (fig. 1.5). The hair is painted with thick, opaque parallel lines. Sahib Ram develops the rendering around the neck using transparent, thin, and uniform parallel lines that follow the contour of the neck. In fact, parallel lines can also be seen in the turban design—though much bolder and used as a repeating pattern—and in the minutely drawn eyelashes. Jewelry elements also form repeating, circular and floral patterns that frame the portrait. As artworks such as this reveal, repetition is the underlying grammar of *musavvari*'s visual language.

Fig. 1.4. Sahib Ram (South Asian, active second half of the 18th century), *Head of Krishna: Cartoon for the Mural of the Raslila*, c. 1800. Ink and opaque watercolor on paper, 27 ¼ × 18 ½ in. (69.2 × 47 cm). Metropolitan Museum of Art, New York. Rogers Fund, 1918, 18.85.2

Fig. 1.5. Detail of fig. 1.4

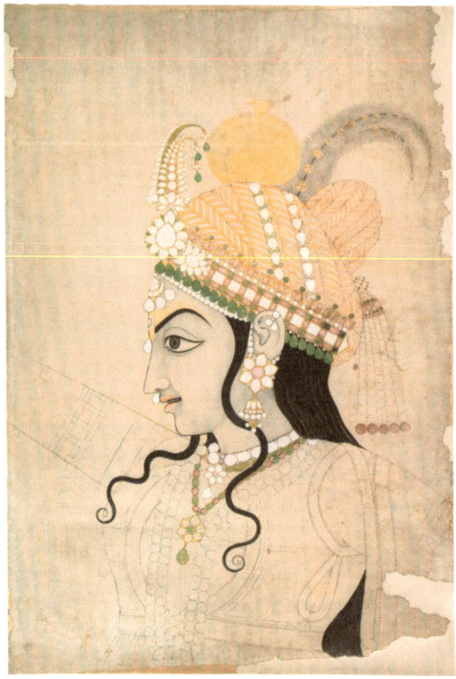

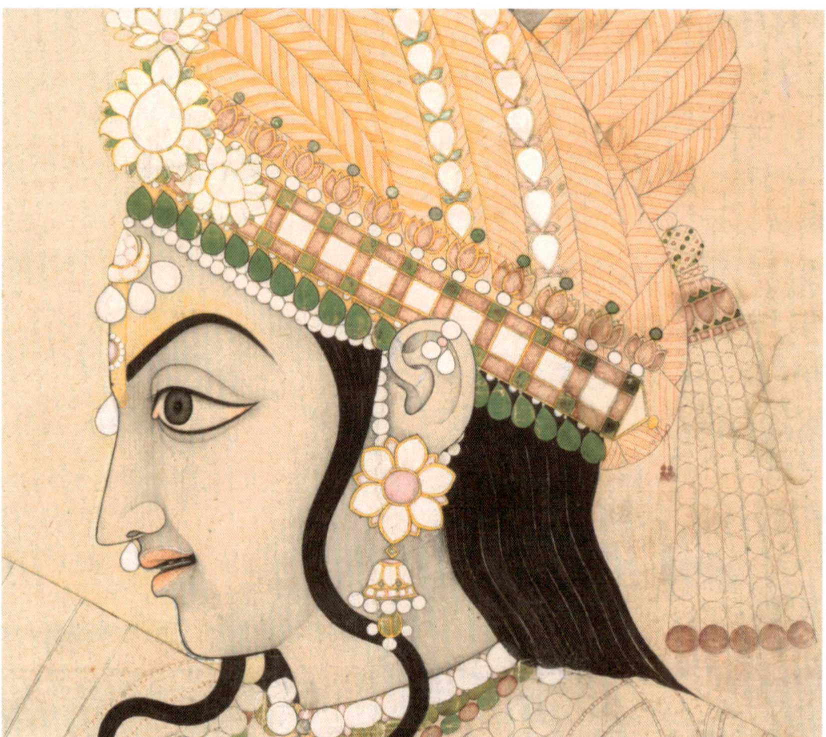

PART 3: WHAT WE LEARNED AT THE NCA

The painstaking accumulation of the stroke, the repetition of the parallel line, learning the art of copying: this is exactly where we as students began our training in the Miniature Painting Department at the NCA. Certain modifications tailor this practice to fit into the curriculum of a modern art college. For instance, instead of practicing with a brush, students initially learn drawing and rendering techniques with customized graphite pencils.[9] The first assignment requires making a grid of 1 × 1–inch squares on a sheet of A4 paper, followed by filling each square with thin lines that form a repeating pattern of vertical, horizontal, and diagonal-lined boxes (fig. 1.6). The aim is to make as light a mark as possible, with straight, unbroken lines drawn close together. These multidirectional lines repeated across the grid instill, from day one, the importance of the repeated stroke, making the art of copying easier to master and appreciate. It also enables new students to focus on minute details while training the hand muscles to work in a completely new, controlled way. As the assignments progress and students start using squirrel-hair brushes, months are spent mastering the *pardakht* technique, beginning with learning how to balance a graded background that is built up with minute stipples. The systematized use of the *pardakht* technique became increasingly common in northern Indian schools of painting from the eighteenth century onward. There are several highly refined examples from

Fig. 1.6. Ivana Mensah-Agyekum, *Untitled* (student assignment for Williams College ARTS 344), 2021. Graphite on paper, 6 × 10 in. (15.24 × 24.4 cm). Courtesy of the artist

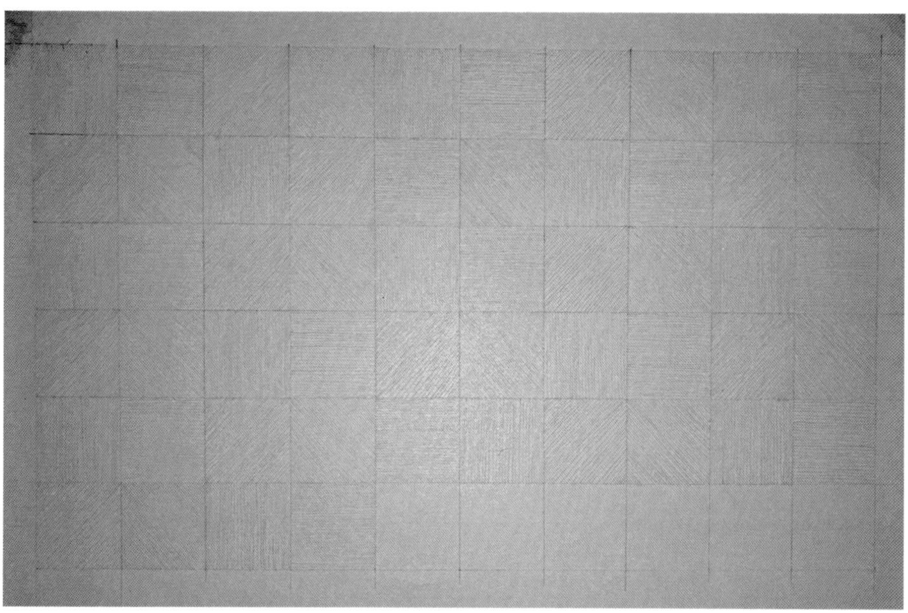

mid-eighteenth-century centers such as Avadh and Hyderabad in which artists used *pardakht* schematically to render portraits.[10] It is likely that the introduction of photography in the nineteenth century, with its black-and-white tints and even gradients, made artists rely even more on *pardakht*.

At the National College of Arts, after the initial assignments that familiarize students with the basic language of miniature painting, a large part of the undergraduate program is dedicated to learning techniques and styles of the major historical schools of painting through making copies. Only later, in the final year, are students encouraged to explore contemporary modes of artistic expression.

The deeply rooted practice of repetition is also evident in the way a typical miniature painting is developed, from the very first preparatory drawing to the final painted and rendered version. The first step is to transfer the drawing onto sized and burnished paper, known as *vasli* paper. This is done using a tracing sheet. Historically, artists would use thin vellum, often made of deer skin. The drawing is traditionally transferred by perforating the sheet along the outlines of the composition and then by passing a powdered pigment, usually carbon black, over it, allowing thin, dotted lines to appear on the *vasli* paper underneath. The transferred drawing is then inked with a light pigment, usually in a light tone of lac red or vermillion. In a work from around 1780, *Krishna Subdues the Serpent Kaliya in the Yamuna River* (fig. 1.7), the female figures have only been partially outlined in red, revealing the coarse underdrawing made with carbon black. Already, even before the rendering process has begun, the artist has repeated the same basic drawing three times: as a sketch, as a tracing, and as the first inked drawing in red on the *vasli*. The next step is to apply a thin layer of opaque white as a primer. Historically, and in most family-based workshops in India today, the white pigment is either a local sandstone or lead-based white. At the NCA, we were taught to use zinc white, a pigment that was most likely popularized during the colonial period. The priming of the *vasli* locks the drawing down and also evens out the surface. Once completely dry, the *vasli* is burnished using a large cowry shell or agate stone. This allows the artist to apply flat washes of pigments and to run the brush smoothly. At this point, the drawing, which is buried under the opaque white wash, is outlined again, but now with a bolder line using carbon black. In this phase, the drawing is finalized and ready to be painted, if the artist is using the opaque watercolor technique, or rendered with light, tinted washes, if the artist is using the transparent watercolor technique of *siah qalam* or *nim qalam*. In the case of the more commonly used opaque watercolor technique, the painter now applies flat washes of color and begins the painstaking process of rendering, starting with the background and foreground, and finally coming to the figures. After this stage, the figures are outlined yet again, one final time. By the end of the entire process of completing a painting, a miniaturist will have outlined the same drawing anywhere between five and ten times.

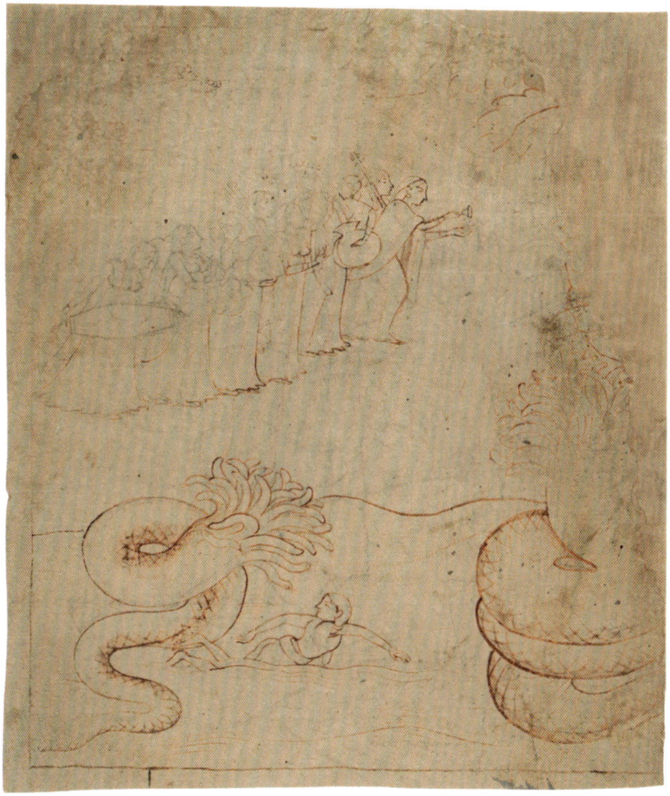

Fig. 1.7. Attributed to a follower of Nainsukh (Punjab Hills, d. 1778), *Krishna Subdues the Serpent Kaliya in the Yamuna River*, c. 1780. Ink and wash on paper, 10⅜ × 9 in. (26.4 × 22.9 cm). Metropolitan Museum of Art, New York. Gift of Subhash Kapoor, in memory of his parents, Smt Shashi Kanta and Shree Parshotam Ram Kapoor, 2008, 2008.359.24

Needless to say, processes and techniques vary subtly from region to region and also change over time. Vellum, for instance, has given way to tracing sheets, which are cheaper and readily accessible. Yet the basic act of repeating and refining the underlying drawing in an artwork has remained surprisingly consistent.

PART 4: CONSERVATION IN TRADITIONAL *MUSAVVARI*

Art historian Chanchal Dadlani explains, "In Mughal India, painters had a historically rooted relationship to tradition with innovation defined through precedent, constantly looking to past examples as the foundations for artistic knowledge."[11] In the historical practice of *musavvari*, there are several ways in which conversing with history helps conserve the art form while also allowing for innovation. Seventeenth-century Mughal albums provide some well-known examples. Reusing older specimens of calligraphy that interact with paintings is one aspect of that. Seamlessly pasting older examples in an album is similar to the way *vasli* paper—the painting surface for a miniature painting—is made, gluing together scraps of paper and then burnishing and sizing the top layer. This all lends itself to the practice of restoring and conserving prized masterworks in an album. The Persian word for

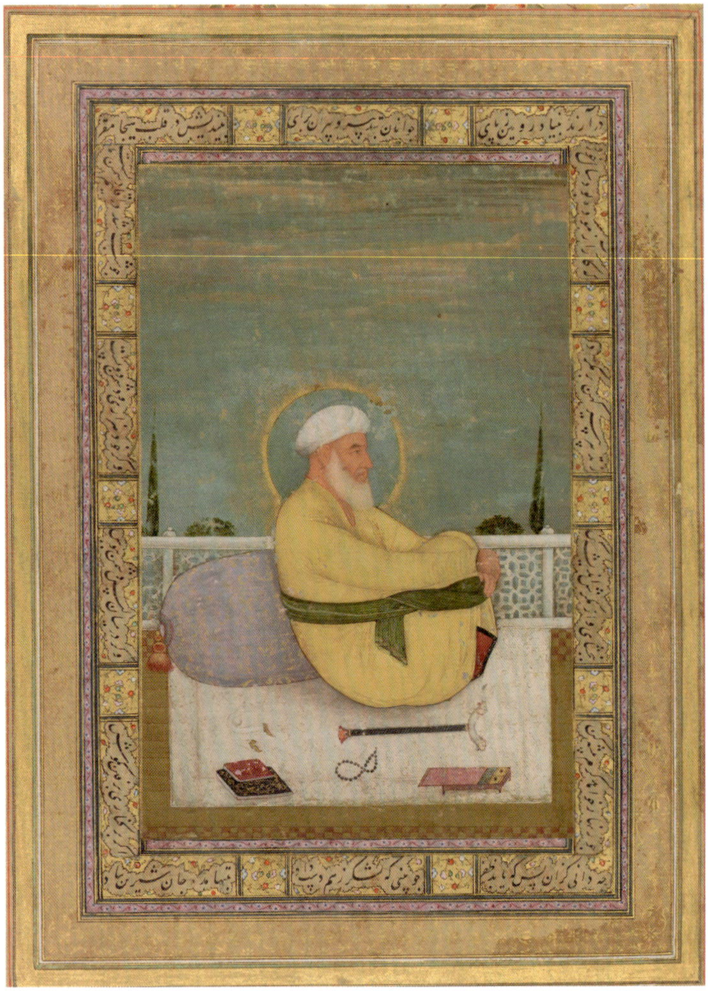

Fig. 1.8. Artist unknown, *Portrait of Mulla Shah*, c. 1655. Album folio, opaque watercolor and gold on paper, 6 1/8 × 4 in. (15.6 × 10.2 cm). Arthur M. Sackler Gallery, Smithsonian Institution, Washington, DC: Art and History Collection, LTS2002.2.4

album, *muraqqa'*, is itself evocative of this concept of reuse and repair. It literally means "patched," and it has strong associations with the patched cloak worn by Sufis and dervishes as a sign of spiritual poverty.

One example of the way remnants of older manuscripts are conserved, reused, and repurposed for a new meaning can be seen in a painting depicting Mulla Shah, a popular seventeenth-century Sufi saint from Kashmir (fig. 1.8). He was influential in Mughal Emperor Shah Jahan's court and was the spiritual guide of two of the emperor's favorite children: the heir apparent to the throne, Prince Dara Shikoh, and the first lady of the empire, Princess Jahanara Begum. The painting was made to fit into a late Shah Jahan–period album by adding thin cartouche strips around the inner border that contain lines from a poem composed by the famous medieval Persian poet and saint Sa'di Shirazi. The calligraphy has been recycled from an earlier manuscript, probably from sixteenth-century Persia. The portion of the verse composed in the central border comes from Sa'di's *Bustan* (*The Orchard*), a Persian classical text narrating short allegorical tales for moral and ethical teaching. The verses in the cartouches are from the first chapter of the book, "On Justice, Wisdom, and Government," from a section titled "On Dealing with Enemies," and resonate perfectly with the subject of the artwork. An early modern Persianate viewer could imagine a wise old man giving advice to a king or prince after the enemy has been defeated and taken captive:

> When he asks for protection, treat him with kindness
> Pardon him, but be aware of his trickery
> From the council of a wise old man turn not away
> For the timeworn [elder] has experience
> And they uproot the stronghold from its roots
> The youth with their strength, and the wise men with their council.[12]

These verses offer a window into an entire cultural ethos, in which an established precedent—in this case the sage advice of an elder—carries wisdom. This mirrors the act of image making within the Persianate world as well, where the superiority of knowledge and skill of past masters is a given, almost to the point of being axiomatic.

The presence of a living saint's portrait in one of the most elite and lavish spaces for artistic expression in South Asia, the Mughal album, juxtaposed with the words of one of the most acclaimed poets in the Persian language, speaks to the growing prominence a living saint could hold in court by this time. It also shows how imperials other than the emperor—in this case, his two children—could project their own standing in the empire through the depiction of their spiritual guide.

In most albums of this kind, examples of folios bringing disparate artworks together to create new meanings through visual interactions abound. In one folio from an album currently in the Bibliothèque nationale de France, the curator/creator/compiler of the manuscript has shown different expressions of Muslim devotion by collaging together three Mughal artworks made by distinct hands within a larger frame of indigo blue and orange bands (fig. 1.9). The album was most likely compiled sometime in the eighteenth century in Muslim South Asia, but the artworks are from an earlier period. The standing figure of an antinomian dervish in the lower-right corner represents a late-Akbar-period style from the 1590s. The depiction of three women performing the Islamic prayer in the lower-left corner is likely from the mid-Jahangir period (c. 1610). The composition at the top showing a congregation of Sufis represents the Shah Jahan–period Mughal style with much more attention given to individualized portraits (c. 1650). As was common for most early

Fig. 1.9. Artists unknown, three paintings mounted on an album folio including *Six Muslim Mystics*, c. 1650; *Muslim Women in Prayer*, c. 1610; and *A Standing Dervish*, c. 1590; album assembled c. 1750. Opaque watercolor and gold on paper, 17 ¾ × 12 ⅝ in. (45 × 32 cm). Bibliothèque Nationale de France, Paris. Réserve Od 44 fol., f.37a

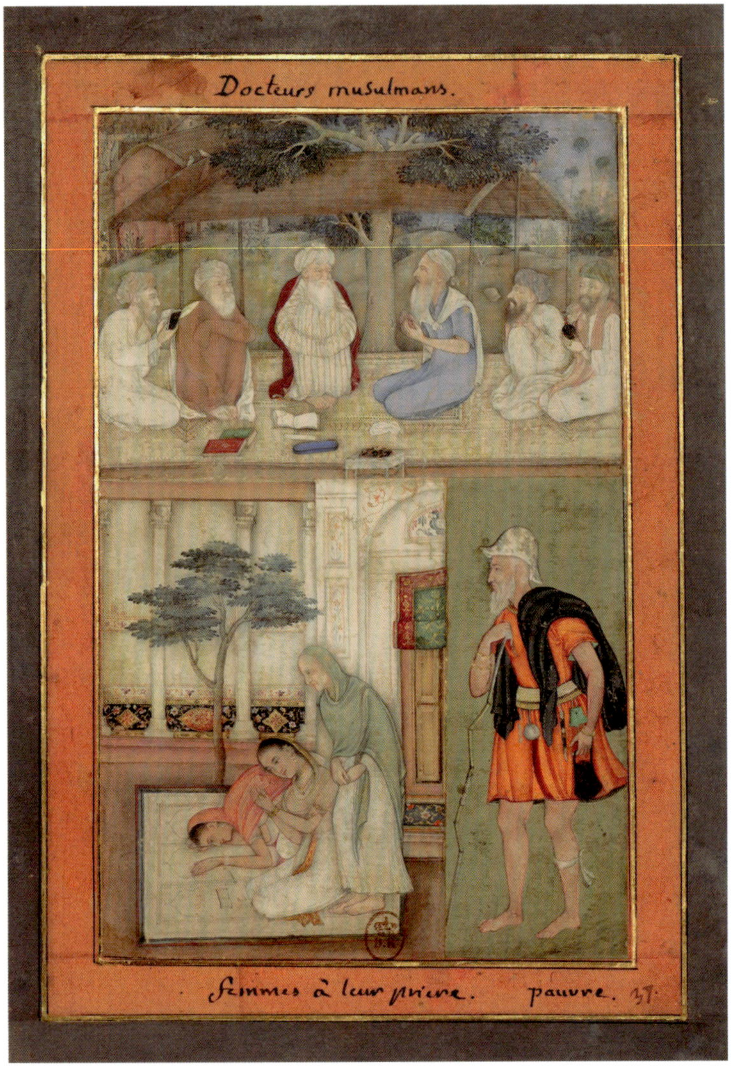

modern albums, gold, black, and red lines along the margins help hide the seams where the artworks were pasted onto the *vasli*. Narratively speaking, the deliberate placement of the three paintings expresses a devotional hierarchy of sorts. The group of mystics at the top represent the more mainstream Sufi type, while the antinomian mystic and female devotees are relegated to the bottom of the folio. An undercurrent of humor is added through the framing of the standing dervish who unwittingly pries into the women's quarters. In purely aesthetic terms, bringing together three distinct styles from earlier periods in one album folio discloses the keen interest that connoisseurs had in their own art history. It is not clear whether the individual paintings were brought together on the page during the Shah Jahan period, nor when the album was compiled in the eighteenth century. Was the compiler also an artist, or purely a connoisseur?

There are other instances in the Indo-Muslim album where artists themselves respond to one another's works through meticulous copying or through reinterpreting the same theme in different ways.[13] In fact, it would be very easy to compose an entire essay based on countless examples that demonstrate the obsession that artists, patrons, and connoisseurs had with conserving and conversing with the past. However, over the last few years I have become more interested in discovering the underlying motivations that instilled this instinctive fervor for conservation, repetition, and imitation. In the final section of this essay, I prize out some cultural and philosophical impulses that helped shape the art of *musavvari* and its passion for preservation.

CONCLUSION: AN ONTOLOGY OF CONSERVATION

One question I have begun to address, both as an educator and researcher and as an artist, pertains to the precolonial, Indo-Persian worldview that fostered and normalized practices such as the art of copying, repetition, and preservation. To what extent were artists, patrons, and compilers of albums conscious of this worldview, in which acts of copying and preserving older masterworks were seen as sources of knowledge? Should this worldview be made relevant today to a contemporary student of miniature painting, and in particular to my students at Williams College, who come from diverse backgrounds and might not be as invested in the art of miniature painting as I was as a student?

I have found early modern album prefaces, or *dibacha*—written in Persian—to be an excellent interpretive lens through which to understand the underlying wisdom behind the practice of *musavvari*. Album prefaces also provide a methodological framework that allows the tradition to speak for itself.

One such text, originally written in the early sixteenth century as an introduction to a treatise on calligraphy but later used as an album preface for a Mughal imperial album in the mid-seventeenth century, is by the famous calligrapher from Herat, Mir'Ali Haravi (fig. 1.10). It is a clear articulation of the Perso-Islamicate cosmology that animated most cultural expressions from this period, as seen through the dual arts of calligraphy and painting:

> Praise without end and laud without limit to a creator, of the traces of whose magnificence and perfection the painted album of the celestial sphere is but a specimen and of whose rays of beauty the illuminated cut-out disc of the sun is but a sample—a craftsman whose creative pen draws the down (*khatt*) of heart-stealing beauties, an innovator whose marvelous brush depicts every form.[14]

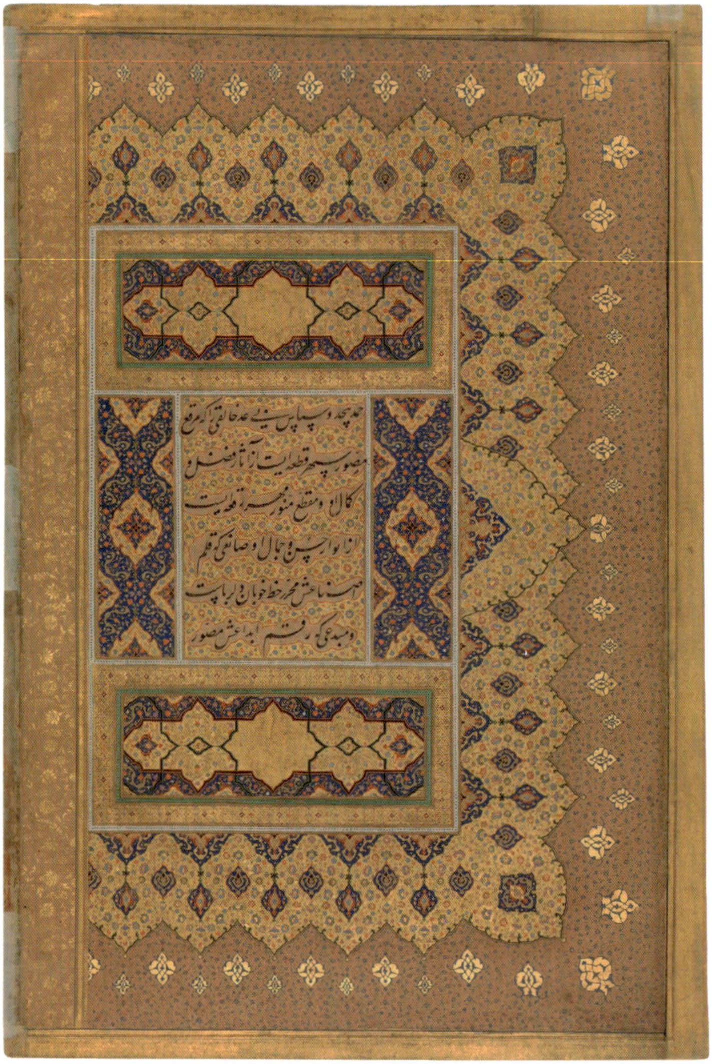

Fig. 1.10. Mir'Ali Haravi (Herat, d. c. 1550), *Unwan* from the *Shah Jahan Album*, assembled c. 1630–40. Ink, opaque watercolor, and gold on paper, 15 ¼ × 10 ¼ in. (38.7 × 26 cm). Metropolitan Museum of Art, New York. Purchase, Rogers Fund and the Kevorkian Foundation Gift, 1955, 55.121.10.41

In the opening sentence, Mir'Ali Haravi explicitly links the act of painting to Islamic cosmology. He draws an analogy between the world of a creator god and a celestial album, of which the earth—with its sun—is but a reflection. All of nature, then, is a trace of this original or archetypal album. In the next section, he elaborates on this ontology of creation through the allegory of the painted album:

> What the "writer of destiny," the unparalleled and unequaled creator, intended ultimately by the "tablet," the "pen," and the things destined in beautiful script in the library of the celestial spheres were the assemblies of depictions on the flat expanse of the dusty earth—just as colorful

> "miscellanies" of flowers and herbs and the elegant "pages" of gardens and orchards are but traces of that intent. The goal of these signs is that sound natures and upright minds should use each and every one to make their way to the original creator and true goal.[15]

Here, Mir'Ali cleverly deploys terms that God uses to describe the act of creation in the Qur'an, such as the "preserved tablet" where all destiny has been prewritten or the "pen" that brings forth all creation into existence.[16] Through the very language of the book, he seems to suggest that images, in fact, are necessary for grasping the word of God, and thereby moving closer to God. The next sentence makes this point even clearer: "True knowledge can be derived only from the miraculous Word of God and the true sayings of the Prophet, but one cannot easily benefit from them until they are 'strung' into writing and 'enchained' in painting."[17]

This preface plays with a long-established Islamic cosmological worldview articulated by medieval scholars and metaphysicians such as Avicenna, Ibn Arabi, and Ghazali, in which a central idea is that human nature and the natural world are similar to the cosmos, in that both reflect God's qualities. Mir'Ali draws an analogy between the macrocosm of God's created universe and the microcosm of the manmade album. Just as God brings together the diversity of His creation into order and unity through His very presence, which pervades all existence, the curator of the album ties disparate folios across space and time into a single bound volume. It is, thus, appropriate that the Shah Jahan–period album that includes this preface opens with a grand sunburst pattern.[18] To put it succinctly, this and most subsequent prefaces follow the Persianate *dibacha* writing convention in which God's act of creation is mirrored in the act of compiling the album. Thus, the curator/creator/compiler is the copyist par excellence, since his act of bringing together diverse folios, calligraphic specimens, and paintings mimics or imitates God's creative act in the microcosm of the album. The compiler reflects the diversity of creation in the act of compilation. The act of reusing and salvaging older artworks also reifies the cosmic hierarchy: just as God's creative act takes precedence over human production, so the artworks of established masters from bygone eras are cherished for having established a precedent for contemporary artists to engage with and respond to. New artistic expressions and fresh meanings are created from this very dialogue between the past and the present.

Could it be that artists and their workshops were conscious of this ontological mirroring that unfolded through the creative brush of the masters? If that is the case, then the language of *musavvari* itself—a language built upon copying and repeating—suddenly takes on a spiritually charged role. Just as the created cosmos is a reflection of celestial archetypes, the artistic act of making a copy is a mirror of God's act of creation.

A later album preface from Mughal India expresses a similar sentiment to that of Mir Ali and appears to hint at this ontologically activated function of the artist. Written by Prince Dara Shikoh, the heir apparent to the Mughal throne, in the 1630s, it states:

> Praise—which the pen is incapable of writing and the imagination unable to visualize—to the [calligrapher who] brings forth the down of the adolescent beards (*naw-khaṭan*[19]) and the painter of the portraits of idols [beloveds/beauties]. For, the master-artist of His [God's] power decorated the page of the sun with golden lines/borders, and the designer of His handicraft fashioned the side-faced/half-faced moon into a portrait. Creatures of the earth in every corner of the land sing His praises, and heavenly beings of every form (*surat*) chant His name with their tongues.[20]

Following Mir'Ali's example, Dara Shikoh uses the language and terminology of album making to describe God's act of creation. The prince acknowledges that artistic creation is God's prerogative. In the Qur'an, He is called *al-khaliq*, the creator, and *al-musavvir*, the painter, artist, or fashioner of forms. The human artist's vocation is thus an extension or reflection of the divine act. It is God who shapes divine archetypes of beauty and gives them the form of human beloveds. More than the making, according to these album prefaces, the beholding of artworks such as portraits of beautiful young men and women is a reminder of God's beauty of creation. In Mir'Ali's words, the artworks help "sound natures and upright minds . . . to make their way to the original creator and true goal."[21] Dara Shikoh sums it up by adding a poem in his preface:

> The Painter [God] of the page of the rose garden
> The maker of portraits of the beautiful ones.
> From the handiwork of his brush/pen,
> the line/down on the faces of the idols—the golden ray of sunlight—is
> immortalized.
> He adorns meaning (*ma'nī*) with form (*ṣūrat*)[22]
> From that [meaning] each form (*ṣūrat*) becomes manifest . . .
> . . . From Him [God] the world became apparent
> Just as paintings [are made manifest] by the painter.[23]

Album prefaces such as those written by Mir'Ali and Dara Shikoh frame underlying motivations—not only that of the album as an object, but also those of the painters and calligraphers who participated in its production. Overall, the

Indo-Muslim, Persianate culture believed in the primacy of a higher reality: God as the first creator. All other creations were believed to be reflections or refractions of that first Divine Act. As an artist, then, the very act of creativity is an act of conserving something of that divine perfection in this world of sensuous forms. According to the famous sixteenth-century Mughal courtier and historian Abu'l Fazl, the arts of calligraphy and painting play two creative roles simultaneously. As loci for manifesting divine light, they at once represent that reality and also act as vehicles that lead people with insight back to that reality:

> A picture (*ṣūrat*) leads to that which it represents [lit. its own master], and this [leads] to the meaning (*ma'ni*), just as the shape of a line leads one to letters and words, and from there the sense can be found out. . . .
>
> In truth, according to the eyes of the lovers of beauty, forms are the loci for the manifestation of light [lit. the place of manifestation where light is captured]. For the farsighted ones, this cup of Jamshid [locus of manifestation] leads to the transcendent.[24] The magic of the line is a sacred geometry that comes forth from the pen/brush of creativity.[25]

In a short section on painting packed with poetic allusion and mystical symbolism, Abu'l Fazl shows how, for an Indo-Perso-Islamic audience, depiction and calligraphy are intrinsically tied to the most important Islamic ideal: God-knowledge.

For the artist working within these culturally specific, ontological parameters, the act of copying and repeating aims at perfection, which is ultimately linked to the divine act of creation, which is considered to be perfect. And in this ontology of creation, certain masters were acknowledged as having achieved a perfection of skill and insight in their own right, and therefore they needed to be copied or referenced in the works of later artists. The fifteenth-century master artist Bihzad from Timurid Herat attained legendary status even in his own lifetime. It goes without saying that not every practitioner would have been aware of this literature, or conscious of its particular ontological reverberations, but Indo-Persian artists were a product of that worldview and thus could not help but channel those values through their practice.

These cosmologies no longer govern artistic practice in a contemporary context, transfigured first by the nineteenth- and twentieth-century colonial turn—when European aesthetics destabilized local production—and then by the more recent postcolonial turn, in which contemporary artists show their work on an increasingly global stage more influenced by Western-centric trends than by local traditions. This is particularly true in Pakistan, where I learned the skill of miniature painting. And yet, through the very process of learning this practice, I believe that traditional wisdom has been preserved, even if left mostly dormant. The practice and process, which is a conservative art form at its very core, contains those seeds of wisdom—a wisdom that celebrates creative expression through copying and repetitive mark making. It thus participates in a larger cosmological scheme that stretches across human and divine temporality.

As I teach this practice in a global context, far away from India or Pakistan, how do I make this ontological intelligence, this unique reservoir of wisdom, present and active today? And, perhaps more importantly, does this embodied wisdom have any value or relevance for contemporary practitioners? These questions do not have easy answers, particularly in relation to *musavvari*'s relevance today. Another important question that could come up is the notion of cultural appropriation in the practice of *musavvari* in a contemporary Western setting, and what that might mean for students who would like to take up this practice more seriously. My own answer is that, in terms of iconography, the art form historically has been a very porous one. Local conventions were regularly in dialogue with non-Persianate elements, such as Chinese and Central Asian landscapes and figures in Timurid Herat, or European prints in the Mughal courts, both of which played key roles in the development of the visual language of *musavvari*. In short, even if conceptually the practice was conversing with its own history and philosophy, iconographically, it has always been open.

One way this art form—which opens up to an entire ethos—can be made relevant is through pluralistic engagement. Most liberal arts institutions have become invested in understanding parallel cultures and their values, often according to those cultures' own epistemologies. In the case of *musavvari*, a pluralistic engagement with the practice offers a window into the Indo-Persianate culture that produced and sustained the practice. And this could provide an alternate worldview that promises to decentralize more mainstream modes of making and thinking, even if momentarily and within the parameters of the classroom. Even then, however, there is no straightforward way to engage with this centuries-old artistic practice, one that was deeply rooted in an established theological tradition. Perhaps one way to approach teaching this art form is to keep an open mind and allow students to connect with it according to their own needs and understanding—in short, to embrace the possibility of multiple outcomes and answers. In this, *musavvari* might prove much like the practice of yoga that lives and thrives in multiple ways in different contemporary contexts, even though it is rooted in a very specific history with a very specific religious and theological expression.

NOTES

1. ARTS 344: Technique and Practice of Indian Drawing and Painting, Williams College.
2. See Alva Noë, "Conserving Ourselves / Creating Ourselves," in this volume, p. 88.
3. Samina Choonara, ed., *"Official" Chronicle of Mayo School of Art: Formative Years under J. L. Kipling (1874–94)* (Lahore: National College of Arts, 2003).
4. *Ustad* is the traditional name for master or teacher.
5. Rukhsana David, "Contemporary Miniature Painting in Lahore 1980–2007" (PhD diss., Lahore College for Women University, 2009).
6. Virginia Whiles, *Art and Polemic in Pakistan: Cultural Politics and Tradition in Contemporary Miniature Painting* (London: Tauris Academic Studies, 2010).
7. Unknown maker, *Gathering of Ascetics*, ca. 1650 (Victoria & Albert Museum, IS.94-1965, under the title *Khwaja Sahib*). For a discussion of this painting, see Elinor W. Gadon, "Dara Shikuh's Mystical Vision of Hindu-Muslim Synthesis," in *Facets of Indian Art*, ed. Robert Skelton, Andrew Topsfield, Susan Stronge, and Rosemary Crill (London: Victoria and Albert Museum, 1986), 153–57.
8. For a demonstration of rendering in Indian painting see, Murad Khan Mumatz, "Tasvir Khana, Lesson 8: Rendering Details," YouTube video, 7:37, Williams College Museum of Art, May 12, 2021, http://www.youtube.com/watch?v=ut-BszDhLYk&t=3s.
9. To see how to prepare a graphite pencil, see Murad Khan Mumatz, "Tasvir Khana Assignment 1: Lines," YouTube video, 22:32, Williams College Museum of Art, February 21, 2021, http://www.youtube.com/watch?v=hDFfsxdr_eM&t=21s.
10. For a highly skilled eighteenth-century example of the use of the *pardakht* technique, see the 1764 painting by Muhammad Rizavi Hindi, *Posthumous Portrait of the Mughal Emperor Muhammad Shah Holding a Falcon* (Cleveland Museum of Art, 2013.347.a).
11. Chanchal Dadlani, "Transporting India: The Gentil Album and Mughal Manuscript Culture," *Art History* 38, no. 4 (2015): 756; see also 760n26 for related readings.
12. Sa'di Shirazi, *Bustan* (*The Orchard*), section 33, translation by the author, http://ganjoor.net/saadi/boostan/bab1/sh33/.
13. For a Mughal example of a folio where multiple artists explore a single composition, see Ebba Koch, "The Mughal Emperor as Solomon, Majnun, and Orpheus, or the Album as a Think Tank for Allegory," *Muqarnas* 27 (2010): 281.
14. Wheeler Thackston, *Album Prefaces and Other Documents on the History of Calligraphers and Painters* (Leiden: Brill, 2014), 40.
15. Thackston, *Album Prefaces*, 40.
16. Qur'an, 85:21–22, 68:1–2.
17. Thackston, *Album Prefaces*, 40.
18. "Rosette Bearing the Names and Titles of Shah Jahan," *Folio from the Shah Jahan Album* (Metropolitan Museum of Art, 55.121.1039).
19. The term *naw-khaṭan* could also refer to the new student of calligraphy.
20. The translation is my own. The album preface is printed in Dara Shikoh, "Muraqqa-i Dara Shikoh aur uska Muqaddima," ed. Muhammad Abdullah Chaghtai, *Oriental College Magazine* (Lahore) 13, no. 3 (1937): 97–103.
21. Thackston, *Album Prefaces*, 40.
22. The persian word *surat* also means face or portrait.
23. Shikoh, "Muraqqa-i Dara Shikoh aur uska Muqaddima," p. 101.
24. The proverbial cup of Jamshid in Persian mythology is a cup that ancient kings of Iran had in their possession and through which they could observe all the seven heavens of creation. It was said to be filled with the elixir of immortality. It is a favorite proverb used often in Persian literature.
25. Translation is my own. Abu al-Fazl, *A'in-i Akbari* (*Annals of Akbar*), ed. Henry Blochmann, vol. 2 (Osnabrück: Biblio Verlag, 1985), 111–12.

CHAPTER 2

THE OVERPAINT-ABILITY OF MADONNAS IN 1300S SIENA

Annika Svendsen Finne

On a summer afternoon in Madrid in 2015, a fly landed on a painting by Francisco de Goya titled *Cats Fighting*, exactly in the sightline of the black cat (fig. 2.1). The painting transformed, temporarily, into *Cats Reacting to a Fly*. By accident, a second narrative emerged, but this accident was possible because of decisions Goya had made. The ambiguity of the cats' expressions allowed the painting to internalize the fly's arrival.[1]

Flies can damage paintings, while conservators try to repair them. However, by tripping a switch within the Goya—by activating content that was latent in the painting, the potential for which had not been obvious beforehand—the fly calls attention to a central aspect of art conservation practice. While the brief for a given treatment is usually fixed in advance—for example, "reweave a tear"—the pathways the mend will take must often be invented along the way through an attentive conversation with the materials that constitute the object, whereby the work's fragilities are carefully accommodated. In certain instances, the treatment seems less an intervention that happens *to* the painting than one that happens *with* it.

This sensitive way of approaching a painting seems at odds with the term "overpainting." By definition, overpaint is paint applied on top of dry paint. In the context of a restoration, overpaint often means that the surface of the artwork has been partially covered up in a heavy-handed effort to hide damages. The sound of the word suggests a kind of ending, as in, an overpainted painting is a painting that is "over," done. It is hard to imagine such an intervention *fitting* within the content and forms of the earlier artwork.

My topic is an overpainting episode from early fourteenth-century Siena, wherein two panel paintings of the Madonna and Child were selectively altered (figs. 2.2, 2.3).[2] This pair of Madonnas share many characteristics: both are over-life-size; both were signed by their respective authors, Guido da Siena and Coppo di Marcovaldo; both date to the latter half of the thirteenth century (making them

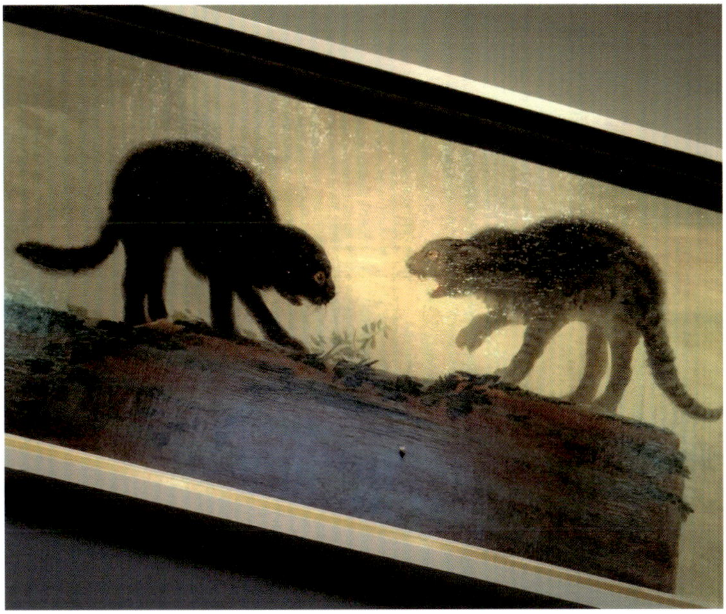

Fig. 2.1. Francisco de Goya (Spanish, 1746–1828), *Cats Fighting*, 1786, with fly in 2015. Paint on canvas, 22 ¼ × 30 ⅜ in. (56.5 × 77.3 cm). Museo del Prado, Madrid. P006323. Photo by the author

roughly fifty years old when they were overpainted); both occupied significant positions in Sienese civic and religious society; and both were owned by prominent mendicant orders.[3] The alterations the figures in the two paintings received also followed a shared pattern.[4] The heads of the two Christ Childs and the faces of the two Madonnas were overpainted in a matching style, and nearly identical soft white veils were placed around the new Madonnas' faces.[5]

The intent of these selective overpaintings does not appear to have been to repair damages, nor to replace Coppo's and Guido's paintings with new artworks.[6] What the interventions aimed to accomplish, it seems, was to update them: to modify the older Madonnas, without changing their identities, in order to bring them into the new brand of Madonna that had become the "face" of Sienese painting after the massive double-sided altarpiece by the artist Duccio, commonly referred to as the *Maestà*, was installed on the high altar of the Sienese cathedral in 1311 (fig. 2.4).[7] The artists responsible for the overpaintings were likely employees of Duccio on the *Maestà* project. The faces they gave to the Madonnas by Coppo and Guido are siblings in look and structure to the face of the Madonna in the *Maestà*.[8]

My aim is not to argue against the explanation of the two overpaintings as Duccesque updates, but to explore a different possibility: that the initial Madonnas could be considered "overpaint-able" — able to *accommodate* later alterations of this kind. In the altered heads of the paintings, the paint handling is unlike that of the unaltered bodies. The most obvious reason for this unlikeness is because these areas

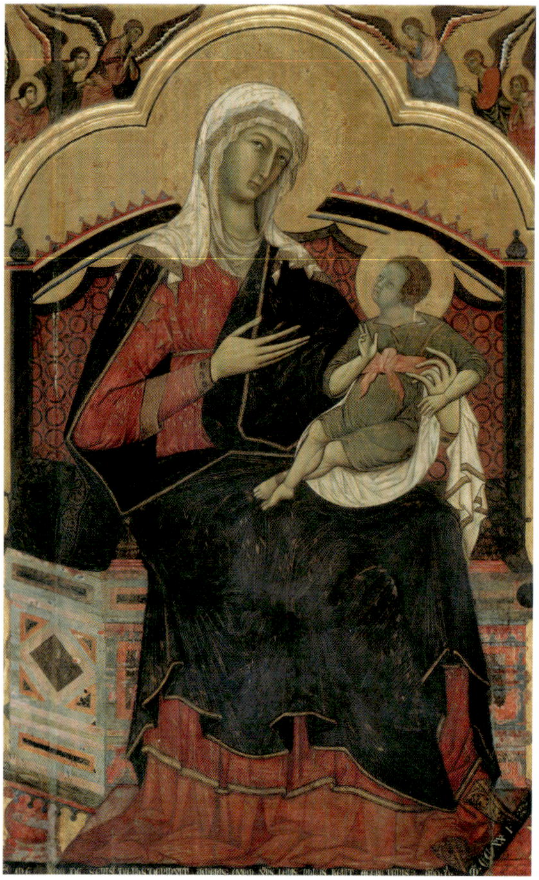

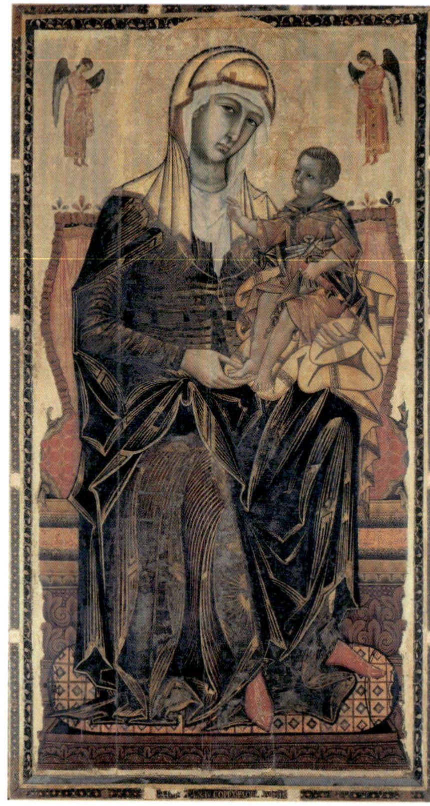

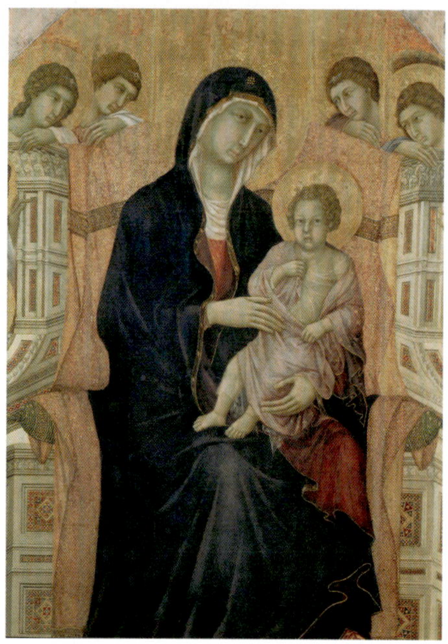

Fig. 2.2. Guido da Siena (Italian, active c. 1250–1300), *Madonna and Child Enthroned*, c. 1270. Paint on panel, 112⅝ × 76 in. (286 × 193 cm). San Domenico, Siena, Italy

Fig. 2.3. Coppo di Marcovaldo (Italian, c. 1220–after 1276), *Madonna and Child Enthroned*, 1261. Paint on panel, 86⅝ × 49¼ in. (220 × 125 cm). Santa Maria dei Servi, Siena, Italy

Fig. 2.4. Duccio di Buonisegna (Italian, c. 1255–before 1319), *Maestà* (detail), 1310. Paint on panel. Duomo di Siena, Italy

were painted by different people, at different times. But what if we release the postulate, cultivated by generations of foundational research on artworks of this period, that when such stylistic dissimilarities appear it means there has been a change in time of origin and/or in authorship, and instead ask: What are some other reasons why there might be unlike zones gathered together in a late-medieval Tuscan painting?[9] Could there be a supportive context for the dissimilarity of head and body introduced by the overpainting, making it possible for the addition of the new faces to have drawn new, latent content *out of* the Madonnas, as the arrival of the fly drew a new story out of Goya's cats?

UNLIKENESS FROM USING PAINT TO SIMULATE NOT-PAINT

One of the reasons why a painting might be commissioned from a late-medieval Italian artist is for paint's ability to mimic more cumbersome and/or expensive materials, as if the medium is a kind of *prima materia* that can be faux-transformed into other substances and mounted on the panel surface.[10] Nonprecious items could also be simulated with this one-to-one representational logic. For example, the late fourteenth-century painter Cennino Cennini recommended that a small wet stick be used to coarsen the surface of the wall when painting wool in fresco: rough cloth calls for/calls forth actual roughness.[11] Where this fictive wool meets fictive skin, there will be a sudden shift, from rough to smooth—a seam line where two zones of paint, which are dissimilar to each other because of how they have been manipulated into fictive versions of unlike substances, meet.

Paint was also used to simulate artworks in other media. By the time Coppo and Guido painted their Madonnas, the industry of making Madonna and Child images had been underway for over 800 years, and many different materials—including ivory, stone, wood, textile, metalwork, and stained glass—had been shaped, woven, carved, and layered into representations of these divinities.[12] Compositional prototypes were recycled and converted from one material into another, even across major changes in scale and function.[13]

Many panel paintings can be seen to contain artifacts of such conversions, skeuomorphic memories of the predecessor medium their imagery was derived from.[14] For example, the gilt halo of Coppo's Madonna does not stop at the perimeter of the flat image field but extends over the underside of the painted frame. Cesare Bradi called this overlap a *riassorbimento*—a reabsorption of a three-dimensional halo, fashioned from a wooden disc, into the two-dimensional picture plane.[15] Another artwork that Coppo may also have been involved in creating, located in the church of Santa Maria Maggiore, Florence, has two large-scale figures of the Madonna and Child selectively built up in polychrome relief, while the remainder of the work is painted.[16] In this part-painting, part-sculpture, the drapery worn by the figures in the flat, painted narrative scenes resembles a flattened, "reabsorbed" version of the

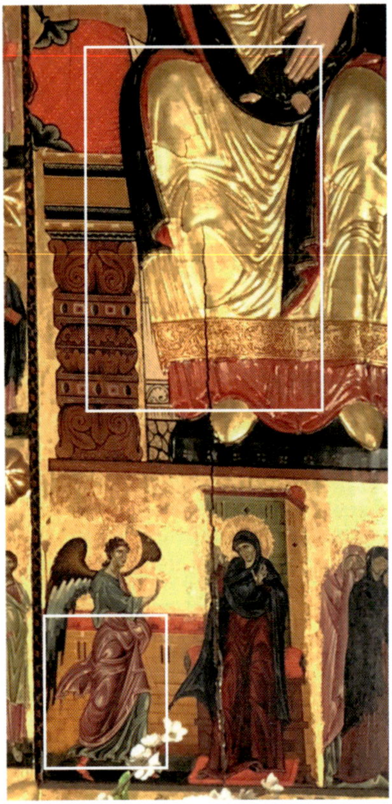

Fig. 2.5. Coppo di Marcovaldo (attr.), *Madonna and Child Enthroned* (detail), c. 1270, annotated to show formal similarity between sculpted and painted drapery. Paint and sculpted gesso on panel, overall 98 3/8 × 48 3/8 in. (250 × 123 cm). Santa Maria Maggiore, Florence, Italy. Photo by the author

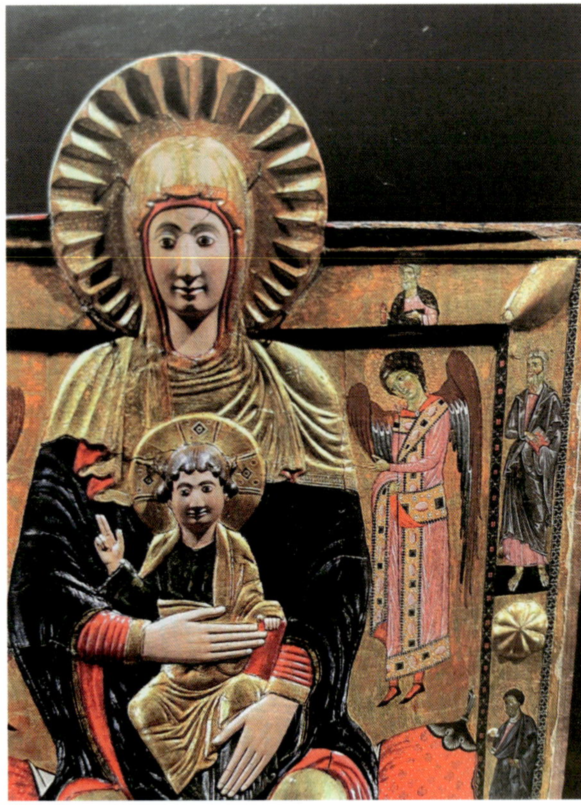

Fig. 2.6. Coppo di Marcovaldo (attr.), *Madonna and Child Enthroned* (detail), c. 1270, during conservation treatment, as reproduced in Marco Ciatti and Cecilia Frosinini, eds., *Immagine antica: Madonna and Child of Santa Maria Maggiore in Florence: Studies and Restoration* (Florence: Edifir, 2003), ii. Opificio delle Pietre Dure photo archive, Florence

three-dimensional drapery worn by the sculpted figures, as the angular, gilt, carved fabric creates a similar pattern of high-contrast shadows next to lines of reflected highlight (fig. 2.5).[17]

The fall of light on the high-relief heads of the Madonna and Child in Santa Maria Maggiore is suggested by gradual, softly blended transitions in their polychromy, from light to mid-tone colors. The heads of the flat figures in the narrative scenes are modeled in a different style, with dark shadow lines laid right next to bright, calligraphic highlights (fig. 2.6).[18] The artist appears to have adapted his painting technique to the curvature of the support. The features of the sculpted head cast their own shadows, removing the need to simulate these shadows in paint.

Scholars have compared Duccio's gently gradated rendering of faces to contemporary Byzantine painting techniques.[19] Without negating these connections, could Duccio's contribution to the art of painting also be understood in relation to the manner of rendering flesh tones intuitively elicited by the task of spreading and stretching color fields over sculpted heads? Duccio was certainly looking at sculptures; it is not unreasonable to think that he was also looking at the techniques used to paint them. He may have even been commissioned to paint a sculpture and apply these techniques himself.[20]

Inconsistencies in style and technique among the various constituent parts of a late-medieval Madonna and Child begin to look normal when set in this context, when seen in relation to the ways zones of paint in these artworks could be selectively made to simulate other materials or absorb nonflat predecessor media. There is a link between this source of unlikeness and the unlikeness source that is time of origin, in that the traces left by three-dimensional substances and media on the painting surface can also be described in terms of befores and afters, precedents and inheritances. Yet such absorptions are built into the artwork by its author, while changes over time are received by the artwork in the absence of its author; the former is closer to a skeuomorph, the latter closer to a palimpsest.

UNLIKENESS FROM USING PAINTING STYLE IN STORYTELLING

The overpaintings of the two Sienese Madonna and Child panels seem to have more to do with form, and less with content: the Madonnas remain Madonnas; they simply look different. But were the artists who overpainted the two Sienese Madonnas operating in a context where there was a clear dividing line between form and content? Shortly after Duccio's *Maestà* was installed in Siena's cathedral, the painter Simone Martini frescoed another *Maestà* in the government headquarters of Siena. In the frame of this fresco is a roundel that depicts Saint Jerome in the act of making a new Latin translation of the Hebrew Bible. While the Hebrew text is represented entirely in paint, a page of Jerome's new Latin text is represented via an actual piece of paper, mounted on the frescoed wall. Simone's artistic conversions—of paint to paper, and paper to paint—visually endorse Jerome's parallel act of translation.[21] The substance of the artwork, its materiality, becomes part of the substance of the story.[22]

Such interplay between medium and message could also happen with divine figures. An analogy can be drawn between using actual paper in a representation of paper and incorporating relics into a representation of a divinity. On the Santa Maria Maggiore panel, the sculpted heads of the Madonna and Child protrude farther than any other element on the artwork. The reason for the higher degree of relief selectively given to these heads is that they are also reliquaries, with small relic pouches held in cavities inside them.[23] Similarly, the sculpted head of a fourteenth-century Madonna in Todi is the only element in relief on the otherwise-painted surface, likely because this head also doubled as a reliquary.[24] The wooden disk that carries the painted head and gilt halo of a very large late thirteenth-century Madonna panel outside of Naples was made from a different kind of wood than the main body of the panel, and within two centuries of its manufacture, a legend had developed that this head disc was itself a kind of relic, a fragment of an older Byzantine icon that had been miraculously saved from iconoclasm and incorporated into a new painting when it arrived in Italy.[25]

In these examples, the dissimilarity of head from body was intentionally constructed to signal a special bond between the painting and its divine prototype. What bodies actually look like—the proportionality and material connectedness that make a real human head seem to fit together with the body it belongs to—was, in these instances, beside the point.[26] The presence of a relic is, moreover, not the only reason why a representation of a Madonna and Child might become willfully disjointed. When one part of a painting is made from a different material or is painted differently than another part, this can destabilize illusionistic effects, calling attention to artificiality of the artwork; in this way, strategically deployed unlikeness can help to prevent idolatrous confusions between actual deity and painted representation. Herbert Kessler has argued that this is the reason for the head/body unlikeness in the twelfth-century fresco cycle at San Pietro in Ferentillo a Vallo, where the head of Christ was not painted in fresco, like the rest of his body, but was instead made on a rigid material mounted onto the wall.[27]

There is another way in which the selective unlikeness in the overpainted Madonnas could have come to chime with the content of the panels. On at least three other large-scale religious paintings made during the generation of Coppo and Guido, between 1260 and 1300, the flesh tones of the main divine figures have a cool, green underlayer, while the flesh tones of the little, marginal angel figures in the corners of the panels have a warm, brown underlayer.[28] The use of a green underlayer was likely understood as a means of enhancing the three-dimensionality of the painted body, so perhaps this switch in layer structure is the painted version of the sculptural technique wherein degree of relief is a way of hierarchically drawing attention to the most important represented figures.[29] Simpler still, perhaps what elicited this unlikeness was just the nonhuman substance of angelic bodies, their natures as a different order of being.

Any of these narratives provide a content-based justification for why the overpainted portions of the Madonnas look unlike the adjacent zones of paint. The subject matter and the particular conventions of representing deities accommodate the dissimilarities delivered by the entry of the new paint layers. Here, instead of the time-telling capacity of style, the storytelling capacity of style—the way in which differences in materiality and technique are made to operate as narrative instruments—becomes another source for unlikeness.

UNLIKENESS FROM HANDLING PAINT AS IF IT IS NOT PAINT

Artworks made by outsider artists may look different from artworks made by commercially successful artists not only because of differences in training, but also because those artworks play entirely different roles in the lives of their makers. This can inflect how tightly the brushes are held, the speed of the strokes, the positioning of the artist's body relative to the canvas, whether the color is pushed or pulled, and any of the near-infinite other sensual factors that will play roles in what the colors come to look like.

A number of paintings from the thirteenth century in Italy have panel supports that are referred to as *scavato*, or excavated, because of how they were fabricated. In these, the framing elements are not attached onto the wooden plank as separate pieces; instead, the frame and the entire interior field that constitutes the main picture plane are carved out of the same plank. Even large panels were prepared with this technique, although the effort required to excavate the flat, recessed interior field would have been significant, and the much easier alternative method of gluing separate framing elements onto the panel was known.[30] It is more accurate to think of the *scavato* panel as a painted relief sculpture than it is to think of it as a painting. The wood of the panel is handled and approached less as a support or carrier for paint layers than as if it were part of those layers, integrally connected to the color films, the way that muscles are integral to skin.

This sculptural sensibility also pervades how the different parts of the paintings are brought together. On the head of a mid-thirteenth-century Madonna in the Accademia in Florence is a crown built up in relief, which means that the crown actually does sit on top of her painted head, in the way that crowns do sit on top of heads. Another mid-thirteenth-century Madonna in the Uffizi sits on a patterned cushion that extends over the edge moldings of the sculpted frame (fig. 2.7), because actual cushions have heft and bulk, and cannot slip beneath frames. Giotto drew an ear for Christ in his Santa Maria Novella crucifix, but this ear is not visible in the final paint layer; hair was painted on top of it, because hair can go on top of ears and cover them.[31] The paint film is handled by the painter as if it has body, as if it is not paint at all.[32]

What would it look like if a late-medieval Italian painter not only approached and used paint films as if those films had sculptural body, but also approached completed, preexisting paintings with the expectation that these works could also behave in three-dimensional ways? In Toulouse, there is a painted crucifix attributed to the early fifteenth-century Florentine artist Lorenzo di Bicci. Within 100 years of its initial construction, the outstretched, painted arms of the crucified Christ were sawn out of the panel, the wood on the back was shaved down, and the thinned-down arms were reattached to the panel in a lowered position.[33] The intervention moved the narrative forward: the figure of Christ was taken from the Crucifixion

Fig. 2.7. Detail of fig. 2.3

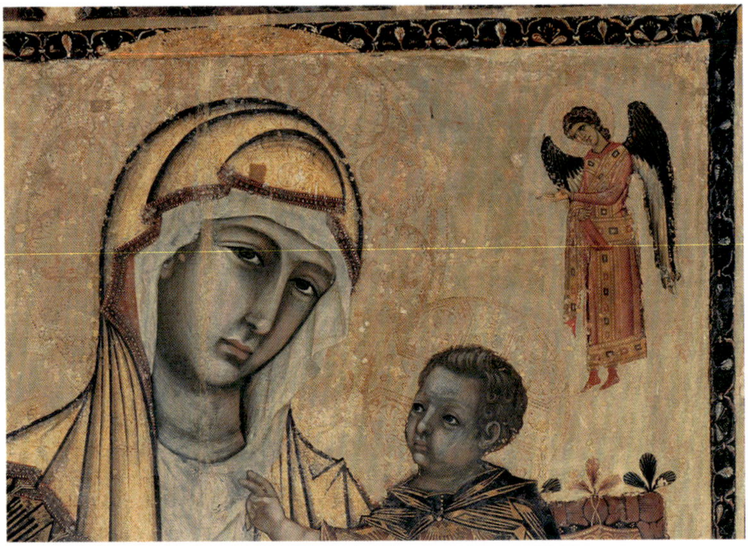

episode of the Passion cycle into the Deposition episode. The painting was altered as if it were, in this case, a sculpture, specifically a mannequin-like, "animated" kind of crucifix, equipped with moveable arms.[34] In Sarzana, there is a twelfth-century crucifix signed and dated by the artist Guillielmus, then overpainted in approximately the mid-thirteenth century. In his account of this intervention, Roberto Bellucci described the overpainter as being so faithful to Guillielmus's contours that the new overpaint layers did not so much give Christ a new face as rather gently rotate his head—again, as if the painting had a head that could turn.[35] In both episodes, it is possible to explain why the preexisting painting was handled the way it was by thinking of that painting as conceptually akin to a jointed sculpture in the minds of its handlers.

In the course of their overpaintings, both Sienese Madonnas were given white veils similar to the one Duccio painted on the *Maestà*.[36] These white veils have finer wrinkles than the headcloths that are painted on top of them, indicating that the veil is made from a light, thin material and the headcloth from a heavier fabric. On Guido's Madonna, the overpainted veil has been executed such that its major folds line up with the folds of the headcloth. The over-painter must have been thinking about the physical impression the heavier headcloth fabric would have left on the thin veil. In addition to having moveable joints, sculpted divinities could have different costumes tacked onto them, sometimes as part of their original conception and sometimes added by later hands. An actual veil, pressed or folded into a preexisting costume worn by a sculpted Madonna, might respond to the pressure of overlying cloth in a similar way.[37]

If an artist sat before a sculpture of a human figure and made continuous drawings of its face over the course of a morning, the appearance of those drawings would gradually change, as changing light on the sculpted face would cause shadows to fall across the features in different patterns, enhancing and diminishing its sense of volume (figs. 2.8, 2.9). Painted shadows on a flat painted face will not move in response to changing light—but they could be made to move, through overpainting. If later interventions could "rotate" painted limbs and heads as if they were fastened onto sculpted bodies, could painted faces be "relit" by an overpainting, as if these were three-dimensional faces responding to a moving sun or candle?

Just as the Guido da Siena overpainter created the white veil he responded to the physicality of the preexisting headcloth that Guido painted, the artist who

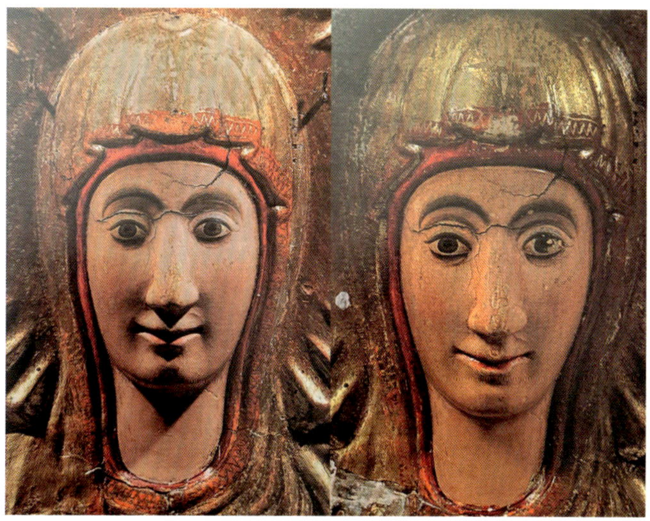

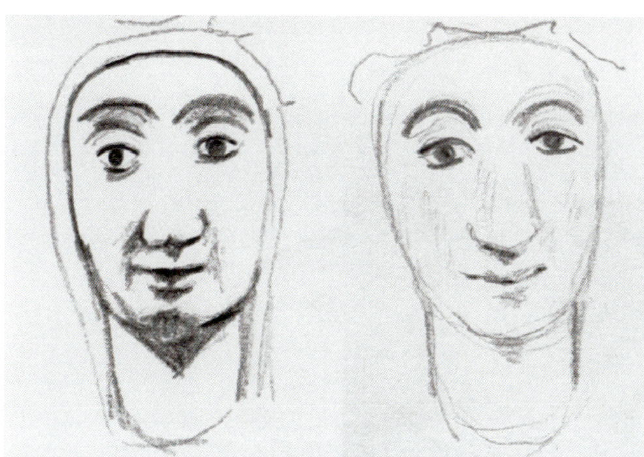

Fig. 2.8. Coppo di Marcovaldo (attr.), *Madonna and Child Enthroned* (details), c. 1270, during conservation treatment, as reproduced in Ciatti and Frosinini, *Immagine antica*, 176. Opificio delle Pietre Dure photo archive, Florence

Fig. 2.9. Illustration, by the author, of the images in fig. 2.8, showing how the same sculpted head can generate multiple, distinct two-dimensional renderings, depending on how it is lit

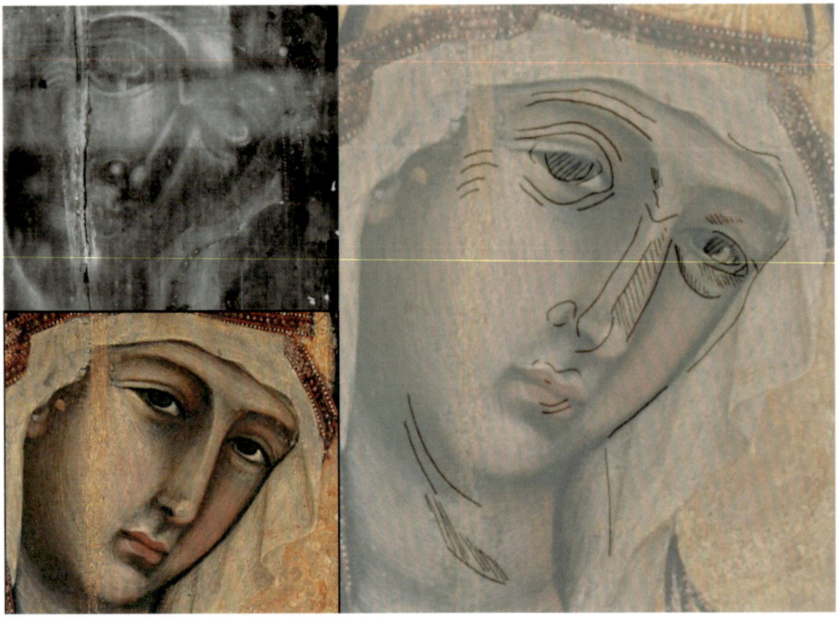

Fig. 2.10. Clockwise from top left: x-radiograph of Coppo di Marcovaldo, *Madonna and Child Enthroned*, 1261, Istituto Centrale per il Restauro; illustration by the author showing drawing of underlying faces visible in the x-radiograph superimposed on the overpainted Madonna's face in Coppo di Marcovaldo's *Madonna and Child Enthroned*, 1261; and Cesare Brandi, "Il restauro della Madonna di Coppo di Marcovaldo dalla chiesa dei Servi di Siena," *Bollettino d'Arte* 35 (1950): fig. 15 (detail of fig. 2.3)

overpainted Coppo's Madonna can be seen to have "listened" to the faces by Coppo that he covered: while he certainly overlaid a Duccesque design upon them, he seems also to have followed their lead. Only the position of the Madonna's nose was shifted by the overpainting, not her eyes or mouth, and even this shift seems also to take its cue from Coppo's nose: the new nose lines up with the shadow cast by Coppo's nose. Even though the position of the nose changed, the contrast-line of the new nose was overpainted where a contrast-line already existed (fig. 2.10).[38] Her features essentially remain stable across the intervention, just as carved eyes and mouths would stay stable under shifting light. Perhaps the overpainting can be re-narrated as this: the Madonna began her existence with Coppo under the hard light cast by a bright, overhead morning sunbeam, and later was moved by the Duccesque overpainter into the soft, ambient illumination of evening candles.

Light was an ingredient of art making in late-medieval Siena.[39] Painters manipulated light to create beautiful effects. For example, a halo around a Christ Child by Simone Martini in the Metropolitan Museum of Art in New York has been textured with a heart-shaped pattern that seems to beat, bright to dim to bright, as the viewer steps from left to right.[40] In front of Simone's *Maestà* in the Sienese council hall, a rope-and-pulley system allowed a set of painted wooden arms attached to the rafters to hold lamps that could be raised and lowered to change the play of light on the fresco, which had a variety of elements embedded in it that would have glittered in reply.[41] Candles were a perpetual expense for the city; over the course of five months in the year 1339, the Sienese commune spent 844 lire on candles for the cathedral, a sum well in excess of the cost of the most expensive Sienese altarpiece from the period on record.[42]

The overpaintings of the two Sienese Madonnas appear set in motion by the installation of Duccio's *Maestà*, but it is also possible that the sculptural ways painters handled paint films *encouraged* the interventions by feeding an intuitive expectation that it would be a natural thing for the flat Madonna faces to exhibit the same illumination-induced dynamism that is automatic for three-dimensional Madonna faces. This would help to explain why the Duccesque face applied to Coppo's Madonna conforms so closely to the earlier face it covers, and how it could be that the communities who prayed and sang before the two overpainted paintings accepted the new faces of their Madonnas. Shadows can fall on objects and people without altering their identities; perhaps shading could likewise "fall" on a painting.

CONCLUSION

The overpainted Madonnas are difficult to attribute and date. Exclusive credit for their making can no longer be given to Coppo and Guido because of the overpainted faces, but neither are they plausible as paintings by followers of Duccio. This ambivalence leaves the continued existence of the overpaintings open to question. In 1990, the art historian Angelo Tartuferi called for art historians and conservators to revisit Coppo's overpainted Madonna and to examine the possibility that, given improvements in photographic technology, the overpaint might be removed from the panel in order to recover the Coppo Madonna painted in its entirety.[43] It is reasonable to imagine that continuing advances in documentation might lead to similar calls in the future, because Tartuferi's desire is understandable: Coppo's Madonna is a touchstone in the history of medieval Tuscan painting, the only known signed and dated work by this artist.

Late-medieval Tuscany was a place and timespan wherein the painted heads of divine figures might look dissimilar to neighboring elements of the artwork not only as a corollary of a later overpainting but as an intentionally constructed aspect of the work's initial manufacture, for manifold reasons connected both to content and to the relations between painting and other media. What if the overpainted Madonnas were appreciated as products of this context, as paintings whose phases can be seen as coordinated even though they were not designed as such by a single artistic personality, rather than as incomplete paintings by Coppo and Guido? By letting go of customary authorship models, it is possible to discover a new way to justify the continued existence of the overpainted Madonnas, through the possibility that, in a more complex iteration of how the fly was taken in by Goya's cats, the Duccesque faces came to *fit* into the half-century older artworks onto which they were painted.

NOTES

1. On openness as an artistic property, see Umberto Eco, *The Open Work*, trans. Anna Cancogni (Cambridge, MA: Harvard University Press, 1989).

2. Enzo Carli and Cesare Brandi, "Relazione sul restauro della Madonna di Guido da Siena del 1221," *Bollettino d'Arte* 36 (1951): 248–60; Cesare Brandi, "Il restauro della Madonna di Coppo di Marcovaldo dalla chiesa dei Servi di Siena," *Bollettino d'Arte* 35 (1950): 160–70.

3. Rebecca Corrie, "Images of the Virgin and Power in the Late-Duecento Siena," in *Art as Politics in Late Medieval and Renaissance Siena*, ed. Timothy Smith and Judith Steinhoff (Burlington, VT: Ashgate, 2012), 83–97; Rebecca Corrie, "The Political Meaning of Coppo di Marcovaldo's Madonna and Child in Siena," *Gesta* 29 (1990): 61–75; Joanna Cannon, *Religious Poverty, Visual Riches: Art in the Dominican Churches of Central Italy in the Thirteenth and Fourteenth Centuries* (New Haven, CT: Yale University Press, 2013), 77–83; and Gianna Mina, "Coppo di Marcovaldo's Madonna del Bordone: Political Statement or Profession of Faith?," in *Art, Politics and Civic Religion in Central Italy: 1261–1352*, ed. Joanna Cannon and Beth Williamson (Aldershot, England: Ashgate, 2000), 237–93. On the special relationship between Siena and the Virgin, see Nicolai Rubinstein, "Political Ideas in Sienese Art: The Frescoes by Ambrogio Lorenzetti and Taddeo di Bartolo in the Palazzo Pubblico," *Journal of the Warburg and Courtauld Institutes* 21 (1958): 179–207; and Hayden Maginnis, *The World of the Early Sienese Painter* (Philadelphia: Penn State University Press, 1997), 32–33, 43–44. For broader context on mendicant orders in Siena as patrons of art, see Victor Schmidt, *Painted Piety: Panel Paintings for Personal Devotion in Tuscany, 1250–1400* (Florence: Centro Di, 2005), 170–73.

4. The throne of Guido's Madonna was also overpainted (a portion of which has been preserved on the left-hand side of the painting), but the time at which this took place is unclear; see Carli and Brandi, "Relazione sul restauro," 254. Carli has been miscited as stating that the throne overpainting took place at the same time as the figural overpaintings; see Cannon, *Religious Poverty, Visual Riches*, 79; Alexander Nagel and Christopher S. Wood, *Anachronic Renaissance* (New York: Zone, 2010), 78; and Cathleen Hoeniger, *The Renovation of Paintings in Tuscany, 1250–1500* (Cambridge: Cambridge University Press, 1995), 22–23.

5. Carli and Brandi, "Relazione sul restauro"; Brandi, "Il restauro della Madonna di Coppo"; Maginnis, *World of the Early Sienese Painter*, 184–86; and Miklòs Boskovits, *The Origins of Florentine Painting 1100–1270*, ed. Richard Offner et al., vol. 1, sec.1, *A Critical and Historical Corpus of Florentine Painting* (Florence: Giunti, 1993), 510. The hands of the figures were not overpainted in this intervention, a misconception stated by James Stubblebine, *Guido da Siena* (Princeton, NJ: Princeton University Press, 1964), 31; Rebecca W. Corrie, "Coppo di Marcovaldo's Madonna del Bordone and the Meaning of the Bare-Legged Christ Child in Siena and the East," *Gesta* 35 (1996): 43; Alessandra Gianni, "Le ridipingere delle Madonne di Coppo di Marcovaldo e di Guido da Siena: Aggiornamento stilistico o esigenze devozioni," *Iconographica* 10/11 (2011/2012): 70; Jaroslav Folda, *Byzantine Art and Italian Panel Painting* (Cambridge: Cambridge University Press, 2015), 148; Gertrude Coor-Achenbach, "Coppo di Marcovaldo, His Art in Relation to the Art of His Time," *Marsyas* 5 (1949): 2; and Cannon, *Religious Poverty, Visual Riches*, 79. The hands of Guido's Madonna were overpainted, but at a later time than the 1300s intervention; see Carli and Brandi, "Relazione sul restauro," 251.

6. Benjamin David, "Past and Present in Sienese Painting: 1350–1550," *RES* 40 (2001): 91; Corrie, "Images of the Virgin and Power," 83; Coor-Aachenbach, "Coppo di Marcovaldo," 2; and Hoeniger, *Renovation of Paintings in Tuscany*, 40–42. The thirteenth-century signatures and dates on both panels were not altered. On the debated dating of the panel by Guido da Siena, see Cannon, *Religious Poverty, Visual Riches*, 79–81; and Nagel and Wood, *Anachronic Renaissance*, 75–80. X-radiographs taken of Coppo's Madonna show that the underlying paint layer beneath the overpainted faces remains well preserved: there are losses along a vertical crack in the woodgrain that runs through the Madonna's cheek, but the Christ Child's face appears intact. X-radiography does not show the initial phase of Guido's figures; see Carli and Brandi, "Relazione sul restauro," 253–54.

7. While it is not obvious whether the overpaintings reflect a conception of stylistic progress in painting or were more connected to maintenance of the Madonnas' religious efficacy, there is consensus that these interventions were a response to Duccio's altarpiece; see Maginnis, *World of the Early Sienese Painter*, 184–86; Bruce Cole, "Old in New in the Early Trecento," *Mitteilungen des Kunsthistorisches Institutes in Florenz* 17 (1973): 229–40; Hoeniger, *Renovation of Paintings in Tuscany*, 24–26 and 40–42; Henk van Os, *Sienese Altarpieces 1215–1460: Form, Content, Function*, vol. 1, *1215–1344* (Groningen: Bouma's Boekhuis, 1984), 22–23; and Nagel and Wood, *Anachronic Renaissance*, 79. Prior to Duccio, there had been a high degree of stylistic coherence among the large panel paintings in Siena; see Hayden Maginnis, "Everything in a Name? or The Classification of Sienese Duecento Painting," *Studies* *in the History of Art* 61 (2002): 470–85; and Corrie, "Images of the Virgin and Power," 87–92. For general discussion of the *Maestà* and its impact, see John White, *Duccio: Tuscan Art and the Medieval Workshop* (New York: Thames and Hudson, 1979), 95–102, 184–200; Keith Christiansen, *Duccio and the Origins of Western Painting* (New Haven, CT: Yale University Press, 2009), 7–19; and Hans Belting, *Likeness and Presence: A History of the Image before the Era of Art*, trans. Edmund Jephcott (Chicago: University of Chicago Press, 1994), 405n89.

8. For a summary of the attributions given to the repainter of the Coppo panel, which include Niccolò di Segna, the Goodhart Ducciesque Master, and Segna di Bonaventura, see Boskovits, *Origins of Florentine Painting*, 510. Luciano Bellosi attributes the Guido overpainting to Massarello di Gilio, see "Il possibile Massarello di Gilio," in *Immagine e Ideologia: Studi in onore di Arturo Carlo Quintavalle*, ed. Arturo Calzona, Roberto Campari, and Massimo Mussini (Milan: Electa, 2007), 386–91.

9. Meyer Schapiro, "Style," in *Anthropology Today: An Encyclopedic Inventory*, ed. A. L. Kroeber (Chicago: University of Chicago Press, 1953), especially 292–95.

10. Marco Ciatti, "Considerazioni sull'oreficeria e le altre arti nella seconda metà del Duecento," in *L'arte a Firenze nell'età di Dante*, ed. Angelo Tartuferi and Mario Scalini (Florence: Giunti, 2004), 158; and Elisabetta Cioni, *Scultura e smalto nell'oreficeria senese dei secoli XIII e XIV* (Florence: Studio per Edizioni Scelte, 1998). See also Elena Bartolozzi and Andrea Santacesaria, "Il supporto 'scavato' del 'Dossale di San Zanobi': Punto di partenza per l'identificazione di una tipologia costruttiva dei dipinti su tavola," *OPD Restauro* 17 (2005): 274–75. For examples of late thirteenth- / early fourteenth-century illusionism, see Schmidt, *Painted Piety*, 141–43; Péter Bokody, *Images-within-Images in Italian Painting (1250–1350)* (Farnham, England: Ashgate, 2015), 38–39; John White, *The Birth and Rebirth of Pictorial Space* (Cambridge: Belknap, 1987), 25–28; and Nagel and Wood, *Anachronic Renaissance*, 72. On *prima materia*, see James Elkins, *What Painting Is* (Milton Park, England: Routledge, 2019), 68–96; see also Caroline Walker Bynum, *Christian Materiality: An Essay on Religion in Late Medieval Europe* (New York: Zone, 2011), 231–39.

11. Cennino Cennini, *Il Libro dell'arte*, trans. Lara Broecke (London: Archetype, 2018), 184; and Roberto Bellucci and Cecilia Frosinini, "Working Together: Technique and Innovation in Masolino's and Masaccio's Panel Paintings," in *The Panel Paintings of Masolino and Masaccio: the Role of Technique*, ed. Carl Brandon Strehlke and Cecilia Frosinini (Milan: 5 Continents, 2002), 39–40.

12. Edward Garrison, *Italian Romanesque Panel Painting: An Illustrated Index* (New York: Hacker Art Books, 1976), 37.

13. Cannon, *Religious Poverty, Visual Riches*, 71; Nagel and Wood, *Anachronic Renaissance*, 75–80; and Corrie, "Images of the Virgin and Power," 85.

14. Klaus Krüger, *Der frühe Bildkult des Franziskus in Italien: Gestalt-und Funktionswandel des Tafelbildes im 13. Und 14. Jahrhundert* (Berlin: Gebr. Mann, 1992): 25–30; 208–10, 219–30; Belting, *Likeness and Presence*, 349; and John T. Paoletti, "Wooden Sculpture in Italy as Sacral Presence," *Artibus et Historiae* 13 (1992): 90. In several early fourteenth-century paintings, it is unclear whether the subject of the painting is the deity or a sculpture of it; see Hayden Maginnis, *Painting in the Age of Giotto: A Historical Reevaluation* (University Park: Pennsylvania State University Press, 1997), 127–28; and Klaus Krüger, "Medium and Imagination: Aesthetic Aspects of Trecento Panel Painting," *Studies in the History of Art* 61 (2002): 73.

15. Brandi, "Il restauro della Madonna di Coppo," 168; and Garrison, *Italian Romanesque Panel Painting*, 88.

16. The authorship and dating of this work is unresolved, as certain pieces of evidence point to a late twelfth-century date and an attribution to an unknown Florentine master, while others point to a late thirteenth-century date and an attribution to Coppo; see Susannah Fisher, "The Tabernacle of the Most High: The Florentine Santa Maria Maggiore Madonna," *Arte medievale* 6 (2007): 75–85; Marco Ciatti and Cecilia Frosinini, eds., *Immagine antica: Madonna and Child of Santa Maria Maggiore in Florence: Studies and Restoration*, trans. Miriam Kimber Barbieri and Diane Kunzelman (Florence: Edifir, 2003); and Boskovits, *Origins of Florentine Painting*, 128–29.

17. Paul Hills, *Light in Early Italian Painting* (New Haven, CT: Yale University Press, 1987), 16–18.

18. Maria Luisa Altamura and Alessandra Ramat, "Painting Technique and the State of Conservation: The Painted Surface," in Ciatti and Frosinini, *Immagine antica*, 109–23. Cleaning and examination did not reveal any interruptions that would indicate the relief and painted portions of the object were manufactured at separate moments; see, especially, Altamura and Ramat, 119.

19. For explanations of Duccio's blended face-painting technique as derived from Byzantine models, see Hans Belting, "The 'Byzantine Madonnas': New Facts about Their Italian Origin and Some Observations on Duccio," *Studies in the History of Art* 12 (1982): 7–21, especially 10; and James Stubblebine, "Byzantine Influence in Thirteenth-Century Italian Panel Painting," *Dumbarton Oaks Papers* 20 (1966): 85–101.

20. Alessandro Bagnoli, "Introduzione," in *Scultura dipinta: maestri di legname e pittori a Siena, 1250–1450* (Florence: Centro Di, 1987), 12–14. The sculptors Nicola and Giovanni Pisano are also commonly cited as influences for Duccio; see Christiansen, *Duccio and the Origins*, 53; and van Os, *Sienese Altarpieces 1215–1460*, 34–43. For a sculpture close in appearance to Duccio's *Maestà* Madonna, see Roberto Bartalini, "La Madonna del convento delle cappuccine e le reazioni senese alla scultura di Giovanni Pisano," in *Scultura gotica in Toscana, Maestri, Monumenti, cantieri del Due e Trecento* (Milan: Silvana, 2006), 67–87.

21. Alessandro Bagnoli, *La Maestà di Simone Martini* (Milan: Silvana, 1999), 74, 146n62; for the commissioning documents for this fresco, see 159–61. For additional interpretation of Simone's use of paper, see Jean C. Campbell, *The Commonwealth of Nature: Art and Poetic Community in the Age of Dante* (Philadelphia: Penn State University Press, 2008), 91–95.

22. For a broader argument on material and message in late-medieval Italian painting, see Anne Dunlop, "On the Origins of European Painting Materials, Real and Imagined," in *The Matter of Art: Materials, Practices, Cultural Logics, c. 1250–1750*, ed. Anne Dunlop, Christy Anderson, and Pamela H. Smith (Manchester: Manchester University Press, 2015), 68–96.

23. Ciatti and Frosinini, *Immagine antica.*

24. Francesco Santi, "Appunti su inediti in Umbria," in *Scritti di storia dell'arte in onore di Mario Salmi* (Rome: De Luca, 1962), 51–60; and Krüger, *Der frühe Bildkult des Franziskus*, 29–30.

25. Walter Angelelli, "La Maesta di Montano d'Arezzo a Montevergine e la pittura su tavola dei secoli XIII e XIV," in *La Maestà di Montevergine: Storia e restauro*, ed. Francesco Gandolfo and Giuseppe Muollo (Rome: Artemide, 2014), 85–106; and Giuseppe Muollo, "Il Progetto e la Tecnica di Esecuzione," in Gandolfo and Muollo, *La Maestà di Montevergine*, 23–61.

26. Paul Barolsky, "Naturalism and the Visionary Art of the Early Renaissance," *Gazette des Beaux-Arts* 129 (1997): 57–64.

27. Herbert Kessler, *Spiritual Seeing, Picturing God's Invisibility in Medieval Art* (Philadelphia: University of Pennsylvania Press, 2000), 104–49. Klaus Krüger has likewise interpreted juxtapositions of scale and deliberate archaism in fourteenth-century paintings as meant to destabilize the veracity of the painted illusions; see Krüger, "Medium and Imagination," 56–81. See also Megan Holmes, *Fra Filippo Lippi: The Carmelite Painter* (New Haven, CT: Yale University Press, 1999), 121.

28. Given that by a conservative estimate over 90% of thirteenth-century panel paintings have been lost (see Edward Garrison, "Notes on the Survival of Thirteenth-Century Panel Paintings in Italy," *Art Bulletin* 54 [1972]: 140), and that the tally of surviving large panel paintings made in Siena between the 1260s and the end of the century comes to only nineteen (as of 2002; see Maginnis, "Everything in a Name," 471), I believe that three examples are enough to establish that a switch in flesh-tone layer structure between marginal and major figures was an established convention. See the dossal in the Memphis Brooks Museum attributed to Rinaldo da Siena by Luciano Bellosi, "Precedenti e contemporanei senesi di Duccio," 40; the Madonna in Siena's Pinacoteca Nazionale, attributed alternately to Guido da Siena and Dietisalvi di Speme by Silvia Giorgi, "Category 1," in Bagnoli et al., *Duccio alle origini*, 52–53; and the Madonna attributed to Guido da Graziano in Montaione by Francesco Mori, "Category 13," in Bagnoli et al., *Duccio alle origini*, 92–95. An earlier, non-Sienese example showing a similar shift in flesh-tone structure is the dossal of Christ in Glory attributed to Pescius or the Maestro di San Felice di Giano, located in the Galleria Nazionale, Umbria; see Garrison, *Italian Romanesque Panel Painting*, 142n369.

29. For a twelfth-century Sienese example of hierarchically organized degrees of relief, see Arturo Carlo Quintavalle, "Rosano e i crocifissi viventi della Riforma, dal Volto Santo di Lucca a Batiló," *OPD Restauro* 20 (2008): 156–57.

30. Bartolozzi and Santacesaria, "Il supporto 'scavato,'" 273–84. An unpublished example is the crucifix in the Acton collection attributed to the Master of Saint Francis and dated to c. 1270, which measures 92 ⅛ × 63 ⅜ in. (234 × 161 cm) but was originally even larger, as this work was cut down in a later intervention. The much-smaller-scale crucifix in the National Gallery, London, also attributed to the Master of Saint Francis, has its framing elements attached as separate pieces, confirming that the artist in this instance was aware of this easier technique and that the *scavato* technique was not the default option. David Bomford, *Art in the Making: Italian Painting before 1400* (London: National Gallery, 1989), 57–58.

31. For discussion of this aspect of the Greve Madonna, see Lars R. Jones, "Visio Divina? Donor Figures and Representations of Imagistic Devotion: The Copy of the 'Virgin of Bagnolo' in the Museo dell'Opera del Duomo, Florence," *Studies in the History of Art* 61 (2002): 45. On Giotto's underpainting, see Marco Ciatti, "Tecnica e stile in Giotto: Alcune riflessioni," in *Giotto e il Trecento*, ed. Alessandro Tomei (Milan: Skira, 2009), 356.

32. Bartolozzi and Santacesaria, "Il supporto 'scavato,'" 275–76.

33. Elisabeth Mognetti, "Marks of Devotion: Case Study of a Crucifix by Lorenzo di Bicci," *Studies in the History of Art* 61 (2002): 354–69.
34. Kamil Kopania, *Animated Sculptures of the Crucified Christ in the Religious Culture of the Latin Middle Ages* (Warsaw: Wydawnictwo Neriton, 2010), 38–40; see also Margrit Lisner, *Holzkruzifixe in Florenz und in der Toskana von der Zeit um 1300 bis zum frühen Cinquecento* (Munich: Bruckmann, 1970).
35. Roberto Bellucci, "La Croce di Sarzana tra materia e immagine," in *Pinxit Guillielmus: Il Restauro della Croce di Sarzana*, ed. Cecilia Frosinini et al. (Florence: Edifir, 2001), 48–50.
36. On the origins of the veil motif, see Joseph Polzer, "Pietro Lorenzetti's Artistic Origin and His Place in Trecento Sienese Painting," *Jahrbuch der Berliner Museen* 35 (1993): 74, 75.
37. Valentina Forni, "Il problema critico delle integrazioni plastiche nella scultura lignea policroma," *OPD Restauro* 10 (1998): 95–111; for examples, see Clara Baracchini, ed., *Scultura lignea, Lucca 1200–1425* (Florence: Studio Per Edizioni Scelte, 1995).
38. The face painted by Coppo visible in the x-radiograph does not appear to show through the overpaint layers like a *pentimento*; this must be because the cool, dark color applied as an underlayer for the Duccesque face has sufficient hiding power to keep Coppo's face obscured. Since the dark underlayer may have limited the visibility of Coppo's face, it is possible that the overpainter had to make an effort to line up the Duccesque features with Coppo's features. This observation was developed in conversation with Mark Aronson.
39. Norman Muller, "In a New Light: The Origins of Reflective Halo Tooling in Siena," *Zeitschrift für Kunstgeschichte* 75 (2012): 153–78; Paul Hills, *Light of Early Italian Painting*, 98; Christopher R. Lakey, "The Materiality of Light in Medieval Italian Painting," in "Medieval Materiality," ed. Anne E. Lester and Katherine C. Little, special issue, *English Language Notes* 53, no. 2 (2015): 119–37.
40. Keith Christiansen, "Simone Martini's Altar-Piece for the Commune of Siena," *Burlington Magazine* 136 (1994): 148–59.
41. Muller, "In a New Light," 167–68; Roberto Bartalini, "Scultori anonimi, tra gli anni venti e quaranta del Trecento," in *Scultura gotica Senese* (Siena: Fondazione Monte dei Paschi di Siena, 2011), 315–21, fig. 16.
42. For the location of Guido's panel within San Domenico, see Cannon, *Religious Poverty, Visual Riches*, 81–83. See Corrie, "Political Meaning," 61–62, 69n2, for the location of Coppo's panel. On the expenditures made by the Sienese commune on candles, see Maginnis, *World of the Early Sienese Painter*, 69, 71.
43. Angelo Tartuferi, *La pittura a Firenze nel Duecento* (Florence: Alberto Bruschi, 1990), 30.

CHAPTER 3
JAPANESE PAINTING
MOUNTING, MEDIATION, TRANSMISSION, RENEWAL

Yukio Lippit

It is often noted that Japan has a highly distinctive culture of art conservation, rooted in practices that extend back centuries. If there is one practice that captures the popular image of this world of Japanese conservation, it is *kintsugi*, or "golden joinery," the practice of mending cracks in ceramics with gold-sprinkled lacquer, in such a way that the repairs remain visible (fig. 3.1).[1] Although admittedly rare, *kintsugi* nevertheless reflects a tendency that applies to many different types of art conservation in traditional Japan: a penchant not to disguise repair but instead to aestheticize it. The artful result not only leaves traces of repair visible but centers them in a manner that reshapes an object's visual profile and biography.

This essay explores the relationship between repair and renewal in the realm of Japanese painting. It does so by examining the mounting apparatus of traditional Japanese painting, and more specifically that of the vertical hanging scroll (fig. 3.2). The hanging-scroll format boasts an ancient history and circulated widely throughout East Asia. Its basic components originated in China and were shared by Chinese and Korean hanging scrolls over the centuries—an important consideration when attempting to understand the specific modes and styles of mounting that developed in Japan. The hanging-scroll mounting can be used to frame a wide variety of display objects, most notably calligraphy, although here painting will be the focus.

The apparatus in which a work is embedded consists of a complex assortment of elements, including decorative silk mountings, backing papers, and a dowel around which to roll and unroll the work; the artwork proper is only one part of this configuration. The painting or calligraphy, typically executed on paper or silk, requires several layers of backing papers, which the mounting helps to hold in place. Strips and fragments of mostly silk or paper surround the painting on all four sides to frame the work (fig. 3.3). The textiles most often include at least two different colors and patterns. These fabrics are affixed to a wooden dowel at top and bottom, around which the painting is rolled and unrolled whenever taken out for display.

Fig. 3.1. Example of *kintsugi*, in which cracked ceramics are visibly repaired with gold-sprinkled lacquer

Fig. 3.2. Unknown painter (Japanese, 14th century), *The Poet Fujiwara Kiyotaka*, 14th century. Hanging scroll, ink and colors on paper, 10 3/8 × 10 1/8 in. (26.4 × 25.7 cm). Metropolitan Museum of Art, New York. Gift of Sylvan Barnet and William Burto, in memory of Setsu Iwao, 2014, 2014.719.1

Fig. 3.3. Diagram of traditional mounting apparatus, from *Japanese Picture Mounting and Restoration—Passing on Paper and Silk Artefacts to Future Generations*, ed. Explore Kyoto in History, Cluster Executive Committee (Kyoto, 2019), 14

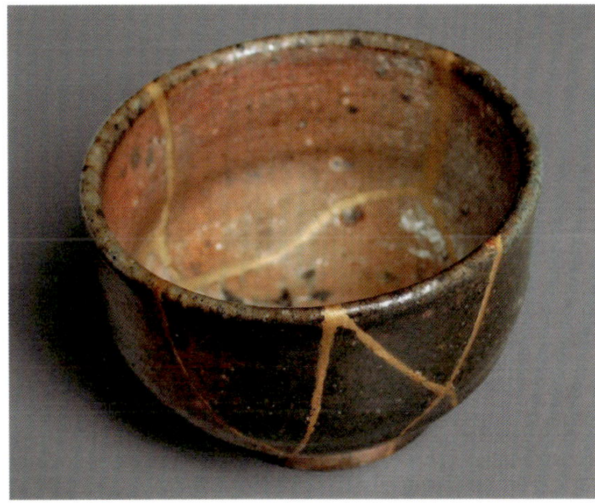

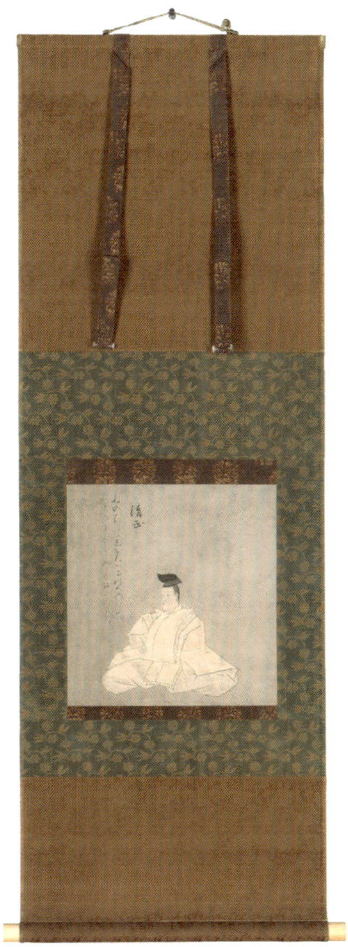

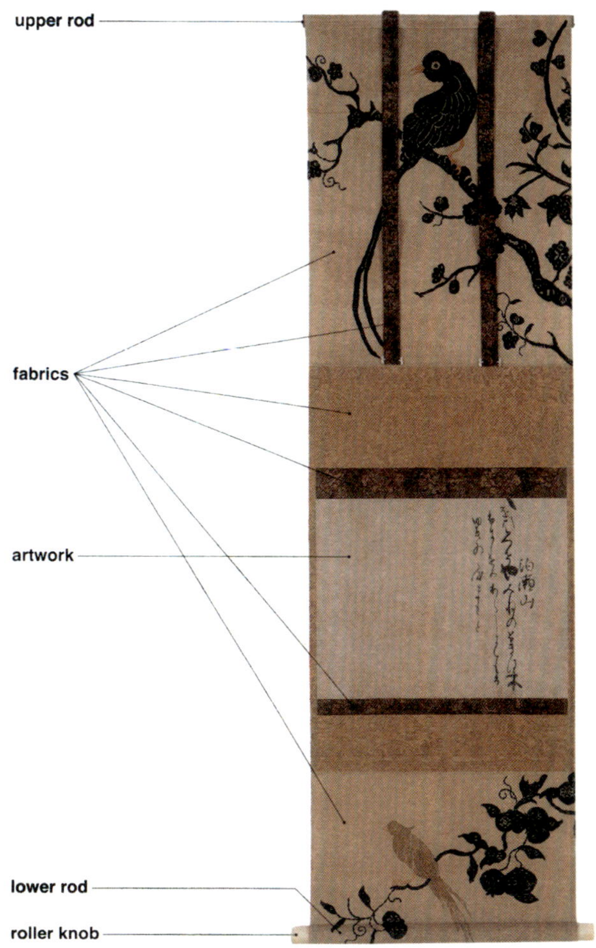

In addition to these basic features, two silk ribbons, known as *fūtai*, are commonly suspended from the top dowel, although they play no particular role other than a decorative one.[2]

The evolution of the mounting apparatus was guided to no small degree by practical considerations. First, it enables ease of rolling and unrolling, which is crucial because until the modern era, Japan had no true culture of public exhibition; paintings were mostly viewed in private settings and only for a brief period. Thus, the display of hanging scrolls was occasion specific. Artworks were typically unrolled only for the duration of a specific event, whether it be a poetry gathering, tea ceremony, social visit, or religious ritual. After a span as short as several hours, the painting was promptly rolled up and stored away. Along with ease of rolling and unrolling, the mounting facilitates compact storage. When a hanging scroll is rolled up around its end-dowel, it forms a cylindrical object that can be placed in a long, slender box and preserved compactly among many similar works.

If maintained within a mounting apparatus in a properly constructed wooden box and storage room, a hanging scroll can be well preserved for centuries. Innumerable antique paintings owe their survival to their mountings, including works that were not initially displayed as hanging scrolls but were eventually framed. When Christianity was banned from the Japanese archipelago in the early seventeenth century, some Christian icons were hidden away and preserved through their placement in mountings. A striking example of a Japanese Christian icon thus preserved is *The Fifteen Mysteries of the Rosary*, now in the Kyoto University Museum.[3]

In this manner, mountings evolved in ways that maximized both ease of display and efficiency of storage, while helping to extend the life of the works they supported. Much more than a physical accoutrement, however, the mounting apparatus was often a carefully curated object in and of itself, a designed environment that was crucial to the aesthetics and meaning of a work. Indeed, the silk mountings, the backing papers, and the dowel constitute something of a parallel history of Japanese painting in which vestiges of the biography, use, and pedigree of the object could be discerned to varying degrees. The mounting apparatus forces us to think in terms of pictorial objects instead of pictures. It constitutes a complex composite that raises fundamental questions concerning the boundaries of a Japanese painting, both physically and conceptually. Where does the artwork end and where do its surroundings begin?

This question comes to the fore whenever a hanging scroll is conserved today. Because the mounting is the zone of first contact between the artwork and its handlers, over time it tends to deteriorate more quickly than the painting itself. With few exceptions, antique paintings that have survived to the present have had their mountings replaced at some point in their history, often several times over. Indeed, present-day mountings invariably bear the imprint of earlier moments of repair and renewal. Numerous works document earlier repairs with inscriptions on the back or on the dowel.[4] Sometimes former mountings are set aside and preserved alongside the painting, visually akin to the shed skin from a molting snake.

This higher rate of turnover on the part of the mounting raises complex questions for the conservation of Japanese painting. In premodern times, mounting could be guided by knowledgeable owners or entrusted to specialized mounters; although professional mounters are still active today, during the modern era, their expertise has increasingly been absorbed into the domain of art conservators. Indeed, during the postwar period, more than a few mounters made an organic transition to art conservation and brought with them a reservoir of knowledge that is now as valuable as ever; in many cases, a conservation project will require the assemblage of an entirely new mounting apparatus for an old painting.[5] At the same time, this convergence of conservation, mounting practice, and art history in practice has developed faster than a mature discursive awareness of the many issues onto which it opens. Before considering these issues further, it is useful to elaborate upon several aspects of the history and nature of the mounting apparatus that underscore its importance to the identity of an artwork.

For centuries, the mounting has conditioned, sometimes to a dramatic degree, the viewing experience of an artwork. This is particularly the case for the mounting silks. The fabrics of the mounting were a focus of attention and admiration, at times on par with or even superseding that of the work they surrounded. Their stature is suggested in historical accounts of art viewings that document, in great detail, the nature of the mountings. Some of these accounts are found in the diaries of practitioners of the *chanoyu* tea ceremony, such as Yamanoue Sōji (1544–1590). In one entry, for example, Sōji records his encounter, during a *chanoyu* gathering, with a landscape by the Chinese painter Yujian. Although he provides a simple sketch of the Yujian landscape in the diary, most of Sōji's entry concerns details of the mounting, and he takes pains to note the color and pattern of each of its components.[6]

Given this level of interest among connoisseurs, it is unsurprising that painters themselves were highly sensitized to the presence and appearance of mounting silks.[7] When the shogunal painter Kano Tan'yū (1602–1674) was asked to authenticate a work by the renowned fourteenth-century Indian monk-painter Yintuoluo, he was apparently as taken with the mounting as he was with Yintuoluo's painting. Tan'yū's divided attention is well captured by a sketch that records this encounter, much of which is devoted to conveying the arabesque peony scrolls that adorned the upper and lower silk bands of the mounting (fig. 3.4).[8]

Despite this attention to the silks that surrounded paintings in traditional viewing practices, the modern discipline of art history has shown little interest in mountings, and it is routine for illustrations in scholarly articles and museum

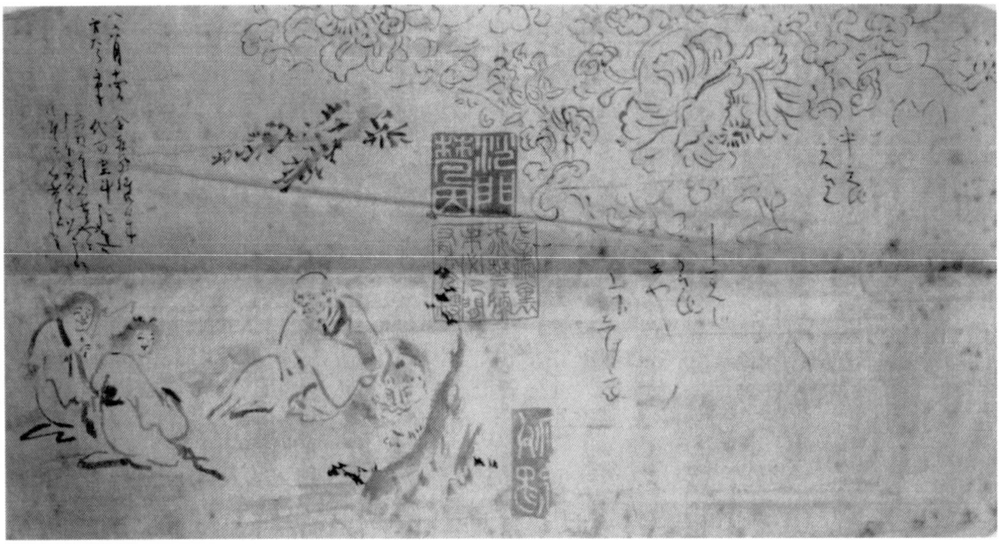

Fig. 3.4. Kano Tan'yū (Japanese, 17th century), *Authentication Sketch of Yintuoluo Painting*, 17th century. Fragment mounted as part of handscroll, ink on paper. Kyoto National Museum. As reproduced in Itakura Masaaki, "'Higashiyama-byōsō' no seiritsu o meguru shōkō," in *Nihon no hyōsō to shūri*, ed. Iwasaki Naoko et al. (Tokyo: Bensei Shuppan, 2020), 92–100

catalogues to crop the mounting out entirely. Most information about the history and practice of mounting is therefore found either among practitioners of *chanoyu* (tea ceremony), which preserves many aspects of premodern connoisseurial practice, or in conservation publications.[9] Only in recent years has art historical attention to the history of mounting ticked upward, and it is now possible to trace, in broad strokes, the stylistic development of mountings throughout the centuries.[10]

Distinctive styles of mounted hanging scrolls can be traced back at least to the fifteenth century.[11] The warrior rulers of medieval Japan, the Ashikaga shoguns, were fond of framing the Chinese paintings in their collections entirely with patterned gold brocade imported from China. Ashikaga Yoshimasa, the eighth medieval shogun, took an especially active role in the design of his mountings, even asking his cultural advisors to procure works to match mounting silks in his possession. The famous triptych *Sakyamuni Descending the Mountain* (fig. 3.5) is now known to have been assembled in the year 1485 under Yoshimasa's supervision.[12] During the subsequent centuries, a number of individual approaches to mounting can be traced among tea masters, aristocrats, and other members of elite status groups. Such examples include the mounting style associated with the tea master and Zen monk Kōgetsu Sōgan (1574–1643), who was fond of using a type of figured silk with a gold

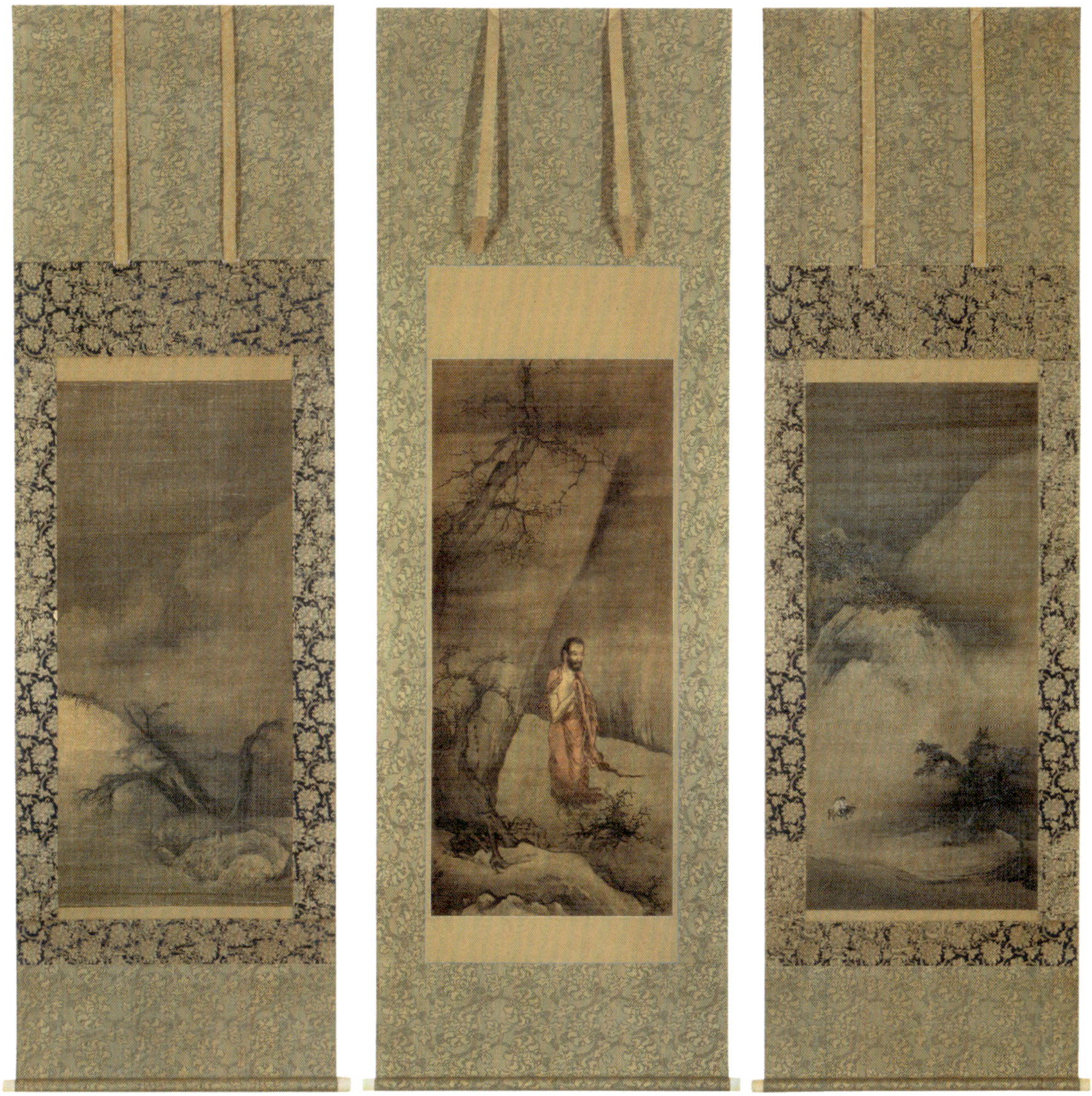

Fig. 3.5. Liang Kai (Chinese, 13th century), *Sakyamuni Descending the Mountain*, early 13th century. Set of three hanging scrolls, ink and colors on silk, 46 5/8 × 20 1/2 in. (118.4 × 52 cm) each. Tokyo National Museum. National Treasure

roundel dragon pattern—the same textile that he chose to use for his own ecclesiastical robe; along with the courtier Konoe Iehiro (1667–1743), who was so focused on this aspect of his collection that he is known to have created at least twenty-eight miniature models of mounting designs.[13]

In the case of literati painting, which became widespread during the eighteenth century, simple and unadorned mountings were considered more appropriate. In contrast to the highly decorative silks that tended to surround other types of paintings in Japan, these works modeled their presentation after the mountings of contemporary Chinese paintings. Accordingly, literati mountings often consisted of plain, unpatterned textiles in silk or satin in subdued colors (fig. 3.6), and without the dangling ribbons (*fūtai*) that had otherwise become de rigueur in Japanese mounting practice.

Mounting styles diversified during the eighteenth and nineteenth centuries, with the spread of pictorial culture. How-to manuals describing the importance of a properly mounted hanging scroll for interior décor served an expanding population of amateur mounters.[14] The fully and splendidly mounted hanging scroll even became a design motif in itself. Beginning in the mid-eighteenth century, one begins to witness women's robes adorned with the motif of mounted hanging scrolls, woven from colored silk threads and distributed across the robe's surface.[15] Within Edo-period visual culture, the entirety of the hanging scroll assemblage was appreciated as an artistic conception in its own right, with no clear boundary separating it from the work embedded within.

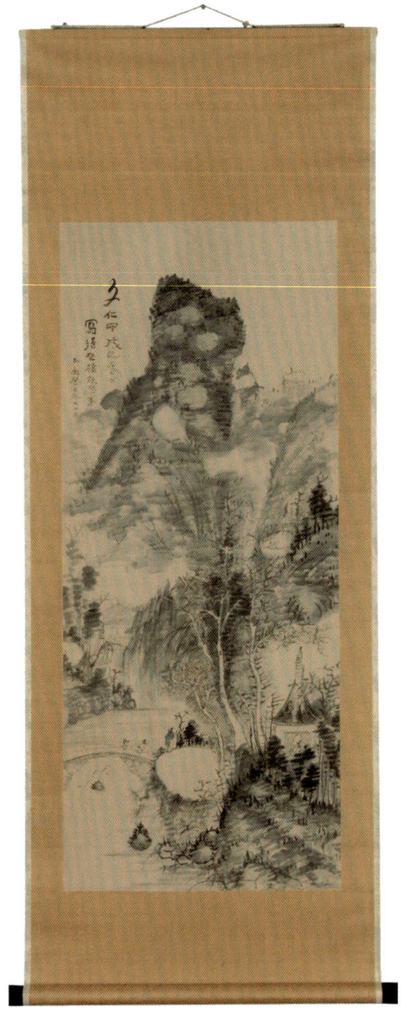

Fig. 3.6. Uragami Gyokudō (Japanese, 1745–1820), *On a Rustic Bridge, Carrying a Zither*, 1814. Hanging scroll, ink on paper, 50 5⁄16 × 21 5⁄16 in. (127.7 × 54.2 cm). Metropolitan Museum of Art, New York. Mary Griggs Burke Collection, Gift of the Mary and Jackson Burke Foundation, 2015, 2015.300.177

In addition to its visual qualities, the material profile of the mounting apparatus was crucial to a painting's function and value. This is especially true in religious contexts, where the sanctity of a pictorial icon could emanate to no small degree from its mounting support. Components of the support could consist of "contact relics"—that is to say, items that once belonged to and were meant to commemorate the deceased. Mortuary portraits were occasionally mounted with fragments from the deceased's robe. And the hair of deceased women was sometimes woven into the mounting, or the painting itself, or placed inside the backing papers on the verso side of a painting.[16] Lists of donors who contributed to the making or remounting of a religious painting, in order to form a karmic connection (known in Japanese as *kechien*), could be included on the back side of a mounting or inside the dowel. Even the metalwork fittings could take the form of Buddhist motifs that enhanced the devotional status of a pictorial object. Such examples suggest that the entire mounting apparatus could be conceptualized as a reliquary, itself a sacred receptacle that intensified the aura of a ceremonial object.[17]

In secular contexts as well, the types of textiles used for the mounting were important to the pedigree and stature of the work as a whole. Prominent families kept albums of valuable textile fragments that could be mobilized toward the remounting of a prized work at any given moment.[18] These albums indicate that the materiality of the mounting apparatus could merit attention equal to that of the work it surrounded, and also that mountings could equally be the focus of collecting activity.

Finally, throughout the history of Japanese painting, mountings participated in the generation of pictorial meaning and could sometimes even change the meaning of a picture. In many examples, as with the mountings of a quartet of paintings *Moons of the Four Seasons* by the artist Mochizuki Gyokusen, the seasonal setting of a work was reinforced by the mounting (fig. 3.7). Here Gyokusen has painted seasonal flowers and plants appropriate to each scroll directly onto the silk mounting.[19] Artists employed this technique of directly painting on the mounting—known as *kakibyōsō*—to generate myriad relationships between paintings and their boundaries. The painted mountings could form a sort of witty or lyrical response, much as with the complementary verses of linked poetry, or complete a form of rebus or picture-puzzle, or provide an aesthetic contrast with the painting that participated in cultural paradigms of high and low (referred to as *gazoku* in Japanese).

In certain cases, the border between painting and mounting was playfully transgressed. An Edo-period ghost painting attributed to the artist Maruyama Okyo (1733–1795) offers a particularly interesting example.[20] Traditionally, female ghosts in Japan were depicted without their feet or legs; the lower half of their body simply faded into the ether. Here, in keeping with this practice, as one moves down the scroll surface, the depicted ghost disappears. But the drama of its disappearance is enhanced by the vanishing of the mounting itself.

The mounting could even serve as a showcase for the artist's agency, a kind of extension of their signature. This was especially the case with the nineteenth-century artists Suzuki Kiitsu and his son Shuitsu (1823–1899), who took the practice of painted mountings to new heights. At times, they took a collaborative approach, whereby Kiitsu created the painting and Shuitsu painted the accompanying mounting. On one occasion, Shuitsu painted all of his many seals on the borders around

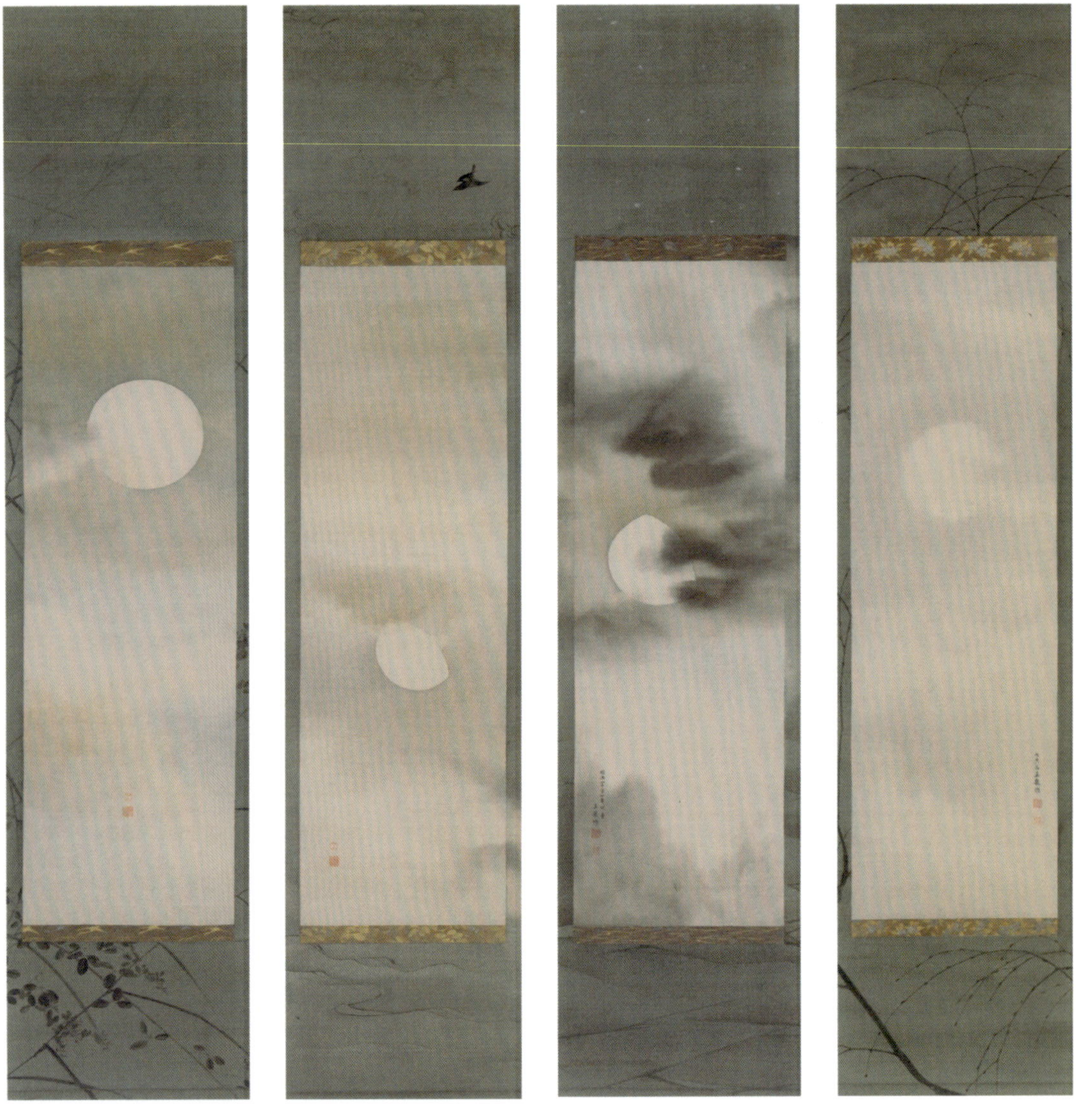

Fig. 3.7. Mochizuki Gyokusen (Japanese, 1834–1913, *Moons of the Four Seasons*, 1911. Set of four hanging scrolls, ink, light color, gold, and silver on silk, 73 ¼ × 17 1/16 in. (186 × 43.4 cm) each. Harvard Art Museums, Cambridge, Massachusetts. Promised gift of Robert S. and Betsy G. Feinberg, TL42147.20

a painting, which were themselves trompe l'oeil paintings of patterned silks, in a playful over-acknowledgement of his own authorship of the work.[21]

Although brief, this survey makes clear that the role played by mountings extended well beyond a merely practical or ornamental one. It is no exaggeration to state that at times the mounting apparatus itself essentially remade or reconfigured the identity of an artwork. This was especially true when painting albums or hand scrolls were excerpted and divided into sets of hanging scrolls.[22] The twentieth-century collector Masuda Takashi (1848–1938), who owned the most celebrated private collection of antiquities in the modern era, owned many such fragments, some of which he cut up himself. For each such piece, Masuda crafted a specially designed mounting apparatus, consisting of rare and valuable historical silks, which reinserted the fragment into a newly consummated composite of pedigreed parts.[23]

Indeed, mounting a two-dimensional object of any kind was a way of elevating its status to that of a notable artwork. There are countless examples of old letters, documents, maps, and lineage charts thus mounted in order to underscore their significance, allowing them to be preserved and enabling their display on occasions of importance.[24] And there are also examples of paintings whose titles or popular monikers derive from their distinctive mountings. Such is the case with the wonderfully nicknamed "Duck Mandala," whose epithet derives from the mandarin duck pattern showcased on its silk borders.[25]

The preceding discussion has attempted to provide a sense of the historical nature and importance of the mounting to the artwork as a whole. In turn, it points to some of the challenges posed by the mounting apparatus for the conservation of Japanese painting today. In recent years, as the mounting itself has emerged as a subject of art historical investigation, and as conservation practices increasingly become the focus of theoretical attention, the issue of how to treat the mounting during conservation has gained in urgency and complexity.

When renewing a mounting, the conservator is confronted by a whole host of considerations that might be broadly defined as aesthetic or art historical.[26] Although many of these considerations overlap and mutually inform any remounting project, it is helpful to examine them individually for expository purposes. The first is the idea that the mounting apparatus should somehow bear a historicist dimension. This is most often expressed through the use of textile fragments from the period in which the work was created, in an attempt to generate an aesthetically coherent or complementary whole. This historicist approach can be witnessed in numerous examples, including an early seventeenth-century calligraphic work by Hon'ami Kōetsu, for which the mounting consists of fragments of a rare textile from Kōetsu's era (fig. 3.8).[27]

A second dimension, which closely relates to the first and might be called contextualist, concerns the potential resonance between the theme of the painting

Fig. 3.8. Hon'ami Kōetsu (calligraphy; Japanese, 1558–1637) and Tawaraya Sōtatsu (painting; Japanese, active c. 1600–c. 1640), ***Poem from the Anthology of Ancient and Modern Poems (Kokin-shū) with Design of Wisteria***, early 17th century. Poem card mounted as a hanging scroll, ink and mica on paper, 50 × 16 ⅛ in. (127 × 41 cm). Museum of Fine Arts, Boston. Gift of Sylvan Barnet and William Burto in honor of Anne Nishimura Morse, 2014.1508

and its borders, and it might lead to a preference for silk mounts decorated with motifs appropriate to a work's subject matter. Yet a third consideration involves color coordination and is centered upon principles of Gestalt psychology. The idea here is that the color and appearance of the silk borders can condition, to no small degree, the manner in which a painting is perceived, and that a well-chosen mounting can resonate with or bring out specific colors and qualities in a work.

And in recent years, the mounting apparatus has become the arena of more adventurous approaches, in which the mounter breaks with convention and designs an environment for the artwork that is bold and surprising. Such is the case for a sutra fragment now in the collection of the Museum of Fine Arts, Boston, remounted by the artist Sugimoto Hiroshi, a famed photographer and interior designer (fig. 3.9). Here Sugimoto has used silver foil—previously unheard of as a material for hanging-scroll mounting—oxidized or tarnished in places to surround a sutra fragment inscribed in silver pigment, one that was famous for having survived a fire at the Buddhist monastery Tōdaiji. Not only does the mounting resonate with the identity and visual qualities of the work, but in this case it self-consciously participates in the domain of contemporary art and design.[28]

One of the great challenges posed by remounting concerns the fact that the subject of conservation often does not reflect any unified conception of time or history. Any given hanging scroll can embody multiple temporalities among its constituent parts. In one example at Zuisenji Temple (Kyoto), a seventeenth-century edict by Emperor Higashiyama (1675–1710) was mounted in the eighteenth century with late sixteenth-century textile fragments.[29] A pictorial object is not necessarily unified in the way in which it manifests a particular historical era or aesthetic regime.

Furthermore, the hanging scroll has become increasingly hybrid as an object of knowledge. That is to say, its different components have become subject to increasingly disparate areas of specialization. The greatest

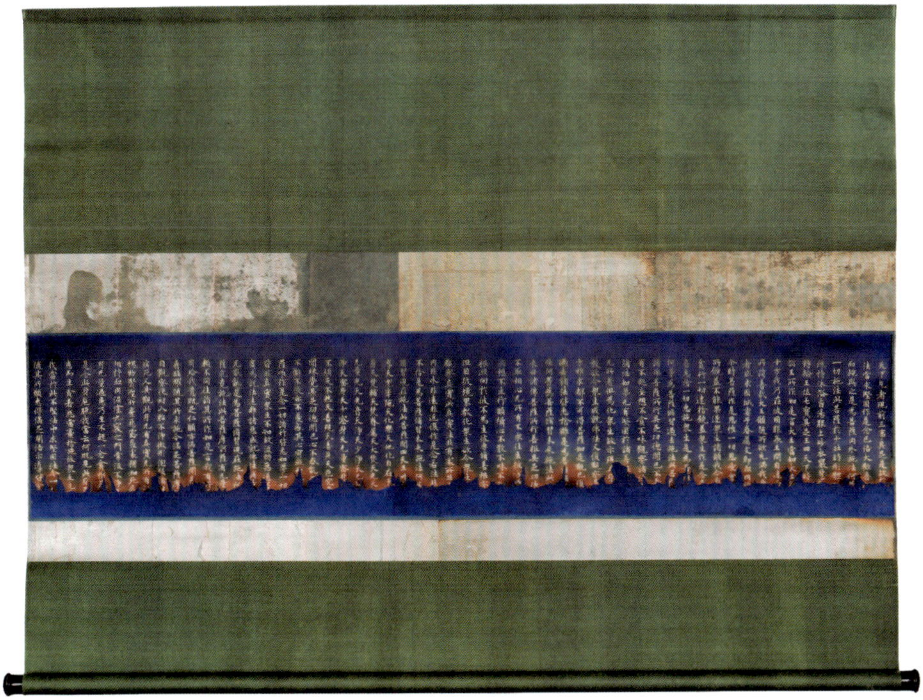

Fig. 3.9. Unknown painter (Japanese, 8th century), mounting designed by Sugimoto Hiroshi (Japanese, b. 1948), *Section from the Flower Garland Sutra (Kegon-kyō), known as the Nigatsudō yake-kyō*, c. 744–52. Section of a handscroll mounted as a hanging scroll, silver on indigo-dyed paper, 33 7/8 × 43 5/16 in. (86 × 110 cm). Museum of Fine Arts, Boston. Gift of Sylvan Barnet and William Burto in honor of Malcolm Rogers, 2014.905

experts of historical mounting practices today are members of the art world whose own professions maintain continuity with traditional crafts and vocations, such as conservators and antiquities dealers. They are the living repositories of "premodern knowledge" about the mounting apparatus, not art historians. Most painting historians are, in fact, poorly informed about mounting history.

This divide is exacerbated by the fact that an increasing number of specialists in painting no longer directly handle works of art. In earlier historical eras, viewers were always also handlers, and direct haptic engagement with a hanging scroll was an organic and central part of the viewing experience. Today, an increasingly greater proportion of the audience for Japanese painting is estranged from a tactile familiarity with the artworks, dimming considerably an awareness and appreciation of the mounting apparatus as a vital component of a work's objecthood.

In the modern era, the movement and redistribution of traditional Japanese paintings into international collections across the globe has added extra layers of

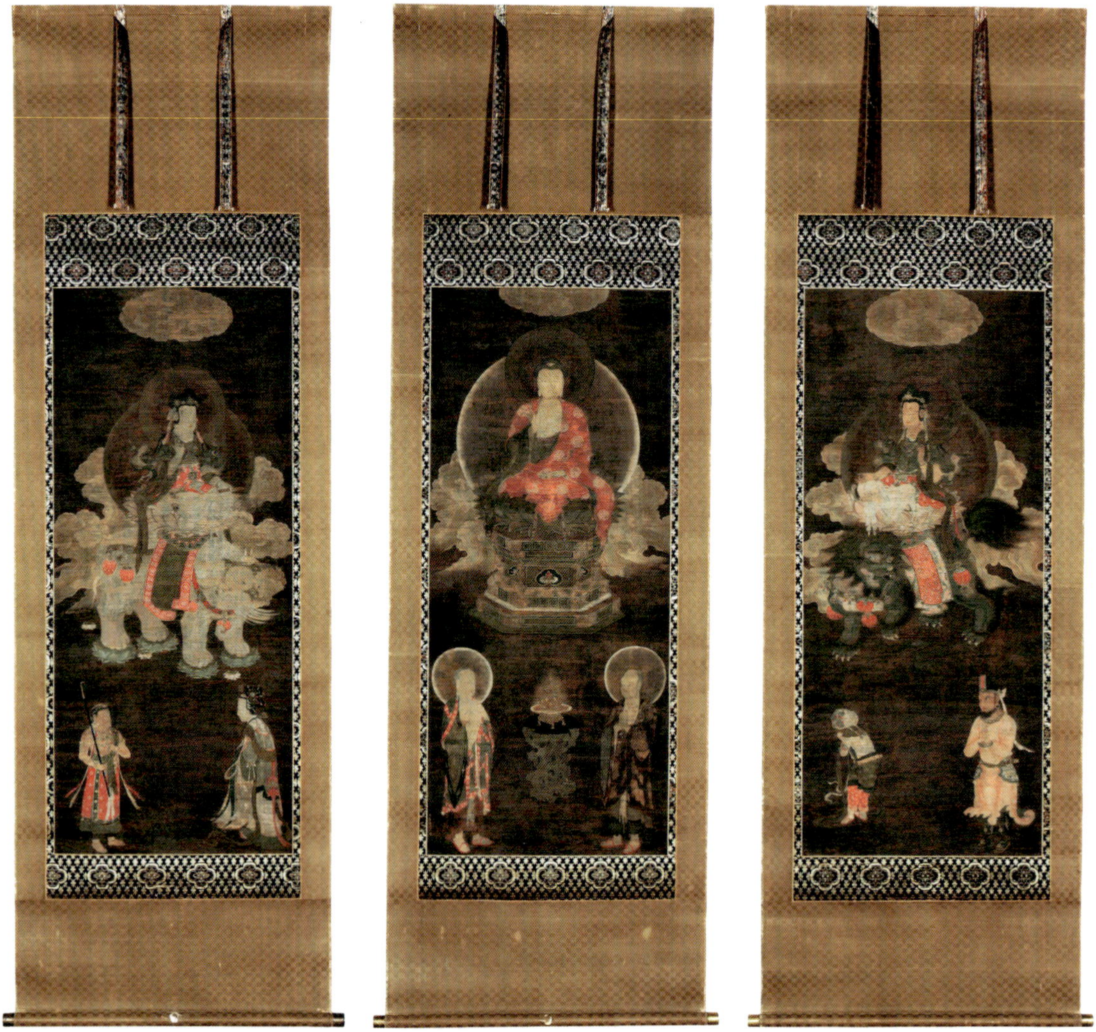

Fig. 3.10. Unknown painter (Chinese, 14th century), *Shakyamuni Triad: Buddha Attended by Manjushri and Samantabhadra*, 14th century. Set of three hanging scrolls, ink and color on silk, 42 1⁄16 × 18 1⁄4 in. (106.9 × 46.4 cm) each. Cleveland Museum of Art. Purchase from the J. H. Wade Fund, 2009.342

complexity to their preservation. During the early twentieth century, for example, large numbers of Japanese paintings settled in distinguished collections at places such as the Museum of Fine Arts, Boston, and the collection of Charles Lang Freer, now housed at the Smithsonian's Freer Gallery of Art in Washington, DC. It was common practice at this time for hanging scrolls to be placed in framed panels, which precluded the ability to roll and unroll them in the traditional manner. Today, however, many of these same scrolls are being systematically restored to the traditional apparatus of a vertical hanging scroll.

The world of East Asian conservation today has even witnessed the emergence of a "politics of mounting." During earlier historical eras, countless scrolls of Chinese and Korean origin circulated in Japan, where they served for centuries as icons for ritual worship or prized works in elite collections. Over time, these imported paintings were remounted—typically multiple times—in Japanese styles and have been passed down to the present framed by the ornate silks and other features of Japanese mounting traditions. As a result, some paintings can be understood to have multiple nationalities. This dual citizenship raises difficult and essential questions when such works are conserved and their mountings require renewal. In what manner should that mounting be carried out? Such questions can become particularly delicate for the many Chinese and Korean paintings of Japanese provenance that have moved into Western collections during the modern era. A good example is a Chinese Buddhist triptych in the Cleveland Museum of Art that still bears its traditional Japanese mounting (fig. 3.10).[30] The very idea of a national style of mounting can be understood as a political one, and the mounting apparatus itself can potentially serve as a space onto which identity politics and the complicated dynamics among East Asian nation-states are projected.

In the case of Japanese painting, a sustained focus on the mounting apparatus underscores the need for an art history that is centered more robustly on the analysis of pictorial objects, rather than merely of pictures. The conceptualization of how time, history, pedigree, and biography are embedded in the hanging scroll may necessitate a reconfiguration, and preferably a convergence, of the fields of knowledge that currently inform the conservation and renewal of hanging scrolls. Such a realignment will help us to understand more holistically, and within a framework that accommodates the complex temporality and objecthood of Japanese painting, how to most meaningfully extend the life of the work.

NOTES

Acknowledgements: This essay would never have been written without the inspiration of the 2021 Conservation | Making | Art | History conference at the Clark Art Institute convened by Caroline Fowler and Alexander Nagel, which was remarkable in every way. It is heavily indebted to conversations with colleagues in the Japanese conservation field over the years. In particular, Iwatarō Oka, Jennifer Perry, and Tanya Uyeda are gratefully acknowledged for reading a draft version of the essay, sharing their expertise, and making valuable suggestions.

1. For a recent overview, see *Flickwerk: The Aesthetics of Mended Japanese Ceramics* (Münster: Museum für Lackkunst, 2008).

2. English-language publications that discuss Japanese painting mountings include Masako Koyano, *Japanese Scroll Paintings: A Handbook of Mounting Techniques* (Washington, DC: Foundation of the American Institute for Conservation of Historic and Artistic Works, 1979); Sondra Castile, "Mountings for Japanese Calligraphy and Paintings," in *The Written Image: Japanese Calligraphy and Painting from the Sylvan Barnet and William Burto Collection*, ed. Miyeko Murase (New York: Metropolitan Museum of Art, 2002), 180–87; John Winter, *East Asian Paintings: Materials, Structures and Deterioration Mechanisms* (London: Archetype, 2008), 127–40; and Philip Meredith and Tanya Uyeda, "Mountings and Painting Techniques of Ukiyo-e Hanging Scrolls," in *Drama and Desire: Japanese Paintings from the Floating World, 1690–1850*, ed. Anne Nishimura Morse (Boston: Museum of Fine Arts, 2007), 223–27.

3. See Iwasaki Naoko, "Bunkazai no shūfuku," in *Gakumon no ishizue o uketsugu—Bunka daigaku chinretsukan kara no shuppatsu*, exh. cat., ed. Kyōto Daigaku Sōgō Hakubutsukan (Kyoto: Kyōto Daigaku Sōgō Hakubutsukan, 2014).

4. The most famous such case is the *Six Realms* scroll in Shōjuraigōji Temple, which bears inscriptions on its dowels of six prior conservations over the course of many centuries. Nōami, a cultural advisor to the medieval Ashikaga shoguns, even inscribed *waka* poetry on the dowels. See Yamamoto Satomi, "Shōjuraigōji-bon Rokudō-e no shūfuku to idō," in *Kokuhō Rokudō-e*, ed. Izumi Takeo et al. (Tokyo: Chūōkōron Bijutsu Shuppan, 2007); and Miriam Chusid, "Constructing the Afterlife, Reenvisioning Salvation: Enma Halls and Enma Veneration in Medieval Japan," *Archives of Asian Art* 69, no. 1 (2019): 21–53.

5. On the relationship between traditional mounting practice and conservation today, see Oka Kōzō, "Hyōgu-shi kara sōkō-shi e," in *Nihon no hyōsō to shūri*, ed. Iwasaki Naoko et al. (Tokyo: Bensei Shuppan, 2020), 20–46. Oka's essay includes valuable anecdotes concerning the mounting culture of the prewar period and traces the changing self-awareness of mounters (*hyōgu-shi*) as conservators (*sōkō-shi*).

6. For a full introduction to the diary and illustrations of Sōji's sketches, see Gotō Bijutsukan, ed., *Yamanoue Sōjiki—Tenshō jūyonen no me*, exh. cat. (Tokyo: Gotō Bijutsukan, 1995). Yujian's reputation among Japanese *chanoyu* practitioners at the time is discussed in Andrew M. Watsky, "Locating 'China' in the Arts of Sixteenth-Century Japan," *Art History* 29, no. 4 (September 2006): 600–624.

7. In addition to tea diaries, another valuable resource for commentary on silk mountings is the diary of the Zen monk Kōgetsu Sōgan (1574–1643) titled *Bokuseki no utsushi* (*Copies of Ink Traces*), which records Zen calligraphy (*bokuseki*) that Kōgetsu viewed and often authenticated over two-plus decades. See Gregory P. Levine, *Daitokuji: The Visual Cultures of a Zen Monastery* (Seattle: University of Washington Press, 2005), 160–221.

8. For an introduction to Tan'yū's authentication sketches, see Yukio Lippit, *Painting of the Realm: The Kano House of Painters in 17th-Century Japan* (Seattle: University of Washington Press, 2012), 145–52. The sketch in question is in the collection of the Kyoto National Museum and cited in Itakura Masaaki, "'Higashiyama-byōsō' no seiritsu o meguru shōkō," in Iwasaki et al., *Nihon no hyōsō*, 92–100.

9. For a comprehensive introduction, see Ishikawa Toshio et al., eds., *Sōkō shi* (Kyoto: Kokuhō Shūri Sōkōshi Renmei, 2011), while a wide variety of historical examples are discussed in Yamamoto Gen, *Hyōgu no shiori* (Kyoto: Unsōdō, 1979), 32–58; and Koga Kenzō, *Hyōsō taikan*, 4 vols. (Kyoto: Yanagiwara Shoten, 1987). A valuable discussion to mountings in tea culture and the issue of reformatting can be found in Andrew Hare, "Reformatting the Context of a Rikyū Letter," in *Around Chigusa: Tea and the Arts of Sixteenth-Century Japan*, ed. Dora C. Y. Ching et al. (Princeton, NJ: P.Y. and Kinmay W. Tang Center for East Asian Art, 2017): 135–55.

10. Two recent publications in particular offer valuable art historical perspectives on the history and practice of painting mounting: Kyōto Bunka Hakubutsukan, ed., *Nihon no hyōsō—kakejiiku no rekishi to yosōi*, exh. cat. (Kyoto: Kyōto Bunka Hakubutsukan, 2016); and Iwasaki et al., *Nihon no hyōsō*. In addition, recent museum activity has increasingly showcased the importance of mountings in the appreciation and meaning of artworks. See, for example, Kyōto Kokuritsu Hakubutsukan, ed., *Bunkazai shūri no saisentan*, exh. cat. (Kyoto: Kyōto Kokuritsu Hakubutsukan, 2020).

11. Although many mountings predate the fifteenth century, it is unclear to what degree they reflect widespread patterns of practice. For an overview of medieval Buddhist mountings, see Taniguchi Kōsei, "Nihon chūsei no butsuga no hyōsō," in Iwasaki et al., *Nihon no hyōsō*, 73–91.

12. See Liu Huanshen, "Chūsei no Ashikaga-ke ni okeru hyōgu 'go-e sanpuku-tsui' ni tsuite," *Dezain riron* 47 (2005): 97–111; and Kihara Toshie, "Kokuhō Shussan Shaka, Sekkei sansui zu sanpuku-tsui to 'Dōyū' no kanzō-in ni tsuite," *Gekkan bunkazai* 525 (June 2007): 37–43.

13. On Kōgetsu's mountings, see Kadowaki Mutsumi, "Kōgetsu Sōgan ni yoru hyōgu no kiroku to seisaku," in Iwasaki et al., *Nihon no hyōsō*, 101–24; many examples of his style are illustrated in Miho Museum, ed., *Daitokuji Ryōkō-in*, exh. cat. (Shigaraki: Miho Museum, 2019). Konoe's approach to mounting is central to a recent doctoral thesis on Edo-period court mounting; see Takada Tomohito, "'Bunkazai' to shite no hyōgu no kenkyū" (PhD diss., Daitō Bunka Daigaku, 2014).

14. Information about mounting had been recorded piecemeal in connoisseurship and tea ceremony texts for centuries, but specialized texts focusing exclusively on mounting began to appear in the late eighteenth century. A good example is Tominokōji Sadanao's *Hyōgu no shiki* (*Methods for Mounting*) of 1796.

15. For the mounted hanging scroll as a design motif, see Hayashi Tomoko, "Kakemono-tsukushi mon'yō kosode-gire," in *Miyako no kosode*, exh. cat., ed. Kyōto Bunka Hakubutsukan (Kyoto: Kyōto Bunka Hakubutsukan, 2011), 245.

16. See Elizabeth ten Grotenhuis, "Collapsing the Difference between Buddha and Believer: Human Hair in Japanese Esotericizing Embroideries," in *Esoteric Buddhism and the Tantras in East Asia*, ed. Charles Orzech et al. (Leiden: Brill, 2011), 876–92; and Carolyn Wargula, "Embodied Objects: Chūjōhime's Hair Embroideries and the Transformation of the Female Body in Premodern Japan," *Religions* 12 (2021): 773, http://doi.org/10.3390/rel12090773.

17. Examples of *kechien* participants listed on the back of a mounting, as well as metalwork fittings in the shape of lotus flowers, can be found in Kyōto Kokuritsu Hakubutsukan, *Bunkazai no shūri*, 14 and 25.

18. The textile albums of many prominent Edo-period families still survive and are surveyed in Gotō Bijutsukan, ed., *Meibutsu-gire—torai orimono e no akogare*, exh. cat. (Tokyo: Gotō Bijutsukan, 2001).

19. See Helen Swift, "Moons of the Four Seasons," in *Catalogue of the Feinberg Collection of Japanese Art*, ed. Rachel Saunders (Cambridge, MA: Harvard Art Museums, 2021), 66–67.

20. The work is discussed in Iwasaki et al., *Nihon no hyōsō*, 103.

21. For these and other examples, see Yomiuri Shimbun, ed., *Suzuki Kiitsu—Edo Rinpa no hatade*, exh. cat. (Tokyo: Yomiuri Shimbun, 2016). Several examples of Kiitsu's painted mountings are also found in Saunders, *Catalogue of the Feinberg Collection*.

22. The practice of fragmentation and remounting goes back centuries in Japan. The Ashikaga shoguns were known to have done so to Chinese album leaves and handscrolls for display as vertical hanging scrolls. A number of examples are illustrated in Nezu Bijutsukan, ed., *Meiga o kiri, meiki o tsugu*, exh. cat. (Tokyo: Nezu Bijutsukan, 2014).

23. The most famous artwork thus excerpted was the set of thirteenth-century handscrolls *The Thirty-Six Immortal Poets, Satake Version* (*Satake-bon Sanjūrokassen*), whose fragmentation into thirty-six separate pictures was overseen by Masuda and a cohort of collectors in the year 1919. The pictures were individually remounted as hanging scrolls and today are dispersed in collections around the world. For a recent account of the incident, see Furuya Tetsuo, "Satake-bon kara mieru sukisha no omoi—hyakunen no ruten no naka de," in *Ruten hyakunen—Satake-bon Sanjūrokassen-e to* ōchō *no bi*, ed. Kyōto Kokuritsu Hakubutsukan (Kyoto: Kyōto Kokuritsu Hakubutsukan, 2019), 18–24. Masuda's mounting designs are abundantly illustrated in Gotō Bijutsukan, ed., *Donnō no me—Masuda Donnō no bi no sekai*, exh. cat. (Tokyo: Gotō Bijutsukan, 1998).

24. A plethora of examples can be found in Iwasaki et al., *Nihon no hyōsō*.

25. The "Duck Mandala" is named for the fifteenth-century Chinese "Duck Gold Brocade" (*oshidori-kinran*) used as its primary mounting material. See Gotō Bijutsukan, *Meibutsu-gire*, fig. 27.

26. Although the conservator is assumed here as the lead figure in any remounting project, the fact remains that many remountings of antique paintings today are still carried out by antiquities dealers and professional mounters.

27. It should be noted that a historicist approach to mounting, while understood here as a modern phenomenon, has roots in earlier practices. As Tanya Uyeda observes, fragments of women's robes, which had been used in mortuary portraiture for centuries, begin to be applied in creative combinations to mountings from the eighteenth century onward. See Uyeda, "To Dress a Beautiful Woman: Painting and Mounting Techniques in Ukiyo-e," in *Painting the Floating World: Ukiyo-e Masterpieces from the Weston Collection*, ed. Janice Katz and Mami Hatayama (Chicago: Art Institute of Chicago, 2019), 314–19.

28. During the modern era, mounting practices in which the designs reflect contemporary art practices can be traced back to early twentieth-century circles of Nihonga, a neotraditional painting genre, and was also prevalent in the Mingei (Folk Art) movement. For the former, see Nakano Noriyuki, "Kindai Nihonga no zairyō to hyōsō," in Iwasaki et al., *Nihon no hyōsō*, 182–228.

29. See Iwasaki et al., *Nihon no hyōsō*, 6.

30. The Chinese triptych dates to the fourteenth century but made its way to Japan during the medieval period. Concerning a similar example that was split up between Cleveland and the Seikadō Museum (Tokyo) during the postwar period and then misrecognized as a Korean work, see Yukio Lippit, "The Original Icon," in *Colorful Realm: Japanese Bird-and-Flower Paintings by Itō Jakuchū* (Washington, DC: National Gallery of Art, 2012), 179–80.

CHAPTER 4

CONSERVATION PRACTICE AND THE APPEARANCE OF JAPANESE PAINTINGS

Iwatarō Oka
Translated by Yukio Lippit

This essay considers, from the perspective of a practicing conservator, how conservation practice impacts the look and appearance of Japanese paintings. Along with the basic techniques and issues of Japanese painting conservation, I will introduce specific types of treatment and issues intrinsic to the material profile of traditional Japanese painting. Accordingly, the essay begins with an explanation of the basic materials of mounted Japanese paintings, as well as the structure of the mounting apparatus itself.

THE MATERIALS AND MOUNTINGS OF JAPANESE PAINTING

Over the centuries, the traditional ground for Japanese painting has consisted primarily of either paper or silk. Paper was most often made from the plant fibers of trees known as *kōzo* (mulberry), *ganpi*, and *mitsumata*, as well as bamboo.[1] Painters chose from among these options based upon the pictorial approach they adopted, as well as the function served by a given painting, whether religious or secular. Recent conservation research has demonstrated that in the case of many early picture scrolls (*emaki*) created during the Heian (794–1185) and Kamakura (1185–1333) periods, the paper ground was composed of finely-cut *kōzo* fibers to which surface pressure was applied through careful pounding. On the other hand, paper made from *ganpi* fibers was popular for large-scale sliding-door panels covered in gold foil. Bamboo paper was frequently used for medieval ink paintings such as poem-picture scrolls (*shigajiku*). Some paper grounds combined fibers from different sources, and rice flour or white clay could be added to enhance the whiteness of the surface. In the case of silk, recent analysis has illuminated the changes in thread thickness and weave density across different historical eras.[2]

A variety of materials constituted the pigments and dyes for painterly and coloristic expression. *Sumi* ink, the most commonly employed pigment for lines and brushwork, is derived from pine soot and rapeseed oil. Colorants are drawn from natural minerals such as azurite (blue, *gunjō*) or malachite (green, *rokushō*); yellow ochre (*ōdo*) or red ochre (*taisha*) from dehydrated clay earth; and shell white (*gofun*) from seashells. Dyes are extracted from plants such as indigo (*ai*), gamboge (*tō'ō*), and cochineal red (*enji*). In order for mineral pigments to adhere to the paper or silk ground of a painting, they are mixed with a binder known as *nikawa*, made from deer antlers or the skin of oxen.[3]

After the painting proper is complete, it is then mounted in a manner appropriate to its format and function. Some are made into hanging scrolls that can be rolled and unrolled vertically; others take the form of handscrolls that open and close horizontally; and yet others end up as sliding-door panels or folding screens that adorn and partition space within architectural interiors. At times, out of necessity or preservation concerns, what was originally a panel, folding screen, or a portion of a handscroll was excerpted and remounted as a hanging scroll.[4]

THE MOUNTING STRUCTURE AND FUNDAMENTALS OF CONSERVATION

Knowledge of the mounting structure of a Japanese painting is crucial to an understanding of how it is conserved. Here I will explain briefly the mounting apparatus for hanging scrolls, handscrolls, folding screens, and sliding-door panels. Hanging scrolls and handscrolls must endure constant rolling and unrolling. When hung on a wall, they must maintain a flat, smooth surface that is not marked by large creases or undulations. When stored away, scrolls must be rolled up in a manner that does not cause further irregularities to appear on the surface. In order to ensure that this is the case, the mounting includes multiple layers of backing papers that consist of traditional Japanese paper (*washi*) of differing degrees of sturdiness applied directly to the back of the painting ground.

The number of backing papers to be applied is ultimately determined by the conservator's sensibility and experience, and in accordance with the qualities of a given painting, most notably its scale, the density of its paint layers, and the thickness and sturdiness of its ground. For a hanging scroll scaled for handling by a single individual, for example, the mounting structure consists of four layers of backing papers in all (fig. 4.1). This includes a sheet of backing paper affixed directly to the back of the pictorial ground (*hada-ura gami*), then an additional sheet that adds a layer of thickness while maintaining flexibility (*mashi-ura gami*), then a layer that connects the painting to the silk border surrounding the painting (*naka-ura gami*), and a final layer that spans the entirety of the mounting apparatus (*sō-ura gami*). The adhesive used to affix the backing papers to the support consists of a paste made by melting wheat starch in water and then heating and stirring it. The resulting substance is known as "fresh paste." An "aged paste," created by storing the fresh paste for about ten years in a cool, dark space until it has sufficiently

Fig. 4.1. The structure of a vertical hanging scroll with four layers of backing papers. Diagram by the author

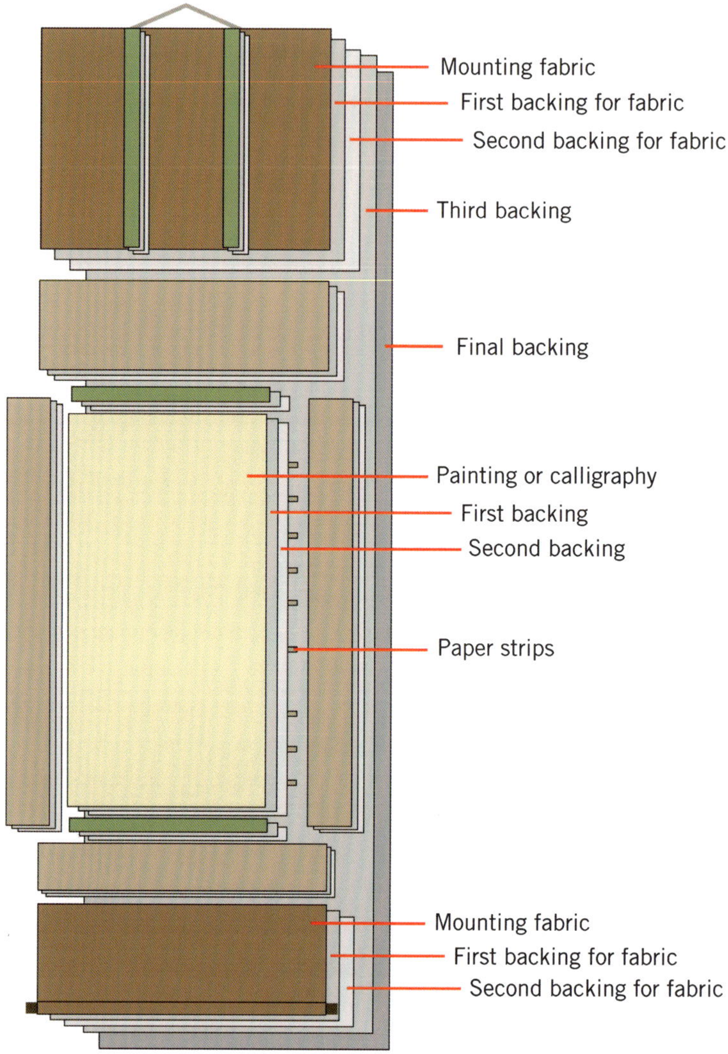

fermented, is used for the second, third, and final backing paper. Through fermentation, the molecular weight of the aged paste lessens considerably, making it less adhesive but also less prone to hardening after drying.

In the case of folding screens and sliding-door panels, which do not require rolling and unrolling, six layers of backing papers are applied to the backside of a painting surface affixed to a wooden core (fig. 4.2). The wooden core has no iron nails, and the backing papers are applied in a manner that prevents changes in the underlayers from adversely affecting the painting on its surface. To complete the mounting, several layers are added to the backside of the wooden core itself to further strengthen its structure. In this way, the painting can sustain long periods of

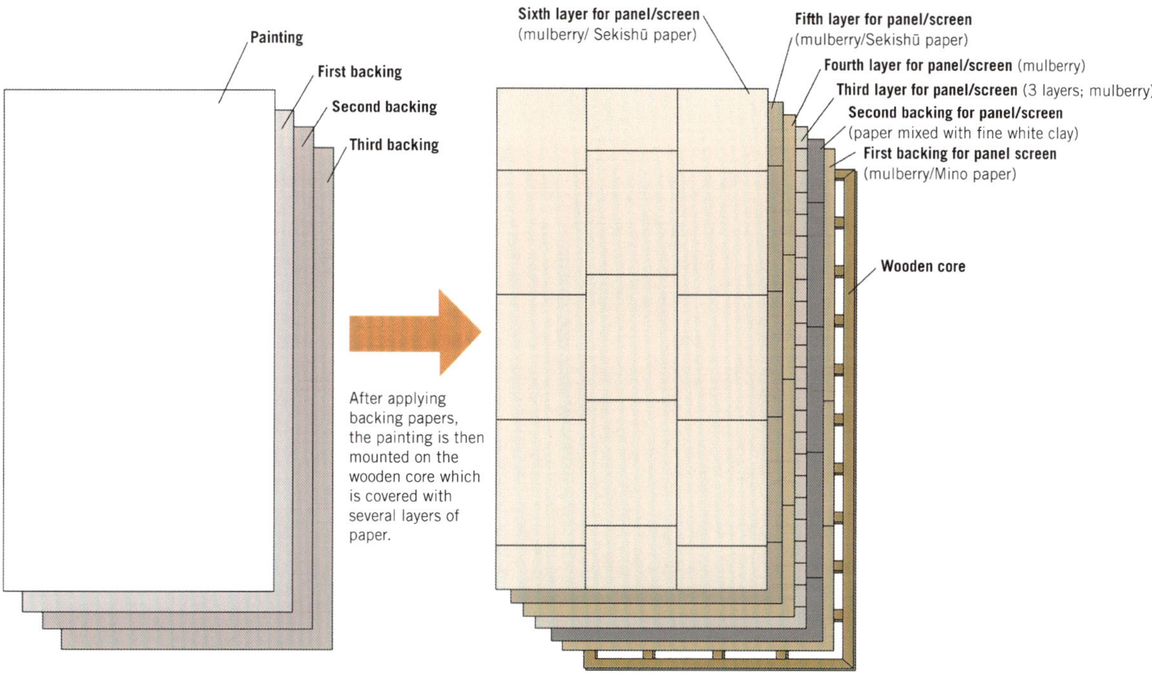

Fig. 4.2. The structure of mounted folding screens and sliding-door panels. Diagram by the author

exposure to the atmosphere or light during traditional annual "airings" (*bakuryō*) of artworks in temples and private collections, as well as repeated acts of folding and unfolding, along with changes to temperature and humidity indoors.

In this manner, the mounting structures of the various painting formats ensure that artworks are supported from the back side by several layers. Through exposure to light and atmosphere, however, or changes in temperature and humidity, the structure of the painting invariably weakens over time, losing flexibility in the process. As a result, small creases, wrinkles, and other forms of damage begin to emerge, leading to the loss of color layers. In addition, the weakening of adhesive starch paste causes backing papers to peel away little by little. If these conditions worsen, it no longer becomes possible to roll and unroll such works, thus necessitating periodic conservation.

The primary aim of conservation is to strengthen color layers and to repair folds and creases, as well as to remove dirt and staining where possible from the painting surface. It is ideal to conserve a painting once every fifty to one hundred years. Doing so requires dismantling the multiple layers of the mounting apparatus. Exposure to light and atmosphere weakens the painting surface, causing loss of pliability, but the same also holds for the *washi* paper affixed to the back side. Replacing the backing papers during the course of conservation with new, sturdy *washi* is necessary to prolong the life of the work into future generations. Because the removal of backing papers is technically challenging, there was once a period when the paper directly on the back side of the painting (*hada-ura gami*) was kept intact, but because older papers kept in place can give rise to folds and creases, it has now become standard practice to remove all layers from the back side.

Silk paintings often have pigments applied directly to the back side of the picture ground. When conserving such works, the innermost layer of backing needs to be removed without compromising this back side coloration, considerably raising the degree of difficulty. Even when the pictorial ground is paper, because of its weakened state, removing the innermost backing layer can potentially damage the ground, and great care is required. It is for this reason that it was customary not to remove the final layer. From the 1970s onward, however, the innovation of a technique known as the Dry Backing Removal Method (*kanshiki hada-age hō*) has enabled this to be done safely and effectively.[5] Today this technique is de rigueur for the conservation of artworks designated National Treasures and Important Cultural Properties.

HOW THE RENEWAL OF BACKING PAPERS IMPACTS THE APPEARANCE OF A PAINTING

Ever since it became possible to safely remove all backing layers during conservation, debates have occurred over the manner in which the color of backing papers influences the appearance of a painting.[6] Depending upon the color one chooses for the backing papers, which typically range from mouse gray to black with varying grades in between, and which can also be dyed in brown tones with diverse vegetal dyes, the appearance of a silk painting in its post-conservation state can be greatly affected. In the accompanying illustration (fig. 4.3), the left half of the silk is backed by undyed paper, whereas the right side is backed by paper dyed with *sumi* ink to a mouse-gray color. As this sample suggests, when dyed papers are applied, the entire painting surface appears darker. This, in turn, obscures the visibility of surface damage, while projecting a more antique atmosphere. Early nineteenth-century documents recording conservation practices for Buddhist paintings indicate that backing papers were frequently dyed to a dark color with *sumi* ink, perhaps for these reasons.

Fig. 4.3. The sample image for the appearance of a silk painting when the color of the backing papers is altered, both black (*right*) and brown (*left*), 2 ⅛ × 9 in. (5.5 × 23 cm)

This practice, however, is not unproblematic, as it also makes delicate ink lines and shading more difficult to discern. Accordingly, as testified by conservators from a generation ago, it was eventually phased out. From the 1970s onward, with the advent of the Dry Backing Removal Method, lighter backing papers dyed to a bright brown color began to replace the darker papers used previously. This dramatic change in coloration led to a greater legibility of the fine details of older paintings. At the same time, it also rendered areas of surface loss or damage, as well as changes made during earlier repairs, more visible. These consequences have led to careful deliberation before deciding upon the color of backing papers in any conservation project. In order to determine the most appropriate color for the backing papers for a particular work, it is now common for a conservator to consult closely with art historians and curators specializing in the type of painting in question.

It is easy to imagine that the color of backing papers was also an important issue for painters in earlier eras. Such concern is reflected in a surviving letter written by the Kyoto literati painter Yosa Buson (1717–1784) to a certain Ōmiya Gohei, which discusses the color of the backing papers to one of Buson's works:

> The backing to this silk painting looks to have been dyed in a light *sumi* ink color. Backing silk paintings with lightly dyed black papers is extremely unfortunate. This would never be done in China. Paintings should be backed with very white paper. When backed with ink-dyed paper, the dignity (*hinkaku*) of a painting is considerably diminished, and the vibrancy of its colors becomes poor. This is truly a pitiful mounting. I implore you to convey this in no uncertain terms to Mister Minakuchi-ya. Twenty-fourth day of the twelfth month. Buson.[7]

Buson's view, recorded here, that silk paintings should be backed by white paper, was not necessarily shared by other painters of his era. A survey of works from this period suggests that many contemporary painters preferred dyed backing papers. The letter does confirm, however, that painters were concerned about the color of such mounting layers.

Similarly, the appearance of paintings with a paper ground can also be influenced by the color of their backing. It is common for the paper grounds of Japanese paintings to become extremely thin over time, in the course of repeated conservation and remounting. Indeed, works on paper often have portions of their backside missing, either intentionally or due to poor conservation technique, resulting in an extremely thin surface. This is often the result of a process known as *aihegi* (splitting and peeling), in which the sum of the multiple layers of plant fibers that constitute a single sheet of *washi* paper are separated and removed. *Washi* paper is made by scooping and layering together plant fibers repeatedly to a desired degree of thickness, so if the proper amount of water is applied, it can be divided into thinner layers by separating and peeling them apart.

When *Scroll of Frolicking Animals* (*Chōjū giga*), a famous twelfth-century set of scrolls designated a National Treasure, was conserved from 2009 to 2012, it was discovered that its third scroll had originally consisted of paintings rendered on both sides of the same sheets of paper that had subsequently been split and peeled apart, and then remounted sequentially as part of a longer handscroll.[8] In prior conservation practice, it was also common to intentionally peel off the back side of the paper to help prevent small folds and creases from occurring when a scroll was rolled or unrolled. In the case of large-scale works such as sliding-door panels and folding screens, thicker paper tends to be used because rolling and unrolling is unnecessary. In the conservation of such works, sometimes the back side of the paper ground is accidentally peeled off with the backing papers because too much pressure has been exerted in the process. Whatever the case may be, when the paper ground of a painting has been thinned, slight changes in the color of new backing papers can engender an even greater transformation in its appearance, underscoring the necessity to carefully consider the choice of color.

Conservators should be wary of making arbitrary decisions on occasions of remounting, especially if the aim is to hide damage or enhance the antique air of a work. Whether paper or silk, the ground of paintings will naturally brown and darken to varying degrees over the centuries. It is therefore crucial to understand in what manner a work has been worshipped or viewed over time in order to determine how best to approximate these experiences or fold knowledge of them into the viewing circumstances of the present, and to choose the backing color accordingly. Indeed, the debates involved in this decision should themselves be recorded along with the conservation for future reference.

ADDING COLOR TO DAMAGED AREAS

Along with the renewal of backing layers, another component of the conservation process that influences the appearance of a painting is inpainting or toning (*hosai*). Because parts of the paper or silk ground are often lost through folds, creases, and insect damage, it is common to fill these areas in during conservation. Simply filling them in, however, does little to obscure areas of damage and can deter from appreciation of the painting. Sometimes it is necessary to add inpainting or toning to the surface. From the late 1960s onward, the policy of the Japanese conservation establishment has been to tone the surfaces of works designated National Treasures and Important Cultural Properties through a practice known as ground-color toning (*ji-iro hosai*). In this approach, damaged areas of the surface are filled in consistently with a color that approximates the ground color of the work, rather than attempting to reconstruct the specific coloration of individual motifs or patches of the surface. Before the late 1960s, missing portions of the surface were filled in with colored pigments, sometimes by an artist, in order to allow them to blend in more effectively with their surroundings. Such retouching can be witnessed in the twelfth-century scroll painting *Minister Kibi Goes to China* (*Kibi daijin nittō emaki*) in the Museum of Fine Arts, Boston. This work was conserved in Japan as part of a commemorative conservation project related to the 1964 Tokyo Olympics. Colored wash was added to missing areas of the front portion of the scroll. Furthermore, when *Portrait of Jion Daishi* (now in the Yakushiji Temple), designated a National Treasure, was conserved during the same period, the renowned painter Yasuda Yukihiko (1884–1978) added color to both eyes to restore their original appearance. When one observes closely these areas of retouching, it is clear that Yasuda carefully avoided coming into contact with the original coloration.

According to conservators active during this period, it was in the moment when backing papers were removed and damaged areas were highlighted that, perhaps counterintuitively, the beauty and power of the painting became most apparent. The policy of ground-color toning was adopted, in part, based upon this collective observation.[9] The policy was made more urgent because conservation records are not regularly made public, and restorative coloration runs the risk of being confused with the original appearance of the artwork. Currently, the approximated ground color added during conservation is determined after extensive consultation between the lead conservator, the owner of a painting, and an art historian. Together, they attempt to select a ground color that best distinguishes damaged areas from their surroundings while avoiding too much obstruction of the legibility and appearance of a picture. Admittedly, this determination is subjective and can be influenced by local lighting conditions or different color preferences among the individuals involved. Thus, it is necessary to use color samples extensively and to consult multiple times with numerous specialists.

A similar problem arises when determining what to do with previously retouched areas or color added from earlier restorations. Premodern repairs leave clear evidence of attempts to hide damage by adding color to damaged areas. Often, these attempts are technically poor and contrast with the artistic expression of the original. At the same time, removing prior repairs entirely can sometimes destroy the balance of the whole, so it is no easy decision whether or not to remove the traces of these efforts altogether.

The complexity of such decisions can be discerned from the conservation of the Buddhist painting *Fudō Myō'ō*, a National Treasure in Manshuin Temple in Kyoto, which was conserved over two years from 2013 to 2015. The accompanying illustration shows the damage on its surface before conservation (fig. 4.4). Parts of the silk ground were missing and had been filled in and painted in prior conservation with silk patches of different weaves and appearances. These additions are particularly notable in the head of the deity (fig. 4.5). On either side of the head, the whirls of the snail-shell curls of the deity's hair are rendered with extremely smooth and even lines. Those rendered in later repairs on the added pieces of silk, however, clearly lack this evenness. Furthermore, although these curls should be rendered in several layers, the ones added through repair consist of only one layer and are iconographically incorrect. The earlier repair was not only clearly inferior to the original, but also inaccurate in its depiction of the hair. That said, its addition effectively allowed the appearance of the head to be preserved in some form until the present. Replacing it with ground color would effectively eliminate the deity's head for posterity. During the consultation surrounding the recent conservation, it was observed that *Fudō Myō'ō* was an art historically important work as well as the most important religious icon at Manshuin Temple. It would be undesirable to change so drastically the appearance of the work as it had been passed down through much of its history. Accordingly, it was decided to leave all the earlier repairs to the head area in place.

With regard to the conservation of arts and crafts, whatever the category, it goes without saying that consistency of approach is crucial. Adhering inflexibly to this principle when determining the course of a conservation project can lead to undesirable results, however, and thus it is not uncommon to choose the approach witnessed in the case of *Fudō Myō'ō*. Watanabe Akiyoshi, the former director of the Tokyo National Research Institute for Cultural Properties, addressed the difficulty of removing the work of earlier repair efforts in a 1996 lecture as follows:

> We conserve works in order to remove elements that are not conducive to preservation, and this is generally acknowledged as a principle of conservation. Even so, we must be aware that we are constantly grappling with the concept of authenticity. We must preserve the entirety of

Fig. 4.4. The Buddhist painting *Fudō Myō'ō*, a National Treasure in Manshuin Temple in Kyoto, showing the brown colored part as the areas of loss and patched with silk in the previous restoration, from 2013 to 2015. 64 × 31 ⅞ in. (162.7 × 80.9 cm)

Fig. 4.5. Details of the head of *Fudō Myō'ō* showing the later addition of the snail-shell curls of the deity's hair

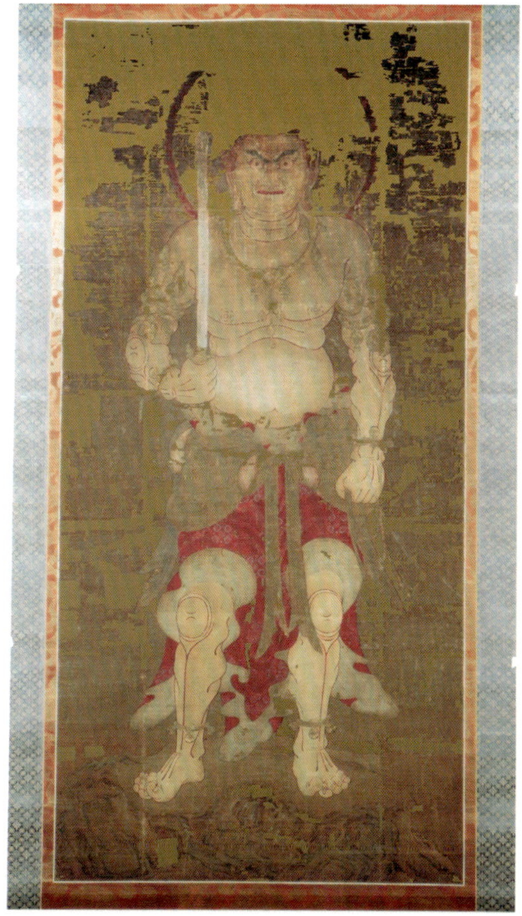

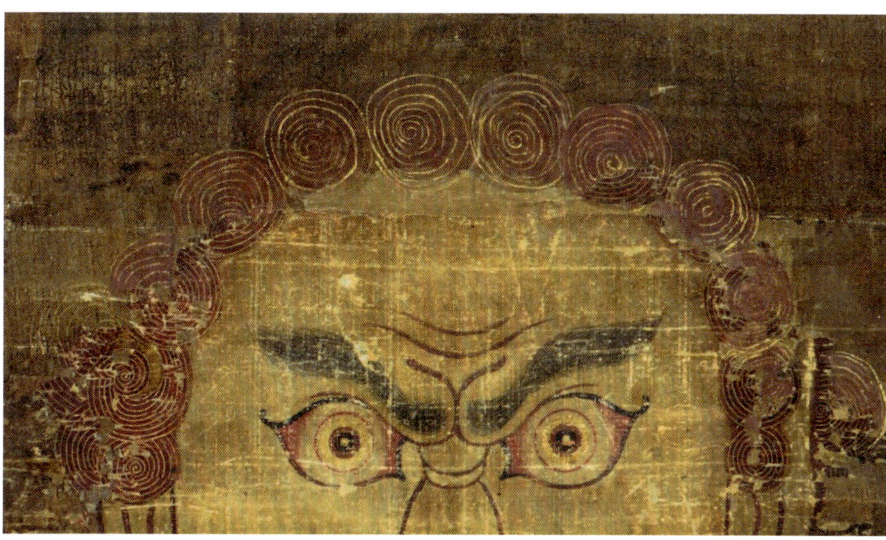

> the original appearance of the artwork, this is obvious; the value of whatever is added later on is low. At the same time, the historical appearance of an artwork has included these elements as well, so when removing them we have to consider how this impacts the overall reception of the work. This is the difficulty of conserving paintings. Evaluating the structural dimension of objects necessarily includes those elements that were added over time, and must include a consideration of their value. Absolute and relative criteria can coexist within the same work, and losing sight of this can lead to grave mistakes.[10]

Accordingly, the conservation approach must be determined based on the contingencies of each individual artwork, and the discussion that determines this policy should be preserved along with the artwork itself and passed on to future generations.

CONCLUSION

This essay has attempted to articulate how conservation affects the appearance of paintings, drawing upon actual case studies. The essence of painting conservation is to repair the wear and tear of time and to prevent new damage from occurring by renewing the structure of the work. Because conservation work can influence the appearance of a painting, its approach must be selected with great care. For example, the color of backing papers can affect the general atmosphere of a work, how light and dark areas are perceived, and details of lines and coloration. Likewise, because the removal of color and lines added in the course of earlier repairs can often affect how the original portions of an artwork are perceived, it has become common to treat areas of damage with ground-color toning.

The primary objective of any conservation project is to repair damage, not necessarily to hide tears or stains. Conservators therefore should not proceed without consulting with specialists as to the proper appearance of a painting, nor without determining the value of transmitting various aspects of its appearance to future generations. In this regard, it is the responsibility of conservators working today to preserve not only the artworks but the discourse surrounding their preservation.

NOTES

1. Like *kōzo*, *ganpi* is a bark fiber known to be drawn from several trees of the *Wikstroemia* species (*W. canescens*, *W. japonica*, and *W. sikokiana*). *Mitsumata*, meanwhile, derives from the species *Edgeworthia papyrifera*.
2. See Izumi Takeo, "Sozai e no shisen: butsuga to eginu," *Gakusō* 34 (May 2012): 201–15.
3. For more on the materials and colorants of traditional Japanese painting, see Takashima Teruyuki and Inoue Takashi, *Zukai Nihonga yōgo jiten* (Illustrated Dictionary of Terms for Nihonga [Japanese Painting]) (Tokyo: Tōkyō Bijutsu, 2007).
4. See, for example, Takashima Mitsuyuki and Inoue Takashi, *Emaki setsudan—Satake-bon Sanjūrokkasen no ruten* (Tokyo: Bijutsu Kōronsha, 1984).
5. See Oka Iwatarō, "A Dry Method for Removing the Backing Papers from Japanese Paintings," *Studies in Conservation* 33 (1988): 69–72.
6. See Oka Iwatarō and Miyajima Shin'ichi, "'Kaiga Nezu bijutsukan zō *Nachi taki zu*, Tōkyō," *Bukkyō geijutsu* 195 (March 1991): 21–38.
7. Ōtani Tokuzō and Fujita Shin'ichi, eds., *Buson shokan shū* (Tokyo: Iwanami Bunko, 1992).
8. See Kyoto National Museum, ed., *Chōjū giga—shūri kara mietekita sekai* (Kyoto: Kyōto Kokuritsu Hakubutsukan, 2016).
9. See Oka Iwatarō, "Kōenroku Kokuhō *Ban Dainagon emaki* to Idemitsu bijutsukan," *Idemitsu bijutsukan kenkyū kiyō* 22 (2017): 237–61.
10. Speech delivered at the Association for Conservation of National Treasures (ACNT) Preservation and Conservation of Japanese Art Training Seminar, 1996.

ENACTING—
TEACHING

CHAPTER 5

CONSERVING OURSELVES / CREATING OURSELVES

Alva Noë

Back in the 1980s, when the California condor was on the verge of extinction, the pioneer environmentalist and conservationist David Brower, who was one of the founders of the Sierra Club, opposed efforts to save the species by breeding it in captivity for later release in the wild. His objection was principled, and activist. A condor is at most five percent blood, brain, bones, and feathers, he said. The rest is environment. A condor bred in captivity, in isolation from its environment, is no condor. Perhaps, he bitterly suggested, it is a flying pig.

Brower appreciated that an organism, in this case a bird, is no mere body. It is a locus of activity, and this activity is world involving. The animal, to borrow Susan Hurley's phrase, is a dynamic singularity.[1] Where do we find it? In its nexus with the wider world.

Every child of refugees knows this is true. Yes, you can hurt an organism, or a person, by inflicting damage on the body—that is, on the brain, blood, bones, and feathers. But it is also possible to alter a living being, irrevocably, by attacking its world. The world of a person, or an animal, is not just a condition causally necessary for its flourishing; it is what philosophers might call a condition of the very possibility of this life at all. It is a transcendental or, what comes to the same thing, an existential condition.

This is one reason, by the way, why the climate crisis is not only terrifying but unfathomable. What is threatened is not merely something we need or value. Our world is much more than that. What is threatened is the background without which we are not even intelligible to ourselves.

But Brower's dogmatism, while philosophically pristine, may have been misguided. By the late 1980s, the population of the California condor in California and Arizona had dwindled to a tiny handful of birds, fewer than thirty, I believe. At that time, it was decided to move all the survivors to zoos for captive breeding with, it now seems, real success. There are today hundreds of individuals of the species living in the wild, all of them offspring of birds born in captivity.

What is the moral? That Brower was mistaken? That we are not constituted by our place in the world? Or that sometimes we need to settle for flying pigs? These questions do not have easy answers.

What goes for organisms goes for artifacts as well. A doorknob *only is* against the setting of a characteristic form of life, to use Wittgenstein's phrase. A doorknob presupposes a vast skein of carings and abilities, needs and interests, dichotomies and values, such as, for example, the importance of keeping ourselves safe *inside* against the threats from the *outside*. Doorknobs, like almost all material culture, are, as we might say, ableist in their core. It is only for a person with the right type of hands, fingers, stature, that the knob affords anything at all—the opportunity to grasp, to hold, to turn, to pull or push, to open, to pass through. Take those abilities away, alter the conditions sufficiently so that the game loses its point, and you do not have doorknobs anymore.

So, Brower's point holds here too. A doorknob, we might say, is five percent metal, ceramic, and latch mechanism; the rest is environment, including us. And just as you cannot, at least according to Brower, raise a condor in captivity—captivity is not compatible with the life of a condor—so you cannot preserve or conserve or maintain a doorknob, or a hinge, or a scythe, on the wall of a museum (for example). Mounted on the wall next to an Impressionist painting, a doorknob is no longer a doorknob.

Or so, at least, Brower's argument would seem to suggest. But can we follow him on this? Granted, the doorknobs put on the wall for display at a museum like the Barnes Foundation in Philadelphia are now devoid of function, removed as they are from the sole setting in which they can perform their defining task and so be what they are. And granted, this function is not intrinsic to the physical makeup of the doorknob but is rather something it possesses by virtue of the way it is put to use by us, the way it is integrated in a larger context or life-world. But far from being *non*-knobs, these disused doorknobs are precisely the remains of knobs, or doorknobs put out to pasture; they are doorknobs the way old men sitting around playing cards are the young boys they once were. Or maybe these museum knobs are a kind of knob-picture. Or might it be that the knobs actually do survive their extraction from the world, just as the condors did? And what would this teach us? That an organism, or an artifact, is world independent in its essence? Or, alternatively, that to preserve an organism is, ipso facto, to preserve its world?

These examples, and these questions, give some of the background against which I would like to explore the question of the preservation, or conservation, not of animals, or artifacts but of artworks which are, I think, in important respects, something else altogether.

My topic today is a simple idea about art and its conservation; like Brower's idea, it is too simple, and that is at least part of what makes it worth discussing.

The idea may be stated easily: art is so much a creature of context, bound up with situations, problems, gestures, rhetorics of exchange that are local and personal and timebound, that the only way to preserve art, or conserve it, or save it, is to save and preserve and hold on to that context, the world of concerns and understandings and assumptions, that alone give the work its standing as significant or important.

But, so the idea continues, this is not possible, we cannot hold on to the past, not any more than we can hold on to and avoid losing our loved ones. Nor is it normally or usually even truly desirable to try to do so. There is something questionable, emotionally, developmentally, and politically, about clinging to the past, about refusing to accept death.

So, we need to let go, accept loss, accept time, accept the destruction and disappearance of even the art that we have come to love, just as we accept, with regret and heartbreak, the loss of people we have loved. We need, then, to renounce conservation, free ourselves from the conservative impulse.

The choreographer Deborah Hay captures the spirit of this too-simple idea I am entertaining, the impulse behind it, when, in a performance lecture in which she reflects on her practice, she uses and repeats the phrase "here and gone, here and gone, here and gone, here and gone, here and gone, here and gone."[2] I take her to mean: art, no less than life, is a phenomenon of the here and gone. You cannot hold it fast; it comes and goes. To have it now is to risk inevitable loss.

Some years ago, I had the opportunity to work as a philosopher in residence with a dance company. I experienced firsthand the unstable, never-the-same, always-shifting, truly ephemeral nature of performance. No performance was ever the same twice. This was so for many reasons operating at many levels. The performances were organized, or conducted, in real time, by the company's artistic director, who communicated with dancers using radio and other forms of signaling. He made different choices every night, sometimes in response to the way things were unfolding on the stage, but also in response to the character or mood of the night's audience; there were improvisational elements built into every scene, so dancers were required to make substantive choices anew each evening; casts were shifting, and different dancers would bring different qualities. And then, finally, the director was quite willing, in collaboration with the dancers, and under the pressure of the need to perform again another night, to tear down and rebuild and make anew what they had been doing. The result: there was tremendous growth and change and variation; sameness of title was no guarantee of sameness of performance. To visit with a performance, even one that had been long in the repertoire, was like meeting a teenager after a few years; metamorphosis was likely to have occurred.

I came to learn, in this setting, that to know dance and to love it was to accept as inevitable some measure of loss, for even after you had done the work to experience the dance—and very often it is hard work to experience an artwork—all you had to show for it was the experience itself, something unfixed, happening, and always, in Hay's phrase, here and gone, here and gone, here and gone.

There is an obvious sense in which dance is the most bodily of the arts; it is the art of the moving, thinking, feeling body itself. But there is also a sense in which it is the least embodied, for it is the least concrete, the least objectual, the least residual, of the arts. Even more so than music, dance refuses to yield up a product, a recording, a record, that can, in any sense, go proxy for the work of dance itself, something that can be bought and sold. Poetry has the book. Music the record album and the conventional score. Dance has only the memory, or the fantasy.

Of course, what goes for dance can be generalized across the arts, even the ones, like painting and sculpture, that are more easily archived or commodified. John Dewey captures this when he writes, in the opening sentence of his book *Art as Experience*: "By one of the ironic perversities that often attend the course of human affairs, the existence of the works of art upon which formation of an esthetic theory depends has become an obstruction to theory about them."[3] It is the existence of art *objects* that deludes us into missing the fact that art is only ever the experience, it is only ever something liquid and becoming, and so uncertain.

But now we are in a position to start to appreciate the way this idea I am exploring—that it is impossible to conserve art and dance, because it is impossible and not even desirable to conserve their ambient context—is not just simple, but *too* simple, as we saw before with Brower's considerations about the condor (and our own about the doorknob).

It is striking that choreographers, as much as they work with movement and time and the live happening of encounter and performance, tend, as a species, to be unsettled by this fact—and unwilling to settle for it. Many choreographers, in my experience anyway, are bent, almost maniacally, on capturing, holding fast, recording, *material*izing, what they do. Very often, dance creators are obsessed with finding a product, a thing of value, something that survives the evening and that deserves to find a place in the archives, or can be deposited in the bank and maybe even, one day, put up for sale.

It is no accident that the company I worked with not only recorded every performance and every rehearsal but went as far as to invent software tools to devise methods to time stamp, index, catalog, label, and organize video not only to view tape of X's solo Y on a given evening, but also every Y solo on every evening, whether performed by X or by other cast members at different times, as well as all the cross-indexed rehearsals, including audio recordings of comments made by the director, the dramaturg, the musicians, or other dancers.

The existence of such a repository of film and annotation is of immense practical value. It is precisely because of the ephemeral, always-only-ever-enacted character of the work that it lives not only in performance but also in its transmission, and this technology supports the teaching and training of new dancers, new casts.

But it does much more than that.

It provides a superstructure of thought and image, of self-representation, in terms of which to comprehend this otherwise liquid and vanishing thing that is the thing these artists do. The self-representing becomes entangled with the doing, so that the doing becomes something different, something more stable, something more substantial, less like a one-off gesture and more like a language; less like a party and more like a culture, or a world.

From this standpoint, we appreciate that choreographies are no more mere happenings in space and time than a chess game is merely a distribution of chess figures on the board. The arrangement on the board of an actual chess game is meaningful, intelligible, built up from known moves according to articulated principles. The dance is a development in a space of ability and understanding; a project inside *a practice*; and it carries the weight of intention, of history, of entanglement with all the reflection of which it is the spontaneous expression. Here we can speak not just of movement, but of a movement *vocabulary*, of grammar and rules.

But this means that the impulse to preserve, whatever its origins, is not primarily reactive at all. It is radically creative. It is not oriented toward preserving what is done, or remaking the past, but oriented to the making of a present that can sustain itself out of the only materials available to us, those with which the past has saddled us.

This belongs to a larger, more pervasive productive phenomenon of entanglement.[4] Every effort to record ourselves—something we have been doing with words and pictures for tens of thousands of years longer than we have been doing it with film and video—is, in effect, the devising of a score by which we can enact ourselves. Every story, every philosophical conversation, every sketch or photograph, ends up laying down paths we might follow going forward.

The artistic past is never really past at all. A drawing, like a writing, is the mere trace of a past movement. But it is not, therefore, relegated to the past. Some drawings are made to be looked at and thought about and end up serving as a resource for understanding the very movement, or style of movement, from which they arose. Such drawings change how we move and see just as writing, which, from this point of view, is a species of drawing, can change how we talk.

It is worth acknowledging that things are very different when it comes to the snail that leaves a trail of ooze as it works its way across the stone path in the garden. The ooze, for the snail, is a mere trace, a by-product, and it is behind and beneath and below the present concerns of the snail. It plays no role in the snail's self-understanding or self-creation (although it may play a role in chemical processes of signaling and "communication" between snails).

But our ooze is very important to us; we use it to enact ourselves.[5]

I have been considering the radically creative and enactive aspect of the act of art preservation, noting how the choreographers' need to represent their work loops down and changes the character of the work, removing it from the domain of mere fleeting and happening and establishing it in a domain of meaning. Something very similar can be said about the creativity of the work of art conservation too. I turn to this now.

To approach this question, it is useful to remind ourselves that what united Brower's California condor and my doorknob was the aptness, in connection with each, of reference to purpose or aim. The doorknob is made for the purpose of fastening and opening doors; it requires that purpose to be what it is. And the condor, too, aims at living and is designed, by evolution, acting under the pressures of natural selection, to achieve the goal for which it is, as it were, perfectly well adapted (at least until we destroyed its habitat)—that is, to life at home. The constitutive relation between the organism and the artifact, respectively, and the world to which they belong, is grounded in purposiveness.

But not so the artwork. Artworks, so I would argue, at least as these are conceived and imagined in the modern European tradition, look like tools, implements with functions—pictures *for* showing or gestures *for* communicating, or whatever—but, really, they are devoid of function. We can never be sure what an artwork is doing or saying; we cannot even be sure whether it is doing or saying anything at all. With artworks—this is the role they play for us—there are no ready-at-hand criteria of success by which to measure their performance. The artwork puts all criteria into abeyance and questions anything we might take for granted about what the artwork is trying to do. Works of art are, if they are tools, *strange* tools.[6] As Kant correctly appreciated, art happens when the artifact has only the form of purposiveness, not actual purpose (*Zweckmaessigkeit ohne Zweck*).[7]

To preserve a heart, you need to keep the organism of which it is an organ alive and healthy. And to preserve the doorknob, you need to maintain human habitual organization with doors, buildings, etc. But to keep *art* alive, to preserve an artwork, what you need, rather, is to preserve the point of pseudo-functionality and resistance. You need to activate, or continue to activate, the artwork's refusal to let habitual modes of being operate undisturbed.

And crucially, this cannot be done conditionally, or without full commitment.

To see what I mean, imagine you wanted to establish a museum of the world's jokes. To do so, it would not be enough that you collected jokes, wrote them down, and displayed them legibly on the walls, or that you ran video loops of people telling jokes from different times and places. Nor would it suffice if you provided all the anthropological background—the cultural stereotypes and assumptions and expectations — the manipulation of which is part of what makes the jokes funny. For understanding the jokes — grasping the words, appreciating the way they play with and disrupt background assumptions, having information about them and the traditions to which they belong — is not the same as *getting* them, and it does not suffice to make them funny, or even interesting. Humor is only achieved when the background assumptions, the way of thinking and looking and assuming that the joke presupposes, are taken for granted, not by them, but by you, that is, by the audience. So, to create a museum of the world's jokes, you would be required first to transform visitors to the museum into the intended audience; to do that, you need to do more than tell them something, give them a bit of context. It is not information they lack. It is attitudes, certainties, assumptions, bigotries, unreflected-upon expectations, ideologies, not to mention languages and customs, they need. For the joke only happens — humor only comes to exist — at that place when what is otherwise mere words, a mere telling, a story, has the effect of setting the listener free from all that (or at least setting such a process of reorganization or emancipation into gear). You need to give them blinkers so they can free themselves to see.

As with jokes, so with art. Before we can genuinely respond to the work of art, we must become its audience. And I am not the audience of a work just because it is intact, there before me, for me look at, watch, or listen to. The art audience is always a participant, a complicit partner, never merely a bystander. To be open to the art in the art, what is required, paradoxically, is that we be prevented from just seeing it, at least straight away; it belongs to the art process that we must learn to see what is there, work to bring it into focus, undergo the passage from not seeing to seeing, or from seeing to seeing differently. For it is that passage that is the undergoing of change and the enactment of self-reorganization. We need to be limited, constrained, organized, and enculturated, before and so that the art can do its work on us — that is, so that the art can disrupt all that, and set us free; art's value, like the joke's humor, happens in that elastic moment of resistance.

Art aims at ecstasy. I do not mean passion, emotion, or pleasure. Its push is for release and its point is to undo the stasis that is our ordinary, our normal, and our most familiar condition. Art is therefore a form of active resistance. The discovery of art is the discovery of paths of resistance.

For this reason, you do not get the artwork, or the joke, just for the price of admission, which is a point that Dewey never tired of making. And, returning to our theme, you do not *preserve* the artwork, or the joke, just by its proper preparation and installation. It is the audience that activates the artwork, and therefore the real job of art preservation — and now I think broadly of all the professions bound up with loving art — is that of creating, and then supporting, the audience.

How do you do this? How do you create an audience?

Actually, there is a familiar term for this work of audience making and support: this is the work of the teacher.

In his dialogue *On the Teacher*, Saint Augustine confronted a paradox—a paradox first articulated by Plato in the *Meno*—that teaching is, in a way, not really possible at all, because the success of the teacher depends on the student's recognition of the truth of what is being taught. It is the student, not the teacher, who is the arbiter of success. But this means that, in a sense, the student must already know what it is that the teacher is trying to teach them. So, the teacher has nothing to teach, after all.

I agree with Plato and Augustine that a teacher—and now I am thinking of the art lover and preserver, but also the artist, as well as the philosopher—needs not so much to impart information as, rather, to encourage the movements of thought and reflection that are what are really required for us to see, to appreciate, to laugh aloud, and to be transformed. But these movements of thought and reflection are almost always *counter*-habitual, and so they may be painful. For this reason, our publics, our students, may offer resistance, turn away, close the book, check their phones, head to the bookshop or the café.

Which gives us our real task: to accept the resistance, to welcome the process and its discomforts, to take our unwilling art lover by the hand without embarrassment, and to try to convince them there is something to do here.[8]

NOTES

1. Susan L. Hurley, *Consciousness in Action* (Cambridge, MA: Harvard University Press, 1998).
2. Deborah Hay, *Using the Sky* (New York: Routledge, 2015).
3. John Dewey, *Art as Experience* (New York: Penguin, 1934), 1.
4. For more on this, see Alva Noë, "Entanglement and Ecstasy in Dance, Music, and Philosophy: A Reply to Carrie Noland, Nancy S. Struever, and Thomas Rickert," *Philosophy and Rhetoric* 54, no. 1 (2021): 64–80; and Alva Noë, *The Entanglement: Art before Nature* (Princeton, NJ: Princeton University Press, 2022).
5. Anna Teresa de Keersmaeker's *Fase*, performed at the Museum of Modern Art, New York, in January 2011, can be thought of as a choreographic exploration of just these themes. In dancing, the artist draws, as the snail leaves ooze. But how much does the dancer's understanding of what she is making organize what she does? See Performance 13: On Line / Anne Teresa De Keersmaeker, January 22–23, 2011, http://www.moma.org/calendar/performance/1580.
6. Alva Noë, *Strange Tools: Art and Human Nature* (New York: Farrar Straus and Giroux, 2015).
7. Immanuel Kant, *Critic of Judgement*, trans. James Creed Meredith (Oxford: Oxford University Press, 1928). It is an interesting question whether these remarks about artworks—about their character as strange tools that, in effect, put us on display—are features only of European art in the tradition that Kant helped us conceptualize, or whether it is the case that art is transcultural. I am drawn toward the latter claim: humans everywhere and always are products of their own organization; art, like irony, is the expression of our effort to free ourselves and reorganize.
8. Thanks to Alexander Nagel and Caroline Fowler, as well as other participants of the April 2021 Conservation | Making | Art | History conference at the Clark Art Institute, for valuable discussion. This paper is a top-to-bottom rewriting of a paper I first presented at Bard, in New York, at a November 2019 workshop, Conserving Active Matter: Degradation as an Aesthetic Value, whose proceedings are being published under the title *Conserving Active Matter*, edited by Peter Miller and Soon Kai Poy. The present paper differs from that earlier paper in content, but there are a few sentences in common. Thanks to Peter Miller, and Soon Kai Poh, and also to Anne Eaton and Ivan Gaskell, who organized the original workshop at Bard.

CHAPTER 6

CONSERVATION AND THE TECHNIQUE OF ART HISTORY

Sven Dupré

Which art histories will we write if, following recent scholarship in conservation, we move skill and technique to the core of the discipline? Skill and technique play a remarkably limited role in the field of art history—with Michael Baxandall's narratives of making, as developed in *Painting and Experience* and *Limewood Sculptors of Renaissance Germany*, arguably the most important exception.[1] One would expect technique to be a prominent concept in technical art history, and skill an important object of study in this field. However, David Bomford (who coined the term "technical art history") embraced a cartesian dualism and clearly positioned the field as dealing exclusively with objects and materials, much less so with subjects and skills.[2] Advocates of the field emphasize its interdisciplinary character and the importance of collaboration, especially with conservators.[3] However, as Marco Cardinali and Emma Jansson have recently observed, despite this emphasis on collaborative research, technical art history lacks a shared methodological and epistemological framework.[4] Here, I will argue that art history can profit from opening a dialogue with the field of conservation and its emphasis on the temporality and processual character of art, as well as further exchanges with anthropological work on "techniques of the body" and research in performance studies.

Whenever a common theoretical language is adopted in technical art history, it is notable that it pivots around materiality.[5] A focus on materials and materiality fosters exchanges with conservators and conservation scientists, and it arguably does work toward overcoming the disciplinary gaps separating art history and conservation (science). It thus avoids the risk of conservators' contributions being "limited to either an appendix or technical entry at the back of a publication, or otherwise remain[ing] inaccessible in the form of an unpublished conservation report."[6] However, more recent thinking on conservation has foregrounded paradigms that are less centered on the object and that question the preservation of material integrity as the sole and universal aim of conservation. Therefore, the development of a common language for technical art history on the basis of materiality runs the risk of privileging a particular conceptualization of the field of conservation, a specific idea of its scope and its epistemology that is not representative of the field in its entirety. If technical art history strives toward a true interdisciplinary exchange with conservation, it would do well to attend to these newer concepts of conservation. In this essay, I argue that such integration of technical art history and conservation can be achieved by promoting "technique" to one of the discipline's central concepts, in addition to materiality.

In the first part of the essay, I will show how the focus on materials and objects is tied to the paradigm of scientific conservation, and how this paradigm engages its own choice of conservation history, which frames the development of the field of conservation as the replacement of craftsmanship and skills by science in the 1930s. This decade thus appears as a crucial period, the epistemologies of which still shape current perspectives on conservation. In the second part of the essay, I will rescue from oblivion the use of the concept of technique in art history during that same decade, when it was in close contact with the field of conservation; and I will connect this idea to contemporaneous, parallel work on technique in anthropology. The history of technique across the disciplines of art history, conservation, and anthropology in the 1930s forms the background to the current problematizing of the epistemologies that emerged out of the 1930s and endure in the contemporary fields of conservation and anthropology.

Here, I will also draw upon recent work in performance studies. Indeed, questioning the role of skill in conservation and art history also raises the issue of the methodology and epistemology of remaking and redoing. Performative methodology, known as reconstruction (the term of preference in conservation studies), reenactment, replication, reproduction, reworking, and other *re-* terms, belongs to the standard toolbox in the field of conservation, while art history is a relative latecomer to the adoption of hands-on methods.[7] In the field of conservation, the emphasis has been on the historical accuracy or appropriateness of materials; only most recently, Leslie Carlyle has highlighted the performative aspects of reconstruction in the field of conservation.[8] In my research to investigate technique in the early modern arts, I have extensively collaborated with conservators. However, in our work on Burgundian-black color technologies and in the reproductions of early modern glass colors, as found in recipes brought together in seventeenth-century books, we moved to spaces outside the laboratory, while conservators' reconstructions more typically take place in laboratory settings.[9] In the third and final part of the essay, I will argue that art historians need to move their reconstruction research outside the laboratory, because these spaces are more appropriate environments for the study of technique. As part of the common theoretical and methodological framework, technical art history should develop epistemologies of reconstruction research, and a key aspect of such epistemologies is how we conceptualize the spaces in which we conduct this research.

CONSERVATION HISTORIES: TECHNIQUE OF CONSERVATION

The field of conservation has developed new theories criticizing claims of truth and objectivity typical of "classical" or "scientific" conservation, in the terminology of Salvador Munoz Vias.[10] Traditionally, conservation was primarily about techniques of prolonging the material life of an object and about permanence, stability, and continuity. Following the processual and dynamic character of contemporary art (such as performances and time-based media), post-classical conservation theories are at odds with the static conception of the object and the idea that change is a threat, which was central to earlier conservation philosophies. There is a growing awareness in the field of conservation studies that conservation has a history—that is, concepts and practices of conservation change over time—and that for some artworks, conservation can be as much about subjects (their values and their skills) as it is about the objects on which "scientific" conservation has traditionally focused. Recently, conservators have challenged the dominant narrative that keepings things for longer is better and argued for the acceptance of loss, damage, and change, contrasted with the focus of scientific conservation on technical analysis and physical intervention. "If conservators re-position their perspective from a commitment to extending the lifetimes of objects to life-experiences generated by them," Jane Henderson has argued, "they can offer a focus in which past inequality rather than future beneficiaries becomes a determining criterion of how long we keep things."[11]

Renée van de Vall has distinguished three different conservation paradigms.[12] The first paradigm is scientific conservation, under which, as mentioned, the material integrity of the physical object is the central aim. More recently, two other models have gained ground: the performance paradigm and the processual paradigm. Under the performance paradigm, the conservator should aim to preserve not the artwork's material authenticity, but its identity. Van de Vall argues that "the core of the work is considered to consist in its concept, which should be realized through the faithful performance of a set of instructions stipulating the features defining the work's identity."[13] In contrast to a performance, a processual artwork does not have a script that needs to be faithfully executed, and it does not have a well-defined outcome. Processual artworks are "all those works that are intended to change according to uncontrollable factors or interventions from inside or outside the work, be it the weather, material decay, visitors' interaction or participation, or collaborative contributions by artists or public."[14] Here, conservation means supporting the continuation of an artwork or maintaining the life of an artwork. And since this might be done by engagement with the public or stakeholders rather than by experts working from instructions, the processual paradigm can mean a serious challenge to institutionalized or professional conservation models. Thus, it is important to recognize the agency of conservators, the epistemic hierarchies of caretakers of objects, and the politics of decision making in conservation.

The boundaries between different types of artworks and between different conservation paradigms are fluid; and while the origins of the processual and performance paradigms reside with conservators of contemporary art, these newer models can also be fruitful for other, older artworks. The point is not, as Van de Vall argues, that there is something inherently wrong with the scientific conservation model; for many artworks, including contemporary ones, preserving their material integrity, obeying principles of reversibility and minimal intervention, makes a lot of sense. It is, rather, that the scientific conservation paradigm is not universally applicable; put differently, it entails the recognition of the plurality of conservation and the importance of the conservator's judgment in deciding which of the different paradigms should be applied in individual cases. Today, conservators have begun to embrace the idea of "cultures of conservation," taking a "cultural turn," and recognizing the cultural specificity and geographical diversity of conservation theories and practices. According to Glenn Wharton, "There is clearly a need for broadly accepted professional ethics based on common values, along with more locally developed documents that are specific to geographies, specialisations, artists and media type."[15] Embracing irreducible cultural differences and diversity, Van de Vall and Wharton have argued for a bespoke ethics and a casuist approach, considering conservation not as a science in the sense of delivering universal knowledge but as a form of practical wisdom (*phronesis*).

Here, I would like to emphasize that conservation is an epistemic practice; it includes research and is fundamentally a knowledge-generating activity. I assume that the articulation of this epistemic ambition is not controversial, but the determination of the kind of knowledge that conservators produce is considerably more contested. Given the history of conservation, its roots in craft and artisanship, and the rise of science-based conservation, it has been not uncommon to consider scientific conservation, and the associated principles of objectivity, authenticity, minimal intervention, and reversibility, as an emancipation from hands-on craftsmanship. "Science came to dominate the methodology of the treatment of objects," according to Miriam Clavir, and she considers the period around 1930 as a key turning point in this shift toward scientific conservation and away from empirical restorer's techniques.[16] However, prior to the period between the two world wars, the professional identity and expertise of the restorer was much contested, and it would be wrong to simply equate the restorer with the craftsman. Rather, the restorer was situated at the crossroads of the different expert worlds. Noémie Étienne has shown that after the French Revolution and the opening of the Musée Central des Arts (the present-day Louvre), the role of the restorer was redefined, taking on the intermediate identity of the "connoisseur-artiste" who had knowledge of the "practical theory" of restoration and who shared the artist's knowledge, yet who was differentiated from the artist by giving up on "genius" and sacrificing their own style.[17] Moreover, recent studies of the history of conservation in the interbellum further complicate the linear progression narrative of conservation shifting from art and craft to science.[18]

It has similarly not been rare to frame the conservation of contemporary art as a theoretical turn, incommensurable with classical conservation, as if contemporary art forms such as multimedia, performance, and installation did not require continuous reenactments in which conservators create meaning, produce knowledge, and rely on skills. However, the re-execution of, for example, Sol LeWitt's Wall Drawings requires a team of professional drafters in possession of a set of technical skills to be able to meet the artist's demanding instructions regarding the result.[19] Moreover, for processual artworks, the conservator's aim of the continuation of an artwork can be dependent upon the transmission of the required skills. The rise of preventive conservation has been associated with the loss of hands-on skills needed for interventive treatment, and conservators likewise have warned against the "danger that the opportunities to learn and maintain the necessary skills for high-level hands-on conservation are diminishing."[20] Jonathan Ashley-Smith identified a certain "snobbery" of conservators as instrumental in this loss of practical skills, as many conservators "resent any element of their professional education being compared to an apprenticeship or their expertise being described as craftsmanship."[21] Such a dismissive attitude toward craftsmanship is served by conservation histories invested in a linear progression from craft to science. However, Ashley-Smith's warning originates in his conviction that craftsmanship, manual skills, and artisanal knowledge are as necessary for the conservator as any other skill or type of knowledge.

To avoid such dichotomies of hand and mind in characterizing the kind of knowledge that conservators generate, Hanna Hölling appropriately describes this knowledge as the *technique* of conservation.[22] The concept of technique embraces the propositional and nonpropositional aspects of knowledge generated by conservators; it is *techne* in the Aristotelian sense of *skill*, different from *episteme*, and for Hölling, in the sense of Heidegger, an expertise exceeding practical skills. Conservation histories depend upon hierarchies of the material and the intellectual and the hand and the mind; and these epistemic hierarchies are still at work in shaping present-day processes of collaboration and tensions between conservators, conservation scientists, and art historians, and their respective attitudes toward craftsmanship and expertise. We argue that the history of conservation, scrutinizing tensions and synergies of expertise, as negotiated in specific historical contexts and settings, should focus on the technique of conservation to avoid unreflectively adopting hierarchies of hand and mind and projecting them back in the ways in which we write conservation history. It can be helpful to look at other disciplines for guidance on how to conceptualize technique.

It is precisely to emphasize the epistemic dimension of practice that the performance theorist Ben Spatz prefers the concept of technique above performativity in his book *What a Body Can Do*. According to Spatz, technique "is a kind of knowledge . . . that moves across time and space . . . in ways deeply influenced but not entirely determined by social power relations."[23] Technique, Spatz argues, is knowledge that structures practice. While practice is not repeatable, technique fundamentally is; it is not bound to a particular place or moment, as people across time and space can rely on "the same knowledge of what is reliably possible given the similarities" of our bodies and environments, nevertheless recognizing that this reliability is relative and our bodies vary.[24] Spatz adopts the concept of technique to focus on what is relatively stable and transmissible in embodied practice. Practice and performance always exceed technique, but it would be wrong to situate the value of art or creative practice in that which remains when one subtracts technique. Spatz thus criticizes the romantic demarcation of art from other practices that would be called "merely technical," thus encouraging us to critically examine the history of technique as a term in art history.

HISTORY OF TECHNIQUE AND TECHNIQUE IN ART HISTORY

The confusion of the technical and the merely technical and the conflation of technique and technology is often observed in assessments of technical art history, which emerged as a field with this name in the twenty-first century. If technical art history is regularly confused with the examination of art with typically new technologies (and technology is here understood as applied science), the "technical" in art history is conflated with technology. Technology, as Eric Schatzberg has recently shown, was the English translation of the German *Technik* in the sense of "the state of the industrial arts," a meaning that only became dominant in the 1930s.[25] Thus, it seems that perceptions of technical art history reside in meanings crafted in the period around 1930, as much as this was a period in the history of conservation and science still consequential for present-day epistemologies of conservation. However, the same decade also witnessed alternative histories of technique in other disciplines.

In the 1930s, the French art historians Fernand Mercier and Henri Focillon argued for an integrated study of the artistic process, supported by a new type of visual expertise.[26] Following the first international conference for the study of scientific methods of analysis and conservation of art, held in Rome in 1930, they distinguished between "external technique" and "internal technique." External technique is visible at the surface of a work of art to the naked eye or photography.

Internal technique concerns the artistic processes that can only be analyzed by application of radiography. Focillon caught the difference between external and internal technique in terms of secret knowledge: "In painting, beneath what one might call the optical layer, there is an infinitesimal depth which cannot be reached by sight, and this is where diverse artifices are elaborated, of which our eyes immediately perceive the results without knowing their secret origins."[27]

This kind of knowledge was not exclusively an affair of the mind. In *L'éloge de la main*, Focillon argued that the hand—touch, not sight—provides us with access to knowledge, and that art is always produced by the hand of the artist.[28] The work of art is not the product of a disembodied mind; it is thought in matter rendered by the hand of the artist, and in this process the artist also produces knowledge, according to Focillon. Thus, Focillon investigated technique as knowledge, and he privileged new imaging technologies (photography and x-radiography) to study external and internal technique; as such, Focillon also foreshadows the conflation of technique and technology that haunts conservation and technical art history today.

This shows how intricately interwoven this history is with shifting notions of technique. The investigation of the concept and meaning of technique is thus crucial to a historical epistemology of technical art history. Citing Ashok Roy in the *National Gallery Technical Bulletin*, Paul Taylor has argued that Focillon's assessment that technique in the visual arts can be studied with the technologies of conservation science has become widely accepted. However, Taylor went on to show that the term *technique* (in French) was first used by Denis Diderot in the mid-eighteenth century to lend the practice of the visual artist aesthetic value—that is, to claim that artistry had value in itself.[29] Similarly, as Marieke Hendriksen has shown at the end of the eighteenth century, Kant adopted the German term *Technik* to explain the reflective nature of judgements of taste.[30] Hendriksen's scrutiny of a wide diversity of German texts from Winckelmann to Goethe reveals that the notion of *Technik* arose in connection with the distinction between processes of making and the works of art themselves. There are then two histories of technique in relation to the aforementioned epistemic hierarchies of body and mind.[31] First, as the term technique was only commonly adopted in histories of art in the nineteenth century, a semantic web of other terms (such as rule, practice, and method) were previously used to refer to the skills of the artist. Second, there is a history of how the term technique lost its aesthetic dimension, and how technique and technology became conflated so as to become similar to Focillon's usage in the 1930s.

In the same decade of the 1930s, the French anthropologist Marcel Mauss established a different line of research on "techniques of the body," in which technique is neither reduced to the merely mechanical nor conflated with technology. Mauss defined technique as "an ensemble of movements or actions, in general and for the most part manual, which are organized and traditional, and which work together toward the achievement of a goal known to be physical or chemical or organic."[32] Several elements of this definition would be up for discussion, but here it is important to emphasize that, for Mauss, technique is knowledge (for example, weaving a fabric supposes and generates knowledge) and can also be learned. Thus, Mauss also considered technique to be transmissible not only from master to apprentice; it can also circulate between societies and cultures, and it is not tied to time and place. Mauss also stressed how technique engages with materiality; it is socially defined, yet it engages with the possibilities offered by the material environment. Finally, Mauss pointed out that most techniques are characterized by the use of tools, but he conceptualized them as techniques of the body because the body is the most important tool for humans.

Mauss's work on technique is consequential in the humanities today. In recent years, historians of science and technology have rediscovered Andre Leroi-Gourhan, who further developed Mauss's framework of techniques of the body, while anthropologists Tim Ingold and Trevor Marchand have studied processes of learning in the crafts and the acquisition of skills in the arts.[33] They describe how artist-apprentices acquire technique; how the judgement of the eye is trained, embedded in a practice of learning in which all senses are involved, in which seeing is coordinated with movements of hand and body, with fast-shifting perspectives and with other sensory experiences, like touch, smell, and taste.[34] Their work offers opportunities for technical art history to open up a historical anthropology of skills and tools as an important field of research. While technical art history reemerged in the 1990s as a polemic movement back to the object, as we have seen in the introduction, I argue for a shift of focus within the field of technical art history, from objects to skills as part of the process of making. Such a shift would be in line with recent, more encompassing understandings of conservation as being as much about subjects as objects. Technical art history offers us the possibility to historicize skills and sensory expertise, and it can (as part of a more comprehensive toolbox) use performative methods of reconstruction, reenactment, and reworking in cooperation with conservators for this purpose. As I will argue in the last part of this essay, this requires specific attention in the design of the *re-* method beyond the use of historically accurate or appropriate materials.

RECONSTRUCTION AND REENACTMENT IN ART HISTORY

Reenactment has been part of the toolbox of art history for a long time. During the same years in which Focillon distinguished between external and internal technique and Mauss coined the "techniques of the body," we find one of the most explicit statements on reenactment in the field of art history in Erwin Panofsky's "Art History as a Humanistic Discipline," published in 1938:

> The humanist, dealing as he does with human actions and creations, has to engage in a mental process of a synthetic and subjective character: he has to mentally re-enact the actions and to re-create the creations. It is in fact by this process that the real objects of the humanities come into being. For it is obvious that historians of philosophy or sculpture are concerned with books and statues not in so far as these books and sculptures exist materially, but in so far as they have a meaning. And it is equally obvious that this meaning can only be apprehended by re-producing, and thereby, quite literally, "realizing," the thoughts that are expressed in the books and artistic conceptions that manifest themselves in the statues. Thus, the art historian subjects his "material" to a rational archeological analysis at times as meticulously exact, comprehensive and involved as any physical or astronomical research. But he constitutes his "material" by means of an intuitive aesthetic re-creation.[35]

While Panofsky's statement clearly embraces a dichotomy between material and meaning, as he emphasized that the art historian engages in *mental* reenactment, Michael Baxandall considered artworks as *thought things* when he engaged in the chiromancy of limewood. Although Baxandall never adopted a performative method, he made room for the application of reenactment as both a bodily and mental act in art history. A second difference with Panofsky concerns the status of the knowledge obtained through reenactment. While Panofsky claimed that through reenactment, the art historian's "aesthetic perception as such will change accordingly, and will more and more adapt itself to the original 'intention' of the work," Baxandall argued that we cannot reexperience the intention. His idea of reenactment is as a method that is self-aware of its distance from the art historical past.

How should technical art historians design reconstructions and reenactments? If the focus of technical art history is on skills, as I argue, other factors than the historical accuracy or appropriateness of materials, to which conservators have paid most attention, are important. Here, again, a dialogue with performance studies can be fruitful. Most recently, the *Routledge Handbook for Reenactment Studies* has observed a shift of the field toward "performance studies, with its emphasis on the body as an evidentiary vehicle for historical knowledge making."[36] Given the centrality of the body and embodiment, models of knowledge production in *re-* practices are based on enactive approaches to perception and cognition. Movements of the body are central to cognition, and perception is based on implicit knowledge of how bodily movement gives rise to changes in sensory stimulation. How bodies are capable of grasping the world "depends upon the possibilities given in the structure of their embodiment, how they have learned from experience, and the affordances of what they encounter."[37] We have taken this as point of departure in designing reconstructions and reenactments in which we are primarily interested in skills and processes of learning in the arts.

While reconstruction in the field of conservation typically takes place in laboratory environments, in consequent reenactments we have moved—following in the footsteps of experimental archaeologists—"in the field," or in open-air spaces with a different range of materials, other technologies, and less control upon the environment, which might be closer to the material conditions under which processes of making have been achieved in the past.[38] However, more fundamentally, how people as embodied minds make sense of the world depends upon the affordances of the things they encounter in their material environments. An affordance means a possibility for action that the sociomaterial environment offers to us; and practices through which people acquire skills generate a selective openness to those affordances, allowing apprentices to follow more experienced practitioners.[39] If we think of skills and their acquisition in this way, it is important to rethink and accordingly materially shape the spaces in which we undertake our reenactments. It is equally important to keep in mind that these sociomaterial environments in the field are still, and by necessity, different from early modern workshops. The cognitive philosopher and artist-architect Erik Rietveld has explored ideas of skills in *The End of Sitting* (2014), a site-specific installation allowing bodies to interact with material structures while exploring what kind of affordances for supporting standing people enjoyed. Rietveld conceives of such installations as "material playgrounds."[40] Following Rietveld, I propose to think of these spaces as material playgrounds in which experts of various kinds—makers, artists, art historians—responding to the affordances of these spaces, co-create art historical knowledge.

Thinking of these sociomaterial environments in terms of playgrounds is useful because the element of play emphasizes the explorative character of this experimental research and the difference and interconnectedness of the past and the present. While *re-* practices are developed upon the premise that our bodies are research tools, we recognize that they are not infallible witnesses. Bodies and our ways of doing are developed in a particular place and time; and thus, our performance engaging with material culture and the embodiment of past practices of bodies will always be partial, and always fail, yet in historically informative ways. Scholars in performance studies, such as Maaike Bleeker, have referred to Katie King's work on reenactments on television, in which she proposes reenactment as a perspective on newly emerging modes of embodied cognition.[41] King argues that reenactments are *pastpresents* producing in their audiences cognitive sensations as they navigate across knowledge worlds. Reenactments thus involve a shift toward the experience of knowledge in the making.

We have arrived at a crucial moment in the history of *re-* research and in thinking about reenactment in art history. To make reenactment sustainable as being productive of art historical knowledge, we will also need to develop epistemologies of *re-* practices; and the ways in which we conceptualize and sociomaterially scaffold the spaces in which we perform *re-* practices are key to such a theory of how they produce art historical knowledge.

CONCLUSION

Technical art history is in need of a shared epistemological framework that moves beyond the accepted wisdom of interdisciplinary methodologies in which conservators, art historians, and conservation scientists currently collaborate. In this essay, I have offered a modest contribution to a (historical) epistemology of technical art history. I also see a dialogue with conservation as crucial to technical art history, but I maintain that such a dialogue should embrace newer, more encompassing definitions of conservation, beyond the focus on objects, material integrity, and physical intervention that is characteristic of scientific conservation. Instead, I have proposed reenactment as an important method and technique as a key concept in the toolbox of technical art history. The origins of the epistemologies characterizing scientific conservation are found in the period around 1930, when the conflation of technology and technique in art history likewise emerged. However, the interbellum was also the cradle of alternative conceptions of technique, foremost in the anthropology of Mauss, whose techniques of the body are still much discussed by performance theorists and can be fruitfully activated in art history. If we move skill and technique to the core of the discipline of art history, technical art historians will need to pay as much attention to the spaces in which they reenact historical processes of making and skills acquisition as they do to the historical accuracy or appropriateness of the materials with which both technical art historians and conservators have been mostly concerned in the past. Conceptualizing this space will be a significant stepping stone toward the development of a historical epistemology of technical art history that moves beyond hierarchies of hand and mind.

NOTES

This research has received support from a European Research Council (ERC) Consolidator Grant under the European Union's Horizon 2020 research and innovation program (grant agreement no. 648718).

1. Malcolm Baker, "Limewood, Chiromancy and Narratives of Making: Writing about the Materials and Processes of Sculpture," *Art History* 21 (1998): 498–530; Michael Baxandall, *Paining and Experience in Fifteenth Century Italy: A Primer in the Social History of Pictorial Style* (Oxford: Clarendon Press, 1972); Michael Baxandall, *The Limewood Sculptors of Renaissance Germany* (New Haven, CT: Yale University Press, 1980).

2. David Bomford, "Introduction," in *Looking through Paintings: The Study of Painting Techniques and Materials in Support of Art Historical Research*, ed. Erma Hermens, Annemiek Ouwerkerk, and Nicola Costaras (Leiden: Archetype, 1998), 9–12.

3. Erma Hermens, "Technical Art History: The Synergy of Art, Conservation and Science," in *Art History and Visual Studies in Europe: Transnational Discourses and National Frameworks*, ed. Matthew Rampley, Thierry Lenain, Hubert Locher, Andrea Pinotti, Charlotte Schoell-Glass, and Kitty Zijlmans (Leiden: Brill, 2012), 151–65.

4. Marco Cardinali, "Technical Art History and the First Conference on the Scientific Analysis of Works of Art (Rome, 1930)," *History of Humanities* 2 (2017): 221–43; and Emma Jansson, "Toward a 'Theory' for Technical Art History," *Materia: Journal of Technical Art History* 1 (2021): 66–72.

5. Ann-Sophie Lehmann, "The Matter of the Medium: Some Tools for an Art Theoretical Interpretation of Materials," in *The Matter of Art: Materials, Practices and Cultural Logics, 1250–1750*, ed. Christy Anderson, Anne Dunlop, and Pamela H. Smith (Manchester: Manchester University Press, 2016), 21–41.

6. Jansson, "Toward a 'Theory,'" 69.

7. Sven Dupré, Anna Harris, Julia Kursell, Patricia Lulof, and Maartje Stols-Witlox, eds., *Reconstruction, Replication and Re-enactment in the Humanities and Social Sciences* (Amsterdam: Amsterdam University Press, 2020), 11–13.

8. Leslie Carlyle, "Reconstructions of Oil Painting Materials and Techniques: The HART Model for Approaching Historical Accuracy," in Dupré et al., *Reconstruction, Replication and Re-enactment*, 141–68.

9. Jenny Boulboullé and Sven Dupré, eds., *Burgundian Black: Reworking Early Modern Colour Technologies* (Santa Barbara: EMC Imprint, 2022), https://doi.org/10.55239/bb001; and Thijs Hagendijk, Marcia Vilarigues, and Sven Dupré, "Materials, Furnaces, and Texts: How to Write about Making Glass Colours in the Seventeenth Century," *Ambix* 67 (2020): 323–45.

10. Salvador Munoz Vinas, *Contemporary Theory of Conservation* (Amsterdam: Elsevier Butterworth Heinemann, 2005), 65–90.

11. Jane Henderson, "Beyond Lifetimes: Who Do We Exclude When We Keep Things for the Future?," *Journal of the Institute of Conservation* 43 (2020): 195.

12. Renée van de Vall, "Documenting Dilemmas: On the Relevance of Ethically Ambiguous Cases," *Revista de História da Arte* 4 (2015): 1–11.

13. Van de Vall, "Documenting Dilemmas," 2.

14. Van de Vall, 6–7.

15. Glenn Wharton, "Bespoke Ethics and Moral Casuistry in the Conservation of Contemporary Art," *Journal of the Institute of Conservation* 41 (2018): 60.

16. Miriam Clavir, "The Social and Historic Construction of Professional Values in Conservation," *Studies in Conservation* 43 (1998): 2.

17. Noémie Étienne, *The Restoration of Paintings in Paris, 1750–1815: Practice, Discourse, Materiality* (Los Angeles: Getty Conservation Institute, 2017), 49–72.

18. Sven Dupré and Jenny Boulboullé, eds., *Histories of Conservation and Art History in Modern Europe* (New York: Routledge, 2022).

19. Van de Vall, "Documenting Dilemmas," 6.

20. Jonathan Ashley-Smith, "Losing the Edge: The Risk of a Decline in Practical Conservation Skills," *Journal of the Institute of Conservation* 39 (2016): 119; and Jonathan Ashley-Smith, "The Ethics of Doing Nothing," *Journal of the Institute of Conservation* 41 (2018): 6–15.

21. Ashley-Smith, "Losing the Edge," 122.

22. Hanna Hölling, "The Technique of Conservation: On Realms of Theory and Cultures of Practice," *Journal of the Institute of Conservation* 40 (2017): 87–96.

23. Ben Spatz, *What a Body Can Do: Technique as Knowledge, Practice as Research* (New York: Routledge, 2015), 38.

24. Spatz, *What a Body Can Do*, 41.

25. Eric Schatzberg, *Technology: Critical History of a Concept* (Chicago: University of Chicago Press, 2018), 97–145.

26. Cardinali, "Technical Art History," 221–43.

27. "En peinture, au-dessous de ce que l'on peut appeler la couche optique, il y a toute une profondeur infinitésimale que la vue n'atteint pas et où s'élaborent des artifices divers, dont nos yeux percoivent immédiatement les résultats sans en connaître les ressorts secrets." Henri Focillon, "Préface," in *Les Primitifs francais: La peinture clunysienne en Bourgogne a l'époque romaine: Son histoire et sa technique*, Fernand Mercier (Paris: Editions A. Picard, 1931), viii.

28. Annamaria Ducci, "Familles de mains: Source d'inspiration dans l'Eloge de la main," in *Henri Focillon: Textes réunis par Pierre Wat* (Paris: Kimé, 2007), 63–70.
29. Paul Taylor, "From Mechanism to Technique: Diderot, Chardin, and the Practice of Painting," in *Knowledge and Discernment in the Early Modern Arts*, ed. Sven Dupré and Christine Göttler (New York: Routledge, 2017), 296–316.
30. Marieke Hendriksen, "'Art and Technique Always Balance the Scale': German Philosophies of Sensory Perception, Taste, and Art Criticism, and the Rise of the Term Technik, ca. 1735–ca. 1835," *History of Humanities* 2 (2017): 201–19.
31. Marieke Hendriksen and Sven Dupré, eds., *The Making of Technique in the Arts* (Turnhout: Brepols, forthcoming).
32. Marcel Mauss, "Les techniques du corps," *Journal de psychologie normal et pathologique* 32 (1935): 271–93. See Spatz, *What a Body Can Do*, 29–33.
33. Marie-Thébaud-Sorger, "Capturing the Invisible: Heat, Steam and Gases in France and Great Britain, 1750–1800," in *Compound Histories: Materials, Governance and Production, 1760–1840*, ed. Lissa L. Roberts and Simon Werrett (Boston: Brill, 2018), 85–105; Tim Ingold, *Making: Anthropology, Archaeology, Art and Architecture* (Hoboken, NJ: Taylor and Francis, 2013); and Trevor H. J. Marchand, "Muscles, Morals and Mind: Craft Apprenticeship and the Formation of Person," *British Journal of Educational Studies* 56 (2008): 245–71.
34. Cristina Grasseni, "Introduction," in *Skilled Visions: Between Apprenticeship and Standards*, ed. Cristina Grasseni (New York: Berghahn Books, 2007), 4.
35. Erwin Panofsky, "Art History as a Humanistic Discipline," in *The Meaning of the Humanities*, ed. Theodore M. Greene (Princeton, NJ: Princeton University Press, 1938), 105–6, quoted in Whitney Davis, "Art History, Re-enactment, and the Idiographic Stance," in *Michael Baxandall, Vision and the Work of Words*, ed. Peter Mack and Robert Williams (Burlington, VT: Ashgate, 2015), 71.
36. Vanessa Agnew, Jonathan Lamb, and Juliane Tomann, "Introduction: What Is Reenactment Studies?" in *The Routledge Handbook for Reenactment Studies* (New York: Routledge, 2020), 7.
37. Maaike Bleeker, "(Re)enacting Thinking in Movement," in *The Oxford Handbook of Dance and Reenactment*, ed. Mark Franko (New York: Oxford University Press, 2017), 225.
38. Allen K. Outram, "Introduction to Experimental Archaeology," *World Archaeology* 40 (2008): 1–7.
39. Tim Ingold, *The Perception of the Environment: Essays in Livelihood, Dwelling and Skill* (New York: Routledge, 2000); and James J. Gibson, *The Ecological Approach to Visual Perception* (Boston: Houghton Mifflin, 1979).
40. Erik Rietveld, "The Affordances of Art for Making Technologies," inaugural lecture, Socrates Chair, University of Twente, April 18, 2019, transcript, 22–31, http://research.utwente.nl/en/publications/the-affordances-of-art-for-making-technologies. For the concept of play in relation to reenactment, see also Petra Tjitske Kalshoven, *Crafting the Indian: Knowledge, Desire, and Play in Indianist Reenactment* (New York: Berghahn Books, 2012).
41. Katie King, *Networked Reenactments: Stories Transdisciplinary Knowledges Tell* (Durham, NC: Duke University Press, 2011).

MATERIALS SURFACING

CHAPTER 7
THE BETTMANN MORGUE
COLD STORAGE, DIGITIZATION, AND ARCHIVES OF RACIAL VIOLENCE

Brian Michael Murphy

INTRODUCTION

I am at the Corbis Film Preservation Facility, where the 14 million images in the Bettmann Archive are stored in a 10,000 square-foot refrigerated vault.[1] I am here to look at many kinds of images, including lynching photography. The archivist is walking toward me, still wearing the heavy parka she put on to be able to withstand the cold of the vault. She is pushing a cart loaded with thick manila folders, some of them full of images of corpses. I pick up a folder and begin looking through the images, every one frigid to the touch. Not only that, but they reek of vinegar syndrome—the smell of decaying negatives. Each glossy black-and-white photo is heavier than it should be, as its back is stacked with stickers from all the times it was licensed and sent out for use by a client. I see castrated and strangled Black bodies, their torsos misshapen by pyres, hands bound with chains and ropes and belts to trees and telephone poles and bridges.

These are the kinds of images that visual culture scholars typically define as lynching images: a Black body, or bodies, at the center of the photo, sometimes surrounded by the white faces of a mob, or a massive crowd gathered to witness the spectacle. These scholars have followed the conceptualization of lynching established in the late nineteenth-century by antilynching activists such as Ida B. Wells, who narrowed the definition of the term lynching so that it referred mainly to Black people lynched by white mobs. But prior to the antilynching campaigns led by people like Wells, the term lynching referred to a wide range of violent acts, including hanging but also forms of nonlethal punishment, such as beating, flogging, and tar and feathering. To be lynched meant to be abducted or taken forcibly, usually by a group of people, and subjected to violence.

In the cold folders of the Bettmann Archive, I found images that so radically exploded the narrow definition of lynching often used by visual culture scholars that I was forced to rethink not only what counts as a lynching image but also

Fig. 7.1. ***Waiting for Dawn and Death***, June 15, 1936

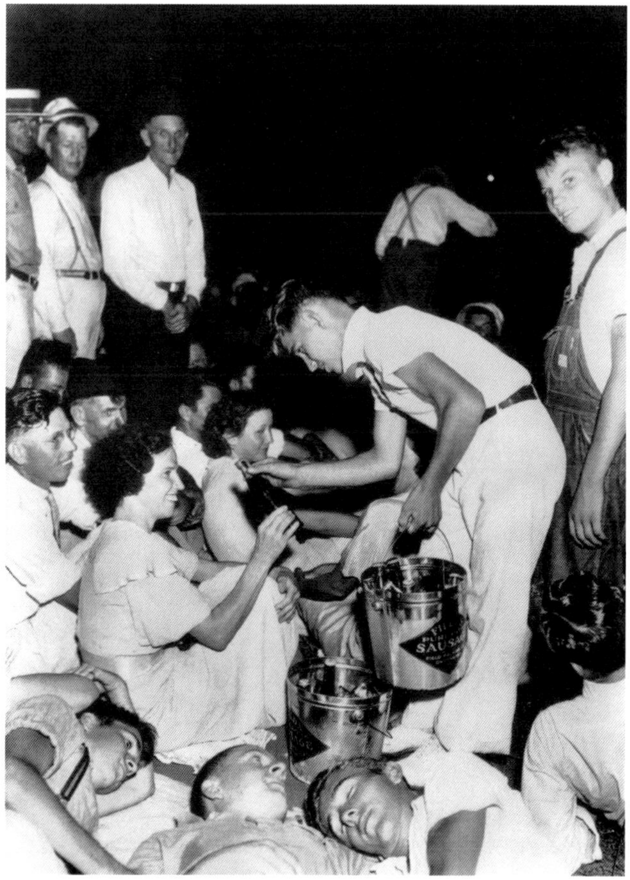

everything about how such scholars have interpreted them.[2] A undated news illustration titled *Female Lynchers*, for example, depicts a group of white women flogging a white man named Kelly Patterson for his "outrageous assault" on one of their young daughters. In a photo from 1934, a "frustrated lynch mob" in Shelbyville, Tennessee, stares into the camera, pistols drawn, just after they failed to break into a courthouse and kidnap their victim. A 1936 photo from Kentucky, titled *Waiting for Dawn and Death* (fig. 7.1), shows a crowd of people enjoying sodas in the early morning darkness, hours away from watching the hanging of a Black man named Rainey Bethea, often described as "the last public execution" in the United States. In the folder labeled "Ku-Klux-Klan: Before 1930," I found a photo of Oren Van Loon, a white pastor who was abducted, held for eleven days, tortured, and branded by the Ku Klux Klan in 1924, in Battle Creek, Michigan.

In this paper, I examine the ways in which the preservation practices of cold storage and digitization shape the proliferation of possible meanings of the Bettmann Archive's lynching images. These preservation practices do not simply save what currently exists, but rather generate entirely new contexts for viewing and interpretation. I argue that the creative categorization and organizational strategies deployed in the digitization of the Bettmann challenge dominant scholarly definitions of historical events and processes. As a case study, I analyze the Bettmann's expanded conception of lynching imagery and elaborate the several ways that this conception productively disrupts long-held scholarly perspectives on historical images of racial violence.

DIGITIZATION AS PRODUCTION

Digitization is a form of preservation by reproduction. Like all forms of preservation, it changes that which it preserves, not simply preserving what already exists but, in actuality, producing something new. Digitization produces many new things: not just a new digital image that did not exist before, which is materially and ontologically very different from the analog photograph it preserves, but also new meanings for both the digital and analog images. Digitization effects this by multiplying the contexts and sites where an image is encountered, spawning vast intertextual webs within databases and search engines, generating the connective tissue of metadata, such as tags. This metadata links images across historical time periods, across the boundaries of previously separate archives, across ostensibly distinct domains of imagery, such as documentary photography from the Great Depression and twenty-first-century commercial stock pictures that are contrived, contextless, and denuded of any ability to represent real life—the opposite of documentary.

Digitization, as much as it sends analog images hurtling around the world and expands the reach of those images, also obscures much of the analog archive. Commercial imperatives guide which images are digitized and which remain only in the analog archive, which is largely inaccessible. Of the Bettmann Archive's 14 million images, less than 300,000 have been digitized. The analog archive thus undergoes redaction through digitization, a narrowing of content that results in different, more limited representations of specific historical events or subjects.[3] Corbis's original selection of which images to preserve through digitization was "based not only on commercial potential but also their historic significance."[4] This valuation has a recursive effect, as digitized images are then more accessible, are used more often, and thus come to authoritatively represent the figures and events they depict. Journalist Sarah Boxer aptly describes the effects of digitizing and making broadly available only two percent of the total images in the Bettmann: "Corbis's most popular photographs—say, the picture of John F. Kennedy Jr. saluting his father's coffin—will become ever more popular. . . . And the more pictures are requested, the more they are requested. Visual history is doomed to repeat itself."[5] Thus, the preservation of the Bettmann Archive is a productive process that recursively reshapes both representations of the archive itself and the overall appearance of American cultural memory, reinvesting specific images with value and iconicity while rendering other analog images less likely to circulate. Digitization as a preservation practice contributes to the production of the very historical and commercial value that is supposedly located in the images themselves, which ostensibly makes certain images candidates for preservation in the first place.

So, in the case of a given category of images, such as lynching photographs, the digital images available in the database are only a fraction of the troubling and strange array of photos in the archive. This broader array of images, when considered all at once and alongside these new digitized versions, disrupts what visual culture scholars have, up to this point, understood the archive of American racial violence to be.

DIGITIZATION AND THE EXPANDED DEFINITION OF LYNCHING

In July 1924, Oren Van Loon, a white minister in Michigan, posed for a news photographer, who focused his lens on the letters *KKK* branded onto Van Loon's back (fig. 7.2). Intraracial violence—white-supremacist violence against white people—was a significant threat in both the Jim Crow South and the North; it was integral to white-supremacist terror and dominance. The case of Van Loon reflects, in ways that conventionally defined lynching images do not, this intraracial violence. Van Loon was not an antiracist agitator, and he had even allowed the Klan to hold meetings in his church. Yet Van Loon had offended the Klan when, in a sermon, he had criticized secret societies and the practice of cross burning, though not the "100 percent Americanism" ideology espoused by the Klan. Van Loon's sermon did not critique the white supremacy at the heart of the Klan's project. Yet they still drugged and kidnapped him, tortured and branded him, as both a punishment and a warning to other white people who might challenge the Klan—not just in terms of their racial ideology, but in terms of their patriarchal dominance that entitled them to do, in their view, whatever they wanted. At the hospital, police guarded Van Loon's room in case the Klan planned to torment the pastor further. He claimed to not remember anything about the incident. His hair, which had been gray before his abduction, an eleven-day ordeal, had begun to turn white.[6]

Fig. 7.2. *Kidnapped Minister Bearing Klu Klux Klan Brand*, July 15, 1924

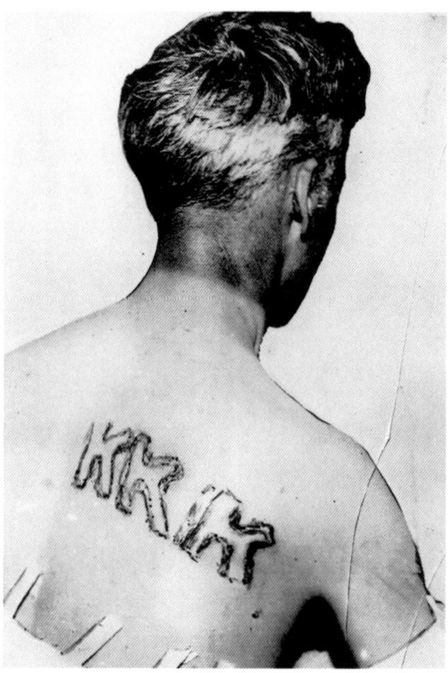

Visual culture scholars have often claimed that lynching photographs, which frequently circulated in the form of postcards, functioned to threaten Black people and consolidate white identity and community. Yet Van Loon's case illustrates an important aspect of white-supremacist violence: its thoroughgoing paranoia about any challenge to white male dominance and the terrorist organizations that took it upon themselves to preserve it. By looking beyond the narrow genre of lynching photos widely recirculated through digitization and instead confronting the Bettmann's more diverse analog holdings, we begin to see how white-supremacist terrorism victimized white *and* Black people in both the North and the South.

White-supremacist violence is and was a patriarchal violence. It is thus entangled with the domestic violence rampant in the United States since before its founding, a violence that reproduces the concentration of power in male hands and most often damages women and children. This means, then, that lynchings, even of Black men and women, also carried a supplemental threat to white people, like Van Loon, who would dare disobey the ever-shifting protocols of white-supremacist patriarchy. Indeed, in the early and mid-1920s, the Klan "not infrequently" targeted white people, "Protestants and females who were considered 'immoral' or 'traitors' to their race or gender," including an Alabama divorcee "flogged for the 'crime' of remarrying then given a jar of Vaseline for her wounds." The Klan attacked other adults for "immorality and failure to go to church," and even lashed girls for "riding in automobiles with young men."[7]

However, in visual culture scholarship, the interpretive frames used to read the archive of racial violence often do not take such dynamics of patriarchal intraracial violence into account. Visual culture scholars have not only defined lynching too narrowly, but also interpreted these images too neatly in asserting that lynching images threatened Blacks with violence and at the same time bound whites together in a sense of community and superiority. Shawn Michelle Smith's analysis of a lynching postcard depicting the burned corpse of Jesse Washington typifies this circumscribed interpretive approach, even as it raises other interpretive possibilities that remain unexplored. Smith describes the white faces of the crowd thus: "These white men and boys (and at least one woman) face the viewer with steady, unflinching gazes, as if daring challengers to defy them."[8] Though she does not classify the "challengers" as either Black or white or both, she maintains a racial division in her interpretation of the effects of the "unflinching gazes" of the mob. For Smith, lynching photographs were "terrifying sites of racial identification for African American men and women, sites which can finally become catalysts for antiracist action."[9] The white eyes seem thus to issue a threat weighted with the charred Black body at the center of the image, a threat that seems, according to this analysis, self-evidently to direct itself at Black people.

But the white eyes simultaneously work to accomplish other tasks in Smith's reading, as they direct their gaze at white people as well, not as a threat, but as an invitation to white self-consolidation and the fortification of the racial bonds and bounds of imagined white community. Smith suggests that the white eyes in these images might look toward other white eyes, and so lynching photographs also functioned "as sites of white supremacist identification." On the back of one postcard is a message written from "Joe" to his mother: "This is the barbecue we had last night. My picture is on the left with a cross over it. Your sone [*sic*] Joe."[10] Joe's gaze, as one of the many in the crowd, serves as a threat to Black men who would challenge white supremacy. But Smith reads the note on the back in a way that suggests it is, at the same time, a tender gaze: "Joe looks directly out at the camera, perhaps anticipating the eyes of his mother. This particular postcard, then, with sender looking out at projected receiver, marks directly the ways in which postcards construct community."[11] So, the same gaze that functions as a threat for Black people is an invitation to community for white people in general, as well as a gaze directed at one white person in particular: Joe's mother.

The very excess of lynching violence depicted in the photograph, however, as well as the frequent repetition of lynching rituals in the Jim Crow era, suggests that the dead body of a Black man—and the photograph of it—failed to suture white familial bonds effectively. The dead Black body establishes not only a path of connection but a point of rupture between mother and son, an insurmountable distance. The Black body convokes a white community of faces whose uniformity diminishes the idealized mother's ability to recognize her own son: Joe had to mark the space above his head with a cross to make himself more easily identifiable. The bond is persistently made and unmade by the violence in the image, for if the white gaze functions as both threat and invitation to identification, then there is always a surplus of each in the other. As Smith says, the "unflinching gazes" are aimed at their "challengers." And as the case of Oren Van Loon demonstrates, each white person was a potential challenger of white supremacy; thus, lynchings and lynching images also issued a threat to white people. If lynchings helped bind white communities together, perhaps they did so through not only the abjection of the Black Other and the performance of racial mastery, but also through the common vulnerability of *white people* to white supremacist violence.

When we consider the pervasiveness of intraracial white violence, including the array of images of lynched white people in the seminal 1999 book *Without Sanctuary* (images that Smith ignores), then the postcard of Jesse Washington necessarily functions as a threat of violence to anyone, of any race, who challenges white supremacy.[12] Terrorist violence directed against Black men in the preservation of whiteness did not occur in a vacuum, but in an environment where Black men and women, *and* white men and women, experienced violence meant to maintain white racial purity and morality.[13] When we assume that interracial violence was the only form of assault that preserved white supremacy, we merely scrape the surface of Jim Crow's overall archive of violence, one that includes images of Van Loon's shoulder branded with *KKK* not as a mark of allegiance, but as a threat and warning to other white people. Nonlethal lynchings like Van Loon's are, in fact, highly similar to those suffered by some Black victims of the Klan, such as Felton Turner, who was abducted by four white youth in Houston, Texas, in 1960, forced into a car, tied to a tree, and flogged about fifty times with a chain. While Turner pretended to be unconscious in an effort to avoid being killed, his assailants carved *KKK* into the skin on his belly, in two different places.[14] I recently found a digitized photograph of a white man bearing the letters KKK on his chest after a similar assault.[15] Such parallels in interracial and intraracial lynchings suggest that a desegregated methodology is now needed to illuminate how white-supremacist violence is, and has always been, more democratic in its thuggery, its threats, its terror, than we have often liked to believe.

Such similarities in nonlethal interracial and intraracial lynchings suggest a different structure of violent dominance than the prevailing one in visual culture scholarship, where lynching is defined as a fatal attack and threat to Black people, enacted by white people who assert their social, racial, economic, and sexual mastery of African Americans through the lynching ritual. Such racially segregated analyses of violence — its threat-effects and affects — skew our historical conception of visualities in the Jim Crow era. Visual culture scholars have tended to focus on the way the deployment of lynching images in different contexts for different purposes points to their semiotic instability, rather than to engage the full complexity of white subjectivity in the historical moment of the images' production, within the broader context of both interracial and intraracial violence.

Lynching images could never function to threaten only Black people in an environment where white supremacists regularly inflicted floggings and beatings on white people as well. Threat does not work so neatly. In his singular essay, "The Future Birth of the Affective Fact: The Political Ontology of Threat," Brian Massumi explains that "the affective reality of threat is contagious," demonstrating how the announcement of a threat "modulate[s] felt qualities infusing a life-environment."[16] Even a young white woman cheering at a lynching of a Black man would have also been subject to patriarchal violence herself. Thus, she could not have wholly inoculated her psyche against the supplemental threat of violence that issued from the male hands knotting the noose, pouring the kerosene, flashing the castration knife, shooting holes of daylight through a charred torso. Those hands were the same hands that bruised her ribs; that knife was the same knife that opened her flesh in places she had to bind and keep hidden. In short, the unspeakably violent men before her carried their terrible capacity with them at all times, and she knew that, and they knew she knew that, and so what Massumi calls the "threat-environment" grew thicker for white people in the wake of lynching spectacles, as lynching postcards and other mementos circulated. The white individuals in the crowd lived amid the hyperviolent white supremacists carrying out the torture and death-work. These men were their brothers, supervisors, lovers, coworkers, classmates, family friends, uncles, cousins, perpetrators.[17]

While there is relatively little in the way of a photographic history of white supremacist violence against white people, there is a significant amount of textual evidence that reshapes the interpretive frame for lynching images, revealing how images threatening violence against Black people could also function as obverse threats to white people who challenged the patriarchal racial order. The "KKK Folder" in the massive Bettmann Archive contains no images that portray physical violence against white victims, besides the photograph of Van Loon. But it does contain one image of "James A. Colescott, Imperial Wizard of the Ku Klux Klan" as he reads a newspaper story about his subpoena to appear before a grand jury investigating a rash of floggings in East Point, Georgia. In the photo, the headline of the front page is legible: "Ku Klux Chief Is Called by Grand Jurors for Questioning in Flogging Probe Here." The investigation of the floggings in East Point began after the flogging and murder not of a Black man, but of Ike Gaston, a white barber. According to an oral history interview with Daniel Duke, the principle investigator for the grand jury, Gaston was "a drinker and he drank and he didn't look after his family but was a likeable fellow." The KKK "decided to discipline him for not looking after his family. So they carried him out there on March 3, 1940, I think. So the next morning they found his body partially frozen, it was cold, with this big whip with the Klan thing carved on it with cleats on it."[18] A few reporters, along with a captain from the county police force and a detective, began investigating the case. The coroner on the Gaston case, Paul Donahue, held a hearing for anyone who had been flogged. Most who came forward were white, and there were several victims, including one who accused the officer taking the report of having been a perpetrator in the flogging. By the end of the affair, three deputy sheriffs were indicted and sent to prison for their participation in the lynchings.[19]

The images of Van Loon's brand and the Imperial Wizard holding the newspaper point to the pervasiveness of intraracial violence in the era of Jim Crow, and they represent a larger archive of material that has been virtually ignored in many histories of racial violence and, in particular, in scholarly literature on lynching images. For example, in 1950, Tabor City, North Carolina, experienced over a dozen terror attacks. In one instance, the Klan kidnapped a white man and woman, forced them "to bend over a car fender," then beat them "with a machine belt nailed to a pick handle. Between blows, the victims were made to pray, and listen to sermons and hymn singing from the Klansmen."[20] An August 11, 1952, *Time* article reports a rash of floggings by the KKK in Columbus County, North Carolina, in 1951. The first victim was a thirty-eight-year-old Black woman: they gagged her with her slip, "tied her legs [to] plow lines and beat her with sticks and gun butts" for the vague offense of "running around with white men." But the overwhelming majority of victims in this spree—ten out of thirteen—were white, punished for varied crimes as defined by the Klan, such as "not attending church regularly, cursing near women," or "drinking too much."[21] The ongoing subjection of white people to such intraracial violence fostered a feeling of threat within white communities with a strong Klan presence. Such intraracial violence and the threat-environment it created have a historical legacy that, like interracial violence, stretches back to the tense days of the mid-nineteenth century and beyond.[22]

DIGITIZING THE LAST "LEGAL LYNCHING"

In 1936, the state of Kentucky carried out the execution of Rainey Bethea,[23] before which a large crowd gathered, a segment of which was captured in *Waiting for Dawn and Death* (see fig. 7.1). By examining this image in both its analog and digitized forms, I will trace the ways that digitization reshapes the meaning of the image itself and the Bettmann Archive's overall representation of that day. While the digitized segment of the Bettmann contains four images of Bethea's execution, visual culture scholars typically do not examine this group of images because, in their strict definition, his death does not qualify as a lynching: Bethea was convicted of rape by a jury, and the execution was carried out by the state, thus making it a legal execution. In contrast to this scholarly distinction, the digital archive firmly establishes Bethea's hanging as a lynching by associating it closely with mainstream lynching images. The digital archive offers an image location tool, a hyperlink that reads "More Images Like This" or "Similar Images." Clicking on the "Similar Images" hyperlink generates an array of lynching images ranked by relevance, many of which firmly fit Smith's definition, from the much-analyzed photograph of Jesse Washington's burned corpse hanging from a tree in Waco, Texas, in 1916, to the prolifically reproduced photo of three Black men lynched in Duluth, Minnesota, in 1920. The digital archive's categorization of Bethea's execution as a lynching accords with numerous historians who have long identified lynchings like Bethea's as falling under the category of "legal lynchings," where a sham trial leads to an unconstitutionally speedy conviction. In Bethea's case, the jury deliberated for all of five minutes.

Digital archives can change quickly and constantly, reshaping the meaning of the images they contain as their content broadens or is reorganized. For example, *Waiting for Dawn and Death* was conjoined with a whole new constellation of images a few years ago, when the Visual China Group purchased Corbis from its sole owner, Bill Gates. The new owners of *Waiting for Dawn and Death* then authorized Getty Images to manage all of Corbis's former assets in North America, including the Bettmann Archive. And so, with Getty's one worthy rival now eliminated, the Getty

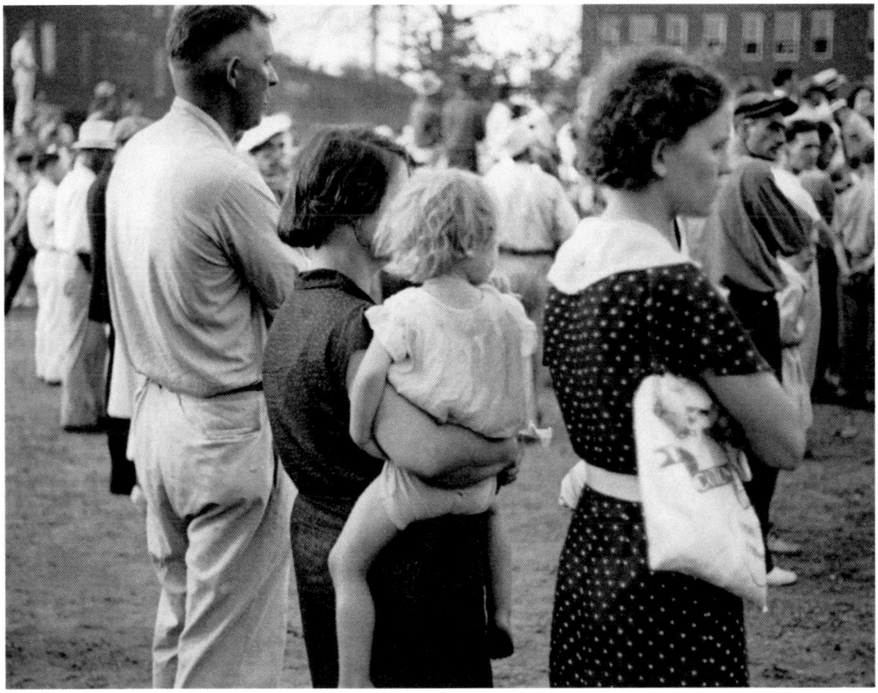

Fig. 7.3. ***Final Public Execution in the USA*****, August 14, 1936**

Images database has absorbed all the digital images that I previously would search at Corbis's website, which is now long gone.[24] *Waiting for Dawn and Death* is now linked through its metadata to other images of the crowd that came to witness the lynching of Rainey Bethea, the conjoining of the Corbis and Getty archives generating a fresh set of contextual connections.

These new contexts should shift the interpretive frames through which we analyze *Waiting for Dawn and Death*, in both its digital and analog forms. In the Getty images of the event, now arriving alongside the Bettmann images in searches, we see the scale of the crowd and how some people struggled to get a clear view of the execution, even climbing atop a telephone pole in some cases. We see that the soda sellers in *Waiting* were not the only enterprising vendors there that day, as a sign visible in one photo advertises "Cold Drinks."

In yet another Getty image, *Final Public Execution in the USA* (fig. 7.3), a woman holds a young child on her hip, both of them looking toward the lynching. In this photograph, we can see the broader, deeper function of this lynching at work, the way racism and white-supremacist terror would get embedded in the body through the act of witnessing this violence in early childhood. Before such an onlooker was even old enough to clearly state her name, a specter was lodged in her endocrine system, in the triggers of neurotransmitters released in the brain that tell her she is safe or threatened or a confused mixture of the two. She was told that the most monstrous act she had ever seen in her short life was not monstrous at all, that it was ridding the world of a monster, and she was told to take her hope and her trust and her love and pour it all into that monstrous power she was forced to witness by her parents, who cannot be monsters. Can they?

I do not know the lives of the people portrayed in *Final Public Execution in the USA*. I don't know if they approved of what they saw or detested it, or were as bewildered by it as the child almost certainly was. I don't know if they arrived there by their own will or if one of them had pressured or even coerced the others to attend. But I know the short story "Going to Meet the Man" by James Baldwin, as well as "A Party Down at the Square" by Ralph Ellison. And I know Kristina DuRocher's chilling book *Raising Racists: The Socialization of White Children in the Jim Crow South*.[25] I know that racism made its way not just into the mind in these moments, but into the body, into the deepest biochemical and affective dimensions of our being. These image sets made possible by cold storage and digitization remind us that what James Baldwin said many decades ago is still true: "American history is longer, more various, more beautiful and more terrible than anything anyone has ever said about it."[26]

"OUR GIRLS STILL PREFERS [*sic*] WHITE HUSBANDS"

While I maintain that the digital database in some ways obscures the broader range of images in the refrigerated analog archive, it also revealed to me images that I did not see in the analog archive, images that must have been categorized and filed in folders I did not request. While looking for lynching images in the old Corbis database several years ago, I came across a photo that opened up everything for me, like a doorway from my personal history into our national past. The image was shot in Mansfield, Texas, in 1956, amid protests against the Supreme Court's order to desegregate public schools. The town of Mansfield ended up defying the court for nearly a decade and eventually integrated its schools only in order to avoid losing federal funding. Mansfield's schools finally admitted Black students in 1965, exactly one hundred years after the end of the Civil War.[27]

In the photo (fig. 7.4), a car sits on the grass in front of Mansfield High School. Racial threats written in white paint mar the car's doors, hood, fenders, and trunk. A fourteen-year-old boy stands behind the open driver's-side door, his gaze barreling directly into the camera and the viewer, evoking the defiant and proud stares of lynch mobs who crowd America's endless morgue files. The car's various inscriptions are mostly concerned with maintaining racial segregation and policing sexual contact between Black and white people. The threats on the car worked in concert with lynched effigies just out of view, one of them hung over the entrance

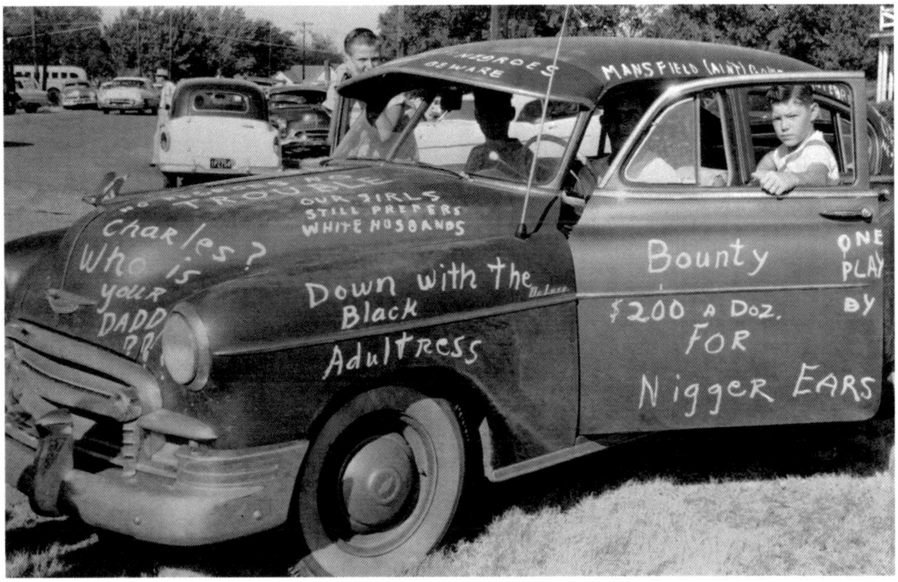

Fig. 7.4. ***Protesting Desegregation*, August 31, 1956**

of the school building (fig. 7.5).[28] Segregationists hung another effigy from a flagpole outside the school and yet another in the center of town, the surrogate body burned and splashed with red paint, bearing signs that read, "This Negro tried to enter a white school," and a message written on its legs: "This would be a terrible way to die." In addition to these effigies, desegregation protesters brandished guns, prevented cars from entering town if their passengers were deemed sympathetic to integration, threatened the Mansfield sheriff, and parked a car covered in white scrawl near the entrance of Mansfield High in August, as student registration began. "Any Negro seen in a Mansfield school will be our next effigy," the trunk of the car read, suggesting both the space in the automobile where a Black person might be secreted on their way to being lynched and burned, and cross-referencing the several effigies hung in various locations in Mansfield.

This extension of the sense of threat from actual lynchings through the effigy and car constitutes what Massumi calls "the mass affective production of felt threat-potential," which "engulfs the (f)actuality of the comparatively small number of incidents where danger materialized. They blend together in a shared atmosphere of fear."[29] In other words, though no living Black individuals were lynched in Mansfield during the desegregation battles in 1956, the threat of lynching and the actual lynchings that had occurred elsewhere in the United States up to that point produced an affective economy that desegregation protesters modulated through the public performance of threats. This threat environment engulfed not

Fig. 7.5. ***Effigy Hanging on Mansfield High School in Texas***, May 31, 1956

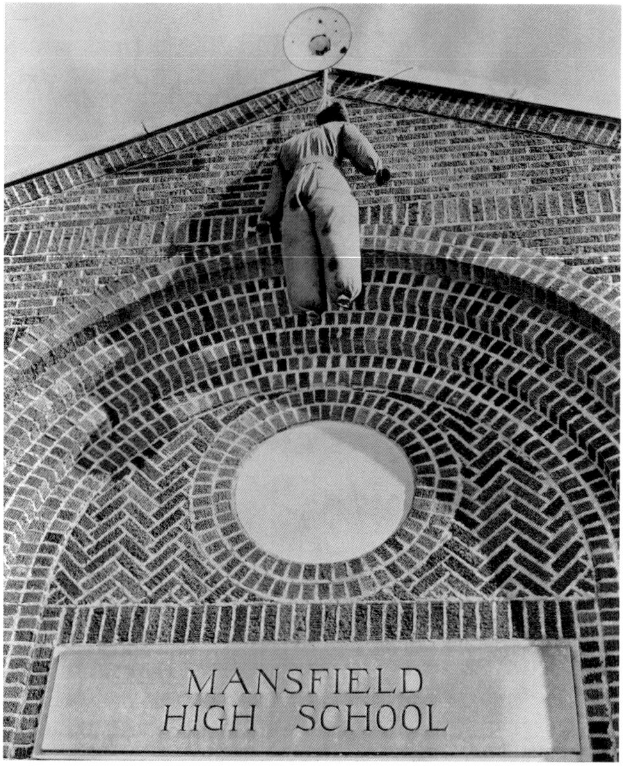

only Black people, but white people as well, although certainly differently. The effigies and cars displayed in Mansfield infused the life-environment with threat, enhanced by cross-referencing the actual mutilations and lynchings of Black bodies in the past ("This negro tried to enter a white school") and simultaneously positioning the effigy as, in Massumi's terms, a "self-renewing threat from the future,"[30] with threats phrased in the future and conditional tenses ("Any Negro seen in a Mansfield school today will be our next effigy"; "This would be a horrible way to die"). When the Bettmann Archive was absorbed by Getty Images, the photograph of the car was directly linked to and appeared in searches with the photos of the flagpole effigy, digitization thickening the context for each one through the others, rendering more fully present the invisible violence of threat in Mansfield that day.

These photographs of effigies are lynching images, as the use of effigies was a form of lynching, of interracial and intraracial violence that served to threaten both Black and white people who dared challenge Jim Crow's racial divisions. In March 1960, white author John Howard Griffith was lynched in effigy from a traffic light at the intersection of Main and Broad Streets in Mansfield, Texas—his hometown. The lynching occurred in response to his publication of the first in a series of articles on his experience posing as a Black man in the South. Griffith used drugs, creams, and tanning to darken his skin, then spent months on the road, walking and hitchhiking through Mississippi and a few other Southern states. (He would later expand his dispatches into the best-selling memoir *Black Like Me*, published in 1961). The effigy's face was painted half white, half black, and was left at the Mansfield dumping grounds, under a sign that read "$25. fine for dumping dead animals." Griffith and members of his family also received death threats in the mail and eventually moved to Mexico for a time out of fear for their lives.[31]

In an attempt to scour the internet for more images and information about the car covered in threats, I turned from Getty to Google, to see what other images digitization had made available. I soon found one more image of the car in the Associated Press database, appearing in Google image search results alongside images from the Bettmann and Getty.

The two girls in *Civil Rights School Integration* (fig. 7.6) are dressed beautifully as they stare at the car and read its grim pronouncements. The flower print and plaid of their dresses are, for me, what Roland Barthes in *Camera Lucida* called the *punctum*, that part of the photo that pierces you.[32] The cascade of tags in the metadata attached to the photo ranges from subject headings including "Education, African-Americans, Human rights and civil liberties, Racial and ethnic discrimination, Social Issues," to keyword labels that are even more disturbing in how they fully strip away all but the innocence in the image: "Standing, Reading, Western Script, Transportation, Childhood." These labels gesture toward, but ultimately fail to convey, the invisible violence that suffuses the photo.[33]

I know that lynchings and the photos and postcards and grisly souvenirs that circulated in their wake were a threat to anyone—Black, white, or otherwise—who challenged heteropatriarchal, white-supremacist power in this country. I know this because of the research I have done, because of the white pastor abducted by the KKK and countless others, from labor organizers to women who "drank too much," who were kidnapped by the Klan and flogged in the middle of the night. But I also know this because I have known it since I was a little boy, when my mom told me a story about her own father, a violent and racist man who disowned her when she married my father.

In the photograph of two girls standing next to the car bearing threats to mutilate and murder Black people, one of the threats is an imperative that refers directly to these bystanders: "Our Girls Still Prefers [*sic*] White Husbands." The girls are around the same age my mom and her best friend Patty were when, one day, they were standing on the sidewalk talking to their friend Henry, a Black boy. My grandfather saw the three of them standing together as he drove up the street and swerved onto the sidewalk in an attempt to run over all three of them. My aunt Denise, all of nine years old, grabbed the wheel and jerked the car back onto the road just in time, saving her big sister, my mother, from severe injury or, possibly, death.

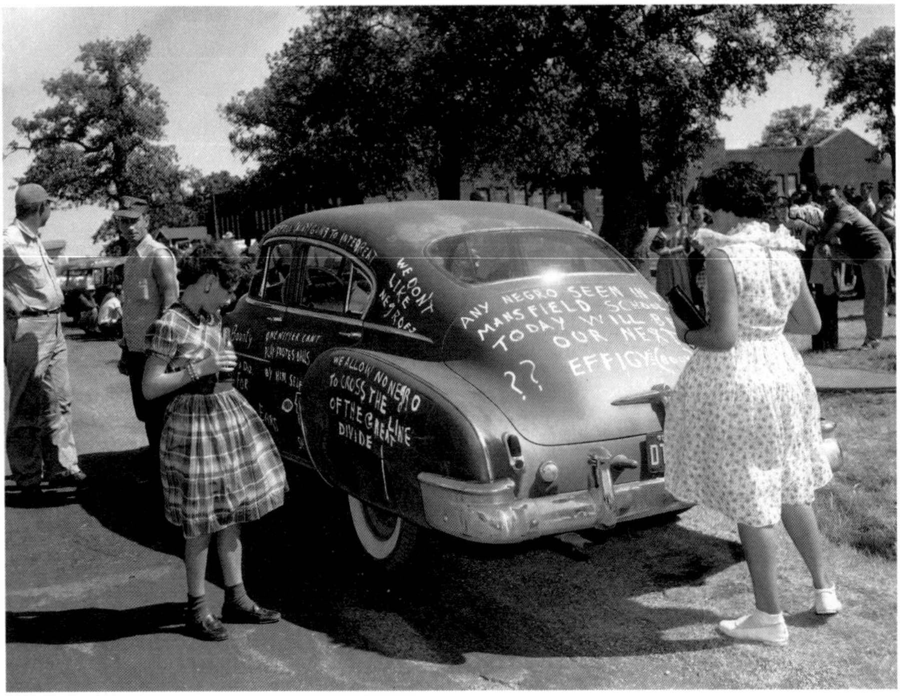

Fig. 7.6. ***Civil Rights School Integration*****, August 31, 1956**

That's a true story, like the story of Heather Heyer, run over and killed in Charlottesville, Virginia, in 2017 by a white supremacist from my home state of Ohio. My brother lives in Charlottesville and knew her, and when he and I talked on the phone about it, I recalled the story our mother told us, and I remembered this photo. We were saddened by Heyer's death, but not surprised, for both he and I had known many white girls caught, like our mother, in the vice of intraracial violence—girls we were friends with, girls we dated, often secretly, knowing that if we were found out, yes, in the 1990s, in Ohio, in the North, those girls would be in even more danger than we would be, at the hands of their fathers and brothers and uncles and cousins. They, like my mother, like the two girls in the photo perhaps, lived in the same house as their monsters, all the more monstrous because the monster professed, at times, endless love for them. Stories like that of my mother, and of Heather Heyer, invade every archive I visit. These stories are already waiting for me there in the cold folders filled with heavy, rotting photos of the living and of the dead, with their frozen threats that inhabit time's suspension and thread together the American archive of racial violence. If we really want to understand that archive's scope and depth, we have to let go of the idea that threat respects the color lines of Jim Crow, and not forget that white-supremacist violence has always also victimized even those white communities it supposedly preserves and protects. For white supremacists are not, and have never really been, at bottom, concerned with protecting the lives and virtue of white children. They have been concerned with power.

The threat of racial violence was never neatly contained by the blood-soaked boundaries of Jim Crow. Threats do not function like bullets or bombs, but like radioactive fallout—they are in the air, in the skin, in the veins, passed on through amniotic fluid. When white supremacists lynched a Black person, when they circulated photographs and postcards depicting the atrocity, it was a threat to *anyone*, Black or white, who would dare challenge the patriarchal racial order. When a family watched a lynching together—and many families watched and participated in lynchings—white children internalized the threat they saw written in the sizzled muscle and charred blood, learning through their own adrenaline, excitement, and shame that they were never to challenge the invisible power they had just witnessed wreck and erase a human body. Long before they learned to read words scrawled in white chalk on a car, they learned to read these glyphs of mutilation, and as they sat on their fathers' shoulders and watched, they were indeed bound to them, through both love *and* threat. The full visual archive of American lynching—refrigerated, buried, decaying, digitized, now re-wrought in light—remembers the way such rituals turn familial love itself into a threat, rendering the very thing we need in order to survive a thing that must itself be survived.

NOTES

Sections of this text were drawn or adapted from essays that originally appeared on the Kenyon Review Blog.

1. The Bettmann Archive contains millions of photos and illustrations, including the entire United Press International Archive and iconic photos like Albert Einstein sticking out his tongue, Marilyn Monroe having trouble with her skirt on a Manhattan sidewalk, and a row of construction workers perched on a steel beam.

2. In her 2007 essay "The Evidence of Lynching Photographs," Shawn Michelle Smith offers a mainstream definition of lynching that informs much of the visual cultural analysis of lynching images: "murder committed by a mob of three or more." Dora Apel and Shawn Michelle Smith, "The Evidence of Lynching Photography," in *Lynching Photographs* (Berkeley: University of California Press, 2007), 15. Leigh Raiford, in *Imprisoned in a Luminous Glare: Photography and the African American Freedom Struggle* (Chapel Hill: University of North Carolina Press, 2011), follows Smith's lead by focusing on white-on-Black extralegal violence, remarking that "the history of lynching in the United States is a long and brutal one," only to circumscribe her temporal scope tightly around the years between 1882 to 1930, which she calls the "apex" of lynching in the United States, and to highlight the fact that 88 percent of the 3,000 lynching victims were African Americans (36). This strict definition limits the archive of "lynching" images to those depicting or referring to interracial, white-on-Black, extralegal, fatal violence.

Historians have long debated the origins of the term "lynching," and the definition of lynching has been highly contentious at various moments. The research and writings of Ida B. Wells deeply influenced the narrowing of the definition of lynching. Wells's narrow and specific definition was important for mobilizing support for an antilynching movement aimed at saving Black lives and freeing Black men and women from the terrorism and threat of lynching. Wells's work clarified the way in which vigilante violence disproportionately victimized often-innocent Black men, an important point to make at a time when other women advocated an increase in the lynching of Black men or—in the cases of many prominent white progressives and suffragists—only hesitantly condemned lynching, or condemned it only because they thought that the barbaric and gruesome nature of lynching degraded the white people who composed the mob.

Manfred Berg, in *Popular Justice: A History of Lynching in America* (Chicago: Ivan R. Dee, 2011), notes that the term "lynching" probably goes back to Virginia in the late eighteenth century, when it mostly referred to nonlethal forms of corporal punishment. He describes floggings and hangings of white abolitionists and other white people accused of inciting slave insurrections in the antebellum South. Lerone Bennett, in *The Shaping of Black America: The Struggles and Triumphs of African Americans 1619 to the 1990s* (New York: Penguin, 1993), discusses the long history of white intraracial violence in his analysis of the establishment of racial hierarchies in the colonial period (74–75). Such practices form the prehistory of white intraracial violence in the Jim Crow era. Jacqueline Goldsby, in *A Spectacular Secret: Lynching in American Life and Literature* (Chicago: University of Chicago Press, 2006), focuses on the fact that Klan violence between 1867 and 1871 functioned to intimidate African Americans but recognizes that it also functioned to "oust northern Republicans from leadership positions across the [South]" (16).

3. It is important to note that Corbis clients can request to use images from the analog archive, even if the clients do not visit the archive in person. Corbis archivists search through the analog archive to locate images to meet the clients' needs. However, the analog images remain far less accessible than those in the digital archive, even if the Bettmann Archive was always private, as Corbis maintains. I am not arguing that the Bettmann should be more accessible; rather, I am interested in accurately assessing the effects of digitization and preservation on the meaning of images and the production and reproduction of history.

4. "Corbis' Film Preservation Facility at Iron Mountain and the Bettman Archive: Frequently Asked Questions, Updated April 2013." After arranging my visit, my host at Corbis sent this document to me via email.

5. Sarah Boxer, "A Century's Photo History Destined for Life in a Mine," *New York Times*, April 15, 2001.

6. JoEllen McNergney Vinyard, *Right in Michigan's Grassroots: From the KKK to the Michigan Militia* (Ann Arbor: University of Michigan Press, 2012), 78; "Branded Pastor Leaves the Hospital," *Gettysburg (Pennsylvania) Times*, July 15, 1924; "Memory of Branded Pastor Still Blank," *Naples (Fla.) Record*, July 16, 1924; and Southern Poverty Law Center, *Ku Klux Klan: A History of Racism and Violence*, 6th edition (Montgomery: Southern Poverty Law Center, 2011), 20.

7. Southern Poverty Law Center, *Ku Klux Klan*, 20.

8. Shawn Michelle Smith, *Photography on the Color Line: W. E. B. Du Bois, Race, and Visual Culture* (Durham, NC: Duke University Press, 2004), 126.

9. Smith, *Photography on the Color Line*, 121.

10. Smith, 122.

11. Smith, 122–23.

12. James Allen, ed., *Without Sanctuary: Lynching Photography in America* (Santa Fe: Twin Palms,

2000). Undoubtedly, the threat, when carried out, looked different in the case of white and Black people, as white individuals were not generally subject to intraracial violence that involved the same kind of ritualistic sexual mutilation that Black men were, and white women were sometimes afforded treatment that Black women were not, even when being punished for behavior that diminished the purity of their own womanhood. In many cases of floggings, for instance, Klansmen would give a white woman salve to put on her back when the flogging was done. However, there are oft-ignored instances of sexual mutilation of white victims. In one case, the Florida Klan castrated a prominent Catholic Priest and left him on the steps of a church. See Billy Townsend, "Ku Klux Klan Met Its Match in Putnam County in the 1920s," *Tampa Bay Times*, October 19, 2012.

13. Furthermore, as Leon Litwack points out and Shawn Michelle Smith reiterates, some white people saw lynching and lynching images as elements that did not consolidate but threatened to disintegrate the imagined white community, as lynching rituals indexed or seemed to portend "the destabilization of the social order and the descent of their region into barbarism" (Leon Litwack, "Hellhounds," in Allen, *Without Sanctuary*, 22). Smith reads the covering of the wounds on Black bodies in lynching images as efforts to limit the visual "evidence of white savagery in minutia" (Smith, *Photography on the Color Line*, 127). She cites Litwack to reinforce her point, and proceeds to examine how the appropriation of lynching images by Ida B. Wells and the NAACP contested "the rhetoric of white civilization and black barbarism" and "provided opposing evidence of white savagery" by documenting "white atrocities" (Smith, 128).

14. See "Flog and Carve KKK on Negro in Texas Because of Protests," *Jet Magazine*, March 24, 1960.

15. "KKK Victim," July 1, 1924, Topical Press Agency / Getty Images, http://www.gettyimages.com/detail/news-photo/nelson-burroughs-who-was-kidnapped-by-members-of-the-news-photo/2643553?adppopup=true.

16. Brian Massumi, "The Future Birth of the Affective Fact: The Political Ontology of Threat," in *Digital and Other Virtualities: Renegotiating the Image*, ed. Antony Bryant and Griselda Pollock (London: I. B. Tauris, 2010), 62.

17. Even in a recent scholarly article that seeks to expand our view of the diversity of racial violence in the Jim Crow era, white subjectivity is oversimplified, and this intraracial experience of violence and its threats is ignored. Kidada E. Williams, "Resolving the Paradox of Our Lynching Fixation: Reconsidering Racialized Violence in the American South after Slavery," in *Lynching Reconsidered: New Perspectives in the Study of Mob Violence*, ed. William D. Carrigan (London: Routledge, 2008), 99, importantly points out the way in which our "fascination with the physicality of lynching or visual, statistical, and print representations of the practice does not help us understand how endemic and varied racial violence was, how people experienced it, and ultimately how horrible it was for victims, their families and descendants." She argues that such a fascination is partially the result of an "intense interest in the extralegal and spectacular components of mob violence by women and men of [the Jim Crow era]," an interest that effectively excluded much discussion of the "more ordinary, individual and private forms of violence that white southerners had used to subjugate African Americans since emancipation." Yet within this illuminating analysis, where she lists off several obscure cases of floggings and beatings of African Americans for challenging white supremacy, she never explores "the more ordinary, private forms" of intraracial violence that would help her to more powerfully demonstrate "how endemic and varied racial violence was." In a footnote on ordinary, nonspectacular instances of violence, Williams reinforces an oversimplified view of white subjectivity in the Jim Crow era: "When I use terms such as 'whites' or 'southern whites,' I do so recognizing that they never constituted a racial monolith. I use 'whites,' and 'southern whites,' and 'white supremacists' here for lack of a better descriptor to refer to those white women and men of the South who used violence to dominate and punish black women, men and children" (117n6). The problem here is not the lack of a better descriptor, but the failure to recognize that the subjugation of African Americans and the bolstering of white supremacy was accomplished not only through pervasive violence and threats of violence (both spectacular and ordinary) against Black people, but against white people as well. One work that does much to address the gap in historical understandings pointed out here is Koritha Mitchell, *Living with Lynching: African American Lynching, Plays, Performance, and Citizenship, 1890–1930* (Urbana: University of Illinois Press, 2011).

18. "Oral History Interview with Daniel Duke, August 22, 1990," interview A-0366, Southern Oral History Program Collection (#4007), Southern Historical Collection, Wilson Library, University of North Carolina at Chapel Hill.

19. In his memoir of his infiltration of the Georgia Klan, *The Klan Unmasked*, ethnographer and activist Stetson Kennedy describes his first meeting on the "flog squad" that carried out the attacks in East Point. He found out that though their most recent flogging had been a Black man who had the habit of "jostling" white women at the bus stop, all their upcoming targets were white men from the North who came south to do union organizing. Stetson Kennedy,

"I Work My Way into the Flog Squad," in *The Klan Unmasked* (Tuscaloosa: University of Alabama Press, 1990), 95–105; originally published under the title *I Rode with the Ku Klux Klan* in 1942. Such attacks on union organizers were not uncommon among white supremacist organizations. In November 1917, the Knights of Liberty kidnapped and assaulted sixteen members of the International Workers of the World, an incident that became known as the Tulsa Outrage. The black-robed Knights lined the "Wobblies" up at gunpoint, lashed their backs with a hemp rope one by one, "then applied hot tar and feathers from a slit pillow." Nigel Anthony Sellars, *Oil, Wheat, and Wobblies: The Industrial Workers of the World in Oklahoma, 1905–1930* (Norman: University of Oklahoma Press, 1998), 108. For more on the Klan's antiunion violence, see Wyn Craig Wade, *The Fiery Cross: The Ku Klux Klan in America* (Oxford: Oxford University Press, 1987), 263–67; "Crackdown on the Klan," *Time*, February 25, 1952; "A Flogging for the Klan," *Time*, August 11, 1952; and Michael Newton, *The Ku Klux Klan in Mississippi: A History* (Jefferson, NC: McFarland: 2010), 27–34, 60–61, 83–86, 106, 151.

20. "Crackdown on the Klan."

21. "A Flogging for the Klan."

22. The 1920s Indiana Klan had predecessors in the whitecappers who would flog women sadistically, from the 1850s to 1889, leaving their victims nearly dead, as punishment for sexually impropriety. Other predecessor organizations that inflicted intraracial violence were the Know-Nothings and the Horse Thief Detective Association, whose members were recruited when the Klan first organized in Indiana. The Indiana Klan's calling card in the Roaring Twenties placed little emphasis on racial dominance or the specific threat of Black men to white womanhood: "Remember, every criminal, every gambler, every thug, every libertine, every girl ruiner, every home wrecker, every wife beater, every dopepeddler, every shyster lawyer, every K of C [Knight of Columbus], every white slaver, every brothel madame, every Rome-controlled newspaper—is fighting the KKK." Quoted in Kathleen M. Blee, *Women and the Klan: Racism and Gender in the 1920s* (Berkeley: University of California Press, 1991), 180.

23. See Renee Montagne, "The Last Public Execution in America," *NPR Morning Edition*, May 1, 2001, http://www.npr.org/programs/morning/features/2001/apr/010430.execution.html; Associated Press, "Nation's Last Public Execution, 75 Years Ago, Still Haunts Town," *Fox News*, August 12, 2011, http://www.foxnews.com/us/2011/08/12/after-75-years-last-public-hanging-haunts-city/.

24. Reuters Staff [Rosmi Shaji], "Visual China Buys Corbis Entertainment," *Reuters*, January 22, 2016, http://www.reuters.com/article/us-corbis-m-a-vcg/visual-china-buys-corbis-entertainment-idUSKCN0V101L. The address www.corbis.com now automatically redirects to www.gettyimages.com.

25. James Baldwin, "Going to Meet the Man," in *Going to Meet the Man: Stories* (New York: Vintage International, 1993); Ralph Ellison "A Party Down at the Square," *Esquire*, January 1, 1997; Kristina DuRocher, *Raising Racists: The Socialization of White Children in the Jim Crow South* (Lexington: University Press of Kentucky, 2011).

26. James Baldwin, "A Talk to Teachers," in *James Baldwin: Collected Essays* (New York: Library of America: 1998), 685–86.

27. Bill Hanna, "60 Years Ago, 3 Black Teens Tried to Enroll in Mansfield High—'Never' Was the Reply," *Fort Worth Star-Telegram*, March 30, 2016, http://www.star-telegram.com/news/local/arlington/article68837362.html.

28. Cars themselves had also long been used as weaponry in lynching spectacles. In Ellison's short story, the Black lynching victim, named Bacote, is tied to the back of a truck and dragged to the site where the lynch mob burns him alive (Ellison, "A Party Down at the Square," 92). "Dragging" was a common form of lynching in Texas, one that preceded the invention of automobiles and continued through the end of the twentieth century. Ashraf H. A. Rushdy, *The End of American Lynching* (New Brunswick, NJ: Rutgers University Press, 2012), 140, quotes "Ester King, an activist in the Houston black community, [who] recalls that his grandmother would relate how 'the favorite way of lynching' when she was growing up was 'to drag Black folks from behind a horse or a wagon or a buggy.'" The most famous case of dragging was that of Jesse Washington in Waco in 1916—until the dragging lynching of James Byrd in Jasper, Texas, in 1998. Three men attacked Byrd, then attached him by the ankles to the back of a pickup truck with a chain they usually used to haul lumber. They dragged him for two miles. By the time they stopped, his head and right arm had detached from his torso. One of Byrd's murderers allegedly asked to get out of the truck partway through the dragging. But the neo-Nazi behind the wheel refused to stop the car and yelled, "You're just as guilty as we are!" Then he made the obverse threat absolutely clear—"The same thing could happen to a nigger lover!" Cliff Redding, "Jasper, Texas: The Road of Infinite Suffering," *The Crisis* (Sept/Oct 1998): 11.

29. Massumi, "Future Birth of the Affective Fact," 87.

30. Roland Barthes, *Camera Lucida: Reflections on Photography* (New York: Hill and Wang, 1981), 26–27.

31. G. Scott Thomas, *A New World to Be Won: John Kennedy, Richard Nixon, and the Tumultuous Year of 1960* (Santa Barbara, CA: ABC-CLIO, 2011), 84.

32. Barthes, *Camera Lucida*, 27.
33. Blee details how threats in the form of a letter or visit from Klansmen were highly effective, so much so that "physical attacks on offending persons were less common" in Indiana, because the Klan, nationally, had such a reputation for violence (80). One white resident in Warren, Indiana, recounted that "in spite of no record of violence there was a general feeling of fear, mystery, and power associated with the Warren Klan. Young girls were warned never to get into a car with men—especially men wearing white hoods!" (81). In other words, the threats issued in Indiana gathered their force from the legacy of a violent organization that had victimized white people in the past, as well as from white-supremacist violence in other places. The fact that KKK members and white supremacists perpetrated and threatened violence against white individuals means that the threat-environment in which lynching photographs circulated was one where some white people would have seen themselves as subject to the threat of intraracial white supremacist violence, not just as witnesses to it or participants in it. Blee, *Women and the Klan*, 80–81, 179–80.

CHAPTER 8

MINIMUM WORLDS

MATERIAL POETICS BETWEEN TIME, DETAILS, AND FRAGMENTS

Gabriela Siracusano

When selecting an artwork for an exhibition or for the pages of a new publication, art historians tend to seek objects with internal coherence that embody an illusion of the organized whole, a control of entropy, the tranquility offered by balance.[1] Curators often exhibit completed and finished work, captured in a frozen, static time. Regarding Spanish American colonial art history, the public and private collections that house these objects weave curatorial stories that favor aesthetic, cultural, and social history, as well as a focus on the objects' uses and functions. Moreover, they are typically selected for their quality and conservation status; objects that are fragmented or in poor condition usually remain in a peripheral area, with little or no visibility for the common spectator. These damaged objects are often held in museum storage facilities, an area constituted as the limbic edge of many museums that hold colonial collections. Works with structural problems, with missing parts, victims of the traces of use in past times, of deterioration by nature or at the hand of man, are precisely the objects that will not be invited to participate in colonial art historical discourse. In this sense, the historiography of art reveals a certain degree of material sectarianism: "We want the work closed! We want you complete! We love your beautiful continuous surface, no breakages, no cracks, no gaps!" But . . . does this impelling desire for completeness not hide a deep fear of dealing with the universe of minimum worlds that make up an object, worlds in which diverse times coexist, together with a fragmented, hidden, ever-changing materiality?

FRAGMENTS OF LOST BODIES

The Museo de Arte Hispanoamericano Isaac Fernández Blanco in Buenos Aires holds one of the most important collections in Argentina of art from the Viceroyalties (sixteenth–eighteenth century) and the Independence period until the mid-nineteenth century, including paintings, sculptures, and furniture from different origins

(Mexico, Peru, Bolivia, Ecuador, Jesuit Missions of Paraguay, and Buenos Aires, among others), along with textiles, liturgical objects, and a large collection of silverware.[2] Since 2000, I have been studying its patrimony with an interdisciplinary gaze that points out the relevance of examining the material histories of these objects.[3] Many of the museum's paintings and sculptures were parts of various projects that I led, in which we studied with noninvasive methods (or by collecting almost imperceptible samples) their supports, preparation, paint layers, and polychromes. We compared this material evidence to descriptions in inventories, manuals, or books of secrets, or with objects from seemingly distant universes of meaning—such as geological rocks or archaeological textiles—in order to understand what I call their minimum worlds. The study of minimum worlds belongs to an "archaeology of the making," in which we bring to light the remnants of forgotten practices. We study an "anthropology of matter," which gives materiality a human dimension, bringing back to our anachronistic gaze the traces left by those who created, manipulated, and consumed those artifacts.[4] Some years ago, I surrendered to the attraction of entering the universe of the broken or fragmented, of that which was never exhibited for its strangeness, apparent lack of value, or simply because it did not follow the curatorial script of the moment. In short, I became fascinated by those objects that, for various reasons, were condemned to sleep in the gloom.[5]

Among those artifacts was a disparate set of wooden hands, arms, and chests. They had been part of sculptures made during the Viceroyalty, when it was a common practice to assemble these parts to form a devotional figure.[6] They could have belonged to some *imágenes de candelero* of the Virgin or a saint (fig. 8.1).[7] They were fragments of bodies that once could have been revered, touched, kissed in an altarpiece, or followed within a procession. If the expertise of a craftsman had been used in their creation, it remained overshadowed by the traces of time and our own ignorance. However, those fragments recovered their lost connection to that past world when, on the occasion of being exhibited in the show *Las entrañas del arte* (fig. 8.2), they fell under the gaze of one person: Héctor Schenone. In addition to having been among the most renowned Spanish American colonial art historians in Argentina and one of the most respected in all of the Americas, Schenone was director of the Fernández Blanco museum for many years between the 1950s and 1970s.

From the moment he stood in front of the exhibition space where those fragments were on display in 2008, they became reunited with their absent bodies.[8] He had often studied, manipulated, and even disarmed some of them (fig. 8.3) as part of his research in various academic and museum contexts. In fact, it is thanks to the publication of *El arte de la imaginería en el Río de la Plata* (1948) by Adolfo Luis Ribera and Schenone that we know about the frequent practice of commissioning and assembling heads and hands to create the imagery of the Viceroyalty. We can

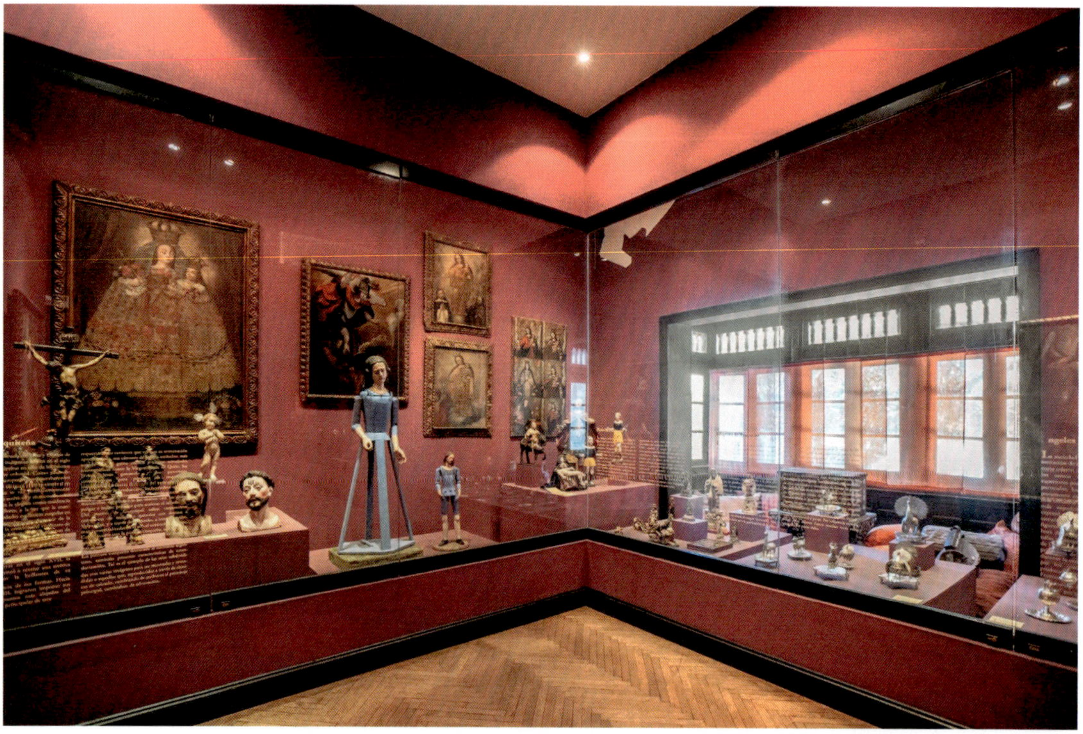

Fig. 8.1. *Candelero* images and heads from the Viceroyalty of Peru, among other South American colonial images, 18th century. Installation view, Museo de Arte Hispanoamericano Isaac Fernández Blanco

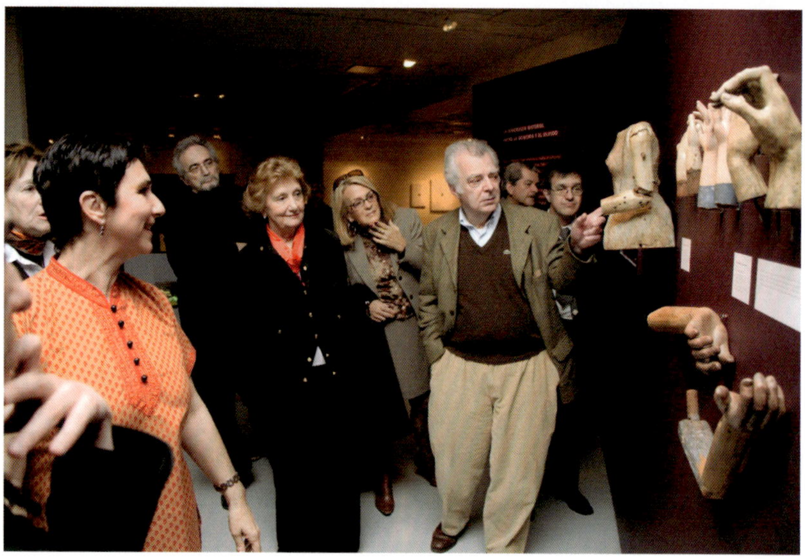

Fig. 8.2. Arms, hands, and chest of South American colonial images from the patrimony of the Museo de Arte Hispanoamericano Isaac Fernández Blanco, on view in the exhibition *Las entrañas del arte*, 2008, Espacio Imago, Buenos Aires

Fig. 8.3. Set of hands from Héctor Schenone's collection

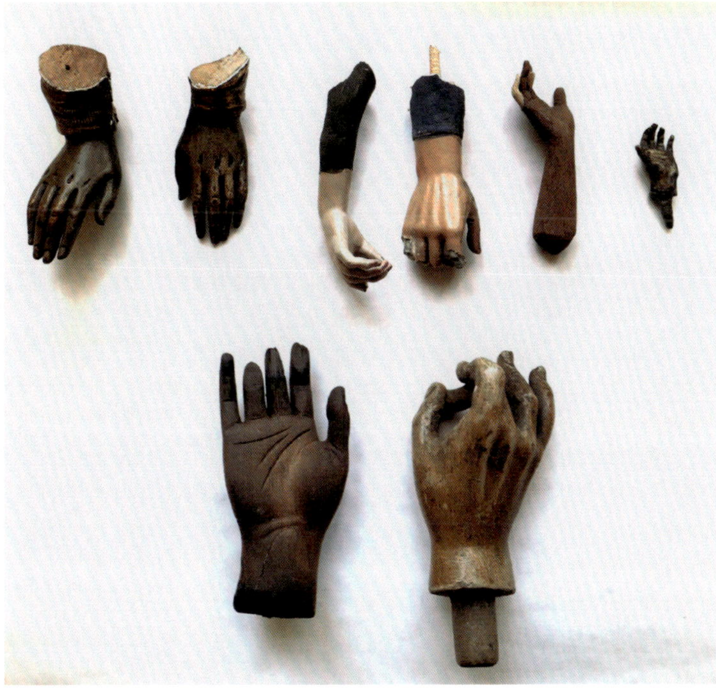

discern, for example, that the image of Our Lady of Sorrows of the Cathedral of Buenos Aires was assembled with a head and hands made in Cadiz, while "the head and hands of the San Ignacio de la Casa de Ejercicios of the same city belonged to a dress figure to which the carving body was added."[9] These two historians cite numerous commissions from Italy and Spain for arms and heads requested in order to complete different images of saints and virgins.[10] For example, the authors cite one passage referring to a ship's cargo: "In 1767, on the ship San Fernando, many religious figures arrived to the port of Buenos Aires, from Europe: a head and hands of San Ignacio, a head and hands of San Estanislao."[11] They also refer to documents regarding the expulsion of the Jesuits, pointing out that Jesuit collections also contained these fragments, including: "A face and hands of St. Theresa 20 duc," "2 faces and hands of S. Xavier," "2 faces and hands."[12]

By the eighteenth century, Buenos Aires received these shipments of heads and chests not only from Europe but also from South America, with loads coming in from Peru, Ecuador, and Bolivia to be assembled into *porteño* River Plate bodies.[13] Among them, the heads from Quito were particularly prized within the River Plate aesthetic because of their high quality.[14] As model parts for assembly, the different fragments were combined to the taste of the consumer, together with clothing and accessories.

Fig. 8.4. José Boqui (Italian, c. 1771–1848), *Halo*, 1799, on the head of a sculpture of Saint Dominic. Silver and bronze, 19⅝ × 23⅝ in. (50 × 60 cm). Museo de Arte Hispanoamericano Isaac Fernández Blanco, Buenos Aires

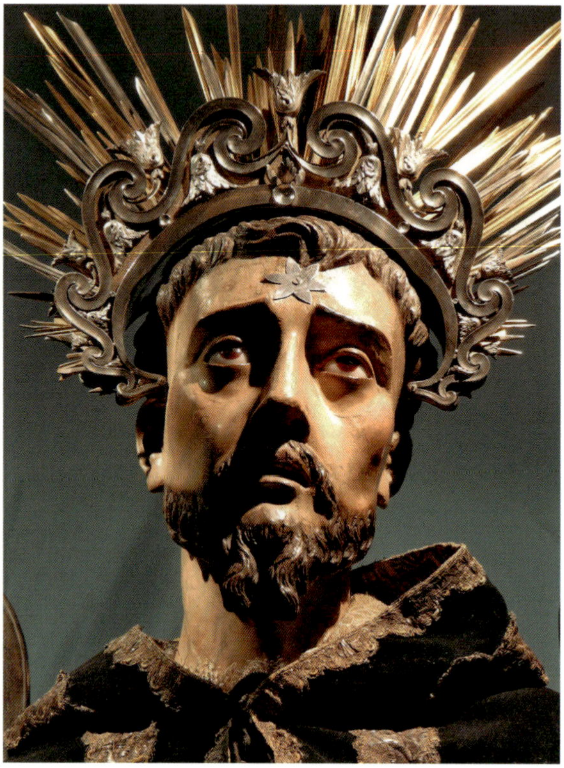

An interesting story is that of a 1799 halo made in Buenos Aires, which belonged to Schenone's collection, that could have been created for the head of a Saint Dominic (fig. 8.4). It consists of several elements (structure and rays of different sizes and materials) that can be disassembled. This work demonstrates a novel system for goldsmithing at the time, as it combined complex mechanical procedures.[15] Its creator was José Boqui, an Italian citizen active in the city of Buenos Aires between 1796 and 1810, who had studied in Madrid and ended his days as an agent of the independence movements in South America.[16] Boqui's halo also includes a trompe l'oeil of a musical score, a coin, and a Dominican shield at the bottom. The piece is inscribed with a signature, date of execution, and a recommendation for its manipulation: "If you want to disarm me / think about it so as not to fail," a riddle appropriate for such a masterful display of artifice and ingenuity.[17]

The halo fits on the heads of both Santo Domingo de Guzmán, from the convent of Santo Domingo of Buenos Aires, and Santo Domingo of Santa Fe. Both heads come from the Southern Andes and now belong to the Fernández Blanco museum. We know this thanks to the archival work and scholarship of Schenone.[18] Due to his knowledge of the museum's heritage, it should come as no surprise that when he stumbled across those wooden fragments at the exhibition, he could recognize to which saints' or Virgins' bodies those hands and other fragments had belonged. To him, those remains were the testimony of the past. They were born as interchangeable fragments that completed bodies of wood, glass, and cloth to satisfy the beliefs of the faithful. Under his gaze, each fragment made sense and embodied a certain figure. They were the minimum synecdoche that enclosed a whole world of pious aesthetic choices and practices.

HIDDEN AND DESTROYED BODIES: MATERIALITY BETWEEN ART AND POLITICS

In the same museum storage facility, two small canvases are kept. One represents *Our Lady with the Child in the Clouds*, which was poorly restored in the past. The other canvas shows some cherubs, also with heavy restorations (fig. 8.5). These two paintings would not have garnered great interest had it not been for a fortuitous event in a research and conservation project on the history of art of the Rio de la Plata region, when these paintings became important for studies around the fragment, art, politics, and iconoclasm in colonial South America.[19]

The church of San Ignacio of Buenos Aires, located in the Manzana de las luces neighborhood, dates from the late seventeenth century, though much of its current construction was carried out in the early eighteenth century. Inside this Jesuit temple are paintings and sculptures distributed between the main altar and the lateral neoclassical altarpieces, made by artists including Miguel Aucell (1728–1795), Isidro Lorea (d. 1807), and Gaspar Hernández (1750–1821), among others. We know from the inventories made during the expulsion of the Jesuit order that the altarpieces were consecrated to the Virgin and to Jesuit saints such as Ignacius of Loyola, Stanislau Kostka, Francis Xavier, John Nepomucene, Philip Neri, and Aloysius Gonzaga.[20] Over time, some altarpieces were replaced by other images, as in the case of the Immaculate Conception, formerly dedicated to Saint Aloysius Gonzaga.

In 2010, on the occasion of conservation efforts on a painting placed in another altarpiece, the priest of the church pointed out to the conservators the presence of something strange under the altar bench. At more than one meter in depth, there was a garbage pile. It looked like the ruins of a canvas (fig. 8.6). Days later, we found a mixtilinear wooden stretcher, with its top almost carbonized, to which some canvas remains were still attached. What was the painting of? Why was it there? How and when did this deterioration occur? Did that mound of rubbish correspond to the stretcher? What minimum worlds were housed in it that could shed light and enable a dialogue between us and the past? Could the preservation of that destroyed body have any interest to anyone? So many questions.

What could have been the painting's primary function—to establish a religious bond with the faithful—was already impossible. Yet, in defiance of that

Fig. 8.5. Artist unknown (possibly Buenos Aires, 18th century), *Cherubs*, 18th century. Oil on canvas, 14 1/8 × 10 3/8 in. (36 × 26.5 cm). Museo de Arte Hispanoamericano Isaac Fernández Blanco, Buenos Aires

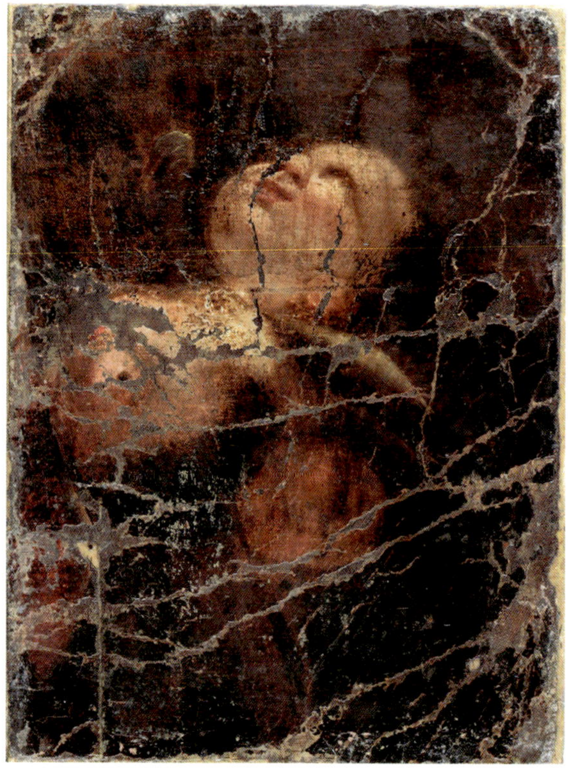

Fig. 8.6. Unknown painter (possibly Buenos Aires, 18th century), *St. Aloysius Gonzaga*, 18th century. Oil on canvas, 65 × 27 1/2 in. (165 × 70 cm). Church of Saint Ignatius of Buenos Aires. Detail showing the ruined state in which the painting was found in 2010

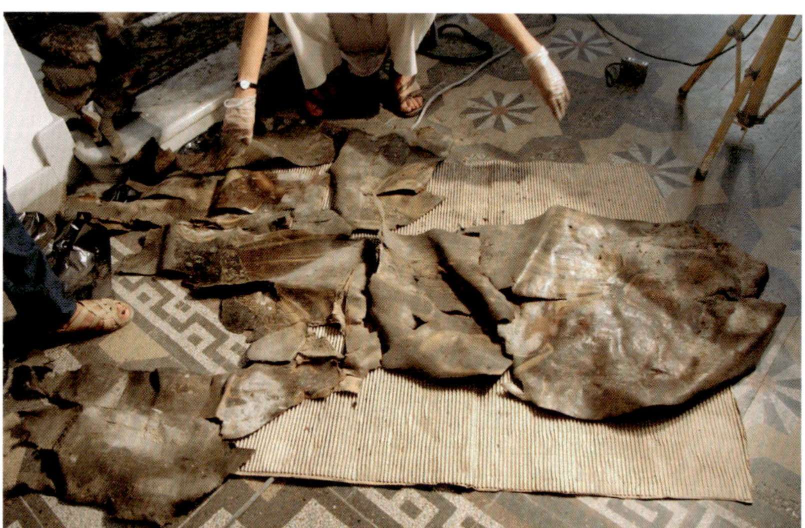

prejudice which implies that fragmentation categorically prohibits an integral understanding, we decided to piece these ruinous parts together, allowing for our own blindness. We spread the fragments first on the floor and then on the table, in order to begin looking at these quasi-archaeological remains from multiple viewpoints; a true interdisciplinary practice between the art historians, conservators, and chemists of our team.[21] The contrast of material, written, oral, and visual data, enlightened by an anthropology of matter and by identifying the overlapping times and the biography of the object, allowed us to trace the different moments, senses, and uses that the painting had gone through before becoming a ruin.

The first iconographic analyses, based on small details in each surviving piece of canvas, indicated that it was a painting representing Saint Louis Gonzaga. It had served to cover and uncover the central sculpture of the altarpiece in its ritual manifestation. Known as the *retablo tramoya*, such paintings moved horizontally or vertically, through a pulley system, generating a spectacular and theatrical effect for the faithful.[22] The church of San Ignacio and others in Buenos Aires still conserve these mechanisms, which were widely used by the Jesuits. Perhaps for liturgical reasons, the practice fell into disuse, which explains why this canvas was sunk into the depths of the altar, leading to its deterioration through the first decades of the twentieth century. Signs of an intentional cut—possibly by thieves—indicate that this action may have caused the detachment and subsequent invisibility of part of the painting. At the same time, we know that by 1944, only the last two fragments remained attached to the stretcher.

Here, the two canvases I mentioned above, together with Héctor Schenone, make their entrance. Rescued by Schenone, these fragments entered the Fernández Blanco museum as two distinct, standalone pieces mounted on separate racks. Considered of little significance, they fell into oblivion in the museum's storage. Yet, thanks to chemical studies carried out on their pictorial layers and their supports, we could corroborate that they were more than just the sum of the parts.[23] They were material links that, although hidden, remained intertwined in a chain of sensory experience embodying religious devotion, loss, and museum histories. Through direct visual examination, techniques such as optical microscopy, organic chemical analysis, and work in archives and libraries, we were able to determine that the remains of fabric attached to the wooden stretcher were made of linen, the same material and textile technique present in the other fragments.[24] Moreover, the stretcher offered its own evidence of multiple overlapping temporalities (fig. 8.7). Its carbonized upper area still demanded attention, and here the inclusion of historical and political variables becomes relevant.

On the afternoon of June 16, 1955, in response to the bombing of the Plaza de Mayo that killed many people and an attempted coup d'etat against the government of Juan Domingo Perón, groups loyal to him burst into the archbishop's palace

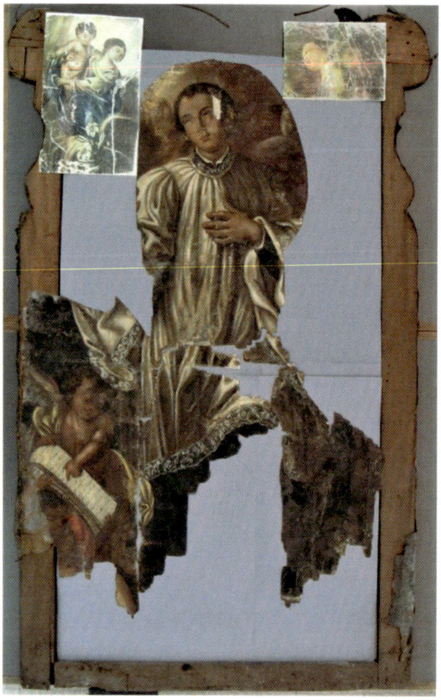

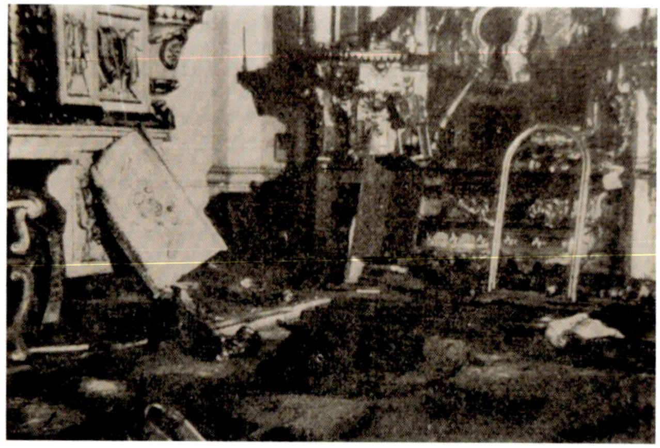

Fig. 8.7. Conservation work on the canvas and burned stretcher of *St. Aloysius Gonzaga*, seen with photocopies of the two missing fragments, which are held in the Museo de Arte Hispanoamericano Isaac Fernández Blanco, Buenos Aires

Fig. 8.8. Destroyed and burned altarpieces in the Church of Saint Ignatius of Buenos Aires, as reproduced in Anibal Rottjer, *El llanto de las ruinas: La historia, el arte y la religión ultrajados en los templos de Buenos Aires, 16 y 17 de junio de 1955* (Buenos Aires: Colegio Don Bosco, 1955)

and the curia. The churches and convents of Saint Dominic, Our Lady of Mercy, Saint Francis, and Saint Ignatius—all in the city center of Buenos Aires—were vandalized and burned inside, causing great material loss.[25] The photographic record of this iconoclastic event revealed that in the church of Saint Ignatius, torches were thrown on some altarpieces, such as that of Saint Aloysius Gonzaga, burning paintings and sculptures next to the altar (fig. 8.8). The fact that the canvas of Saint Aloysius lay at the bottom of the bench, paradoxically, saved it from the fire—although the top of its stretcher, the area most exposed to it, burned.

In the museum's storage today, there is another canvas rescued from the flames by Schenone: an Annunciation, attributed to Miguel Aucell, from the convent of Saint Dominic. Despite being one of the few extant paintings by such a renowned painter of the late eighteenth century in Buenos Aires, its fate took it to storage, which it has left only once.[26] In short, deteriorated objects—fragmented, hidden, and devoid of their primordial function—often become condemned to oblivion. An archaeology of making gives such objects new forms of existence in the world; they become testimonies of various cultural practices in successive and overlapping times, embodying histories not only of eighteenth-century religious practices but also of twentieth-century political strife and uprising.

THE SURVIVAL OF TERROR: THE FATE OF TWO MEISSEN PORCELAINS

Finally, I would like to discuss another small set of pieces—two eighteenth-century Meissen porcelain figurines depicting dancing couples—also in the storage of the same museum. Although they are not a South American production, the case deserves attention. These are very fragile objects, due to the technique with which they were made; one couple is completely destroyed (fig. 8.9). Porcelain—invented in China—is composed of two fundamental elements: kaolinite, a white clay; and petuntsa, a feldsopathic rock. These two elements are heated to high temperatures (approximately 1,450°C) and vitrified in order to produce thin, translucent layers on a solid structure. Porcelain's entry into European culture came around 1707 in Saxony, with experiments linked to alchemical practices carried out in the environment of the Elector Prince of Saxony Augustus II (1670–1733).[27] It should be noted that experimentation and serendipity are linked to the discovery and development of many artistic techniques and materials, as in the case of Prussian blue, created in Berlin by the same time.[28] But could the porcelain technique itself have led to such deterioration and, as a consequence, destroyed these dancers?

The embassy of the State of Israel in Argentina used to be located on Arroyo Street, at its intersection with Suipacha Street, near the city center. On March 17, 1992, at 2:45 p.m., a terrorist attack totally destroyed it, leaving 29 dead and 242 injured.[29] It is one of the most tragic events in Argentina's history, along with the attack on the Argentine Israelite Mutual Association (AMIA) two years later. The shockwave from that bombing hit a Catholic school and a church in front of the embassy building. A few meters away, on Suipacha street, the Fernández Blanco museum's

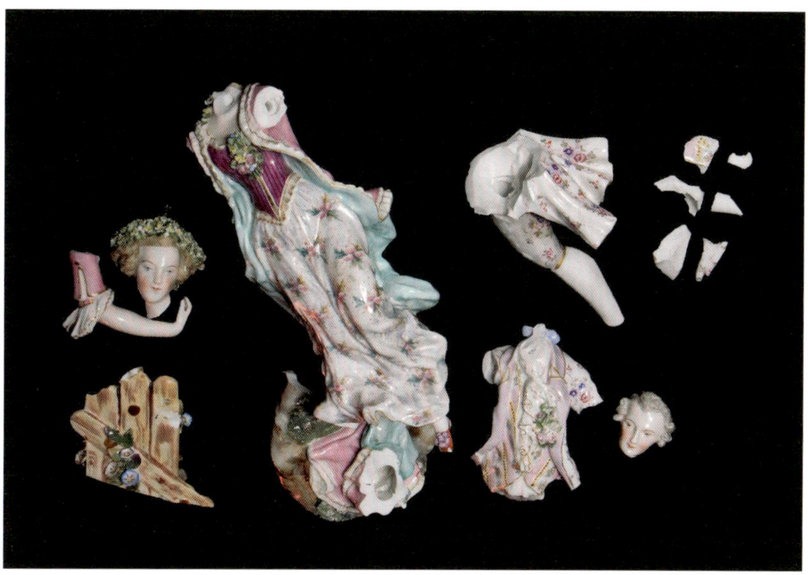

Fig. 8.9. Unknown sculptor, *The Summer*, 18th century. Meissen porcelain, 14 ½ × 9 ⅞ × 7 ⅛ in. (36.75 × 25 × 18 cm). Museo de Arte Hispanoamericano Isaac Fernández Blanco, Buenos Aires

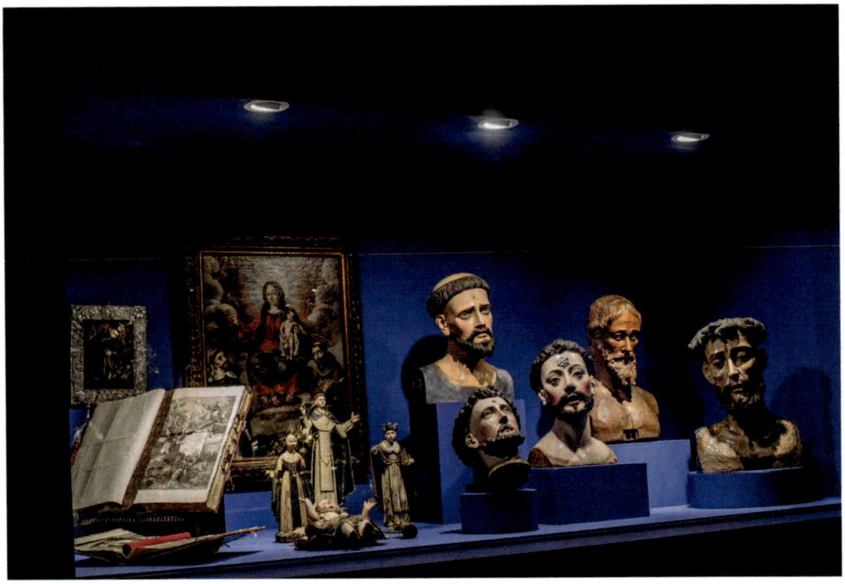

Fig. 8.10. The head of Saint Dominic of Buenos Aires (*upper row, first on the left*) within a group of other South American colonial heads. Installation view, Museo de Arte Hispanoamericano Isaac Fernández Blanco, Buenos Aires

galleries and storage spaces were not exempt from the destruction. Many objects were damaged and, subsequently, restored, including the Meissen porcelains, resulting in a set of dismembered, broken, and torn clay bodies. Their resemblance to the tragic effects on the lives of so many innocent people is astonishing. Do these fragments of memory not deserve to be on display? Does their brutal materiality not show a deeper significance than the one they had when they were a harmonious and complete whole?

The shockwave of the embassy bombing did not just bring destruction. Paradoxically, it enabled the opening of a room in the Fernández Blanco museum that had been closed and locked for years. Inside, and to the surprise of the employees, there stood a number of chests and arms that matched many of the wooden fragments—hands and heads—mentioned in our first case (fig. 8.10).[30] As noted above, the person who had rescued them from destruction and oblivion four decades earlier was the same one who could mentally rejoin them when he saw them exhibited within *Las entrañas del arte*: Héctor Schenone.

Paying attention to such objects through an immersion in their broken and overlapping histories, in their material poetics, in their connection with human and social practices—in other words, in their minimum worlds—is a challenge that we must face if we want to write more textured stories that go beyond the limits of completeness and stability.

NOTES

To the memory of Héctor Schenone (1919–2014), great lover of fragments.

1. This research is part of the project "La interpretación del fragmento: El archivo Héctor Schenone y la colección de fragmentos de obras escultóricas como indicios de la materialidad artística," Código 32/19 80120190100242TF, director: Gabriela Siracusano, 2020–2021 Scientific Program, UNTREF.

2. I mean, in this case, the collections housed in the Noel Palace within the museum.

3. Gabriela Siracusano and Agustina Rodríguez Romero, "Materiality between Art, Science, and Culture in the Viceroyalties (16th–17th Centuries): An Interdisciplinary Vision toward the Writing of a New Colonial Art History," *Art in Translation: Connecting Art Histories* 9, supplement (April 2017): 69–91.

4. Gabriela Siracusano, *El poder de los colores* (Buenos Aires: Fondo de Cultura Económica, 2005), 5–25.

5. Gabriela Siracusano, *Las entrañas del arte* (Buenos Aires: Imago, 2008).

6. In Spanish, the phrase *el alma de madera* refers to the core of an image being made of wood; *alma* means "soul."

7. *Imágenes de candelero* refers to figures with a simple structure that were created to be dressed.

8. See Gabriela Siracusano and Gustavo Tudisco, *Elecciones y selecciones de un maestro: Un programa intelectual* (Buenos Aires: Museo de Arte Hispanoamericano Isaac Fernández Blanco, 2009).

9. Adolfo Luis Ribera and Héctor Schenone, *El arte de la imaginería en el Rio de la Plata* (Buenos Aires: Instituto de Arte Americano e Investigaciones Estéticas, UBA, 1948).

10. Ribera and Schenone, *El arte de la imaginería*, 316.

11. Ribera and Schenone, 43.

12. AGN, Temporalidades, Compañía de Jesús, varios años, s. IX, C.VII, A. 10, n. 4, in Ribera and Schenone, 44.

13. *Porteño* indicates "of Buenos Aires origin."

14. Flamenco artists had been present in Quito since the beginning of the viceroyalty. See Ribera and Schenone, *El arte de la imaginería*, 23.

15. See Siracusano and Tudisco, *Elecciones y selecciones*, 24–25.

16. José Torre Revello, "Un Documento Relativo al Orfebre José Boqui," *Revista de Historia de América*, no. 43 (1957): 107–9, http://www.jstor.org/stable/20137147.

17. "Si me quieres desarmar / piénsalo para no errar." The translation is mine.

18. The Centro de Investigación en arte, materia y cultura (MATERIA) at the Universidad Nacional de Tres de Febrero holds Schenone's archive, which consists of letters, diaries, paper cards, artistic tools, etc., thanks to a generous donation from his family.

19. See Agustina Rodriguez Romero, Gabriela Siracusano et al., "Image, Ruin, Fragment, Document: Vestiges in the Canvas of Saint Aloysius Gonzaga for Interdisciplinary Research," in *Materia Americana: The Body of Spanish-American Images (Sixteenth–Early Nineteenth Century)*, ed. Gabriela Siracusano and Agustina Rodriguez Romero (Saenz Peña: Eduntref, 2020), 419–33.

20. See Héctor Schenone, Isaura Molina, and Jorge Santas, *Inventario de Bienes Muebles: Ciudad de Buenos Aires* (Buenos Aires: Academia Nacional de Bellas Artes, 1998).

21. This research was developed within two projects: "Imágenes en peligro: Arte, ciencia y tecnología para el estudio del deterioro del patrimonio colonial artístico nacional," Diálogos entre las ciencias, UNSAM, under the guidance of Gabriela Siracusano and Beatriz Hallac, 2013–14, and "Arte, ciencia, tecnología y conservación: Imagen y cuerpo material en la producción artística colonial sudamericana," PICT 2011-1327 ANPCT, under the guidance of Gabriela Siracusano and Marta Maier, 2012–15.

22. Adolfo Luis Ribera and Héctor Schenone, "Los lienzos corredizos y breve noticia del pintor Miguel Aucell," in *Archivium* 2, no. 1 (1944): 333–45.

23. These studies were carried out by Beatriz Halac and Mariel Reinoso.

24. Ana Morales, Damasia Gallegos, Gabriela Siracusano, Agustina Rodriguez Romero, and Fernando Marte, "Alternative Methodology for Traditional Interventions: A Colonial Painting and Its Lining with Nap Bond Method," *Journal of Cultural Heritage* 18, no. 1016 (March–April 2016): 362–65.

25. Héctor Schenone rescued many paintings and sculptures during that fateful day, some of them still kept at the Fernández Blanco museum.

26. It was shown in the exhibition *Las entrañas del arte*.

27. G. Savage, "Pottery," *Encyclopedia Britannica*, August 18, 2020, http://www.britannica.com/art/pottery.

28. See Gabriela Siracusano, *Pigments and Power in the Andes: From the Material to the Symbolic in Andean Cultural Practices 1500–1800* (London: Archetype, 2011).

29. See the Fototeca object record, "Sección AR-ARGRA-I-MEI- —Muestra Atentado a la Embajada de Israel," http://www.argrafototeca.com.ar/index.php/atentado-a-la-embajada-de-israel.

30. I am very grateful to my colleagues and friends from the Fernández Blanco museum Gustavo Tudisco and Patricio Lopez Méndez for sharing this rich information with me. Within those fragments stood the body of Saint Dominic of Buenos Aires. That allowed the conservators to unite the saint's head with its limbs and torso.

INSTITUTIONS WORKING

CHAPTER 9
THE ARTS OF THE SAME

Fernando Domínguez Rubio

THE PROMISE OF THE SAME

Light births objects anew. This much becomes clear when you take a nightly walk in a museum. In the absence of light, the museum morphs into an extraordinary space populated by bright shadows and unknown contrasts that transform familiar objects into unfamiliar ones (fig. 9.1). Here we can fully understand what Emily Dickinson meant when she wrote that some objects only exist within "a certain slant of light,"[1] as the dullest of objects become the most intriguing, while the most beautiful become utterly terrifying.

However, unless you are a museum (or art gallery) worker, it is unlikely that you have had the opportunity to experience the manifold objects that this slant of light can give us. Chances are that your experience of art has been restricted by the diktat of sameness that dominates contemporary art spaces with an iron fist. To enter an art space today is to come into a space where everything is designed so that each encounter is like the previous one and like the next one. Everything has been meticulously engineered to eliminate variation so as to guarantee that we always experience art objects in exactly the same way: under the same light, the same temperature and humidity, the same type of air, the same odor, as well as the same type of silence. It is as if artworks had been suspended in a seemingly eternal pause beyond time.

Today, when experiencing this kind of sameness in art spaces is as surprising as doing grocery shopping in a supermarket, this may seem perfectly normal. But we may ask: Where does the commitment to this radical form sameness come from? Why the need to keep artworks and our experience of them "the same"?

To answer these questions, we need look at the promissory nature of the modern art space. When we walk into one of these spaces, we are not simply promised an encounter with an artwork; we are promised to encounter and experience the *same* artwork the artist originally produced. In other words, we are promised a

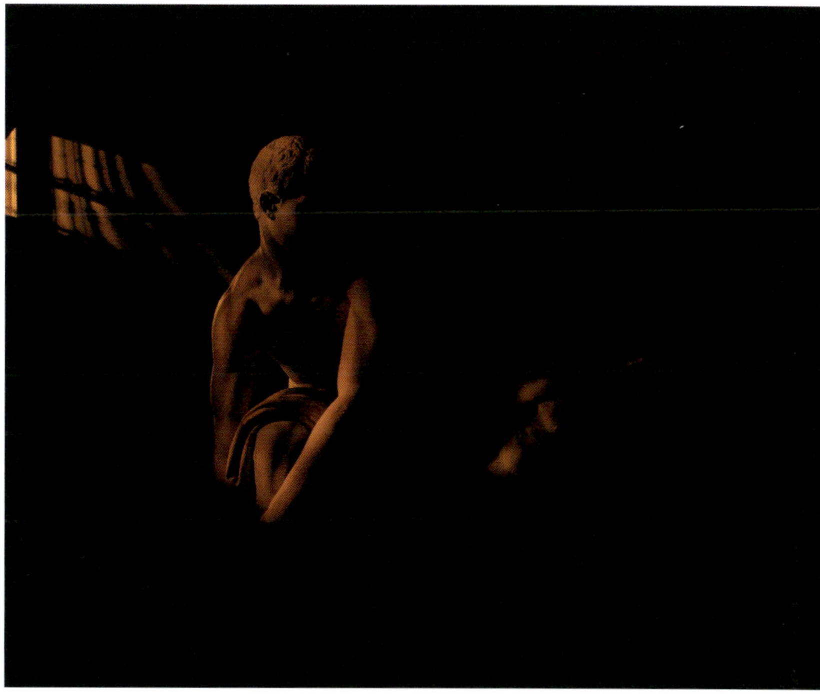

Fig. 9.1. Fernando Maquieria, *Real Academia de Bellas Artes de San Fernando, Madrid, Hermés abrochándose una sandalia, Cincinato, escultura griega, ca. 300 a.C., 27-11-2013 /00:27,* 2013, from the series *Guía Nocturna de Museos.* Courtesy of the artist

true and authentic object. Any art space worth its salt must fulfill this promise. Museums must make sure that what you see is the exact same artwork that the artist produced. Should they fail to do this, they could be accused of creating a fraudulent object or an inauthentic experience of the object. Just imagine, for example, the public scandal that would erupt if a museum like Reina Sofía or the Louvre were to alter Pablo Picasso's *Guernica* (1937, Museo Nacional Centro de Arte Reina Sofía, Madrid) or Leonardo's *Mona Lisa* (1503–19, Musée du Louvre, Paris).

At first sight, it may seem that fulfilling this promise of "the same" should not be an overly complicated task, since it is just a question of avoiding interference with how the artwork looks. In other words, it may seem that not intervening or meddling with the artwork would be enough to fulfill the promise of offering "the same" object.

If only!

As it turns out, fulfilling the promise of sameness is an impossible task. There are different reasons for this. One has to do with the inherent variability of our encounters with things, which always happen amid ever-changing environments, with varying lights, temperatures, air quality, smells, and sounds. As a result, we rarely, if ever, encounter the same thing under the exact same conditions twice. A second reason why the promise of sameness is impossible to fulfill is the inherent variability of things themselves. Things are constantly changing over time, deteriorating, crumbling, cracking, and oxidizing, until they eventually disappear. In other words, they do not remain "the same" for long. What all this means is that if art spaces were to adopt a simple principle of "noninterference," they would quickly find themselves with artworks that not only would be experienced in very different ways each time they were presented but would also look very different from how they originally did, as a result of physical deterioration.

"The same" is not something that exists by default or *au naturel*. It is something that needs to be artificially engineered, built into the world, and tirelessly maintained. This is precisely what modern art spaces do: they artificially build sameness into the world. To do so, they must engineer *unnatural ecologies* that are able to sustain the very particular environmental and perceptual conditions under which an artwork can be kept and be experienced as (more or less) "the same." Crucially, producing and sustaining the conditions required by these unnatural ecologies is not an easy task but a complicated one involving a variety of actors, forms of labor, technologies, and infrastructures. It also requires the ceaseless labor of conservators, x-radiography, infrared reflectography, organic chemistry, and material science to prevent artworks from collapsing. It requires controlling organic and inorganic processes and taming biological life such as killing bugs and insects. And it requires creating and managing massive storage rooms and a vast atmospheric infrastructure to quarantine artworks so they can be kept the same forever—or at least trying to do so.

Interestingly, most of the elements composing these unnatural ecologies have barely registered in contemporary writings and thinking about art. Part of the reason for this is that the work involved in producing these unnatural ecologies has been seen as lacking any aesthetic, let alone political, value, given its simple charge to make sure that everything remains "the same." Yet this is not the case. If these unnatural ecologies are important, this is not because they complete or supplement the main narrative of art with narratives about its context or environments. Rather, they reveal how the promise of keeping "the same" is behind the extractive system and uneven geographies of power and dispossession that organize how art is narrated today, where it is narrated, and, more importantly, by whom.

But to do this, we must first understand what exactly we mean by "the same."

THE CURIOUS CASE OF THE MODERN ART OBJECT

If we are to understand what the promise of the same entails, we need to turn our attention to the origins of the modern aesthetic regime of art that began to emerge in the European seventeenth century.

Broadly defined, the modern aesthetic regime of art is a particular way of producing form, meaning, and imagination organized around a series of practices (for example, painting or sculpture), actors (artists, curators, collectors), institutions (museums, galleries, academies, art markets), objects (such as artworks), and categories (such as authorship, authenticity). Exploring in detail all the elements composing the modern aesthetic regime of art would take us well beyond the purview of this short chapter.[2] However, we can focus on what is perhaps its most idiosyncratic element: the "art object."

Today, art objects are a common and ordinary part of the furniture of the contemporary world, alongside bicycles, plastic bags, condoms, cellphones, printers, or cars. The contemporary normalcy of the art object conceals how strange—one could even say anomalous—these types of objects are. If we adopt a Braudelian *longue durée* approach for a moment, the modern art object appears as a quaint and relatively new addition to the family of objects. In fact, outside the narrow precincts of Western modernity, the notion of the art object does not have a real equivalent. It is true that we can detect a certain family resemblance in other types of objects like, say, the sculptures of Western antiquity, Chinese Gongbi paintings, Kongo ivories, Renaissance paintings, or contemporary Maori kowhaiwhai patterns. However, despite these family resemblances, none of these objects have existed or circulated in quite the same way as the modern art object.

One of the elements that sets the modern art object apart from other aesthetic objects is the rather particular relation that these objects enjoy with their creators. In the modern aesthetic regime, the art object is considered to be an externalization, and thus a *material* extension, of the artist's individual self. I emphasize "material" because, in the secular cosmology of the modern aesthetic regime, the art object is a literal, not merely figurative, extension of the self. This has several important implications.

The first one is that when we talk about the modern notion of the "art object," we are talking not about a particular type of thing but about a particular type of *relation* between things and a particular kind of subject: an artist. The second implication is that this relation makes the art object unique, irreplaceable, and irreplicable, since no other object can claim to be a material expression of an artist's self and labor—this is what separates a perfect replica from the original. This brings us to the third implication, which is that, as an externalization of the artist's self, the art object is considered to be an inalienable possession of the artist. That is, the art object always belongs to the artist and cannot be separated from them. The inalienability of the art object is important because it places the object in a position between people and things. As a material expression of the artist's self, the art object is more than a thing but less than a person. This peculiar in-between ontological position is what separates art objects from any other types of objects and what defines how they are treated, how they circulate, and, more importantly, what can and cannot be done to them. This brings us to a fourth and final implication, which is that in the modern aesthetic regime of art, the inalienable relation uniting the art object and the artist is considered sacrosanct. It can never be altered or defaced. The art object must always remain the same as what the artist originally intended. In other words, it must be and always remain *true to its author*. This peculiar in-between ontological status of the artwork has been codified since 1928 in modern Western law under a new type of rights, *moral rights*, which recognize artworks as inalienable extensions of the self and prevent any change that could deface such objects' sacred relationship with their author.[3]

Needless to say, the notion of authorship is not a modern invention—despite post-structuralist claims to the contrary. Sculptors and painters, among others, have been recognized, eulogized, and historicized in different aesthetic regimes, both within and outside the Western tradition.[4] What defines the modern aesthetic regime of art is how authorship is attached to the production of inalienable, unique, and unalterable objects, and how this peculiar relationship of authorship depends upon, and is maintained by, a vast array of institutional systems devoted to circulating, exhibiting, and preserving unique artworks, ranging from art markets and legal systems to museums, fairs, and galleries.[5]

The democratic tyranny of entropy poses a problem for the modern aesthetic regime of art and its dreams of unique and unalterable objects. Because, as we all know full well, in this sublunar world of ours, entropy is the law of life, which means that things, including artworks, are always deserting us as they relentlessly come undone, heaving, cracking, oxidizing, and breaking apart, until they eventually disappear. As the artwork is consumed by entropy, the bond between the artist and her creation is bound to be eroded and, eventually, broken. Now while we can always get another sock, frying pan, or pair of glasses when entropy consumes them, we cannot do this with artworks in the same way. In other words, if Vincent van Gogh's *Starry Night* (1889, Museum of Modern Art, New York) breaks down, we cannot simply substitute it with a new one. The sacrosanct relationship between artwork and artist does not allow for substitutions or replacements. This also applies to contemporary art forms, like ephemeral performances or replicable installations. Because even though these types of artworks can exist through different material combinations, the fundamental relationship of identity between the artist and the art object remains immutable and unaltered. This is why, for example, you cannot use lollypops, or candies of a single color, or a different total weight of candies, in Félix González Torres's famous *"Untitled" (Portrait of Ross in L.A.)* (1991, Art Institute of Chicago), or why you cannot disrupt one of Carol Schneemann's performances when or as you please (unless you are given permission), or why you cannot appropriate one of Tania Bruguera's collaborative and socially engaged artworks into your own individual project. When these types of artworks are reproduced, it cannot result in anything new, a different object, nor even an interpretation of one. It must produce a (seemingly) perfect repetition, a return of the same—or, at least, something that works and looks like the same. In other words, the fact that these artworks are open ended, multiple, relational, collaborative, or can be endlessly repeated does not mean that you can break the umbilical cord that links them to their authors. The artwork must always remain true to its author.

The question then is: How can this be done?

To answer this question, we need to explore what I call mimeographic labor.

MIMEOGRAPHIC LABOR AND THE MODERN DISAVOWAL OF LOSS

As I will define it here, mimeographic labor is any form of labor aimed at producing and sustaining the same. Or, differently put: it is the form of labor that makes it possible to sustain the identity of something as a particular kind of object: to keep your house as a house, your cellphone as a cellphone, or to keep an artwork as an artwork.

The importance of this kind of mimeographic labor should be obvious. Were it not for this labor, those meaningful objects that furnish our lives, as well as the systems of meanings, value, and temporalities that are generated through them, would simply collapse before our eyes. One of the idiosyncrasies of this mimeographic labor is that the work of creating the same is never finished. Things are constantly changing and degrading, and we are condemned to be ceaselessly engaged in the mimeographic labor of trying to keep them alive. This is why a great deal of our daily toil (and our budgets!) is spent in the Sisyphean work of mending, repairing, adjusting, tweaking, and modifying things so that they can remain legible and effective "working objects" capable of generating the kind of functional or semiotic work they are supposed to perform. Were it not for this constant mimeographic labor, the physical fabric of the world would be redescribed until it would no longer be possible to claim that the objects in front of us are what they were; and you would be forced to find new names for them, like "junk," "waste," "ruins," or maybe even "heritage."

Here, we may be tempted to dismiss this mimeographic labor as irrelevant since, after all, it is simply in charge of "just" keeping the same. This, however, would be a mistake. For one, there is not such a thing as *just* keeping the same, because there is never a self-evident definition of what counts as the same. There are always competing, often incommensurable, definitions of what counts as the same and how it should be maintained. This is evident if we look at how different aesthetic regimes have defined "the same" and the different logics of mimeographic labor they have deployed to achieve it. For example, in some aesthetic regimes, the mimeographic labor of keeping "the same" entails not preserving stuff but creating a repetition that can generate the image of a return of the same. A case in point is the famous example of the Ise Jingu shrine, which has been rebuilt every twenty years for the last 1,300 years.[6] In this case, "the same" is achieved by separating the fate of the object—the Ise Jingu shrine—from the fate of the things that compose it—the wood making up the shrine. As a result of this separation, the inevitable loss of things (that is, the wood) does not necessarily entail the loss of the object (that is, the shrine).

In other aesthetic regimes, keeping the same is achieved not through repetition but through multiplication. In these aesthetic regimes, the original often functions as an "archetype" or a "model" that can exist in multiples through a chain of replications.[7] This is the case, for example, of sculptures in the ancient Greek and Roman traditions (fig. 9.2)[8] or the Pakistani musawwir paintings, to name just two. Importantly, replications in these aesthetic regimes do not necessarily occupy a subservient position as mere copies of the original. Instead, they often operate as equivalents of the original, which exists as a "distributed object" through its different iterations. Moreover, these iterations do not necessarily need to be identical with the original and can incorporate variations and interpretations. This allows these aesthetic regimes to recognize the possibility that "the same" can exist not only through multiple and equivalent instantiations, but also through multiple forms of authorships—that is, it is possible to recognize the author of the original archetype while simultaneously recognizing the mimeographic authorship of those who introduced their own variation while still keeping the object the same. The result is a series of things that, while different, are understood as the same.

In other aesthetic regimes, the acceptance of variation and change into the definition of the same goes even further. An example is the case of *kintsugi*, the Japanese art of repair, which works by accepting deterioration and incorporating it into the definition of the object, rather than trying to return things to some mythical original and pristine identity. Somewhat similarly, much of the mimeographic labor in the Western tradition up until the nineteenth century was not necessarily beholden to the idea of keeping or recovering some original pristine form. In fact, over much of this period, preserving paintings and sculptures typically involved trimming and modifying them to "modernize" them.[9]

This brief list, which could go on and on, is simply meant to illustrate the plurality of ways in which different aesthetic regimes have established what counts as "the same." What is important to underline here is that each of these definitions establishes not only a canonical description of what counts as a "working object" and how it should be upheld but also the conditions of their existence and circulation, as well as the types of interventions and transformations to which they can be subjected while still being considered "the same." With this in mind, it is easier to understand the uniqueness—one could even say the weirdness—of the logic of mimeographic labor under the modern aesthetic regime of art.

The modern aesthetic regime implies a radical departure from these other logics by creating a form of mimeographic labor organized around a radical

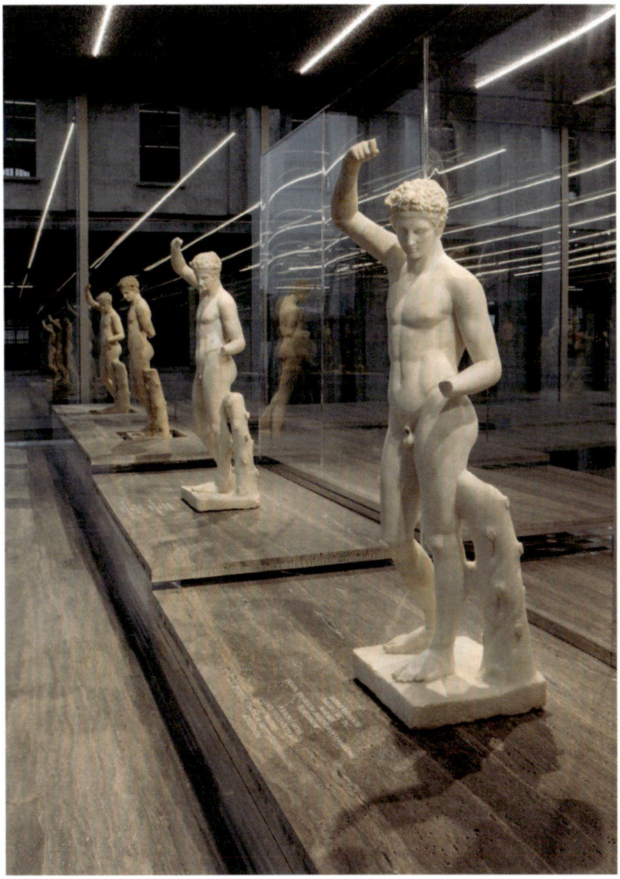

Fig. 9.2. Installation view of *Serial Classic* at Fondazione Prada, Milan (2015). Courtesy of Fondazione Prada

disavowal of loss. To explain what this disavowal means, we need to remember that the modern aesthetic regime is predicated on the idea that an art object must always remain the same as how it was when it was originally produced. The mimeographic labor in this regime, it follows, is devoted to keeping artworks the same as their authors wanted them by preventing, as much as possible, any change or loss. Thus, for an artwork like Picasso's *Les Demoiselles d'Avignon* (Museum of Modern Art, New York), this means that it must be preserved as it was in 1907 when Picasso originally made it. And for an ephemeral and replicable artwork, like *"Untitled" (Portrait of Ross in L.A.)*, it means that the pile of candies has to be reproduced each time exactly as Félix González Torres conceived it.

Of course, no one in their right mind would think that it is possible to avoid change or loss. *Les Demoiselles d'Avignon* will age over time, losing some colors while gaining others, just as every time *"Untitled" (Portrait of Ross in L.A.)* is re-produced, the pile of candies will necessarily be different from its previous iteration. This is why

I have described this logic as a "disavowal," and not as a *denial*, of loss. A disavowal is a refusal to acknowledge something and take responsibility for it. Thus, when I say the modern aesthetic regime is based on a disavowal of loss, it does not mean that this regime denies change and loss, but rather that it refuses to acknowledge them and operates *as if* it were indeed possible to avoid their consequences—that is, *as if* artworks could exist unchanged forever, *as if* time did not pass, *as if* we could have a lossless past, all while fully knowing that all this is simply impossible.

What I want to claim here is that sustaining this disavowal, this *as if*, is the fundamental organizing principle of the modern aesthetic regime of art. But how is this sustained?

This is where the museum enters the scene.

The modern art museum is the mimeographic machine in charge of sustaining the disavowal of loss upon which the modern art world is predicated. To be successful in this endeavor, the museum must create unnatural ecologies that meet two different but tightly related objectives. First, it must generate unnatural ecologies to prevent, or at least minimize, the inevitable decay and deterioration that artworks undergo. This task entails organizing the museum *as if* it were a perpetual-motion machine in which artwork could exist forever in suspended states. Second, the unnatural ecologies organize the museum *as if* it were possible to provide the same experience of the artwork, a task that entails producing unmediated and untainted access to the art object.

Let's see how the museum meets these two objectives.

STILLING LIFE

Despite the privileged position in which modernity has placed them, there is no difference whatsoever between the things inside the museum and what lies outside it. If this sounds strange at all, this is simply because we have naturalized and internalized the modern metaphor that imagines a discontinuity separating cultural objects, like artworks, from natural objects, like rocks. But there is no such discontinuity. What we call artworks are just things among things, physical knots made of seeds, minerals, wood, cotton, cellulose, crystals, or plastic, subjected to the same chemical and mechanical processes as the rest of the natural environment.

Even if artworks inside the museum are exactly the same as the stuff outside it, they cannot be treated in the same way. For one, and as we have seen, in the secular cosmology of modernity, artworks are not mere things but the externalization of the artist's self, carrying different forms of aesthetic, cultural, and economic value that grant them a unique and extremely privileged position. In fact, under the aegis of the modern aesthetic regime, artworks have become so special and unique that their loss is seen as a tragedy—so much so that we take as inherent the existence of a *collective* moral obligation to care for them and prevent their

Fig. 9.3. The museum's mechanical lungs, main boiler room, Museum of Modern Art, New York

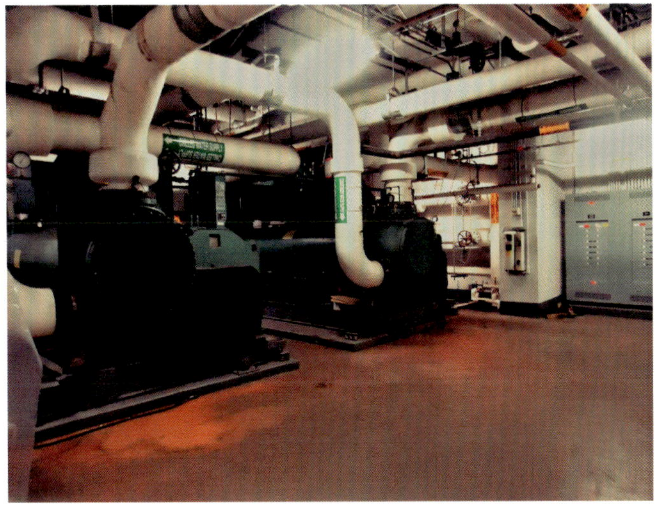

disappearance. If you think I am exaggerating, just consider what happens during war, when artworks are cared for and protected to the same extent as human life itself, and their loss is mourned just like human deaths.[10]

The task of the museum is to fulfill this obligation by trying to prevent artworks' death. If I say the museum "tries," this is because this task is, of course, impossible – it would require stilling life itself. But, while the museum cannot still life, it can at least aspire to *defer* their death. This is done by artificially quarantining a part of the natural environment and trying to control and slow down the chemical and mechanical processes that take place within it. That is, in essence, what a museum is: a machine to still life.[11]

Producing and, more crucially, sustaining, these conditions is something that requires a vast machinery. One of the most important parts of this machinery is the exhibition room. At first sight, exhibition rooms may look like regular rooms that happen to contain art objects. But exhibition rooms are far from regular rooms: an exhibition room is a highly sophisticated aesthetic machine designed to look *as if* it were just a regular room. In a way, exhibition rooms are to the museum what intensive care units (ICUs) are to hospitals. Artworks are delicate beings that can only survive within a very specific range of temperature, humidity, air, and lighting conditions. This is achieved through various technologies, including the powerful HVAC systems (fig. 9.3) that keep exhibition rooms at 20°C (68°F) and 50% of relative humidity (RH), with variations ideally within the ±2%RH range and a maximum of ±5%RH. Since the 1970s, this "20/50 rule" has become the de facto official environment of art, since it is the range that functions for a broad spectrum of artworks. But not all of them. The most fragile ones, like photographs, watercolors, textiles or prints, carry even more specific requirements, which is why many are displayed in separate rooms or exhibited in individualized display cases that, like neonatal incubators, provide them with the kind of stable, personalized microclimates needed for their survival.

In addition to maintaining these hygrothermal conditions, exhibition rooms are also equipped with powerful air filtration systems designed to make the environment as aseptic as possible. This is particularly important in museums situated in corrosive urban environments where gaseous pollutants can cause abrasion, discoloration, and the blackening of artworks. To avoid this, museums need to operate as relatively closed-off and stable atmospheric "aesthetic envelopes" shielded from their surroundings. This shielding is done by relying on recycled air and by minimizing the intake of outside air through filtration systems that remove particles before getting into the exhibition rooms.

Creating these atmospheric conditions is a necessary but not sufficient condition to sustain the disavowal of loss that these unnatural ecologies are designed to uphold. Light is another key element in this process, because light—especially sunlight—is a curse for modernity and its dreams of sameness. Sunlight contains ultraviolet (UV) light, a natural "fuel" for the photochemical reactions that render things unstable and restless, and it produces radiant heat, which leads things to expand and crack. The life expectancy of an object is inversely proportional to the time that it is exposed to light. This is why most artworks can only be on display for very short spans of time and always under very specific lighting conditions. Oil paintings, for example, should only be displayed in a light that does not exceed 200 lux and no more than 80% of UV radiation. To avoid damaging the artworks, when sunlight is brought into the exhibition room, it is done through specially coated windows that eliminate up to 99% of UV radiation. For the most part, however, exhibition galleries tend to shun sunlight as much possible and rely on artificial light that is engineered to minimize damage.

Even with all these technologies in place to control temperature, humidity, air quality, and light, most artworks can only remain in exhibition rooms for so long. The exhibition room is a hostile environment for many of them, especially light-sensitive artworks like photographs and prints, which should not be on view more than three or four months per year. This is why the vast majority of artworks spend most of their lives in storage.

This takes us to an important but often-neglected fact, which is that exhibition galleries are only the tip of the iceberg of the museum's unnatural ecologies. In most large museums, the art on view in exhibition rooms rarely constitutes more than five to ten percent of the collection. And yet, even though most artworks live in storage, you will be hard pressed to find any discussion about the role storage spaces play in art. As Ann Temkin, the Museum of Modern Art (MoMA)'s chief curator of painting and sculpture, once wrote in *Artforum*, storage remains "the dirty little secret of the art world."[12]

Storage facilities are part of the huge, but mostly invisible, geography that runs parallel to the visible art geography of museums, art galleries, fairs, and biennales. These facilities are not merely important for storing artworks not on view, but also for defining how art circulates in the world today. The kind of unnatural ecologies storage areas need to produce are the same, sometimes more strenuous, than those of the exhibition room, especially those containing delicate artworks, like films and watercolors, which require purpose-designed, deep-storage conditions to keep these objects as close as possible to a state of chemical and mechanical latency. Many of these objects require individualized conditions that can only be produced in autonomous, self-contained vaults. For example, vaults containing black-and-white prints are kept at a constant 7°C (44.6°F) and 30% RH, while those containing color prints—which are more chemically unstable—are placed just above freezing, at 1.7°C (35.06°F).

Despite this massive technological and infrastructural apparatus, the unnatural ecologies created by these storage spaces can never achieve a complete disavowal of loss, since things, *qua* material processes, can be slowed down, but they can never be fully stilled. That is why this massive mimeographic infrastructure needs to be complemented by an equally massive effort of mimeographic labor. This labor is visible every day before the museum opens its doors and after it closes them, when conservators revisit all the exhibition rooms to check how they are doing—much like doctors checking on their patients every day in a hospital—taking light and temperature measurements, checking the hygrothermographs in the rooms to make sure that the vital conditions of the room are stable enough for the artworks to survive.

Despite this ongoing mimeographic effort to contain them, artworks continue to relentlessly unfold and decay, until one day, the discrepancy between the thing that we see and the object it once was becomes all too evident. It is at this point when conservators typically intervene. In the modern aesthetic regime, these interventions are geared to making sure that the artwork remains as close as possible to what the artist originally created. Achieving this requires, among other things, cleaning any dirt or grime that may have accumulated on the artwork; removing aging varnish that may distort the artwork's appearance, as well as any interventions by others actors (such as conservators) that may distort the original intent of the artist; or even repairing and filling up losses to bring the artwork as close as possible to how it was when it was first produced by the artist.

Crucially, the conservator working within the modern aesthetic regime of art is tasked not only with making sure that the artwork remains true to the artist but also with doing this work *invisibly*. If their mimeographic labor becomes visible, it can call into question the status of the artwork as an expression of the author's creative labor and intent. It is not by chance that most modern conservation polemics have emerged when this mimeographic labor has become visible and has raised the question of whether the repaired artwork can still be considered the same that its author created, or whether conservators have ended up creating a different object.[13]

A massive ensemble of mimeographic technologies and labor is required to sustain the disavowal of loss upon which the modern aesthetic regime is predicated. Thanks to this mimeographic labor and infrastructure, artworks that would, if left to their own devices, have died in a matter of weeks or years can now remain more or less the same for several centuries. Of course, everybody working in the museum is fully aware of the fact that all these objects will eventually die. The task of this mimeographic labor is not to defeat death but simply to delay it, keeping objects artificially alive for as long as possible, *as if* the museum could indeed make good on its promise to keep artworks the same forever.

But this is only one part of what is needed to sustain that promise. If the museum is to deliver on that promise, it is not enough that it keeps the remains of artworks (more or less) the same over time; it must also make sure they look and are experienced as the same. Which means that the museum needs to build sameness not only at the level of things but also at the level of perception by transforming the artwork into a (more or less) fixed object of experience.

THE ANAESTHETIC VOID

Creating a (more or less) fixed object of experience also requires producing an environment that is not perceived as interfering with the art object: a "neutral" environment that can be seen as providing unmediated and untainted access to the art object. Achieving this effect requires engineering what I call an "anaesthetic void": a controlled, neutral, and invariant environment designed to suppress, or at least mitigate, any "sensory pollution" that might alter the conditions of perception and the encounter with the art object.

Producing and sustaining this anaesthetic void involves eliminating the variance inherent to any naturally occurring perceptual environment and removing (or at least diminishing) anything that could be perceived as sensory pollution. One of these elements is smell, which has been traditionally considered to be the basest sense as well as one of the most disruptive to the kind of encounter that is foundational to the modern aesthetic regime of art, because, as the philosopher of art Monroe Beardsley put it, smells cannot "construct objects with balance, climax, development or pattern."[14] This is why museums smell of nothing (or at least they try to). Removing or mitigating smells is achieved through a variety of methods, like, for example, using HVAC systems to recycle air and filter odor particles, or by creating negative pressure in exhibition rooms to prevent odor molecules from entering into rooms. Another element that needs to be controlled to generate a fixed object of perception is sound, which has also been deemed to pollute the experience of art. Controlling sound pollution is done by detaching the interior space of the museum from its surrounding noisy environments and by mitigating sound inside the museum as much as possible. This is achieved through different architectural technologies, which include, among other things, sound-buffering systems installed in walls, windows, and floors; attaching headphones to sound-based artworks; or relegating audible artworks to black cubes.

Perhaps the most important, and unruly, element in the production of this anaesthetic void is light. The reason for this is that light cannot be cancelled or suppressed in the same way as smell or sound, for the simple reason that light is the very condition of possibility for most artworks. Cancel light and you cancel most art. Art needs light but, crucially, not just any light. Art needs a neutral light that does not affect or alter how an artwork is perceived. The difficulty here is that, as any photographer would tell you, there is no such thing as neutral light. Every light has, to quote Emily Dickinson again, "a slant." What we have come to associate with "neutral" light is a rather particular *moment* of sunlight, which corresponds to the midday light of a sunny spring day. Yet, this natural light is very damaging for most artworks. Hence the paradox: the light that we associate with seeing a true object is the one that most undermines the conditions of that true object.

To solve this problem, museums have to engineer a natural-like light capable of sustaining the aesthetics of neutrality. This is done in two ways. One is by engineering complex lighting infrastructures, which are often hidden in museums, roofs and ceilings, that blend sunlight with artificial light. The second, and more common, solution is to manufacture a working image of natural light in closed-off white cubes. This is what museums do through track-lighting systems installed in the ceilings of exhibition rooms. Museums use light racks equipped with lenses and diffusers to create a neutral color effect, which is achieved by avoiding any hues that may be seen as creating "moods" or "atmosphere" and thus distorting our access to the true artwork.[15]

These are some of the technologies required to transform exhibition rooms into the kind of scentless, soundless, unnaturally acclimatized and neutrally lit voids that can sustain the modern promise of an encounter with the same artwork. Arriving at this point, one may be tempted to say that, while all this may be interesting, these are nonetheless purely "technical" questions about the types of environments in which art is displayed but have no bearing on art per se. This, I am afraid, is far from being the case.

The production of these unnatural ecologies is a deeply political and aesthetic operation that shapes the uneven geographies of circulation and exchange, which, in turn, shape how art is narrated, where it is narrated, and, more importantly, by whom it is narrated. Let me explain why.

THE (OFTEN-UNHEEDED) POLITICS OF THE SAME

To understand the politics underlining the unnatural ecologies described in the previous section, we must begin by noting that they are not optional, but compulsory. To begin with, most loan agreements today demand as preconditions to lending artworks that the receiving institution is able to sustain specific hygrothermal and lighting conditions during the display, transport, and storage of the loaned artwork. Those museums and galleries that cannot demonstrate their ability to sustain these values are excluded from participating in the circuits of exchange through which art circulates today. Moreover, museums are internationally categorized according to how well they meet the standards required to produce these unnatural ecologies. In the United States, for example, the American Society of Heating, Refrigerating and Air-Conditioning Engineers (ASHRAE) developed in 2003 a specific chapter for museums, which ranks them from Class AA (precision control) to Class D (relaxed control).[16] In different countries, these standards are prerequisites to receiving a museum accreditation, as well as to receiving grants and public funding. For example, in the United States, grants from the National Endowment for the Arts are tied to a museum's ability to meet the conditions laid out in the National Environmental Policy Act and/or the National Historic Preservation Act.

Critically, producing and sustaining these unnatural ecologies is not within the means of every museum. This is essential to understanding the specific set of inclusions and exclusions that shape this "global" geography of art. Many museums and art galleries from the Global South, as well as small and regional museums from the Global North, cannot afford the costs associated with sustaining these unnatural ecologies. We must remember that these unnatural ecologies do not simply comprise the exhibition rooms in the museum, but also include every element that makes possible the circulation and preservation of artworks, from storage spaces and crating to shipping trucks and conservation labs. This can help to explain why putting together a medium-sized exhibition today can easily run into several hundred thousand dollars in shipping costs alone. Moreover, sustaining the "20/50 rule" in exhibition spaces required by many loan agreements can be extraordinarily difficult and expensive for museums located outside Northern climates—hence, the bitter complaint of Maxwell Anderson, director of the Dallas Museum of Art, that museums like his, located in climatic areas that make it almost impossible (or exceedingly expensive) to guarantee production of the required climatic conditions, are considered to have "no business asking for loans, and cannot be trusted."[17]

The cost associated with producing these unnatural ecologies is central in shaping the asymmetrical nature of contemporary global geographies of art and helps to explain why, for example, most exchanges proceed in almost exclusively in two directions: south to north, and north to north; why global art circuits run between New York and Berlin, but not between New York and Quito or between New York and Addis Ababa; or why we routinely see exhibitions of artists from the Global South in the main museums and galleries of the Global North, but it is almost impossible to see exhibitions in the Global South made of artworks from collections of the Global North.

The asymmetry generated by the costs associated with producing and sustaining these unnatural ecologies affects not only the logistics of contemporary art circulation but also the logic of the material accumulation of art. When artists, private collectors, and artists' estates sell or donate their collections, they often choose museums that have the resources to guarantee them to be kept the same. This explains why large museums in the Global North often receive massive gifts of entire private collections and artists' estates. This is also how many artworks from the Global South end up locked in the storage spaces of powerful institutions of the North. And this is also why it is so difficult to see these objects displayed as part of collections and exhibitions. Because for many of these objects from the Global South, entering the holdings of the wealthy institutions of the Global North entails a devil's bargain: they are promised to be cared for and kept the same for eternity and beyond, but in exchange they must accept invisibility, since they rarely play a part in the hegemonic narratives created in these powerful institutions.

By now, it should be clear why the production and management of these unnatural ecologies is never merely a "technical issue." The imbalance of the exchanges these unnatural ecologies create results in an uneven playing field that grants wealthy institutions in the Global North an undue power to extract, exhibit, and narrate art from the Global South. At the end of the day, the wealthy institutions at the center of the art world in the Global North have the financial power to create the unnatural ecologies that are required to borrow, display, and store art objects. In this sense, these unnatural ecologies are at the heart of the extractive system behind the uneven geographies of power and dispossession that organize whose memories are being narrated today, where they are narrated, and, more importantly, by whom.

This, however, is not the only way in which these unnatural ecologies are extractive. They are likewise extractive in the sense that these ecologies are not only extremely expensive but also extremely dirty. The need to sustain the artificial environmental conditions of these unnatural ecologies 24 hours a day, 365 days a year has transformed art museums into some of the most unsustainable buildings on earth. For example, the 747 institutions included in the Arts Council England's National Portfolio Organisations (NPOs) emitted an average of 153.3 tons of carbon dioxide in 2018–19.[18] A museum like the Metropolitan Museum of Art in New York, uses the same amount of electricity as 10,000 homes, while MoMA's main storage area consumes an average of almost 5 million kWh per year—for reference, its energy consumption per square meter (328 kWh/m2) is higher than that of a large hospital (313 kWh/m2).

What these numbers reveal is that sustaining the art world's unnatural ecologies comes at an extraordinarily environmental cost. In fact, few objects today are as energy hungry and environmentally demanding as the modern art object, because few objects need the vast and unsustainable machineries that artworks need simply to exist and be experienced as "the same." Of course, this is not to suggest that art is as polluting as the fuel or transport industries, or the booming and polluting cryptocurrency infrastructure. But it is important to remember these numbers to dispense with the notion, still common today, that art is detached from the natural environment and that environmental problems are caused by other sectors. Fortunately, these notions have been changing in recent years as museums have gained consciousness of how unsustainable and polluting it is to produce these unnatural ecologies.[19] However, exceptions aside,[20] most of these discussions have been framed through the lenses of sustainability. In other words, as a question of making the existing model more sustainable, rather than questioning the model that forces the creation of unsustainable unnatural ecologies in the first place, chasing impossible dreams of timeless objects and lossless pasts.

ART BEYOND THE SAME

Art occupies a special place in the contemporary imagination. While other modern artifacts, like the market, the nation state, or even science, have been harshly criticized for their universalizing and colonizing logic, art has, until very recently, enjoyed a diplomatic immunity of sorts that has spared it from the same type of criticism. This license has allowed the peculiar categories and logic of the modern aesthetic regime of art to slowly colonize every corner of the modern imagination and how we think of the past, present, and future. Art has become so hegemonic and so entangled with the dominant common sense that aesthetics is often assumed to be some sort of neutral lingua franca. It has become entirely normal to describe all sorts of practices from different aesthetic regimes, past and present, as art, and to describe their objects as artworks, even in cases where that concept is completely absent in the originating context.[21]

One of the places where this is particularly evident today is in how different past and present aesthetic regimes are forced to abide by the logics and categories of the modern aesthetic regime of art, and to be organized around the same disavowal of loss that organizes this now hegemonic regime. All sorts of museums today, from ethnographic museums and science and technology museums to popular culture museums or design museums, are organized around the same unnatural ecologies and the same disavowal of loss that dominates the modern art museums. Moreover, many of the objects in these museums whose mode of existence entails multiplicity, substitution, multiple authorship, nonlinearity, or change are forced to fit within the canon of the modern art object.[22]

In this context, where the logic and categories of art are encroaching upon other aesthetic regimes, it is more important than ever to decolonize our imagination. We can do so by remembering what the modern aesthetic regime of art makes us forget—namely, that the modern aesthetic regime of art is just one among many different aesthetic regimes, one that is organized around a radical disavowal of loss and an obsession with keeping things exactly the same. What I have tried to show in this chapter is that chasing this obsession comes at a great cost, as it requires creating vast unnatural ecologies that are at the heart of the extractive logics, forms of exclusion, inequalities, and polluting infrastructures that organize how we deal with and preserve objects, both inside and outside art, so that they can be fixed in time as aesthetically and economically valuable objects. The modern grammar of authenticity, authorship, originality, and uniqueness locks contemporary objects into ever-tighter institutional and legal enclosures that constrain their circulation in logics of profit making in the name of keeping them the same—with the recent emergence of non-fungible tokens (NFTs) as the latest example of this logic.

This raises the question of whether it is responsible at all to pursue this modern obsession with disavowing loss. Maybe the cost of sustaining the disavowal of loss is simply too high. Maybe we should accept change and deterioration as part of life rather than pursuing an impossible image of timeless objects and a lossless past. Accepting change and decay does not mean that we should abandon the valuable objects that hold our relations, memories, narratives, and histories. Because, as we have seen in this chapter, there are numerous aesthetic regimes that keep those objects without the need to disavow loss. If anything, the modern aesthetic regime of art is an exception in this regard. And maybe it is an unnecessary exception that we can no longer afford as we become increasingly aware of its environmental and economic costs. And if that is the case, perhaps it is time to reverse the logic and allow art to be the thing that is colonized, infiltrated, and short-circuited by the logics and categories of these other aesthetic regimes, and to accept that perhaps it is not necessary to require unique and authentic objects to build meaning, narratives and imagination; or that perhaps it is perfectly possible to use copies, replicas, or imperfections. And if we do so, perhaps it is possible to begin to imagine art beyond the tyranny of sameness that it has been subjected to by the modern aesthetic regime, and to enable (or recover) forms of building meaning and imagination that allow for multiple, changing, collective objects and nonlinear narratives.

NOTES

1. Emily Dickinson, "There's a Certain Slant of Light" (320), in *The Poems of Emily Dickinson*, ed. R. W. Franklin (Cambridge, MA: Harvard University Press, 1999).

2. For a deeper look at the emergence of the modern aesthetic regime of art, see Paul Kristeller's classic formulation in Paul Oskar Kristeller, "The Modern System of the Arts: A Study in the History of Aesthetics (II)," *Journal of the History of Ideas* 13, no. 1 (1952): 17–46, http://doi.org/10.2307/2707724. Stefanie Buchenau has written a detailed account of the historical and intellectual roots of the modern aesthetic regime with a focus on German aesthetics. See Stefanie Buchenau, *The Founding of Aesthetics in the German Enlightenment: The Art of Invention and the Invention of Art* (Cambridge: Cambridge University Press. 2013). Larry Shiner provides a lighter but illustrative history of the emergence of the modern aesthetic regime in Larry Shiner, *The Invention of Art: A Cultural History*, 2nd edition (Chicago: University of Chicago Press, 2003).

3. World International Property Organization, *Berne Convention for the Protection of Literary and Artistic Works*, 2008, http://www.wipo.int/treaties/en/text.jsp?file_id=283698. See also Mark Rose, *Authors and Owners: The Invention of Copyright* (Cambridge, MA: Harvard University Press, 1995); and Stina Teilmann-Lock, *The Object of Copyright: A Conceptual History of Originals and Copies in Literature, Art and Design* (New York: Routledge, 2015).

4. Alastair Minnis, *Medieval Theory of Authorship: Scholastic Literary Attitudes in the Later Middle Ages*, 2nd edition (Philadelphia: University of Pennsylvania Press, 2009); J. J. Pollitt, *The Art of Ancient Greece: Sources and Documents*, 2nd edition (New York: Cambridge University Press, 1990); Brenda G. Jordan and Victoria Weston, *Copying the Master and Stealing His Secrets: Talent and Training in Japanese Painting* (Honolulu: University of Hawai'i Press, 2002); James Francis Cahill, *A History of Later Chinese Painting: 1279–1950*, vol. 1–3 (New York: John Weatherhill, 1992), http://www.worldcat.org/title/history-of-later-chinese-painting-1279-1950-3-the-distant-montains-chinese-painting-of-the-late-ming-dynasty-1570-1644/oclc/489578631&referer=brief_results.

5. On the role of art markets, see Michael North and David Ormrod, *Art Markets in Europe, 1400–1800* (Aldershot, England: Routledge, 1995); and Svetlana Alpers, *Rembrandt's Enterprise: The Studio and the Market* (Chicago: University of Chicago Press, 1995). On legal systems, see Rose, *Authors and Owners*; and Teilmann-Lock, *The Object of Copyright.* On museums, see Tony Bennett, *The Birth of the Museum: History, Theory, Politics* (New York: Routledge, 1995); and Oliver Impey, *The Origins of Museums: The Cabinet of Curiosities in Sixteenth- and Seventeenth-Century Europe*, 2nd edition (London: House of Stratus, 2001). On art fairs and galleries, see Caroline A. Jones, *The Global Work of Art: World's Fairs, Biennials, and the Aesthetics of Experience* (Chicago: University of Chicago Press, 2017); and Hans Belting, "From World Art to Global Art: View on a New Panorama," in *The Global Contemporary and the Rise of New Art Worlds*, ed. Hans Belting, Andrea Buddensieg, and Peter Weibel (Karlsruhe: ZKM / Center for Art and Media Karlsruhe, 2013), 178–85.

6. Cassandra Adams, "Japan's Ise Shrine and Its Thirteen-Hundred-Year-Old Reconstruction Tradition," *Journal of Architectural Education* 52, no. 1 (1998): 49–60, http://doi.org/10.1111/j.1531-314X.1998.tb00255.x.

7. Hans Belting, *Likeness and Presence: A History of the Image Before the Era of Art* (Chicago: University of Chicago Press, 1996); and Alexander Nagel and Christopher S. Wood, *Anachronic Renaissance* (Cambridge, MA: Zone Books, 2010).

8. Elaine K. Gazda, ed. *The Ancient Art of Emulation: Studies in Artistic Originality and Tradition from the Present to Classical Antiquity* (Ann Arbor: University of Michigan Press, 2002); Miranda Marvin, "Copying in Roman Sculpture: The Replica Series," *Studies in the History of Art* 20 (1989): 29–45; and Ellen Perry, *The Aesthetics of Emulation in the Visual Arts of Ancient Rome* (New York: Cambridge University Press, 2011).

9. Alessandro Conti, *History of the Restoration and Conservation of Works of Art* (Oxford: Routledge, 1973); and Noémie Étienne, *The Restoration of Paintings in Paris, 1750–1815: Practice, Discourse, Materiality* (Los Angeles: Getty Publications, 2017).

10. Dario Gamboni, *The Destruction of Art: Iconoclasm and Vandalism since the French Revolution* (London: Reaktion Books, 2007).

11. Fernando Domínguez Rubio, *Still Life: Ecologies of the Modern Imagination at the Art Museum* (Chicago: University of Chicago Press, 2020).

12. Ann Temkin, feature in "The Museum Revisited," *Artforum* 48, no. 10 (Summer 2010): 312–13.

13. Since the 1990s, conservation has acquired more visibility in the public surfaces of art thanks to, among other things, various educational initiatives and the new architectural layouts of some museums, which have made conservation labs visible to the public (as at the recently renovated Harvard Art Museums and the Lunder Conservation Center at the Smithsonian Institution). However, this new visibility of the practice of conservation does not translate into the conservation work itself, which still needs to be invisible to be successful. You can see the conservator at work, but not the conservator in the work.

14. Monroe Beardsley, *Aesthetics: Problems in the Philosophy of Criticism*, 2nd edition (Indianapolis: Hackett, 1981), 99.

15. Fernando Domínguez Rubio, "On the Discrepancy between Objects and Things: An Ecological Approach," *Journal of Material Culture* 21, no. 1 (2016): 59–86, http://doi.org/10.1177/1359183515624128.
16. S. Michalski, "The Ideal Climate, Risk Management, the ASHRAE Chapter, Proofed Fluctuations and toward a Full Risk Analysis Model," ed. Getty Conservation Institute (Los Angeles: Getty Conservation Institute, 2007), 1–19.
17. Maxwell Anderson, quoted in Julian Bickersteth, Jerry Podany, and Richard Kerschner, "Climate and Conflict—the Complex Question of Environmental Conditions in Museums," 2014, paper presented at the 42nd annual meeting of the American Institute for Conservation, http://www.icssydney.com.au/media/docs/AIC_2014_Paper_-_Climate_and_Conflict.pdf.
18. Adele Redmon, "NPOs Carbon Emissions: New Report Reveals Good Intentions but Little Change," *ArtsProfessional*, January 23, 2020, http://www.artsprofessional.co.uk/news/npos-carbon-emissions-new-report-reveals-good-intentions-little-change.
19. Bickersteth, Podany, and Kerschner, "Climate and Conflict."
20. Jennie Morgan and Sharon Macdonald, "De-growing Museum Collections for New Heritage Futures," *International Journal of Heritage Studies* 26, no. 1 (2018): 1–15, doi: http://doi.org/10.1080/13527258.2018.1530289; and Beatrix Ruf and John Slyce, eds., *Size Matters!: (De)Growth of the 21st Century Art Museum* (London: Koenig, 2017).
21. Alfred Gell, "The Technology of Enchantment and the Enchantment of Technology," in *Anthropology, Art, and Aesthetics*, ed. Jeremy Coote (Oxford: Clarendon Press, 1994).
22. Miriam Clavir, *Preserving What Is Valued: Museums, Conservation, and First Nations* (Vancouver: UBC Press, 2002); Petrina Foti, *Collecting and Exhibiting Computer-Based Technology: Expert Curation at the Museums of the Smithsonian Institution* (New York: Routledge, 2018); and Marion Leonard, "Staging the Beatles: Ephemerality, Materiality and the Production of Authenticity in the Museum," *International Journal of Heritage Studies* 20, no. 4 (2014): 357–75, doi: http://doi.org/10.1080/13527258.2012.754367.

CHAPTER 10

ART HISTORY AND THE CONDITION REPORT

Caroline Fowler

There are many ways to begin a description of an artwork. For example, I might consider recounting the drawing pictured here (fig. 10.1) with the following sentence: "With black charcoal on paper, the draftsman focuses on the lower half of a kneeling figure, examining the movement of drapery."[1] From these prosaic terms, I might convey the particular qualities of the drawing, discussing the brisk outline of a torso that gives way to a more detailed rendering of cloth, gathering around the knee with stiff crinoline-like folds frozen in place. What might give me pause, as I attempted to make the historical work palpable for a reader, would be the presence of the paper's slow degradation and the transformative effects of time on the drawing.

These features are not intrinsic to the original drawing, although they are now inseparable from its physical appearance. In particular, the paper holds a textured pattern of ripples and bumps across its surface (known as cockling), a disturbance that has become central to its visual impact. This corrosive effect mirrors the fall of drapery in some places, such as the creases around the lower leg. The cockling also reminds the viewer that paper (made from textiles in the sixteenth century) contains its own crinkling and torquing, like the drapery contained within the study. Although it is an anachronistic intrusion, the cockling unintentionally draws attention to the pleats and gravity of textiles as containing a force independent of human action. It also creates a distinct texture within the surface of the paper that competes with the representation of the drapery. The paper object and the representation of textile come together in a new work to form a study of the potency embedded in materials, presenting a dynamism distinct from human time. Yet the artist certainly never intended for this routine workshop study to be considered in relation to the internal corrosion of the support. Moreover, to attend to this particular quality of the paper does not illuminate the historical context of the drawing within the Renaissance. Instead, it draws attention to its institutional histories of care, storage, and preservation. For this reason, attention to the paper's surface and decomposition

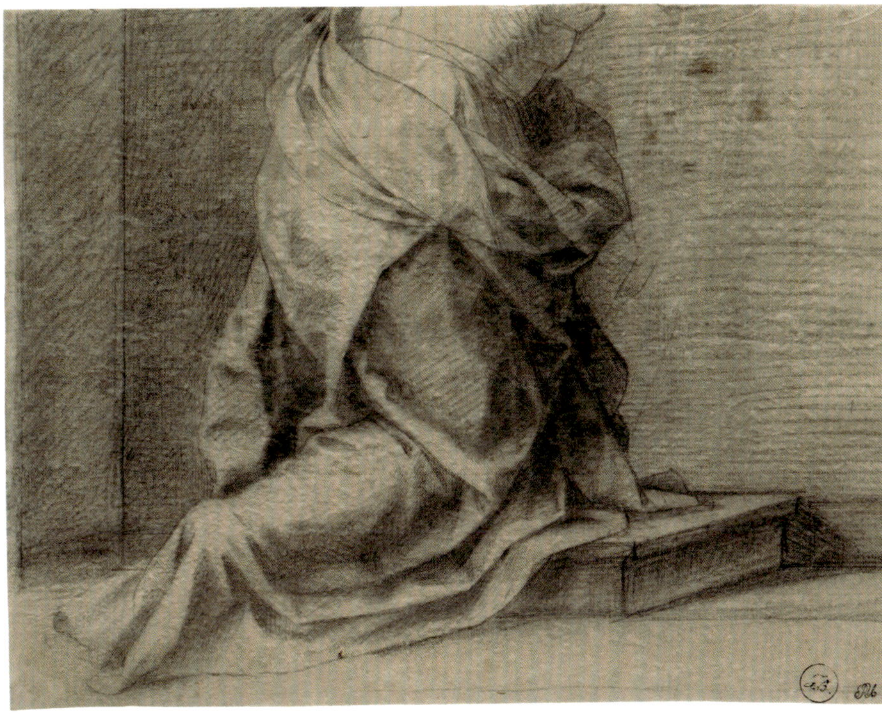

Fig. 10.1. Unknown artist, Italian (Florentine), *Study of Drapery*, c. 1530–50. Chalk on paper, 10¼ × 13⁷⁄₁₆ in. (26.1 × 34.1 cm). Clark Art Institute, Williamstown, Massachusetts. Acquired by Sterling and Francine Clark, 1919, 1955.998

often occurs within a discrete register of art historical description, known as the condition report, which introduces the object as not only a product of the sixteenth century but also of time. The drawing was produced both by its original draftsman and by later collectors and conservators, traveling from sixteenth-century Tuscany to a twenty-first century climate-controlled storage vault in the Sterling and Francine Clark Art Institute in Williamstown, Massachusetts. The cockling, while not intrinsic to the original drawing, is part of its physical appearance today—although many art historians might not engage with this temporal intrusion. The surface abrasion introduces complicated histories of mounting, preservation, and care, forcing a recognition that multiple factors, such as how objects are kept in storage and put on display, impact the writing of art history. While historically the conditions of display, storage, and institutionalization remain little acknowledged in art historical analysis, increasingly scholars are attending to both the condition of a work and its museum presentation, as exemplified in the work of Fernando Domínguez Rubio, included in this volume, and scholars such as Avinoam

Shalem, who attends to the often-overlooked category of the museum label as a form of ekphrasis.[2]

In part, this heightened awareness emerges from changing styles of image reproduction. New imaging technologies are transforming the language of description. Whereas early exhibition and collection catalogues often presented works (such as prints and drawings) in grainy black-and-white photographic reproductions with occasional color inserts, new capabilities in image rendering have created a reproductive aesthetic focused on surfaces in raking light, infrared and ultraviolet imaging, or two-dimensional reproductions that captures the work's physical weight and depth. For example, a photographic reproduction of a drawing today might include the paper's shadow cast on the table, marking its structure and presence as a three-dimensional object in the world. Accompanying these imaging technologies is a turn toward attending to a work's condition in descriptive practice.

This acknowledgment of the contemporary condition of a work is grounded within the institutional exercise known as the condition report, a mode of description that has remained discrete from the ekphrastic labor that defines art historical writing. As conservators and museum registrars are the primary authors of condition reports, these administrative documents are often overlooked as a central descriptive mode within art history, for the bureaucratic paperwork of museums often remains separate from the theoretical labor of the academic art historian. Condition reports also often depend upon a photographic reproduction, on which the conservator or registrar might write a series of annotations across the surface of the image. This mode of description therefore challenges typical art historical analysis in its strong reliance on images to make visible contours that might otherwise not be rendered legible in words. Whereas art history struggles with translating sensory experience into verbal ekphrasis, condition reporting embraces the limits of language. Whereas art historical description engages with the boundaries of language to convey a visual work in text, condition reporting depends upon an established language that communicates the manifold variations of loss.

Condition reporting plays a key role in the institutional structures that determine which works may go on display or remain in storage, which can be transported across the globe, acquired into a collection, or deaccessioned. The condition report informs art historical discourse as it shapes the selection of artworks displayed, exhibited, and taken out of museum storage. The language of the condition report, with its focus on loss, surface, and photographic evidence presented within a paradigm of scientific objectivity, has bestowed upon art history a specific vocabulary and visual form with which to convey the intrinsic transformation of materials as they degrade over time, a descriptive mode and viewpoint that remains unexamined. A consideration of this descriptive mode offers a moment to reflect on the institutional histories that create states of viewing and presentation that remain invisible.

This essay is not an exhaustive history of the condition report, nor a reflection on methods of conservation directly, but instead a consideration of how the language and visual methods of conservation impact the writing of art history.

According to manuals on object registration, a condition report depends upon both "brevity and accuracy." Some defects, such as splits, tears, holes, or stains, may be quantified—measured and assigned a specific location. Yet some, such as "abrasion, grime, cleavage, weakness, brittleness, dullness, and so forth are not easily measured, and adjectives must be used."[3] These qualitative terms include: negligible, slight, moderate, marked, and extreme. The language of the condition report is premised around loss and dominated by adjectival ways to express damage. An object may be deemed "insecure" due to weak material or mechanical stresses. An object may be injured with "losses or ruptures" or "by mechanical or physical violence or chemical change." Disfigurement occurs through "dirt, stains, discolored coatings, or poor restorations."[4] The standard vocabulary of terms for damage includes: abrasion, accretion, bloom, blister, chalking, cockling, crack, crease, dig, discoloration, dog-ear, embrittlement, fading, flaking, foxing, gouge, insect damage, loss, mat burn, mold, silked, soil, stain, and tear. As discussed, condition reports often accompany photographic documentation to highlight and further illustrate the areas of loss and disfigurement. This precise vocabulary of terms, therefore, becomes a means to visualize losses and, perhaps, barely discernable damage.

Outside the internal files in museums, the language of the condition report appears in other ubiquitous sites, such as catalogues and monographs. In the catalogue raisonné *Drawings from the Clark Art Institute*, incisive remarks on condition occupy the space between materials and provenance in the catalogue's tombstone. For an Albrecht Dürer drawing (fig. 10.2), the author records: "Laid down, metalpoint lines and white partially oxidized; sheet trimmed on all sides; upper left corner missing but repaired." These markers of the drawing's age and handling are cordoned off within the tombstone, keeping the material wear separate from the drawing's analysis, which is devoted to the affective potency of Dürer's work: "The impact of the face is not simply a result of carefully rendered details; it derives more from the enigmatic expression and a sense of potential change."[5] Within this exposition, there are two forms of description (although art history tends to pay attention to the latter rather than the former). There is the consideration of the work's temporal condition and its repairs. In turn, there is the articulation of the work's atmospheric and elusive qualities. These two modes of description are maintained within separate registers, so that the latter does not interfere with the former. The physical separation of the accounts also allows condition reporting to remain distinct from the art historical exercise of description.

This observational distance is necessary to the method of the condition report, as institutions rely on it to determine the viability of a work for acquisition,

Fig. 10.2. Albrecht Dürer (German, 1471–1528), *Head of a Young Man*, 1503. Metalpoint and pen and brown ink with white on gray prepared paper, 8¾ × 7⅛ in. (22.3 × 18.1 cm). Clark Art Institute, Williamstown, Massachusetts. Acquired by Sterling and Francine Clark before 1955, 1955.1835

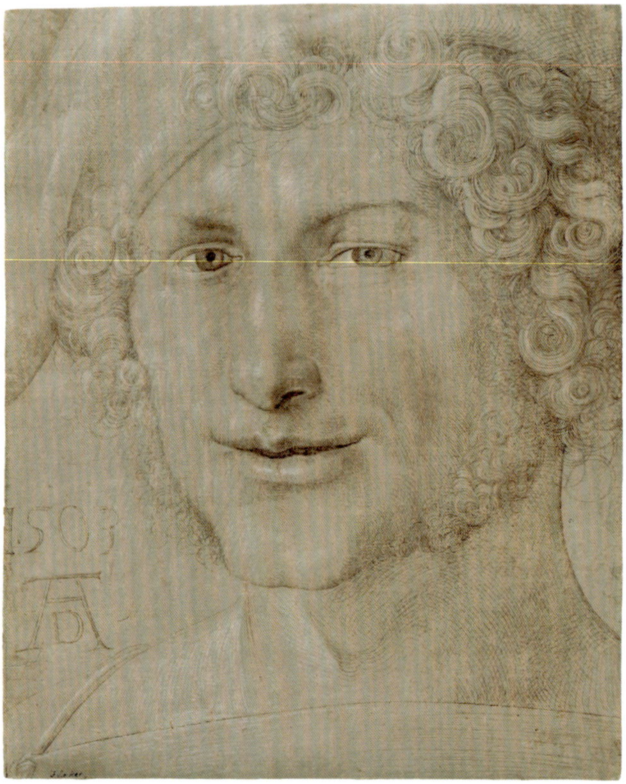

Fig. 10.3. Photograph by Charles Thurston Thompson (English, 1816–1868), with annotations by Richard Redgrave (English, 1804–1888), *Raphael Cartoons: The Healing*, 1858/1860s. Albumen print from a collodion negative, 23¾ × 34¾ in. (60 × 88 cm). Victoria & Albert Museum, London, 76598

Fig. 10.4. Photograph by Charles Thurston Thompson, with annotations by Richard Redgrave, *Raphael Cartoons: Christ's Charge to Peter*, 1858/1860s. Albumen print from a collodion negative, 23¾ × 34¾ in. (60 × 88 cm). Victoria & Albert Museum, London, 76599

deaccessioning, and travel. It is the registrar's duty to write a report when an object leaves a collection, travels to an exhibition, and then returns. The condition report also plays a central role in insuring works of art and placing claims, should works be damaged in transit. The history of condition reporting is also inseparable from the early institutionalization of the museum in the nineteenth century and the establishment of protocols around collections care. While a condition report may be written for many reasons, the transportation of artworks and its possible deleterious impact on objects is central to the report's historical development.

Richard Redgrave (1804–1888), surveyor of the queen's pictures and first keeper of paintings at the South Kensington Museum (now the Victoria & Albert Museum), innovated condition reporting when he combined the photographic representation of an object with brief descriptions of its condition (figs. 10.3, 10.4).[6] Redgrave's engagement with condition reporting was central to his position as he was instrumental in establishing the parameters for heating, lighting, ventilation, and collection management at South Kensington.[7] One of his major projects was the installation of the Raphael cartoons (1515–16) from the royal collection, which had been kept in adverse conditions at Hampton Court Palace. Redgrave advocated

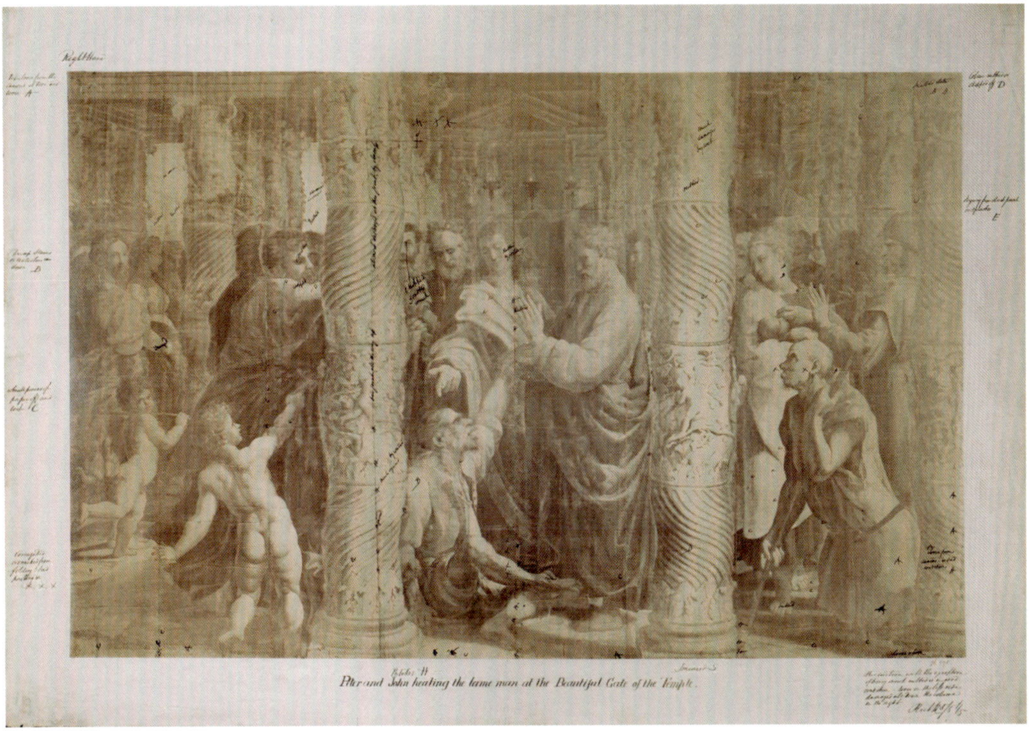
Peter and John healing the lame man at the Beautiful Gate of the Temple.

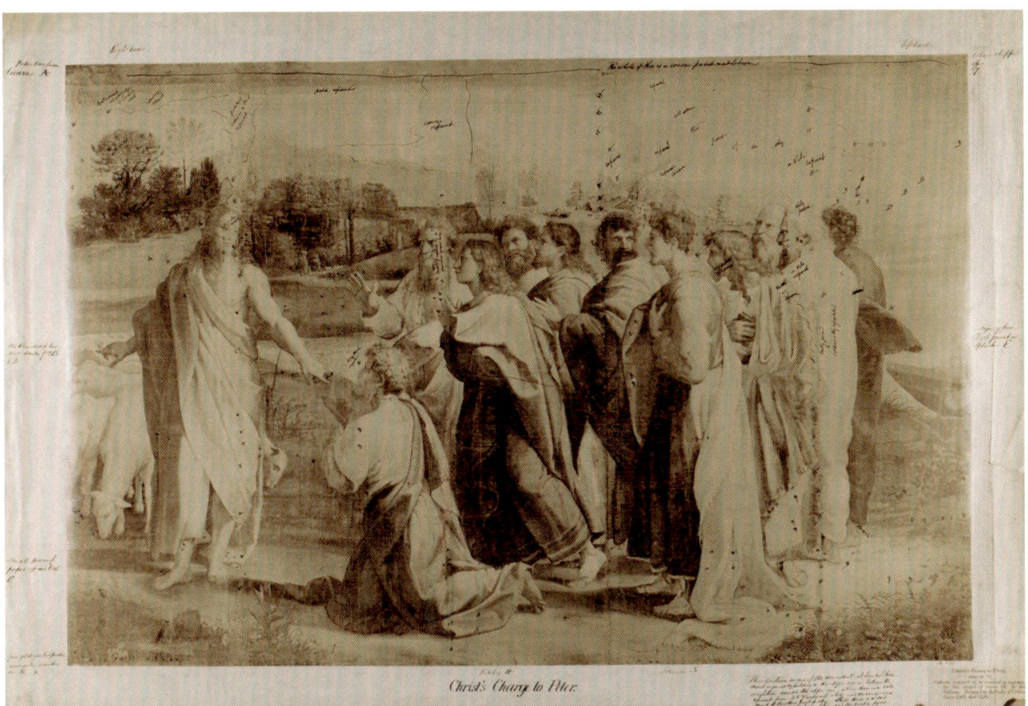
Christ's Charge to Peter.

to move the cartoons to South Kensington where they could have the proper lighting conditions, heating systems, and a protective coat of glass to preserve their delicate surfaces. In conjunction with the transportation of the cartoons from Hampton Court to South Kensington, Redgrave documented the impact of the journey on the drawings by bringing together photographic imaging with short descriptions of losses.[8] Just as novel imaging technologies today are transforming the attention to materiality and the condition of objects in art historical analysis, so for Redgrave the invention of photography allowed for a new means by which to archive, represent, and theoretically engage with material wear and tear on objects.

Despite their size and precarious paper condition, the cartoons were designed to travel.[9] Depicting the Acts of the Apostles, they were also made to be punctured, incised, and amended, as they were models for tapestry weavers for the Sistine Chapel. The paper models were sent to the workshop of Peter van Aelst (c. 1495–c. 1560) in Flanders, where the cartoons were cut into long strips to accommodate the looms. After the finished tapestries were sent to the Vatican, the cartoons traveled among various workshops in the sixteenth and seventeenth centuries, only to arrive in England in the 1620s, acquired by Charles I of England (1600–1649) from an agent in Genoa. Under the reign of William III (1650–1702), the cartoons transformed from rolled-up strips of paper held in storage to monumental works of art mounted on canvas and displayed in a gallery at Hampton Court. The cartoons then traveled to Buckingham House in 1763 and Windsor Castle in 1787–88, only to return to Hampton Court in 1804.

In 1858, with the aid of Charles Thurston Thompson (1816–1868), first official photographer of the South Kensington Museum, Redgrave began an extensive photographic campaign of the cartoons. He likely intended that the photographs would serve as models in place of the original works, as he notes with concern that they were often transported to various institutions, such as the Royal Academy, where they were copied "to the great injury of the dry and fragile paper."[10] Yet it was not only the frequent peregrinations of the cartoons that concerned Redgrave, but also their installation at Hampton Court, which opened to the public in 1838 and included few measures to protect the works from the foot-traffic, shifting temperatures of the gallery, and lighting conditions. As Redgrave notes: "Through this gallery during the year some 200,000 people passed, raising clouds of dust which gradually was deposited on the surface of the cartoons."[11]

Accompanying Redgrave's description of concern for the state of the cartoons are Thompson's photographic reproductions, which document them as objects marked by discrete losses. Many of the images focus on details, allowing a close examination of Raphael's affective vocabulary and his attention to gesture and emotion. Yet these detailed renderings also convey the mark of time on the painted surfaces. In the photograph of Peter from the *Miraculous Draught of Fishes*, Peter

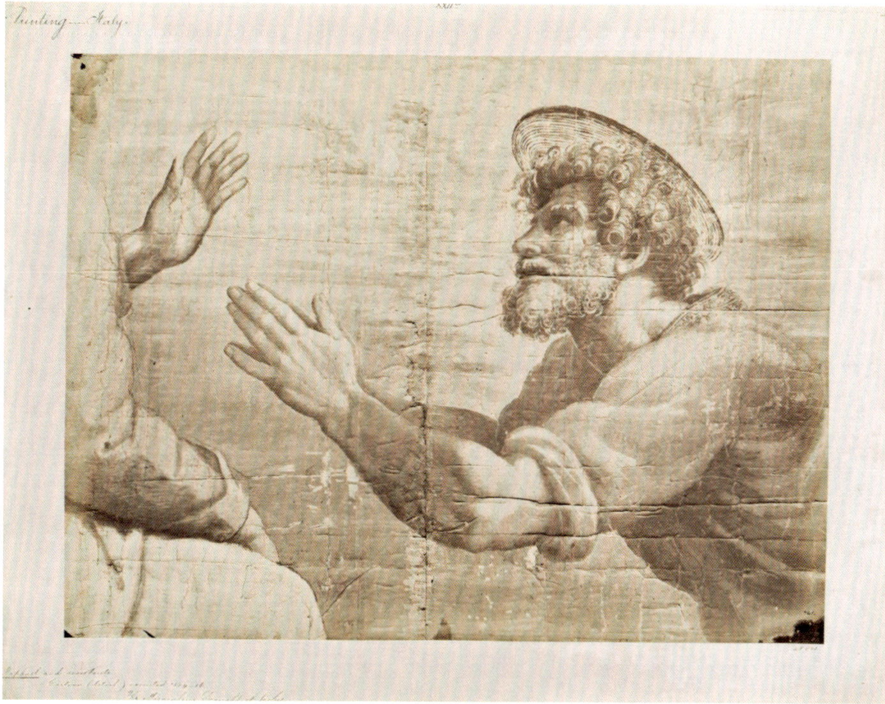

Fig. 10.5. Photograph by Charles Thurston Thompson, *Raphael Cartoons: Detail of Peter from "Miraculous Draught of Fishes,"* 1858. Mounted albumen print, 21 5/8 × 27 3/8 in. (54.5 × 69.5 cm). Victoria & Albert Museum, London, 48830

beseeches Christ with his hands in prayer (fig. 10.5). Thompson captures the delicate joining of Peter's hands extending from the strong musculature of his forearms to the breadth of space between his gesture of prayer and Christ's hand raised in blessing. Yet the photograph also pictures the seam of the paper where the cartoons were originally cut into strips, only to be mounted and reunited centuries later. The reproduction represents the surface of the cartoon and the patterns of cracking and lines in the paint extending from the multiple histories of incisions and remounting.

While Thompson's photographs capture the expressive potency of Raphael's cartoons, they also display the works' condition. The photographic documentation of the cartoons was therefore central not only in making the works more widely dispersed and accessible to a larger audience but also in displaying the temporal degradation of the Renaissance masterpieces. This history of documenting decay, impairment, and scratched surfaces became the foundation for Redgrave's condition reports. As the innovations in capturing likenesses of works of art, the photographic images presented the cartoons as objects inseparable from their material erosion.

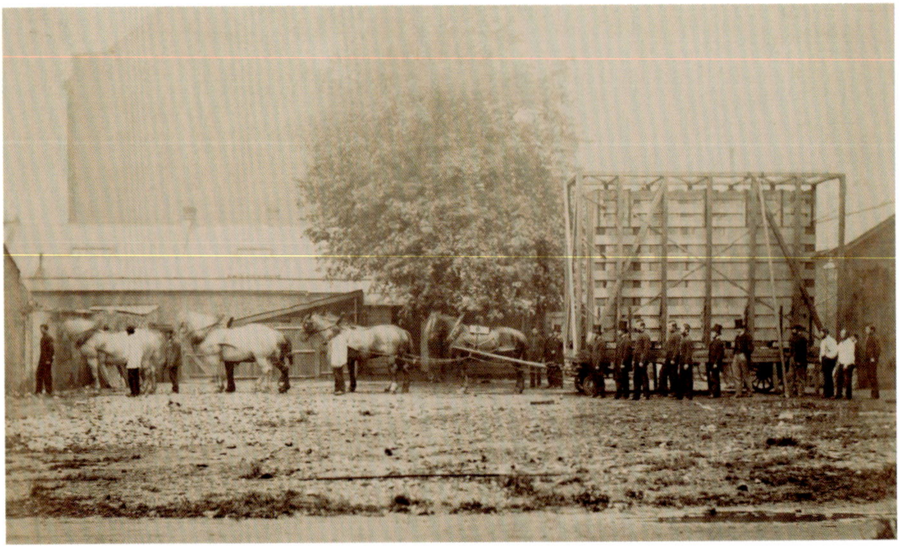

Fig. 10.6. Photograph by Charles Thurston Thompson and Lance Corporal B. L. Spackman, *Side View of Packing Case and Horse-Drawn "Van" for Transport of Raphael Cartoons from Hampton Court to South Kensington Museum*, 1865. Mounted albumen print, 15 × 21 in. (38 × 53.3 cm). Victoria & Albert Museum, London, 44413

To counter the deterioration of the cartoons at Hampton Court, using the evidence of their extensive damage displayed in the photographs, Redgrave advocated for their installation at South Kensington, where he could control the heating and lighting conditions.

In preparation for the transportation of the cartoons from Hampton Court to South Kensington, Redgrave employed Francis Fowke (1823–1865), an engineer and architect with the governmental Department of Science and Art, who was also responsible for designing many of the first galleries of the South Kensington Museum, to build a special carrier that would minimize damage during the journey (fig. 10.6). Redgrave also wanted to gauge the condition of the cartoons after their journey, so he made brief descriptive notations on the Thompson photographs after the cartoons' arrival at South Kensington. As he remarked about the condition reports: "It was necessary to take careful notes of the state of the whole on their arrival, in order what injuries they have heretofore suffered may be carefully noted, as well as the natural decay of age."[12] This was the first photographic and textual record created in relationship to the transportation of a work of art with the assumption that the journey would negatively impact its material. Inscribing brief phrases and signs directly on the photographic images, Redgrave demarcated the areas of loss, abrasion, and discoloration.

In these early condition reports, Redgrave created a format of description that combined photographic documentation and a specific vocabulary centered around losses. These reports are presented on Thompson's photographs of the cartoons in their entirety, in which the material wear and tear is less visible, rather than on his photographic renderings of details. Therefore, the losses and abrasions are primarily made visible through Redgrave's own textual annotations. With the photographic apparatus and a cryptic system of signs and terms, Redgrave created a form of viewing that assumes erosion and loss, and that acts as a means to archive the material destruction of artworks as they circulate within the institution of the museum. In his condition reports, the cartoons do not exist as discrete works from the Renaissance, extending their presence untouched from Raphael's hand to the contemporary museum viewer. Instead, they become highly mediated works. They are inseparable from the emotive grace of Raphael's distinct style. Yet they also carry their history as models for weavers, icons of eighteenth-century art theory, and prized objects in royal collections. Within Thompson's photographs and Redgrave's reports, the gestures of Raphael's figures are indivisible from the wearing away of their paint layers, so that they become historical works made in both sixteenth-century Italy and nineteenth-century England. The condition reports present the cartoons in a continuous process of unmaking and reconstituting. Redgrave's condition report and the accompanying photographic images demarcate an art history defined by micro-histories of loss, wear, tear, and preservation. The condition report, therefore, speaks to a formation of historical understanding that unfolds from the continuous transformation of materials under the conditions of transport, display, and storage.

CONDITION REPORTING AS ARTISTIC PRACTICE

Until recently, the condition report as a descriptive mode has remained little remarked upon, a form of rote reporting typically under the purview of conservators and registrars. Yet a critical engagement with condition reporting as a method has emerged in the practice of the contemporary artist Glenn Ligon, beginning with a response to his own painting *Untitled (I Am a Man)* (fig. 10.7), for which Ligon created a condition report.[13] In the original painting, Ligon reproduced the phrase and lettering of the signs held by workers during the Memphis Sanitation Workers' Strike in 1968. It was during his trip to Memphis to participate in these protests that Martin Luther King was assassinated, but Ligon references this pivotal moment in American history directly through the words of the workers, not through King.

In this engagement with the conservation exercise, Ligon made a reproductive image (a screenprint) of his original painting *Untitled (I Am a Man)* in order to inscribe the marks of loss and abrasion that accrued on his work. Yet the language of Ligon's condition reporting draws attention to the specific vocabulary employed

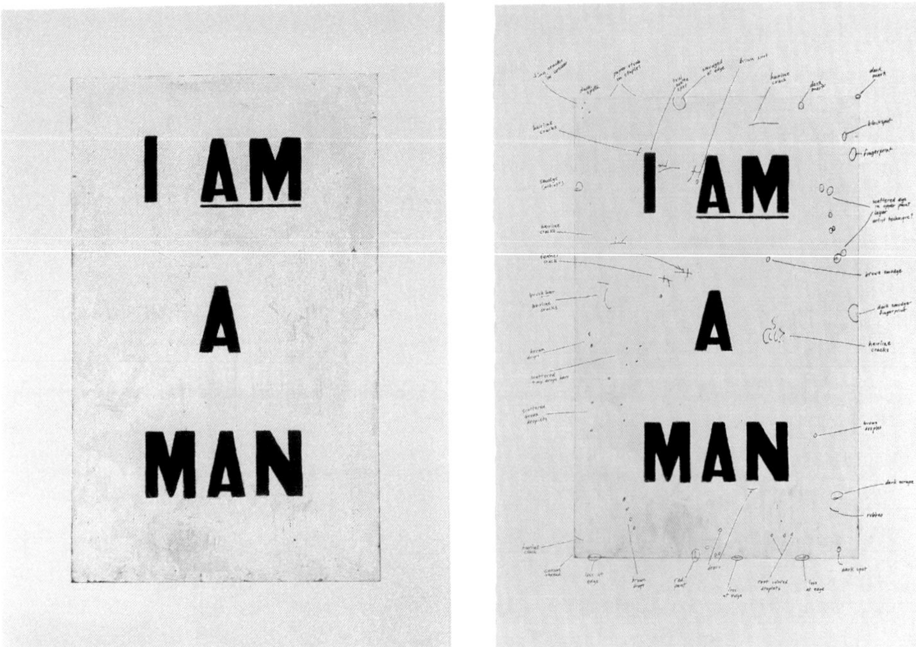

Fig. 10.7. Glenn Ligon (American, b. 1960), *Untitled (I Am a Man)*, 2000. Iris print, screenprint, in two parts, each: 31 7/8 × 23 in. (81 × 58 cm). Tate Gallery, London. Lent by the American Fund for the Tate Gallery 2007, L02822

to define material losses and depreciation. He focuses on a series of verbalizations that point toward amorphous intrusions of brown and dark against the white-painted ground, phrases such as "brown drips," "brown drops," "brown droplets," "scattered brown droplets," "brown spot," "brown smudge," "dark smudge—fingerpaint," "smudged at edge," "dark spot," "dark spots," "dark scrape," "dark mark," and "brush hair."

The actual droplets often remain invisible within the reproductions of the screenprint, and are only made visible by the artist's annotations, including a series of black-pen marks encircling the accretions deemed by this later hand as not intrinsic to the original work. While Ligon demarcates specific geographic locations, his terminology also draws attention to the ambiguity in the language of the condition report. His concentration on "brown" and "dark" as nebulous nomenclatures to delineate accumulations of pigment against the white ground suggests that the lexicon of the condition report does not hold the proposed neutrality of the empirical observer.

While the style and formal qualities of Ligon's report adhere in visual and formal terms to the established genre exercised by the registrar or conservator, the specific adjectival play in Ligon's language disrupts the presumed objectivity undergirding the history of condition reporting. His condition report obliquely questions the limits of a neutral language within the bureaucratic machine of the museum, and its determination of criteria for damage, loss, and care. For example, in another account of the surface of Ligon's canvas by a different author, the focus is on the craquelure pattern in the thickly layered paint and the glimpses of multiple colors underneath the white ground, ranging from orange and red to green and blue: "Thick application of paint cracking all over in a web pattern. A single strand of hair stuck on the surface. Grey, blue and green tints are visible through the layers of the white."[14] This portrayal of Ligon's work and its condition is remarkably different than Ligon's own. Ligon's attention to a vocabulary around demarcations of brown and black smudges against a white surface, in a work that explicitly addresses the long history of American racism, suggests that the scientific purview of the conservator cannot easily be disentangled from the institutionalized racism that structures most museums.

Ligon returned to this technique in 2015 and again in 2019, performing a condition report on a paperback copy of *Black Rage*, a landmark book published in 1968, in which the psychiatrists William H. Grier and Price M. Cobbs document the impact of persistent racism on the everyday interactions, failures, successes, and psychological traumas of Black lives in American society (figs. 10.8, 10.9). In this format, Ligon's engagement with the condition report significantly differs, as it becomes a means to visualize the accumulations of minute traumas on physical and psychic bodies. Instead of documenting a singular painting, Ligon produced a condition report for a mass-produced paperback made particular through its own history of handling, reading, and marking pages. In his 2015 condition report, Ligon's vocabulary focuses on "ballpoint pen marks," "cracks with media loss," "dents," "scratch," "bends in spine." Describing the single Black man standing on the title page, Ligon marks: "abrasion to face and arm."

While *Black Rage* is grounded within a series of contemporary case studies, Grier and Price articulate that the conditions of their subjects are formed not only by workplace discriminations in the present but also by the longer arc of American history, which for the African American is determined by erasure. As Grier and Price write: "History is forgotten. There is little record of the first Africans brought to our country."[15] Their introduction clarifies that the current condition of Black life in the United States is inseparable from a history that has yet to be written: "The black experience in this country has been of a different kind. It began with slavery and with a rupture of continuity and an annihilation of the past."[16] Ligon's performance of the condition report, therefore, inscribes making within a temporality that understands the past and the present not as discrete events separated by ruptures. Condition reporting on the paperback marks history as a force held within and imposed upon bodies, psyches, spines, book covers, and torn pages.

Fig. 10.8. Glenn Ligon, *Untitled (Front Cover: Condition Report for Black Rage)*, 2015. Digitally generated screenprint on paper, 11 × 8 ½ in. (28 × 21.6 cm). British Museum, London, 2015,7068.1

Fig. 10.9. Glenn Ligon, *Black Rage; or, How I Got Over; or, Sketches of the Life and Labor of Glenn Ligon*, from the series *The Life and Adventures of Glenn Ligon, A Negro*, 1993. Etching printed in black ink on greenish chine collé on white wove paper, plate: 21 ⅞ × 15 ¼ in. (55.6 × 38.7 cm). Detroit Institute of Arts. Founders Society Purchase, Friends of Modern Art Fund, 1996.61.8

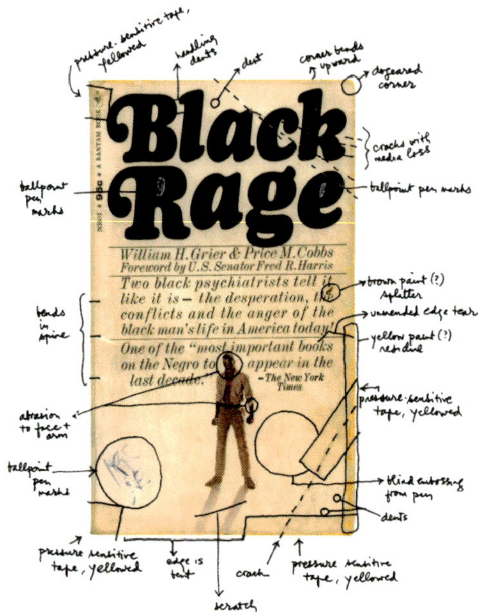

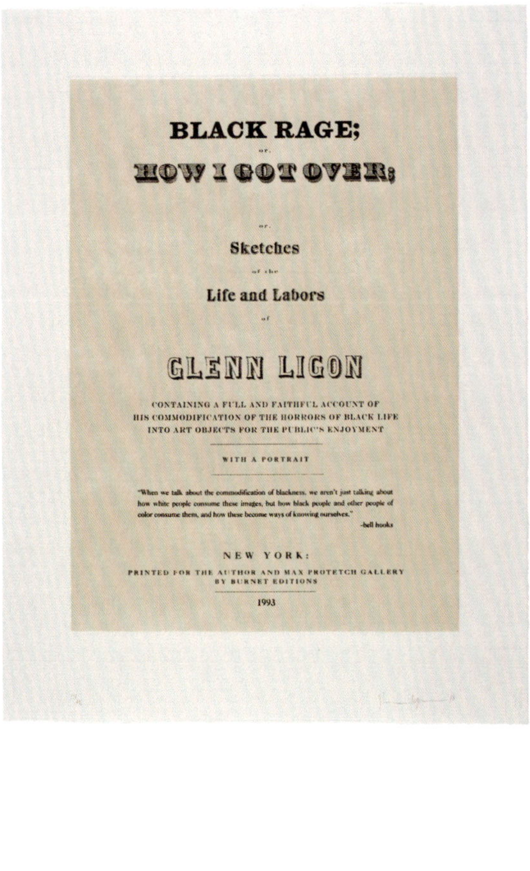

Grier and Price state that slavery is structured within the annihilation of the individual and communal histories of the Africans who were brought to the United States, and their own case studies testify to how these historical erasures cause extensive damage in the psyche. In this wake of absent histories, Grier and Price diagnosed physical symptoms in their patients as part of a larger psychic condition of trauma created through the denial of African and African American histories in the American psyche. By performing a condition report on *Black Rage*, Ligon turns the process into a metaphoric means by which to visualize the effects of trauma on the bodies of those whose ancestors were transported across the Atlantic to form the dominant labor force for the economic development of the United States. In his condition report for *Black Rage*, Ligon examines how surfaces are eroded through their interactions with the world in small ways that often remain unattended to, mirroring how persistent racism causes psychological trauma and exhaustion.

The physical and psychic damages outlined by Grier and Price may be further understood in relationship to the theoretical work of Lauren Berlant and the terms *slow death* and *crisis ordinariness*, language she offers to counter the shock-and-awe news cycles of endless crisis. Berlant argues that contemporary everyday life carries minute traumas, exhaustions, and feelings of radical vulnerability, and she attends to the resulting ubiquity of minute wear and tear. Crisis operates through the ordinary in embedded conditions of precarity. Berlant defines slow death as occurring not in a traumatic, discrete, time-framed event but instead "in temporal environments whose qualities and whose contours in time and space are often identified with the presentness of ordinariness itself, that domain of living on."[17] In his attention to demarcating the losses on a popular paperback, Ligon illustrates that existing in the world is inseparable from minute losses, accretions, and traumas that can be both discretely located and also might unfold across an entire surface of the psyche, like cockling across a sheet of paper. In turn, the method of condition reporting presents an engagement with history that demands an acknowledgment of objects, bodies, and lives formed in the domain of "living on."

While the condition report has remained invisible as a mode of description in art history, it highlights a process of visibility that attends to fissures, cracks, and losses that accrue through use and capital. It makes perceptible the damage that increases when works are in circulation; when they are bought, sold, and traded on an open market. The condition report demands a practice of reckoning with the abrasions and accumulations that occur over a process of exhibition, commodification, display, and travel, placing these minute crises within the everyday functioning of the museum. For the writing of art history, the condition report is an overlooked formal language that becomes a means to make visible the invisible labor that determines what is seen and what is not, as it governs the actual works on display within museums and in circulation for exhibitions. Yet even more, it defines an understanding of art history as determined by fissures, cracks, and losses. Demarcating these erosions and accretions offers a method of art historical description that recognizes institutional histories as central to determining methods for care, preservation, and the historiography of art history. As a mode of description, the condition report demands a new historical reckoning that attends to these institutionalized histories, recognizing that methods of care, curation, and exhibition are often synonymous with exploitation and the accumulation of losses that remain invisible until they are circled, marked, and named.

NOTES

1. Egbert Haverkamp-Begemann, Standish D. Lawder, and Charles W. Talbot, *Drawings from the Clark Art Institute: A Catalogue Raisonné of the Robert Sterling Clark Collection of European and American Drawings, Sixteenth through Nineteenth Centuries, at the Sterling and Francine Clark Art Institute, Williamstown* (New Haven, CT: Yale University Press, 1964), cats. 5, 8.

2. See also Fernando Domínguez Rubio, *Still Life: Ecologies of the Modern Imagination at the Art Museum* (Chicago: University of Chicago Press, 2020); and Avinoam Shalem, "On the Art of Beholding, Display, and the Transformative Museum, and on Why We Need Another Museum for the Arts of Islam," in *Dynamis of the Image: Moving Images in a Global World*, ed. Emmanuel Alloa and Chiara Cappellatto (Boston: Walter de Gruyter, 2020), 329–52.

3. Richard D. Buck, "Inspecting and Describing the Condition of Art Objects," in *Museum Registration Methods*, ed. Dorothy Dudley and Irma Bezold Wilkinson (Washington, DC: American Association of Museums, 1979), 239.

4. Buck, "Inspecting and Describing," 238.

5. Haverkamp-Begemann, Lawder, and Talbot, *Drawings from the Clark*, cats. 2, 4–5.

6. On Richard Redgrave, see Susan P. Casteras and Ronald Parkinson, eds., *Richard Redgrave* (London: Victoria & Albert Museum, 1988).

7. On the history of the V&A, see Julius Bryan, *Designing the V&A: The Museum as a Work of Art (1857–1909)* (London: Lund Humphries, 2017); and John Physick, *The Victoria & Albert Museum: The History of Its Building* (London: Victoria & Albert Museum, 1982).

8. John Physick, *Photography and the South Kensington Museum* (London: Victoria & Albert Museum, 1975); Simon Fleury, "Mattering: Richard Redgrave and the Curious Practice of Drawing on Museum Objects," *Conservation Journal* 64, *V&A Blog*, July 17, 2017, http://www.vam.ac.uk/blog/caring-for-our-collections/mattering-richard-redgrave-and-the-curious-practice-of-drawing-on-museum-objects; Clair Battison, "Back to the Future: Revisiting Richard Redgrave's Condition Reports," *Conservation Journal* 64, *V&A Blog*, April 27, 2017, http://www.vam.ac.uk/blog/caring-for-our-collections/back-to-the-future-revisiting-richard-redgraves-condition-reports; and Simon Fleury, "Reticulation," *Various Small Fires* no. 26, October 4, 2014, http://varioussmallfires.co.uk/2014/10/04/one-photograph-26-reticulation-by-simon-fleury/.

9. On the Raphael cartoons and their multiple peregrinations, see John Shearman, *Raphael's Cartoons in the Collection of Her Majesty the Queen, and the Tapestries for the Sistine Chapel* (London: Phaidon, 1972).

10. Richard Redgrave, "Report on the State of the Rafaelle Cartoons on Their Removal from Hampton Court Palace in April 1865," in *Report of the Commission on the Heating, Lighting, and Ventilation of the South Kensington Museum* (London: George E. Eyre and William Spottiswoode, 1869), 83.

11. Redgrave, "Report," 83.

12. Redgrave, 84.

13. Huey Copeland, "Untitled (Jackpot!)," in *Glenn Ligon: Some Changes*, ed. Wayne Baerwaldt and Thelma Golden, exh. cat. (Toronto: Power Plant, 2005), 122–23; Darby English, "Glenn Ligon: Committed to Difficulty," in *Glenn Ligon: Some Changes*, 31–78; and Darby English, *How to See a Work of Art in Total Darkness* (Cambridge: MIT Press, 2007), 201–54,

14. Gregg Bordowitz, *Glenn Ligon: Untitled (I Am a Man)* (Belgium: De Keure, 2018), 13.

15. William H. Grier and Price M. Cobbs, *Black Rage* (Eugene, OR: Wipf and Stock, 1992), 25.

16. Grier and Cobbs, *Black Rage*, 28.

17. Lauren Berlant, "Slow Death (Sovereignty, Obesity, Lateral Agency)," *Critical Inquiry* 33, no. 4 (2007): 759; see also Lauren Berlant, *Cruel Optimism* (Durham, NC: Duke University Press, 2011).

CHAPTER 11

BUT WHO DECIDED?

ON THE EPISTEMES AND POLITICS OF PHOTOGRAPHIC DECAY

Jennifer Bajorek

Of course, the very definition of the word "history," its meaning in Western discourse, was not always compatible with the way time was measured in Africa. In contrast to the monstrousness [*le gigantisme*] of Western materiality, Africa had its palaces of earth, destined to disappear with their inhabitants. It would be necessary to use a different method. But who decided that a history, that history as such, must be a visible accumulation of ruins? A thing that one can reach out and touch with one's hands?

—Simon Njami

My research on photography in West Africa has focused on the images and practices of West African photographers and on archives and collections that remain physically in West Africa. Working in collections in four cities—Dakar and Saint-Louis, Senegal; and Cotonou and Porto-Novo, Benin—I have become particularly intrigued by certain challenges posed by West African histories of photography to dominant histories of the medium, told from Western and Northern perspectives. Many of these challenges invite us to reconsider our very notions of both photography and history. These same challenges raise unique issues with regard to the conservation and preservation of photographic collections—not only in West Africa but, I would argue, all over the world.

Fortunately, both scholars and practitioners have become increasingly attuned to the many complex factors impacting approaches to conservation in diverse collections globally, as the framing of the 2021 Conservation | Making | Art | History conference and this volume attest.[1] If we want to do decolonial work, however, this complexity cannot be understood only in terms of local or regional differences in conservation practice or resources; it must take into account broader geographic, cultural, and economic factors, which exist in epistemological and political (and not only in climatic or chemical) domains. This is what I understand Simon Njami to be suggesting when he reminds us that our definition of history was decided (but by whom?), and it is this I am urging us to consider by attending to both the epistemes and the politics of photographic decay.[2] The materiality of what remains, how it remains, and how we engage with both loss and duration are not just neutral or apolitical categories or concepts. They are entwined with histories of violent conquest, colonial occupations, and ongoing colonial preoccupations.

To begin with an example that looms large for my West African research, it is more or less well known that the life of a photographic print in a tropical or subtropical zone is significantly shorter than that of a photographic print in a temperate one.[3] But what matters is not simply the so-called difficulty of tropical and subtropical climates for photography. We must also consider, alongside this shorter life, the fact that the structures and infrastructures that have been developed to look after photographic prints in rich countries—museums and archives, conceived as fortress-like structures with stone walls, doors, windows, temperature and humidity control, vaults, and lab-trained personnel—are actually, in most of the world, colonial institutions, and are perhaps particularly likely to be so in the tropics.[4] I use the word "colonial" here in the deepest sense, to underscore that the practices that have evolved in tandem with these structures and infrastructures are linked to and informed by colonial histories, and that colonial institutions often, still today, directly regulate access to photographic collections in many parts of the world. They regulate access *physically* in many parts of the postcolony, namely through state-sponsored museums, archives, and other official repositories of photographs, which are often housed in buildings that were previously seats of colonial government or colonial museums. They also regulate our access *epistemologically* in terms of the very structures of knowledge that determine what we understand to be a photograph.

If we want to decolonize our approaches to conservation, we must acknowledge that these approaches have been developed in tandem with, and often to serve, colonial institutions, and in epistemological and political domains that have been powerfully shaped by colonial histories. How might our approaches to conservation and preservation acknowledge more fully the ways in which colonial histories and institutions remain deeply entangled, not just with photography histories, but with our very conceptions of photographic materiality and time? How might they acknowledge more fully, and begin to respond more explicitly to, coloniality's entanglements with the duration of the photograph itself? These are questions about decolonizing not just photography's history but also its future.

BETWEEN THEORY AND METHOD: ACCEPTANCE OF LOSS

In both Senegal and Benin, my research has often followed questions about the production, circulation, serialization, reproduction, and remixing of photographs. The reproduction of photographic prints through serial rephotography is an excellent example of a practice that has left a distinctive mark on local collections, against the backdrop of this wider reproduction and remixing. In contexts where, for much of the twentieth century, negatives were not kept, in which they were particularly vulnerable to mold and mildew, or where they were recycled immediately after printing (particularly common in the case of glass-plate negatives, which remained in regular use in much of West Africa through the 1950s), and in a notoriously difficult climate, in which the life of a print on paper is significantly shorter than in temperate zones, it was not unusual for families and other keepers of photographs to bring their prints to local studio photographers to be rephotographed, throughout the twentieth century, at regular intervals.[5] The frequency of these intervals has varied according to particular circumstances and conditions, but it is not uncommon to see photographs in West African collections that have been rephotographed over many iterations, sometimes as often as every ten to twelve years. Those that were rephotographed very frequently, such as this portrait of Oumou Khady Guèye (fig. 11.1), were often those that were particularly cherished. A photograph such as this one confronts us, aesthetically and conceptually, with an "acceptance of loss" (to cite a phrase invoked during the Conservation | Making | Art | History conference). It also suggests that reproduction through serial rephotography is or was an ingenious method of photographic preservation—one that was very well suited to local conditions, and one that raises a number of fascinating questions for our evolving thinking about conservation and preservation in a global context.

Which print (is there one?) are we seeking to preserve in this case? How do we date the photograph? Who is the author? Which is the photograph / photographic technology, material, or process on which we should focus our research or that we should privilege in our documentation? Finally, how might reproduction through serial photography inform our approaches to photographic preservation or conservation such that they acknowledge loss more fully, or that they can even be predicated on an "acceptance of loss"?

Photographic conservation and preservation initiatives often begin, whether implicitly or explicitly, with the assumption that one is working on a print that has remained self-identical over time, that has remained relatively stable or weathered minimal damage, and that needs only to be rehoused and stored in certain conditions (conditions often associated with optimal temperature and relative humidity ranges that are unattainable in much of the world).[6] Such initiatives often presuppose the existence of written documents or forms of notation providing contextual information or details about a print's provenance, authorship, date, and process. In the case of silver prints, they often assume that a negative is still extant. And yet, from the moment that a photograph has been reproduced through serial rephotography, questions of provenance, authorship, date, and process, are irrevocably clouded, as we have seen, and dominant (Western) definitions of authorship

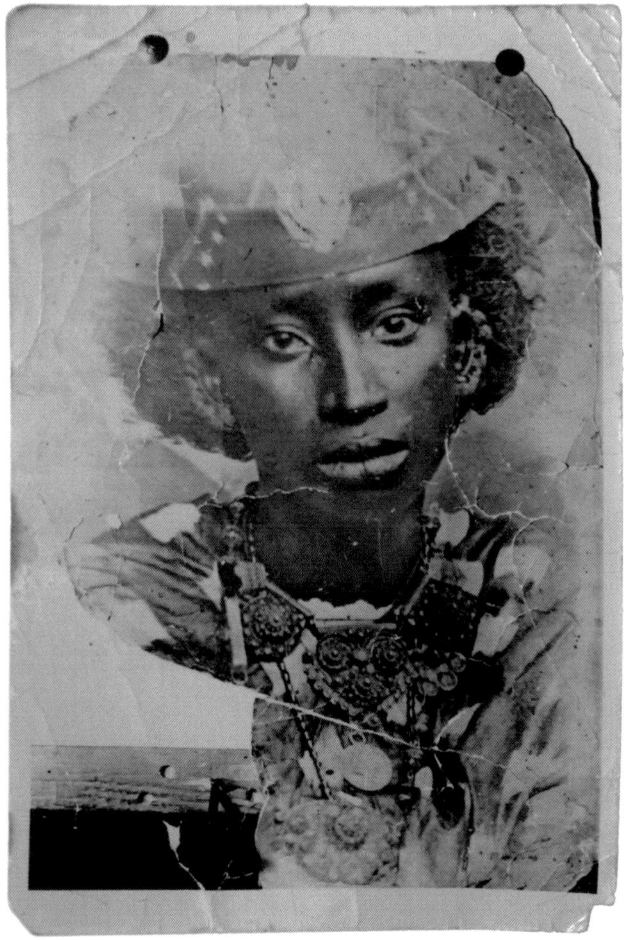

Fig. 11.1. Photographer unknown (Dakar, Senegal), *Portrait of Oumou Khady Guèye*, early 1930s (first vintage print). Gelatin silver print, approx. 7 × 5 in. (17.8 × 12.7 cm). Collection of Ibrahima Faye and Khady Ndoye

and practices of dating are often irrelevant or mismatched to African contexts. This mismatch, already apparent in serial rephotography, is only amplified by practices such as collage or montage, which have also played a significant role in West African photography histories and in the larger landscape of remixing. Finally, from the moment that a photograph has been reproduced through serial rephotography, we can assume that a negative is not extant. In order to make space for West African photography histories, we must query some of the most basic tenets of conservation and preservation practices.

Equally powerful here is the example of modifications made directly on the surface of the print: drawing or writing on prints, hand tinting or colorization, infilling of details with graphite, ink, or pigment, and tinting with gouache. These practices started with the very first photographs in the nineteenth century, and overpainted photographs, or those that have been inked, shaded, tinted, or inscribed upon, can be found in collections across the region. Vitally, and distinguishing many prints in family- and community-based collections in West Africa from those in other parts of the world, these and other modifications made on the surface of the print have been carried out not only by photographers, understood elsewhere as the principal or final authors of the image, but also by family or community members caring for the photograph in domestic or communal contexts: what Erin Haney has called the photograph's "creative audiences."[7] These practices have only rarely been treated by scholars, and few have recognized them as the acts of multigenerational and collective curation and conservation that they are. Such practices challenge positivist notions of the photographic index, so cherished by Western approaches to photography. They require us to expand the frame of the photograph's plasticity, inviting deeper and more sustained reflection on the intersections of photographic plasticity with other modes of cultural expression, African methods of historiography, and related economic, social, and political forces.[8] Ultimately, these practices help us to understand how local values, aesthetics, and conceptions of photography can, and should, impact our very definition of the word "history," as per Njami.

Take, for example, the significance of orality. Orality, which is widely understood as a privileged mode of cultural expression and method of historiography in West Africa, has clearly had consequences for photographic interpretation in the region.[9] Orality pulls us away from oversimple understandings of the photographic image's capacities for inscription, dating, chronology, and periodization; it challenges the distinction between the tangible and the intangible; and it exposes cultural preoccupations with monumentality. Surely all these consequences must be taken into account for photographic conservation and preservation initiatives. Orality might itself even be considered a tool or technique of conservation well suited to the conditions of radical ephemerality that, I would argue, characterize all photographic prints and negatives today—insofar as orality expands possibilities for the transmission of fine-grained historical information (about a particular photograph or its meanings), as well as for the transmission of broader cultural values.

I am thinking, here, of the discussions I had about a photograph of two women in Saint-Louis, Senegal (fig. 11.2). Local interlocutors saw, in this image, significant aspects of precolonial Senegalese history: the women's clothing (of imported lace) signified, for them, forms of elegance and beauty associated with precolonial wealth accumulation; their necklaces (of a metal alloy associated with traditional artisans from Mauritania) signified broader regional and trans-Saharan exchanges; their pearl bracelets signified wealth amassed through transatlantic trade.[10] And yet the photograph itself dates, we think, from the first two decades of the twentieth century. Other twentieth-century photographs, too, were interpreted for me by

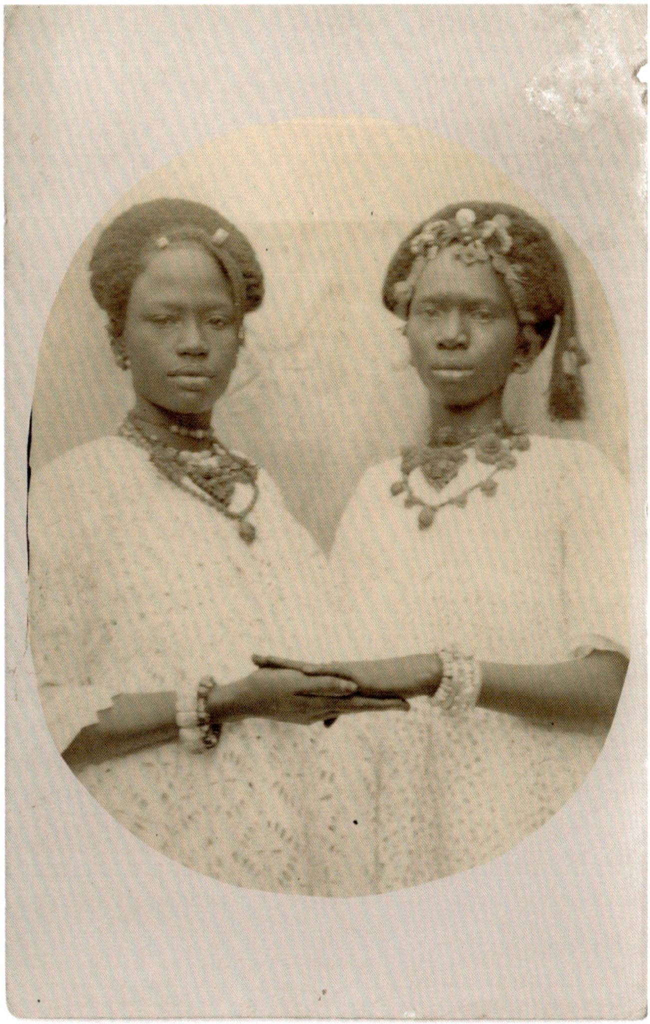

Fig. 11.2. Photographer unknown (Saint-Louis, Senegal), *Portrait of two women in lace*, late 1920s / early 1930s. Photographic print on postcard stock, approx. 5 × 7 in. (12.7 × 17.8 cm). Collection of the Centre de Recherches et de Documentation du Sénégal, Saint-Louis, Senegal

local interlocutors as evidence of Saint-Louis's status as a center of wealth accumulation, again, during the transatlantic slave trade.[11] It is worth thinking more about what is happening when twentieth-century photographs are used to narrate precolonial histories and to render visible more complex temporalities and longer timescales. At a minimum, these other temporalities and longer timescales suggest a more expansive understanding of a photograph's capacities for inscription and dating, and, by extension, for the transmission of historical knowledge.

We might return, here, to the portrait of Oumou Khady Guèye (see fig. 11.1). I saw this portrait in the personal collection of Ibrahima Faye, a high-ranking civil servant and regional governor in Senegal in the immediate postcolonial period. The photograph, taken in Dakar, was rephotographed at frequent intervals. In interviews with Faye, I learned that those intervals could be roughly mapped onto his successive relocations to the capital cities of the regions of which he was governor: Mbour, Ziguinchor, Kaolack, and Saint-Louis. There is, therefore, contained within this portrait, a kind of latent regional geography of postcolonial Senegal and a latent chronology of decolonization. Faye's relocations were determined by his service in the government of the newly created postcolonial state, and they led, each time, to a new iteration of this photograph.

I have explored these questions at length in my research and writing.[12] As an activist, I have explored these questions from different perspectives, and it is to this activist practice that I will turn now.

IN PRACTICE: LET THE WIND BLOW THROUGH

In 2014, I helped to organize and participated in a four-day workshop focused on photographic preservation in photographic collections in Africa. The workshop, which was held in Porto-Novo, Benin, was called the 3PA [*Préservation du patrimoine photographique africain*]: West African Image Lab, and provided technical and hands-on training to people looking after photographic collections in an array of contexts in Africa (fig. 11.3). The workshop also opened a broader dialogue about the future of African collections, which are, in West Africa as in many other parts of the continent, widely considered to be "endangered" — due to climate and environmental factors (high temperatures, high relative humidity, and extremely variable humidity), but also due to precarious institutional structures, scarce preservation resources, and accelerating rates of export of prints and negatives abroad. For those not familiar with the West African context, the global vogue for West African studio portraiture — sparked when photographic portraits by Seydou Keïta, taken in Bamako mainly in the 1950s, began to be exhibited in Western galleries and museums in the 1990s — has had a huge impact on the export rate of both vintage prints and negatives.

I organized the initiative in collaboration with Erin Haney (another scholar of photography in West Africa and cofounder and codirector, with me, of Resolution Photo), Fatima Fall (director of the Centre de Recherches et de Documentation du Sénégal [CRDS], a museum and research institution that houses an extensive photographic archive in Saint-Louis, Senegal), Franck Ogou (a scholar, senior curator, and cultural heritage professional at the École du Patrimoine Africain, our host institution in Porto-Novo), and a distinguished team of professional photograph conservators from the United States and France: Debra Hess Norris (professor and Henry Francis Du Pont Chair of Art Conservation, University of Delaware), Nora Kennedy (Sherman Fairchild Conservator of Photographs in the Department of Photograph Conservation at the Metropolitan Museum of Art, New York), and Bertrand Lavédrine (former director of the Centre de Recherche sur la Conservation

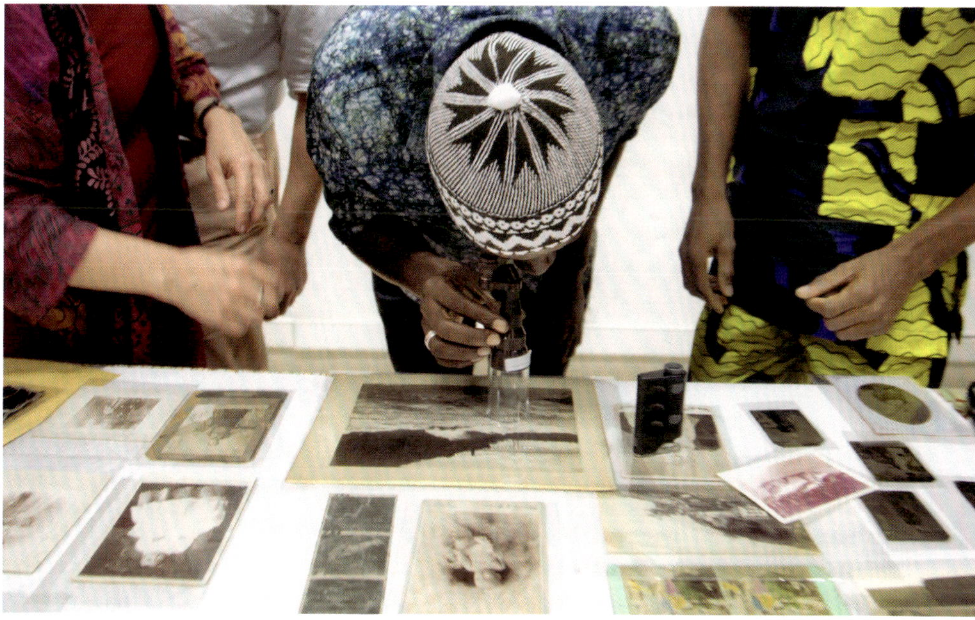

Fig. 11.3. Senegalese photographer (and workshop participant) Ibrahima Thiam working with the teaching collection during the 3PA: West African Image Lab workshop in Porto-Novo, Benin, in April 2014

des Collections, France).[13] The workshop enrolled twenty participants representing collections in nine countries in sub-Saharan Africa: Benin, Burkina Faso, Côte d'Ivoire, Ghana, Mali, Nigeria, Senegal, Uganda, and Zimbabwe. Approximately half of all participants were trained cultural heritage professionals looking after collections in institutional settings. The other half were looking after community-based collections, often held by photographers' families or individuals with strong ties to those families, or they were themselves photographers to whom significant community-based collections had been entrusted.

The core curriculum, focused on preventive conservation, was drawn from a course our French and American partners had designed for use in the Middle East Photograph Preservation Initiative (MEPPI). MEPPI is a training program for conservation professionals in the Middle East that the conservators we worked with (Norris, Kennedy, and Lavédrine) have been teaching since 2009. In Porto-Novo, we were incredibly lucky to be able to draw not only on the conservators' deep technical expertise, but on this curriculum they had already created and refined.[14] This core curriculum was supplemented by sessions led by our African partners: Fall, of the CRDS, and Ogou, of l'ÉPA, focused on the particular challenges faced by museum and heritage professionals in Africa; Haney and I focused on the history of photography in the region; and the participants themselves presented on their own collections and the particular challenges they faced. The core curriculum consisted of a unit on the value and significance of photographs (participants were asked to articulate why their collections had value); a unit on handling prints and negatives (in which participants worked with an encyclopedic teaching collection, containing examples of numerous photographic processes, although it lacked examples drawn from African collections); a unit on the identification of prints and on basic photochemical processes; a unit on photographic negatives, and on identification of silver prints; a unit on the main risks for twentieth-century photographs, taught by Lavédrine (which included discussion of image deterioration examples — immediately familiar to African participants and often closer to the norm than the majority of images in the teaching collection); a unit on storage materials (emphasizing DIY approaches to storage materials, produced from everyday items available in the local market); a unit on climate and assessment; and a unit on emergency planning.

The workshop was, by all measures, a huge success. It was truly unprecedented as an initiative, and for the majority of participants (including museum professionals), it was their first exposure to basic concepts and methods of photographic preservation (fig. 11.4, fig. 11.5). The entire workshop was underwritten by a general acknowledgment and collective affirmation that actual conservation methods and techniques favored by Western and Northern institutions are not always appropriate to African contexts. Yet the horizon of Western and Northern museum practice was never absent, leaving some aspects of our approach much too limited and even problematic. What would it take to sharpen our awareness of this horizon and, hopefully, begin to dismantle it? We took away several lessons:

Intra-African collaboration is essential. While the transfer of basic knowledge (for example, knowledge of photochemical processes, handling of prints and negatives) and organizational philosophies (for example, articulating value and significance, assessing risk) worked well in teaching and discussions between European/American and African partners, the most promising ideas for practical solutions arose from intra-African conversations. While this is not surprising, it is vital to consider ways to create this space, and to continue to refine the protocols for international collaborations, so as to maximize this potential. For example, in the formal teaching sessions led by photograph conservators informed by Western and Northern photography histories, institutional infrastructures, and ideas about storage conditions, it was easy to become preoccupied with the unattainability of key benchmarks — particularly, vis-à-vis storage conditions — and this could feel demoralizing. The most powerful rejoinder to this demoralized feeling came through the recognition of microregional or subregional affinities between African participants and conversations about local approaches to shared solutions. Specifically:

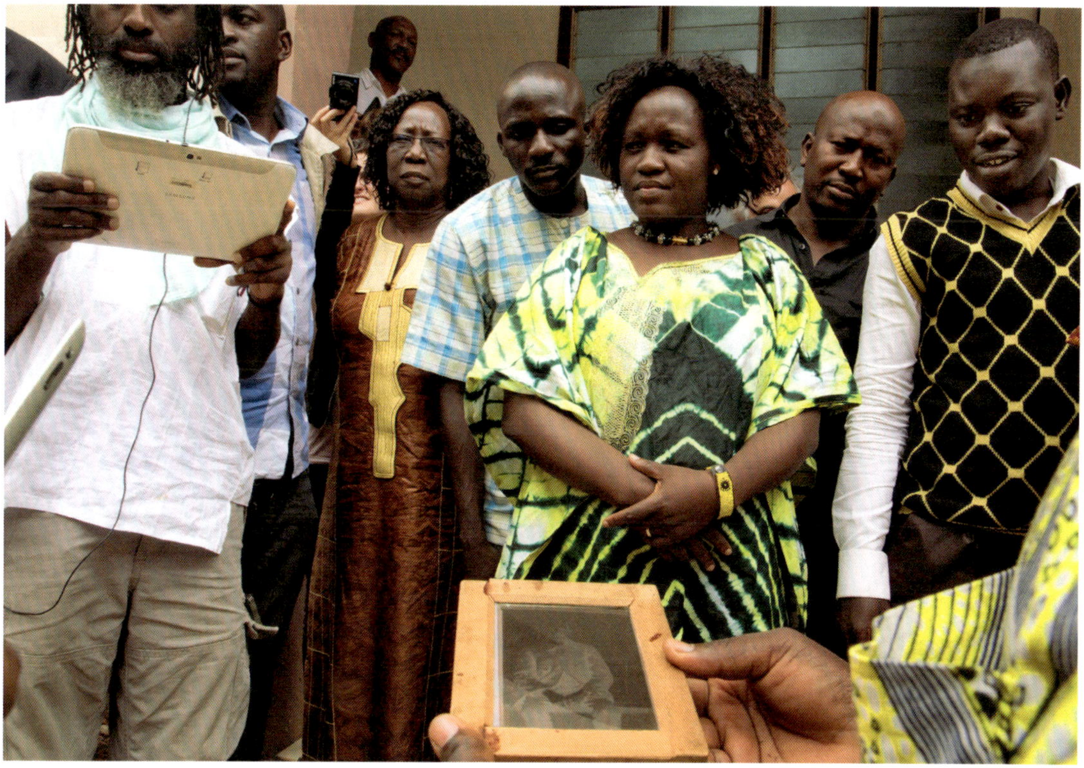

Fig. 11.4. Participants watching a demonstration of the salted-paper print process during the 3PA: West African Image Lab workshop in Porto-Novo, Benin, in April 2014. Bertrand Lavedrine, director of the Centre de Recherche sur la Conservation des Collections (and workshop instructor), led the demonstration

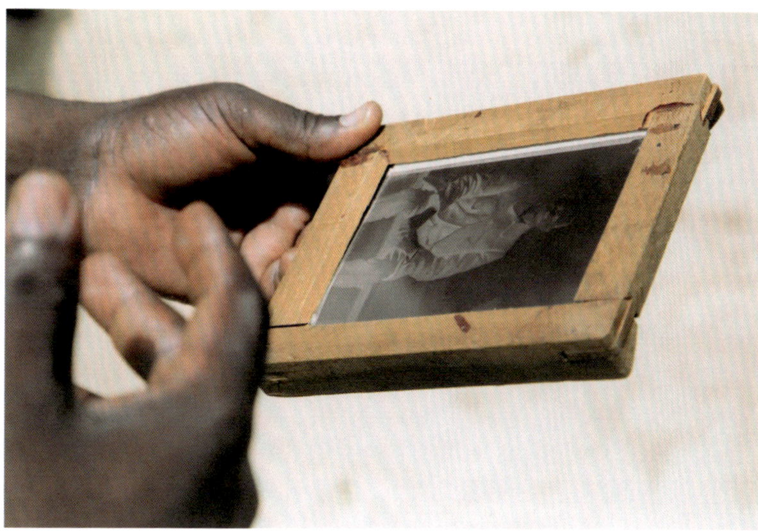

Fig. 11.5. Beninese photographer (and workshop participant) Léonce Agbodjélou holding the salted-paper print during the 3PA: West African Image Lab workshop in Porto-Novo, Benin, in April 2014

Collaboration between institutional and community-based collections is particularly important. Among the most exciting forms of collaboration we saw emerge was that between institutional collection keepers and those looking after community-based collections, many of whom, even if they lived in the same city, had never met before. Particularly promising were conversations that emerged between *photographers* looking after family- or community-based collections and cultural heritage professionals working in museums or archives. While collection keepers based in museums and archives were in a position to invite the photographers to deposit copies of materials from their collections (often those of a family member or a photographer-elder), the photographers were in a position to share technical knowledge of photographic processes that the cultural heritage professionals generally lacked.[15] In West Africa, where many studio photographers also worked for the government or for individual politicians, such collaborations have the added advantage, often, of rejoining "two halves" of a photographer's archive and of facilitating collaborative research and knowledge production (identifications, etc.).

Collaboration between Francophone/Anglophone collection keepers across colonial linguistic borders is also particularly important. Another untapped potential was that of collaborations between Francophone and Anglophone workshop participants, most of whom were neighbors. Vitally in this regard, we ran the workshop in both French and English, with simultaneous interpretation (fig. 11.6). This was the most expensive line item of the workshop budget, and we faced considerable pressure to eliminate this cost by doing two separate events (one in French and one in English). Yet working across these linguistic barriers, which were created by colonialism, is absolutely essential to doing decolonial work. The case must constantly be made to Western funders to support this type of bilingual and multilingual event, complete with costly simultaneous interpretation; funders must be educated as to the significance of these linguistic fractures and the value of bridging them.

In a promising example of what can happen or be imagined through cross-border conversations, participants from Benin and Nigeria (which share a border but are divided by language) hatched an idea for the development of solar-powered refrigeration technologies for negatives. Rolling blackouts and intermittent electricity supply are daily occurrences in both countries, meaning HVAC systems used in European and North American museums and archives to control temperature and humidity rarely work in the handful of African institutions that can afford them. The solar tech industry, however, is booming in West Africa. Benin boasts a growing solar-cell assembly sector, supported by German and Chinese investment; Nigeria has a booming culture of tech entrepreneurship. Why not explore solar-powered mobile refrigeration units for negative storage? Such units could be developed and manufactured locally, precisely in the context of a

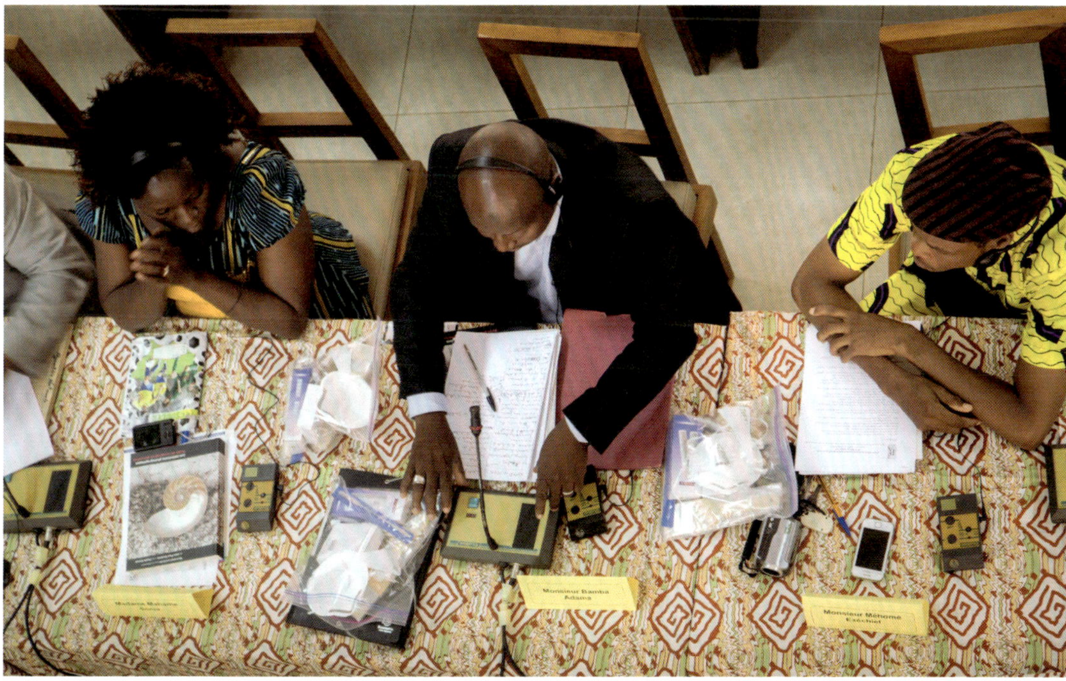

Fig. 11.6. Workshop participants Sonia Mahamé, Adama Bamba, and Ézéchiel Méhomè during the the 3PA: West African Image Lab workshop in Porto-Novo, Benin, in April 2014

Beninese-Nigerian collaboration, and they would be a cheap and viable alternative to centralized systems powered by a notoriously unreliable grid. It is difficult to imagine photograph conservators at institutions in Paris or Amsterdam or New York initiating this conversation, as they live on more reliable grids. Yet one can imagine that those in Brazil, El Salvador, Barbados, or Mauritius might be very interested in joining this conversation. The geography is postcolonial, but the approach is rigorously decolonial, insofar as it frames ways of working that are practically unimaginable from the vantage point of Western and Northern institutions and that have the potential to undo the hegemony of those institutions.

Solutions designed to address challenges specific to African collections have the power to transform the field. This was already evident in the example of the solar-powered mobile refrigeration unit. It became even more so in discussions of using traditional earthen architecture—rather than colonial-era buildings or those of more recent vintage—for storage facilities. Colonial-era architecture is the norm for many storage facilities in West Africa, yet such architecture has often failed miserably in terms of facilitating both temperature control and ventilation adequate to photographic storage. These buildings may have walls of stone, but it is erroneous to assume they have doors and windows that can be sealed to the elements or to the outside world, and it is not possible to create in them storage conditions equivalent to those in European and North American institutions.

Here, we learned an important lesson from our colleagues in the Beninese National Archives, in Porto-Novo. After years of purchasing expensive air conditioning units that broke all too quickly, that were difficult to maintain, or that (due to rolling blackouts) rarely worked, they found the best way to improve storage conditions in their central facility was to stop using air conditioning and transition to a natural ventilation system, using louvered windows. In the mornings, when the temperature increases, they leave the windows closed to retain the cool night air. In the afternoon, when the temperature decreases, they open the windows (located on opposite sides of their building) for several hours, allowing the wind to blow through.[16] This method turns out to be much more effective for both temperature and humidity control. Not only is it more cost effective than buying air conditioners, but it is more sustainable and environmentally friendly from the standpoint of energy consumption, and it has all but eradicated mold and mildew growth.

This approach, too, is rigorously decolonial. For it illuminates, and effectively eliminates, the colonial errors undergirding approaches to conservation and preservation that are blind to colonial histories. It also emulates many features already present in traditional earthen architecture (Africa's "palaces of earth"), marking a return to Indigenous architectural knowledge. During the Conservation | Making | Art | History conference, questions were posed about the prospects for bringing Indigenous knowledge and practices into the conversation about conservation. All too often, these questions were framed as if Indigenous actors were being brought into a static colonial context, the museum or archive conceived as a colonial institution: a fortress-like structure with stone walls, doors, windows, temperature and humidity control, vaults, and lab-trained personnel. Here, the return of the Indigenous is at once more subtle and more radical, insofar as it puts this structure into question, illuminating its epistemological and political as well as its practical limitations and throwing it wide open.[17] These are only some of the lessons we might draw from contemporary approaches to photographic collections in West Africa, lessons I sincerely hope we can allow into our evolving thinking about conservation and preservation in this critical moment.

NOTES

Epigraph: Simon Njami, *C'était Senghor* (Paris: Fayard, 2006), 119.

1. Speaking specifically of changing approaches to conservation and preservation in photographic collections, a number of successful initiatives, such as those organized by the Middle East Photograph Preservation Institute, the Arab Image Foundation, or the Alkazi Foundation, attest to greater awareness of local and regional differences in conservation practices and resources.

2. I am not alone in urging us to pay attention to the epistemological and political dimensions of photographic decay in Africa. Liam Buckley has written magisterially about this question, in Liam Buckley, "Objects of Love and Decay: Colonial Photographs in a Postcolonial Archive," *Cultural Anthropology* 20, no. 2 (2005): 249–70. Achille Mbembe, although he does not write explicitly about photographs, addresses this question from a political-theoretical vantage point in a well-known essay: Achille Mbembe, "The Power of the Archive and Its Limits," in *Refiguring the Archive*, ed. Carolyn Hamilton et al. (Dordrecht, Netherlands: Kluwer Academic, 2002), 19–26.

3. Hans van der Hoeven and Joan van Albada report a difference in the stability of paper, between the tropics and temperate zones, of a factor of ten: "In tropical climates, as has been established, it may take records, even if of long-lasting paper, only 100 to 200 years to become dust. Before that, they cross the no-use line (identical to a no-research line) and, shortly after, the no-touch line (identical to no-reformatting line or past-lamination line). In moderate climate zones, the no-research line may be crossed after 1,000 years and the no-reformatting line after 1,500 years. . . . The no-research line of unstable paper will be crossed in the tropics within 100 years, in more favorable climates within 400 years." Hans van der Hoeven and Joan van Albada, *Memory of the World: Lost Memory: Libraries and Archives Destroyed in the Twentieth Century* (Paris: UNESCO, 1996), 21.

4. A spate of recent research and activism reminds us that museums have often been and remain colonial institutions not only in colonized space but also in the capital cities of Europe. See, for example, Dan Hicks's excellent recent volume on the British Museum as an instrument of colonial violence: Dan Hicks, *The Brutish Museums: The Benin Bronzes, Colonial Violence, and Cultural Restitution* (London: Pluto, 2020). For an earlier and trailblazing analysis of how the collecting and display of African art in particular has been inextricable from colonial conquest in Europe, see Sally Price, *Primitive Art in Civilized Places* (Chicago: University of Chicago Press, 1989); as well as Sally Price, *Paris Primitive: Jacques Chirac's Museum on the Quai Branly* (Chicago: University of Chicago, 2007). See also, for more on the role played by the collecting and display of African art in the construction of French identity in both the colonial and postcolonial periods, Joëlle Busca, *L'art contemporain africain: Du colonialisme au postcolonialisme* (Paris: L'Harmattan, 2000). See also the numerous actions taking place in New York City under the umbrella of Decolonize this Place and Strike MoMA, which have been careful to acknowledge the status of the present-day United States as colonized space.

5. Van der Hoeven and Van Albada, 20–21. On what she calls the "remaking" of photographs through rephotography and other techniques, see Erin Haney, *Photography and Africa* (London: Reaktion, 2010), 80–82.

6. A guide to the preservation of photographic material published by the British Library's Preservation Advisory Centre recommends that photographic materials not be stored at temperatures above 25°C (77°F) and not above a relative humidity (RH) of 60%. Yet in Saint-Louis, Senegal, one of the four cities on which I have concentrated in my research, the average annual temperature is 31–32°C (88–90°F), and the average RH is 65%. (Saint-Louis is located in the north of Senegal and is therefore relatively arid. The average RH for Senegal is 76%.) The capacity for temperature and humidity control is limited in Senegal, even in comparatively well-resourced institutions and facilities, meaning that it is generally not possible to attain the conditions recommended by the British Library. Susie Clark, "Preservation of Photographic Material Guide" (British Library, 1999; rev. ed. 2021), http://www.bl.uk/conservation/guides.

7. Erin Haney, "Film, Charcoal, Time: Contemporaneities in Gold Coast Photographs," *History of Photography* 34, no. 2 (May 2010): 119.

8. I have written at greater length about these questions in Jennifer Bajorek, *Unfixed: Photography and Decolonial Imagination in West Africa* (Durham, NC: Duke University Press, 2020), 1–31.

9. Orality is, of course, also an important factor to consider in many other parts of the world and not only in Africa.

10. Pearls were harvested off the coast of Venezuela by enslaved African divers.

11. That is, the "original" vintage prints dated from this period, even if the prints to which I had access were reproductions produced, precisely, through serial rephotography.

12. See, among other publications, Jennifer Bajorek, "Decolonizing the Archive: The View from West Africa," *Aperture* 210 (Spring 2013): 66–69; Jennifer Bajorek and Erin Haney, "Vital Signs: 21st-Century Institutions for Photography in Africa," in *The African*

Photographic Archive: Research and Curatorial Strategies, ed. Christopher Morton and Darren Newbury (London: Bloomsbury, 2015), 215–29; and, again, Bajorek, *Unfixed*.

13. Additional teaching, technical expertise, and support were provided by Peter Mustardo, a photograph conservator working privately (and who generously supported the workshop), the late Henrike Grohs (director of the Goethe Institut-Abidjan, Côte d'Ivoire), and Marie Lavandier (former director of the Centre de Recherche et de Restauration des Musées de France, Paris). I gratefully wish to acknowledge their collective support.

14. In addition to their significant commitments in the Middle East, Norris, Kennedy, and Lavédrine have all taught and worked with conservation professionals in several other regions of interest, including Southeast Asia (Vietnam), Latin America (Brazil), and South Africa.

15. This is particularly important to note, given that the inclusion of community-based collections and collection keepers in our workshop was something that several of the Western funders and international partners we approached actively objected to—whether on the basis of arguments about "peer institutions" or on other grounds. In this sense, Western funders (albeit unconsciously) were invested in policing the very distinction between "making" and "conservation" that this conference and volume are seeking to contest.

16. Bertrand Lavédrine, one of our distinguished team of photograph conservators, noted while we were in Porto-Novo, in 2014, that similar revelations with regard to the benefits of natural ventilation have recently reoriented major cultural heritage initiatives in Vietnam.

17. Other promising examples of more radical or more rigorously decolonial approaches that we saw in Porto-Novo in 2014 included experiments being conducted at the École du Patrimoine Africain, then under the direction of Baba Keïta, focused on the production of natural insecticides, derived from cassava or manioc root, which could be used to preserve documents.

NATION
FORMING

CHAPTER 12

CAN CONSERVATION BE DECENTERED?

Noémie Étienne

Today, museums are under heightened scrutiny in light of increasing requests for objects to be returned to their country or community of origin, along with growing questions about whether and how to display certain collections. Conservation practices are also changing and now include multiple experts and stakeholders when determining the most appropriate methods to preserve material culture. In this spirit, several research projects about the conservation of art and material culture have been carried out since the 1990s.[1] When the National Museum of the American Indian (New York City and Washington, DC) opened on the National Mall in Washington and broke ground for its storage facilities in Maryland, for instance, the museum sent questionnaires to members of various nations represented in the collection inquiring about the way items should be conserved and stored in the new institution. In response, Edmund J. Ladd, author, researcher, and member of the A:shiwi (Zuni) Nation, for example, recommended that his community be allowed to provide food for certain objects, such as masks: "Zuni masks must be fed once or twice a year by their people, male and female; to let the museum's staff do this would be to neglect our responsibility and would not do any good."[2]

From the museum conservators' point of view, the influx of perishable goods into the storage facilities raised the risk of attracting insects. This would be detrimental to the physical stability of the objects, which was until recently the focus of most practitioners trained in a Western tradition of conservation. For many Indigenous cultures, however, the proper idea of care pivots around use and impermanence. The rhetoric pitting a purportedly universal ideal of conservation (a term in itself potentially homogenizing, and a practice based, broadly speaking, on European philosophical and technical standards) against usage practices that pose a danger to the stability of artifacts took shape during the French Revolution, and it is still employed today. As I will show, this is often advanced as an argument against the restitution of objects to the originating cultures, suggesting that artworks could only be well preserved in the Western museum.

Beginning with the writings of Austrian art historian Alois Riegl, there has also been an approach that attends to the handling and preservation of objects depending on context. In 1903, Riegl analyzed the conservation of monuments, underscoring the existence of "values" attributed to an object or building. For instance, religious believers attribute a utilitarian value to their place of worship (it is for regular use in their eyes), which determines the kind of renovations they would like to see carried out there.[3] The utilitarian value, however, may stand in contrast to other values—artistic value, for instance. Many conservation theorists, such as Miriam Clavir,[4] Salvador Muñoz-Viñas,[5] and Erica Avrami,[6] have embraced and developed Riegl's recognition of these contrasting values, employing the terms "function," "meaning," and "significance" in their approaches. The theory of values is notably mobilized to explain controversies in the realm of conservation that are rooted in the contrasting ideals that the different groups (for instance, Indigenous people versus Western conservators) bring to the table.

Nevertheless, various scholars in the field of critical heritage studies have stressed the reductive, even simplistic character of an overly strict dichotomy between Western and non-Western approaches to cultural legacy, as it is sometimes implied in the charters of large international organizations like the Nara Document (1994).[7] Dividing lines are certainly cultural, but also political and contextual, as demonstrated by Kavita Singh in this volume. That is, they vary according to historical periods, individuals, and milieus (secular, religious, etc.). In this essay, I use the term conservation to describe practices that both preserve and afford access to objects. The broader questions I will ask are the following: Is conservation sometimes an alibi for museums to preserve the status quo and prevent objects from circulating? And, more importantly, can we decenter conservation through a study of its multiple histories and related theories? Indeed, the tendency to analyze conservation as a Western science with specific values is already blinding us to other, alternate approaches to conservation (or, one could also say, ways of caring), that might include restitution or even loss. In knowing them even better, and integrating them into routine practices, museums are currently transitioning from a logic of keeping to an ethic of caring.

WAYS OF CARING

In 1928, a funeral totem pole (fig. 12.1) commissioned in 1872 by Chief G'psgolox (Paddy McDonald) was cut up in the village of Misk'usa in the northwest of what is today British Columbia. The piece was first cut off at its base, then sawed into sections and transported to the Museum of Ethnography in Stockholm; the inhabitants of the site were not present for its removal.[8] Six months after it arrived, the totem

Fig. 12.1. Funeral totem pole commissioned in 1872 by Chief G'psgolox in Misk'usa, British Columbia, 1928. Museum of Ethnography, Stockholm, 0279.0002

Fig. 12.2. Derek Wilson, Henry Robertson, Barry Wilson, and Patricia Robertson with their copy of the totem pole at the Museum of Ethnography in Stockholm, September 2000. Museum of Ethnography, Stockholm, 1046.0114

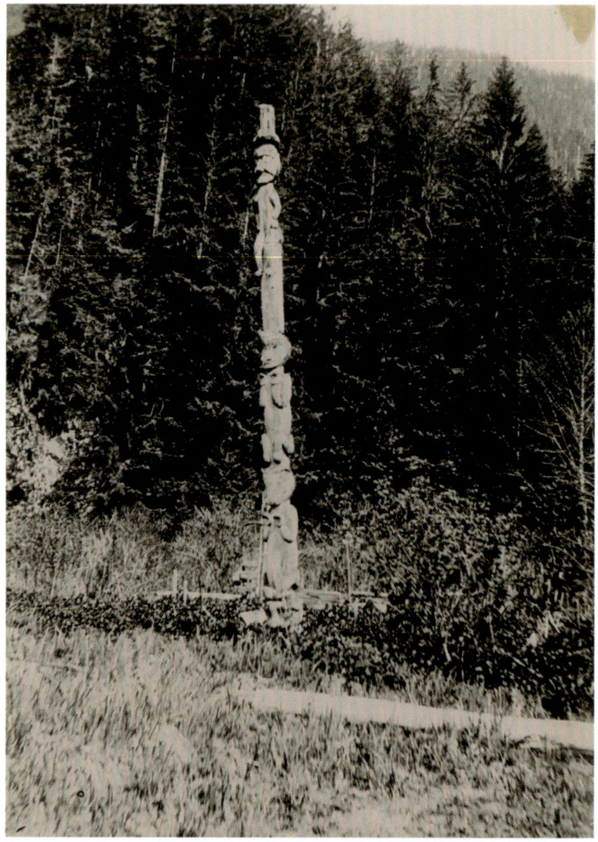

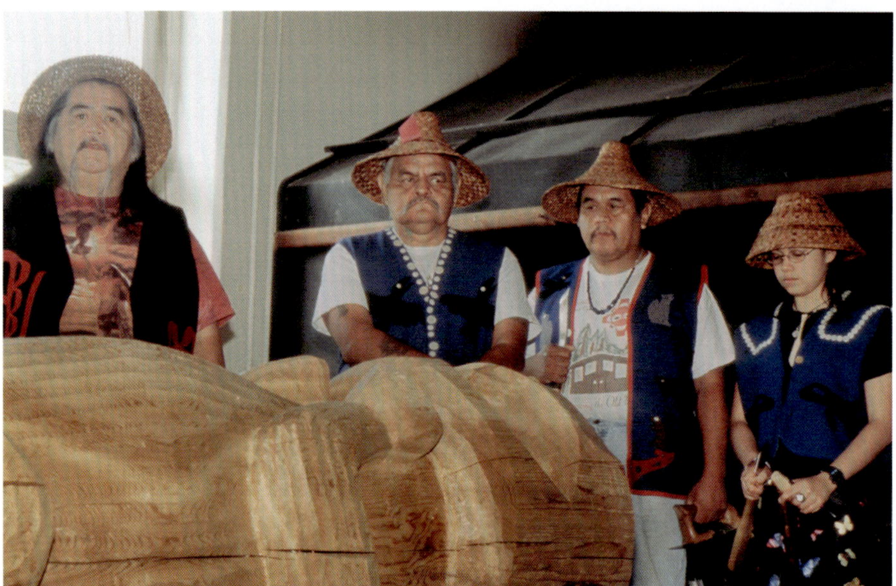

pole was placed in the museum's storage area before being cleaned and soaked in insecticide. Conservators applied varnish to unify the sculpture and lend it a well-aged look. The museum finally put the totem pole on display in 1980. The Haisla, a First Nation that today comprises the Kitamaat (Haisla) and the Kitlope (Henaaksiala),[9] made their initial request that the totem pole be returned in 1991. They sent four delegates, Gerald Amos, John Pritchard, Louisa Smith, and David Peerla, to conduct negotiations. Par Kaks, the director of the Museum of Ethnography from 1991 to 2002, was in favor of restitution. However, for legal reasons, the Swedish government wanted the return of the piece to be considered a gift, not a restitution. In 1992, the Haisla proposed carving a replica of the piece for the Swedish museum. In the early 2000s, the Henaaksiala sculptors Henry Robertson, Patricia Robertson, Barry Wilson, and Derek Wilson produced two replicas (fig. 12.2). One replica was transported to Stockholm and the other raised on the former location of the funeral monument. The ethnography museum issued demands concerning the conditions for conserving the original totem pole, requiring that it be kept in a building providing "climate-controlled facilities" upon its return. The steep cost of building and opening such a place delayed the restitution process considerably. Finally, financing arranged through private foundations, institutional support, and fundraising campaigns allowed the Haisla to raise the necessary funds.[10] In 2006, the original totem was repatriated and installed in a shopping center not far from the village. In 2012, however, despite the agreement reached with Sweden, the descendants of Chief G'psgolox decided to have the totem transferred to the cemetery (burning site) of the former village of Kemano (Henaaksiala) so that the work could recover its original funerary function and eventually disintegrate.[11]

In a film from 2004, the director of the Stockholm museum justifies his request, asserting that the totem pole belonged to a world cultural heritage that ought to be conserved: "I wanted to give it back. . . . The only condition we had . . . having kept the pole for so many years and tried to make it survive . . . was that together we could look upon the pole as the property of mankind. I would be very unhappy if [they] put the pole back according to [their] traditions because it would be destroyed."[12] This case study makes clear the polarity between a museum professional dedicated to physical preservation and a community focused on material life cycles and an embrace of the ephemeral.

Yet it is also simplistic to assume that the Haisla community is uninterested in conservation practices. Gerald Amos (Haisla) stressed the violence done to the totem pole when kept in a gallery for display, where it was held upright with wires and a metal yoke.[13] In a press release published by the Haisla Nation when the totem pole returned in 2006, concern for the harm done to the object's material integrity by its violent seizure is clear.[14] The press release states that the pole was "exposed to wind and weather for approximately six months" (fig. 12.3) and also "placed

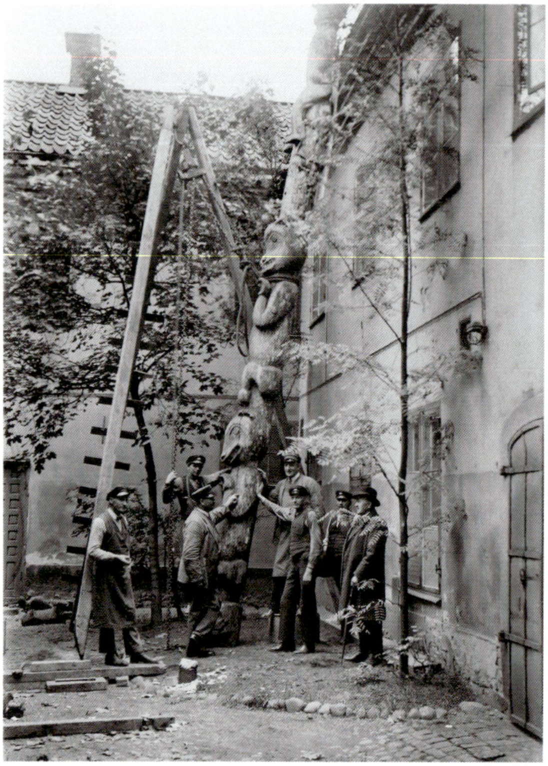

Fig. 12.3. The relocated totem pole standing outside the Museum of Ethnography, c. 1929. Museum of Ethnography, Stockholm, 1046.0096

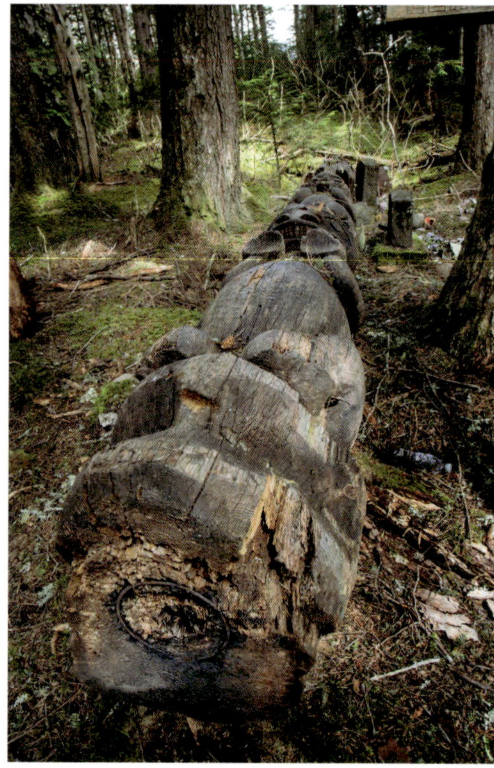

Fig. 12.4. The totem pole in 2014, after it was returned to the descendants of Chief G'psgolox by the Museum of Ethnography in 2006 and transferred, in 2012, to a cemetery in Kimano, Kitlope Valley. Museum of Ethnography, Stockholm, 0962.0019

horizontally in an unheated storeroom for more than 40 years." These facts suggest that the museum's practices around 1930 ran counter to the standards of conservation the institution advocates and seeks to impose today.

In turn, the press release quotes the "Indian Agent" Iver Fougner, who wanted to purchase the totem pole for the Swedish consul Olof Hanson in 1927 in order to preserve it against its adverse installation conditions within the reservation: "The reserve is uninhabited and very isolated. Chances are that the pole, if not removed, after some time will fall down and be destroyed."[15] The dispossession is justified by the idea of safeguarding the monument. The museum is presented as the savior of an object that would be condemned to decay if allowed to remain in place. For those who carved the totem pole, however, it *ought* to disintegrate to fulfil its monumental and memorial function.

These debates reflect different understandings of heritage and conservation. For an A:shiwi intellectual like Edmund Ladd, quoted in the introduction, the standards of classification and display upheld in museums prevent one from giving objects the care they need to survive. Ladd, for instance, advises against using plastic containers because they do not allow the materials to breathe: "It is not the fact that the material actually breathes, but the fact that the spiritual content of it, the condition of it, has to breathe through some means of its own not to be hampered by plastic or being constrained by having it in a container."[16] The norms of preventative conservation and storage imposed by the museum therefore threaten the survival of objects, which have to eat and take in air to live. Other Indigenous stakeholders, however, take different positions. In a report by the National Museum of the American Indian, John Flint of Nohwike' Bágowa (White Mountain Apache Cultural Center and Museum, Whiteriver, Arizona), for example, states that for him, museum norms pose no problem: "Standard museological treatment acceptable."[17]

These distinct approaches to heritage and conservation exist not only in cultural but also in historical and political contexts. The press release published by the Haisla Nation upon the return of the totem pole clearly shows how this conservation argument may be, at least for a time, reappropriated and turned against the European museum, whose practices from the past are recalled several times. Initially, in the early 2000s, the Haisla Nation accepted the museum's conditions for the totem pole's return. The chair of the Haisla totem pole repatriation committee Gerald Amos declared, "Our children will be able to touch something their ancestors carved and that is very important for the future of the Haisla people."[18] Yet the totem pole was nonetheless brought back to the Kemano funerary site several years after it was returned to British Columbia, to fulfill its original function (fig. 12.4). Although the original material object is currently decaying—as it was made to do—the craftmanship and traditional techniques that produced it are still alive and well, as demonstrated by the carving of the two replica totem poles. These Haisla and A:shiwi examples demonstrate the variety of arguments swirling around the conservation of cultural goods: each group involved in a given debate can defend a conservation project while accusing the other of damaging the object. A museum can also be suspected of mistreating its collections when an alternative understanding of conservation is presented that runs counter to predominantly Western museological standards, which some deem harmful. In the second part of this essay, I would like to offer a historical perspective and show how these arguments have been framed since the early nineteenth century in the context of Napoleonic imperialism and the rise of nationalisms in Europe.

ART SAVED BY THE MUSEUM?

The links between conservation, museums, despoliation, and restitution go back centuries. Over two hundred years ago, after the French Revolution and during the age of Napoleon, French emissaries in newly conquered European countries sent hundreds of works of art, books, natural history specimens, even technical and scientific instruments to France. The rhetoric accompanying these forced changes of address was that of a repatriation.[19] Works of the human spirit, of genius and ingenuity, were simply being returned to the homeland to which they naturally—if not geographically—belonged. *La France* and, in particular, Paris, the mother that had given birth to freedom, was the only city worthy of gathering in her arms the arts signifying and displaying the genius of civilization. The assembled works were restored and installed in a new museum that opened in 1793, the forebear of today's Musée du Louvre. Different actors, however, took a stand on these transfers and restorations (the latter word in keeping with the terminology of the age).

In 1797, the German writer Friedrich Johan Lorenz Meyer initially came out against this new state of affairs. He developed an argument that hinged on the specificity of the works, linked, as they were, to their original function as religious objects created for specific locations.[20] However, five years later, Meyer advanced, in a second publication, a completely different analysis, now centered on a work of major art historical importance, Raphael's *Transfiguration* (1516–20, Vatican Museums). According to Meyer, this work of art was wonderfully installed in the new museum and bathed in an ideal light that set it off in all its beauty, unlike the dark and sooty grime in which the painting had been held previously, in the Roman church of San Pietro in Montorio.[21] A comparative analysis of these two arguments formulated by one writer just a few years apart reveals two modes of perception reflecting two distinct systems of value attributed to works of art. However, such values, meanings, or functions are not frozen in time but are liable to change.[22] Around 1800, *The Transfiguration* was put on display in the restorer's studio (prefiguring the great contemporary mises-en-scène of the work carried out by conservators in publicly visible studios). In such spaces, opinions are formed and, importantly, transformed, in front of the artwork and supported by various display mechanisms—the frame, the light, and so on (fig. 12.5). Thus, judgments and expectations are not necessarily preconceived and grounded in fixed cultural traditions; they also depend on the political context (particularly in the case of spoliation) or the ways artworks are displayed.

After the fall of Napoleon and the First Empire, followed by the Treaty of Vienna, *The Transfiguration* returned to Italy. Significantly, the painting was not brought back to the church where it had originally been on view. Like so many pillaged works that had been displayed in France, Raphael's picture was stored in the Vatican and formed the core collection of what would become the Pinacoteca Vaticana. Another work by Raphael, *The Crowning of the Virgin* (1502–4, Vatican Museums), was likewise kept in Rome after its return from France. Originally, the painting belonged to the Oddi Chapel in the Church of San Francesco al Prato in Perugia. It was displayed in Paris next to *The Transfiguration* and had been exhibited half-cleaned in the

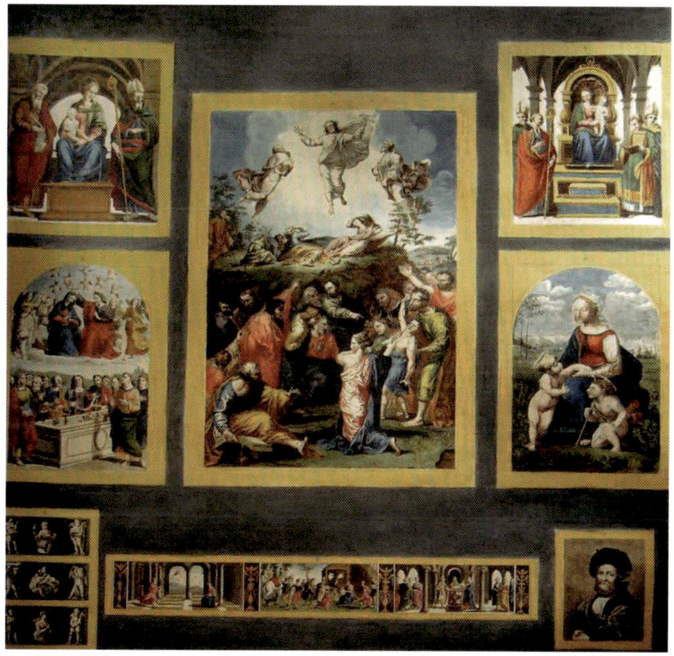

Fig. 12.5. View of the Musée du Louvre, enhanced with watercolor, in Julius Griffiths, *Vue de la galerie du Louvre*, with engravings by Maria Cosway (Paris, 1802), unnumbered plate

Louvre—proof, in the eyes of the French, of the poor conditions in which the paintings had been kept in their Italian churches. (The official report concerning the unpacking of the crates suggests, however, that the work was damaged while in transit to Paris.) The former owners penned many letters to the Pope in an attempt to recover the piece. In particular, they advanced the argument of the picture's prior restoration. They even appended a note by the restorer, one Francesco Romero, to evidence their efforts to care for the work.[23] The owners underscored the good conditions in which the object was kept, contrary to what the French museum was asserting. The care taken to conserve the painting thus legitimized their ownership of the object. Conservation and ownership function mutually and reinforce each other. That is, ownership of the artwork implies its conservation, while conservation guarantees its ownership.

International (in particular German, Italian, Flemish) reactions to the planned French restorations were negative at first, but became positive once the work was carried out around 1800, and again turned negative following Napoleon's downfall. With the 1815 Treaty of Vienna spelling the end of the old order, the practice of transferring works of art from their original (often wooden) support to canvas, for instance, crystalized differing opinions. During the transfer process, the original wooden support of a painting was entirely removed (generally physically deconstructed from the back). Then, the remaining paint layer was glued onto a new canvas. Thus, the painting became flat, and the weave of the canvas appeared under the paint layer. For Parisian restorers, however, this transfer immortalized the painting, and the operation was carried out overwhelmingly in Paris, notably on works by Raphael.

The practice of transfer both physically relocated the works to a new support and symbolically placed them in another, different history with a brand-new provenance. The restoration thus re-localized the objects. It also transformed church altarpieces into a different kind of object, transfiguring heavy wooden panels created for sacred architectural spaces into paintings for the museum: lighter, easier to transport, and reduced to an image—nothing but the actual paint layer. In addition, the restored works were an integral part of the canon of art history, a discipline that was only then taking shape. Indeed, restorations focused on the works that were deemed the most important, playing a role in constructing the canon. Rid of its deposits of soot left by the smoke of church lamps and candlelight, the painting became an object worthy of the museum as well as a showpiece in art history.

The practice of transferring works of art from one support to another sparked scathing criticism when the paintings were returned to their home countries in 1815. While several of Raphael's Spanish panels were awaiting transport, French restorers proposed changing their support. They indicated they were both guaranteeing the works' conservation and making transportation to Spain easier. The paintings' owners, however, were of quite a different opinion. The Roman restorer Pietro Palmaroli, called as an expert witness in the ensuing negotiations, wrote: "They think they are rendering the works of such great masters eternal through this operation but I think the opposite [is true]."[24] For Palmaroli, along with many others, removing the original support was tantamount to destroying the painting.

The different actors in this post-Waterloo debate over conservation approaches had incompatible, even antagonistic positions in terms of how best to care for the objects in question. To the cultural dividing lines between these Italian, Spanish, French, and German figures we can add other, contextual borders connected with the milieus (religious, secular, etc.) that gave rise to the actors in these clashes. We should also not underestimate the political context and the rise of nationalisms in Europe. When the crates were broken open as artworks were returned to their country of provenance following the end of the First Empire, the paintings were inspected in detail. To criticize the restorations carried out in France was a way to deconstruct the French logic that had justified the pillaging of paintings and sequestering them in the museum space under the pretense of conserving them.

In the third part of this text, I discuss the continued advocacy for the museum in its European form as a model in terms of how objects are conserved. In turn, the effect of this standard complicates the procedures for returning works of art, which are subject to specific and occasionally unsuitable clauses. Indeed, the standard reflects a Eurocentric understanding of conservation that today some are calling into question.

WHAT DOES CONSERVATION MEAN?

Conservation evolved throughout the twentieth century. Today, new developments are becoming standard, such as using less-toxic products and adopting practices that are more environmentally friendly.[25] Moreover, since the Burra Charter (adopted for the first time in 1979 by the International Council on Monuments and Sites–Australia, and revised since), consulting with source communities (the people who produced the object or objects to be conserved, or their descendants) is recommended, although this is not always carried out in practice. At the same time, many conservators articulate the negative, harmful consequences of a universalist understanding of conservation, which can impose norms the communities that originally generated the objects cannot or do not wish to respect.[26] Consequently, new ways of working have taken shape, especially in the United States and Canada, but also in Switzerland, Belgium, and Germany.[27]

Yet decolonial conservation projects raise several questions in terms of their methods and finality.[28] The imperative to conserve, as it is defined and determined in European and North American museums, complicates the circulation and return of objects. Since the 1980s, several instances of restitutions, long-term loans, and donations of works have taken place in Switzerland, a country whose legal framework does not preclude deaccessioning collections. European museums also often establish a framework according to which objects can be returned in controversial cases involving colonial despoliation as well as contested acquisitions involving the art market or even donations.

In 1985 in Geneva, Jean-Paul Barbier-Mueller purchased a Makonde mask from René Garcia, a Parisian art dealer who had acquired it the previous year under conditions that remain uncertain (fig. 12.6).[29] That same year, according to information from the Centre universitaire du droit de l'art in Geneva, the National Museum of Dar es Salaam in Tanzania reported to the International Council on Museums (ICOM) and Interpol the theft of a very similar mask, along with sixteen other objects.[30] In 1990, at the instigation of the Italian professor Enrico Castelli, the Musée Barbier-Mueller contacted ICOM to inform the organization that the museum had in its possession an object that might have belonged to the Dar es Salaam museum. In 1997, ICOM published the piece in an index of objects pillaged from Africa. According to Laurence Mattet, the director of the Musée Barbier-Mueller, the Dar es Salaam museum was late to report the burglary and failed to prove that the mask was the same object. Nevertheless, the director of the National Museum and House of Culture of Tanzania Achiles Mujunangoma Bufure affirms that there has never been any doubt about

Fig. 12.6. Makonde mask, Tanzania

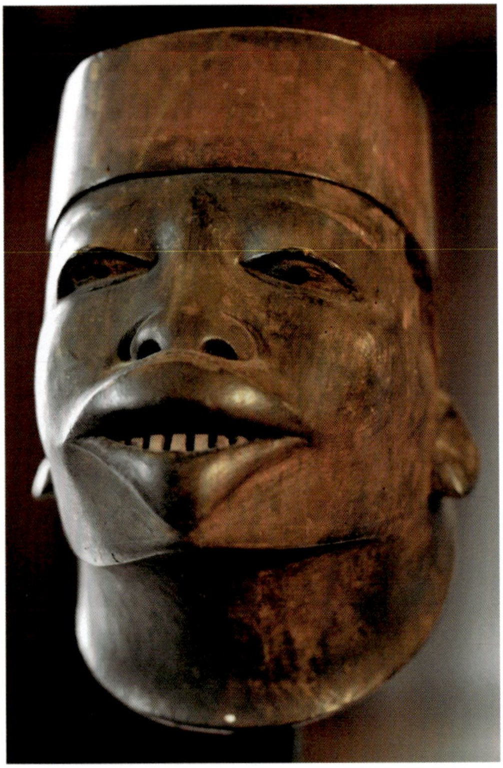

the identity of the mask. He added that a positive outcome for the case and the return of the mask would represent an important event for Tanzania and for the local communities.

In 2006, the United Republic of Tanzania referred the case to UNESCO in order to recover the object. The Musée Barbier-Mueller appealed to UNESCO in turn and brought suit against the republic. In 2010, the mask was donated—that is, not officially *returned*—by the Genevan museum to Tanzania on the condition that it would be put on display and properly guarded.[31] The Musée Barbier-Mueller requested that the mask be stored in a secure showcase during the day and a safe at night. In 2021, however, during a tour of the museum, members of the Swiss embassy noted that, contrary to the agreement reached by the two parties, the mask was not displayed but rather stored in a safe located in the museum's underground floors. Achiles Mujunangoma Bufure explained that the selection of objects on view depends on the subjects currently being highlighted by the museum, and that the mask would be shown when that made sense in terms of the chosen theme and the particular narrative the institution was presenting to the public. The director of the African museum also stressed that conservation and restoration of objects are a

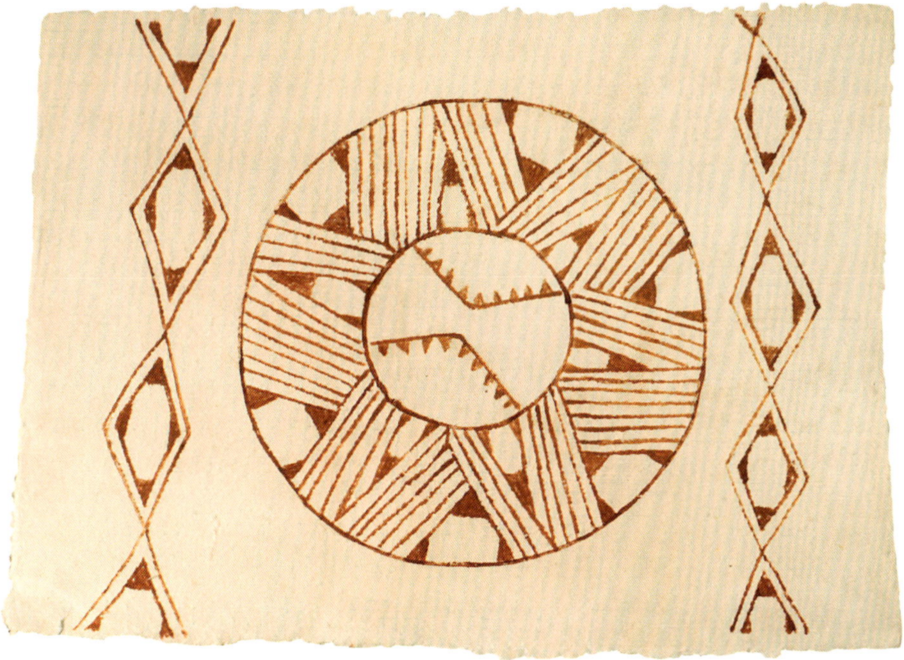

Fig. 12.7. Unrecorded maker(s), Wauja Nation (Brazil), ornament, Apairumá, n.d. Urucu on paper, 19⅝ × 27½ in. (50 × 70 cm). Museum der Kulturen Basel, Switzerland

priority for him. Thus, while first-world museums may determine the conditions under which an artifact is to be returned, those conditions are not necessarily followed nor respected once the property has been transferred.

In other instances, Indigenous communities have not been able to meet the conditions for conserving their own artifacts required by repatriation agreements, and the objects have instead been donated to the museums in the large capital cities of the country of origin (regardless of the rights granted to the Indigenous peoples by the governments of these same countries). Such is the case, for example, in a dispute involving Switzerland, Brazil, and the Wauja, an Indigenous people living in the Upper Xingu River in the Amazon rainforest. In 2000, the Museum der Kulturen in Basel was bequeathed a collection of Wauja cultural goods by the Brazilian ethnographer Vera Penteado Coelho (fig. 12.7).[32] The Basel museum accepted the donation in principle, but the objects were still in Brazil, where the anthropologist's mother lived. In 2001, the Museum der Kulturen received a letter of protest from a teacher and member of the Wauja community. The Museu de Arqueologia e Etnologia Universidade of São Paulo also contested the departure of the ethnographer's collection, which contains drawings, objects, and photographs.

In 2003, after all the parties had met and spoken, it was decided that the objects would remain in Brazil. To give the decision a legal framework, the Swiss museum proposed accepting Penteado Coelho's bequest and then, in turn, donating the objects to the São Paulo museum.

Quickly, however, the Wauja submitted a request for the photographic materials and the drawings in order to open their own museum in a former missionary's house in the village of Canarana at the entrance to the Xingu Indigenous Park.[33] A fax dating from October 2003 ordered the São Paulo museum to return the objects to the Wauja from the villages of Piyulaga and Aruak. (This message was later disavowed and attributed to an anthropologist involved in the region, although I am unable to confirm this information or the validity of the fax, nor is the conservator from the Weltmuseum in Basel who shared this information with me able to do so). In 2008, the agreement established between the two museums and one of Penteado Coelho's beneficiaries stipulated that if the Wauja, who were only present during the signing of the document as witnesses, introduced conservation conditions deemed adequate (namely, that they open their own museum), they could become owners of the objects once again. Nevertheless, the concrete forms this possible restitution might take are not defined in the agreement.

In this example, the museum remains the benchmark of preservation, upheld as the only possible and legitimate form of conservation. The Wauja were offered privileged access in the 2008 agreement, enabling them to see their cultural heritage in order to pass on their knowledge, but they were not deemed capable of preserving it directly. It seems that one of the challenges in the field of conservation and restoration stems from the possible exploitation of any collaborations with source communities, with agreements that ultimately serve the interests of the institution that holds the artifacts. As it is currently defined, conservation can become—often involuntarily and in spite of the care professionals give to objects in their charge—one of the obstacles that makes it difficult to take the wishes and desires of the producers of cultural artifacts into consideration. The rightsholders may thus find themselves involved in perpetuating a logic of conservation that is not self-evident.

CONCLUSION

Conservators are everyday more explicit and innovative in their own practices. In ethnographic institutions, for instance, but also in private studios, objects conservators are taking groundbreaking initiatives toward more inclusive and more ecological actions. They often consult with different stakeholders and limit as much as possible their use of toxic products. When possible, they also try to learn about earlier care traditions in order to better interpret the material history of the objects they are treating. In parallel, artists and activists are considering the multiple ways in which material fragility and politics intersect.[34]

Indeed, conservation today faces a triple challenge. First, it is important to critically reconsider the norms and standards that have taken shape in the museums of Europe and North America, to avoid imposing practices that claim universality yet are in reality culturally and historically determined. It is a question of taking into account the culturally specific expectations of the producers of goods without either reifying or simplifying them, but rather understanding the power relations in which those expectations exist. As I pointed out, dividing lines are not consistent but are clearly located in a given context. Values are not simply infused into an esthetic object or an artifact of a people's material culture; they are also mobilized pragmatically in discussion and conflicts.

The second challenge lies in the instrumentalization of conservation. The supremacy of the museum as the ideal place for conservation became the norm after the Treaty of Vienna in 1815. Yet there are other approaches to consider, including non-European forms of museums, such as the museums of the chiefdoms in Cameroon, where objects are preserved and used. Use is integral to their conservation practice, or, to put it differently, to their care.[35] As I stated in the introduction, a logic of caring for collections rather than keeping them is currently shifting the conception of what conservation is and shall be.

The third challenge is the need to develop models for alternative conservation practices. For example, within certain contexts, using objects can be a form of preservation. Taking these different approaches to conservation into account might make it possible to broaden and decenter conservation. This would entail not only sharing scientific methods among institutions and inviting source communities to tour the storage areas of museums with the idea of making room for their outlook, but also redefining what falls under the province of conservation itself, including a variety of practices ranging from nonprofessional repairs to uses that lead to the loss of the material object. Significant historical work lies ahead, and art history can help further this work. In this perspective, knowing the past better might help to forge the future.

Finally, the question of "care," imagined critically, is at the center of progressive museum practices.[36] Accumulating objects in museum storage rooms in Europe, the United States, and Canada and accruing the enormous energy costs involved in maintaining their material existence at any price no longer seem like realistic or desirable ambitions today, as Fernando Domínguez Rubio demonstrates in his work. The concepts of instability and impermanence must continue to transform both object conservation and art history. Acknowledging and welcoming the fragility of things and people might allow us to keep telling even more stories of humans and nonhumans: narratives of reshaping, destruction, and losses, but also of survival, repair, and resilience.

NOTES

1. See, for instance, "First People and Artifacts: Heritage and Conservation Issues," Queen's University at Kingston, Art Conservation Training Programs, Professional Papers, Ontario, May 9, 1992; Christina F. Kreps, *Liberating Culture: Cross-Cultural Perspectives on Museums, Curation, and Heritage Preservation* (London: Routledge, 2003); *Préserver le patrimoine autochtone: Approches techniques et traditionnelles, Actes de congrès, Ottawa, September 24–28, 2007* (Ottawa: Institut canadien de conservation, 2008); Alison Richmond and Alison Bracker, eds., *Principles, Dilemmas and Uncomfortable Truths* (London: Victoria & Albert Museum, 2009); and Frances Lennard and Patricia Ewer, eds., *Textile Conservation: Advances in Practice* (London: Routledge, 2010). Groundbreaking initiatives are also carried on by independent objects conservators or institutions such as the Bard Graduate Center in New York City.

2. Edmund J. Ladd (A:shiwi [Zuni]), in "The Way of the People: Native American Tribal Museum and Center Survey on Storage, Care and Access," National Museum of the American Indian, Washington, DC, unpublished report, Master Facilities Program: Suitland, vol. 2, April 23, 1993, VII. 442, consulted at the National Museum of the American Indian, New York.

3. Alois Riegl, *Der Moderne Denkmalkultus: Sein Wesen und Seine Entstehung* (Vienna: W. Braumüller, 1903).

4. Miriam Clavir, *Preserving What Is Valued: Museums, Conservation, and First Nations* (Vancouver: UBC Press, 2002).

5. Salvador Muñoz-Viñas, *Contemporary Theory of Conservation* (Amsterdam: Elsevier, 2005).

6. Erica Avrami, Susan MacDonald, Randall Mason, and David Myers, eds., *Values in Heritage Managment. Emerging Approaches and Research Directions* (Los Angeles: Getty Conservation Institute, 2019).

7. Kavita Singh, *Museums, Heritage, Culture: Into the Conflict Zone* (Amsterdam: Reinwardt Academy, 2015).

8. The Haisla Nation published a group of texts touching on this case, notably the speeches given during the return ceremony: http://www.turtleisland.org/culture/culture-haisla.htm. Additional information and a chronology of the events are available at the Na Na Kila Institute (a not-for-profit association that first began working to have the totem pole returned in 1993), in the village of Kitamaat. The spelling in the transcription of names varies among the different sites. See also Noémie Étienne, "Les statues mangent aussi: Repenser la conservation-restauration," in *Trouble dans les collections* 2, ed. Lotte Arndt (2021) http://troublesdanslescollections.fr/2021/07/26/article-5/ and Noémie Etienne, "Who Cares? Museum Conservation Between Colonial Violence and Symbolic Repair," Museums and Social Issues, 2022, https://doi.org/10.1080/15596893.2022.2057413

9. Anne-Marie Pedersen and John Pritchard, "Haisla (Kitamaat)," *L'Encyclopédie Canadienne*, October 16, 2011, http://www.thecanadianencyclopedia.ca/fr/article/haisla-kitamaat.

10. Stacey R. Jessiman, "The Repatriation of the G'psgolox Totem Pole: A Study of Its Context, Process and Outcome," *International Journal of Cultural Property* 18, no. 3 (2011): 365–91.

11. The return of the totem pole to Misk'usa in 2012, rarely mentioned, is reported in Anders Björklund, "The Case of Chief G'Psgolox's Totem Pole: 'Rescuing,' Keeping, and Returning," *Baltic Worlds* 1 (June 18, 2018): 72–76, http://balticworlds.com/the-case-of-chief-gpsgoloxs-totem-pole/.

12. Excerpt from the documentary *Totem: The Return of the G'psgolox Totem Pole*, National Film Board, 2004, http://www.youtube.com/watch?v=05C5Ub19exM.

13. Jessiman, "Repatriation of the G'Psgolox'Totem Pole," 371.

14. "G'psgolox Pole Returns Home after 77 Years, First Totem Ever to Be Repatriated from Overseas," press release, April 26, 2006, http://ecotrust.ca/gpsgolox-pole-returns-home-after-77-years-first-totem-ever-be-repatriated-oversea/.

15. The quotation appears in a press release from the Haisla Nation. The archive reference (which I was unable to consult firsthand) is Iver Fougner to the Secretary, Dept. of Indian Affairs, Ottawa 16.12 1927, RG 10, vol. 4087, file 5077-2B, Public Archives, Indian Affairs, Ottowa.

16. Ladd, quoted in *Way of the People*, Phase 2.

17. John Flint, quoted in *Way of the People*, Phase 2.

18. "The Haisla Prepare to Welcome Their Totem Pole Back Home," Turtle Island Native Network website, June 27, 2006, http://www.turtleisland.org/culture/culture-haisla.htm.

19. Edouard Pommier, *L'art de la liberté: Doctrines et débats de la Révolution française* (Paris: Gallimard, 1991); and Dominique Poulot, *Musée, nation, patrimoine, 1789–1815* (Paris: Gallimard, 1997).

20. F. J. L. Meyer, *Fragmente aus Paris in VIten Jahr der französischen Reppublik* (Hamburg: Karl Ernst Bohn, 1797), 2:186.

21. F. J. L. Meyer, *Briefe aus der Hauptstadt und dem Innern Frankreichs* (Tübingen: Gotta'schen Buchandlung, 1802), 1:91.

22. Léonie Hénaut, "L'interprétation comme activité de travail: Matérialité et signification de l'oeuvre," *Sociologie de l'art* 1 (2009): 15–34.

23. Camerale II, Antichità e Belle arti, b. 2, fasc 95, April 24, 1834, Archivio di Stato di Roma (ASR), Rome.

24. Pietro Palmaroli, testimony written from Rome, April 19, 1815, Foreign Affairs Archives, Santa Fede Section, leg. 738, no. 103, Archive and Documentation Service, Prado, Madrid.

25. See, for instance, Towards a Sustainable Practice

in Paintings Conservation: New Insights into Reducing Solvent Toxicity during Cleaning and Cold Relining, workshop at the École nationale supérieure des arts visuels de La Cambre (ENSAV), Belgium, May 17, 2021, online lecture at http://www.lacambre.be/fr/actualites/categorie/ateliers.

26. Dean Sully, ed. *Decolonising Conservation: Caring for Maori Meeting Houses outside New Zealand* (Walnut Creek: Left Coast Press, 2007); and Glenn Wharton, *The Painted King: Art, Activism, and Authenticity in Hawai'i* (Honolulu: University Press of Hawai'i, 2012).

27. Robin O'Hern, Ellen Pearlstein, and Susan Elizabeth Gagliardi, "Beyond the Surface: Where Cultural Contexts and Scientific Analyses Meet in Museum Conservation of West African Power Association Helmet Masks," *Museum Anthropology* 39 (2016): 70–86; Caitlin Mahony, *Conserving a Yup'ik Mask*, Metropolitan Museum of Art, video, January 28, 2019. See also the online symposium proposing a decolonization of and by conservation, Share the Mic: Decolonizing an African Museum, Fowler Museum at UCLA, March 23, 2021, http://www.fowler.ucla.edu/event/share-the-mic-decolonizing-an-african-museum/.

28. Just like the term "to decolonize" in the curatorial discourse. See, for a comparison, a 2017 text that calls into question the very possibility of decolonizing the museum: Sumaya Kassim, "The Museum Will Not Be Decolonized," *Media Diversified*, November 15, 2017, http://mediadiversified.org/2017/11/15/the-museum-will-not-be-decolonised/.

29. Part of the information in this paragraph comes from a telephone conversation with the current director of the Musée Barbier-Mueller Laurence Mattet, May 14, 2021, as well as an exchange of emails with the director of the National Museum of Tanzania Achiles Mujunangoma Bufure in June 2021. I would like to thank Flower Manase, an exhibition curator in Dar es Salaam, who kindly answered my questions in June 2021.

30. Anne Laure Bandle, Raphael Contel, Marc-André Renold, "Masque Makondé—Tanzanie et Musée Barbier-Mueller," Plateforme ArThemis, Centre universitaire du droit de l'art, University of Geneva, April 2013, http://plone.unige.ch/art-adr/cases-affaires/masque-makonde-tanzanie-et-musee-barbier-mueller/fiche-2013-masque-makonde-2013-tanzanie-et-musee-barbier-mueller.

31. Lucie Agache, "Le musée Barbier-Mueller rend un masque Makonde à la Tanzanie," *Connaissance des arts*, May 11, 2010, http://www.connaissancedesarts.com/archeologie/actus/breves/le-musee-barbier-mueller-rend-un-masque-makonde-a-la-tanzanie-84322.php.

32. Part of the information in this paragraph comes from a telephone conversation with Alexander Brust, curator of the America Department, Museum der Kulturen, Basel, on May 27, 2021. See also Brust's article "Nur eine Frage der Ethik: Erben und Shenken in der Museumspraxis zwischen Brasilien und der Schweiz," *museums.ch*, no. 8 (2011), http://www.museums.ch/assets/ebooks/museums-n6/files/mobile/index.html#110. Wauja is sometimes rendered as "Waurà."

33. See Caroline Renold, Anne Laure Bandle, Marc-André Renold, "Case Waurà Indians Collection—Museum der Kulturen Basel, Penteado Coelho Heirs and Museu de Arqueologia e Etnologia Universidade de São Paulo, Waurà Indians," Platform ArThemis, Centre universitaire du droit de l'art, University of Geneva, April 2013, http://plone.unige.ch/art-adr/cases-affaires/waura-indians-collection-2013-museum-der-kulturen-basel-penteado-coelho-heirs-and-museu-de-arqueologia-e-etnologia-universidade-de-sao-paulo-waura-indians/case-note-2013-waura-indians. Alexander Brust told me the story of the fax in an exchange of emails in June 2021, but he cannot confirm the anecdote's veracity.

34. At the Ateliers de la pensée in Dakar in 2019, a panel called Réparations, résilience et dévulnérabilisation (Reparations, Resilience, and Devulnerabilization) brought together Karima Lazali, Kader Attia, Nafissatou Dia, and Christiane Taubira. The day's talks are available online at http://www.youtube.com/watch?v=o8FlaBiASbc. The panel in question begins at 3:01. I would like to thank Lotte Arndt for having pointed out this reference to me.

35. Honoré Tchatchouang Ngoupeyou, "Sauvegarder le patrimoine en Afrique subsaharienne: l'interdépendance entre le patrimoine culturel immatériel et le patrimoine culturel matériel," *Patrimoines: Revue de l'Institut national du patrimoine de Paris*, no. 16 (2020–21): 43–50.

36. See, for instance, the Europe-based project Taking Care: http://takingcareproject.eu. For a critical approach of the notion of care, see Bonaventure Soh Bejeng Ndikung, *The Delusions of Care* (Paris: Les presses du réel, 2021).

CHAPTER 13

CONSERVING MONUMENTS, REVIVING TEMPLES

COMMUNITIES, MONUMENTS, AND POLITICS IN SOUTH INDIA

Kavita Singh

In the past decades, as the field of heritage conservation has tried to decolonize itself, practitioners and theorists have questioned the universal applicability of the conservation philosophies that were dominant throughout much of the twentieth century. Rather than invoking a universal but abstract "humanity" for whose sake sites and monuments must be entrusted to professional hands—professionals who will determine how sites will be maintained, what meanings they will bear and how they will be used—the field has begun to foreground the role and rights of local communities to have a more intimate relationship to "their" monuments. These may be communities that claim descent from those who had brought the monuments into being, or they may simply consist of the population that lives in or near particular heritage sites. But by virtue of their close connection to the monuments and sites, these communities are now understood to have a right to determine the meanings of those monuments and the manner in which they are to be used and maintained.

In this new paradigm, the heritage structure that constitutes tangible heritage forms only one part of what needs to be conserved. The beliefs, customs, values, and practices in which monuments are embedded constitute the other crucial dimension of the sites' intangible heritage. And, as Gustavo Araoz has observed, "The core values of heritage are now increasingly deemed to reside in the cultural meanings and values humans invest in monuments and landscapes, not their physical substance."[1]

In this essay, I want to examine this emerging understanding of the relationship between monument and community in the context of India. I will take us to the southern tip of the subcontinent, to the province of Tamil Nadu, whose landscape is dotted with thousands of temples, large and small, old and new, many of which lie neglected. Here, a group of heritage enthusiasts have taken it upon themselves to conserve and restore crumbling Hindu temples. Abandoned by faith communities, the temples have fallen out of worship and have also failed to attract the attention of the conservation authorities of the state that might have preserved these buildings as secular monuments. In this context, the actions of this volunteer group, as they repair the temples and then reinstate worship within them, seem wholly laudable—and seem well aligned with the new currents of thinking about a decolonized heritage regime. Yet, upon closer observation, the group's project becomes less benign. Acts of restoration become implicit denunciations of those held responsible for the decay, straining the already-fraught social fabric of present-day India; invocations of heritage and tradition help to broaden social fissures between religious communities; and the rhetoric of community revival begins to align with the ascendent right-wing majoritarianism that would turn India into a theocratic Hindu state.

THE TEMPLE CLEANERS

One morning, a group of men set out for a road trip from the city of Chennai. From the highway, they turn off onto unpaved village tracks as they search for forgotten temples scattered across the Tamil landscape. Some of the temples they seek out are quite recent, but many were founded as far back as the Chola period (from the ninth to thirteenth centuries); some have remarkable carvings or house important bronze sculptures, while others are quite plain; some are currently used for worship, but most of the temples they look for are forgotten, ruined, and overgrown.

On this trip, they go to a village called Venkadu. They find what was once a temple, now reduced to a heap of stones and overgrown with brambles. As they explore the ruin, a group of villagers comes to see what they are doing. The city dwellers speak to the villagers about the value and importance of the temple and the need to take care of it (fig. 13.1). Together, they begin to clear the bushes and explore the

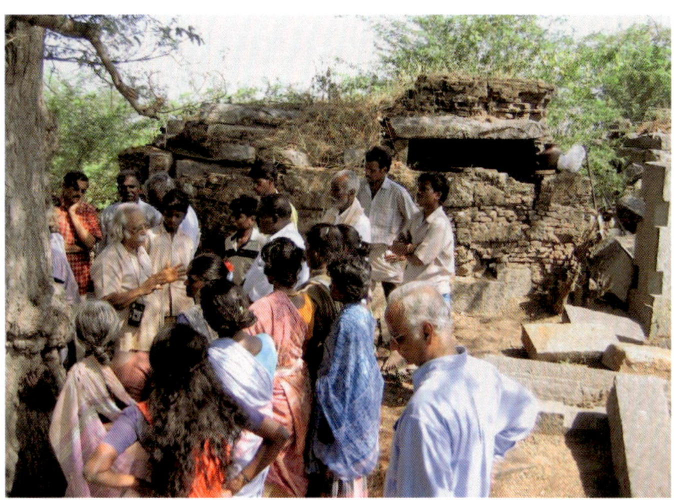

Fig. 13.1. REACH Foundation volunteers speaking to the residents of Venkadu about the value of the ancient and ruined temple in their village, February 2006

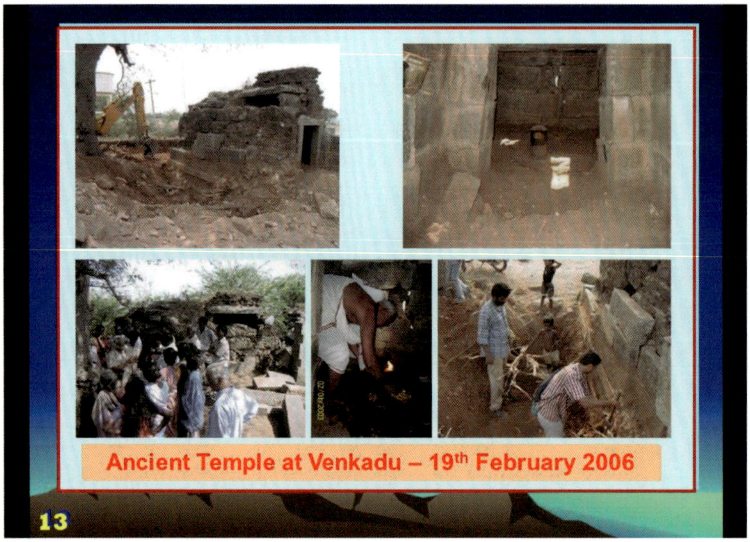

Fig. 13.2. A composite image showing various stages in the REACH Foundation's activities for the conservation project for the temple at Venkadu, February 2006

site. When they push through to the shrine, they find that the old icon is still present amid the rubble. They immediately offer worship.

A few weeks later, the group returns. They are pleased to find that the village community has been at work; they have cleared the area of vegetation, and they have hooked up an electricity line to the site. This time, the urban volunteers have come with earth-moving equipment, which they use to uproot trees, unearth pillars and sculptures, and dig around the temple to find the original level of the base. Over time, this group of volunteers will involve private foundations and local communities and enlist government support to repair the temple, salvaging and restoring what they can find. They will do it well. They will document the building and decipher its inscriptions and research its historical significance. As they repair the structure, they will take care to use lime mortar to join the stones rather than modern concrete, they will not use sand-blasting machines to clean the surfaces, as some others do, for this abrades them. They will adhere to accepted conservation norms in the repair work they conduct, and they will engage *sthapatis*, or traditional sculptor-architects, to make the most faithful substitutes possible for the parts that are missing and need to be replaced (fig. 13.2).[2]

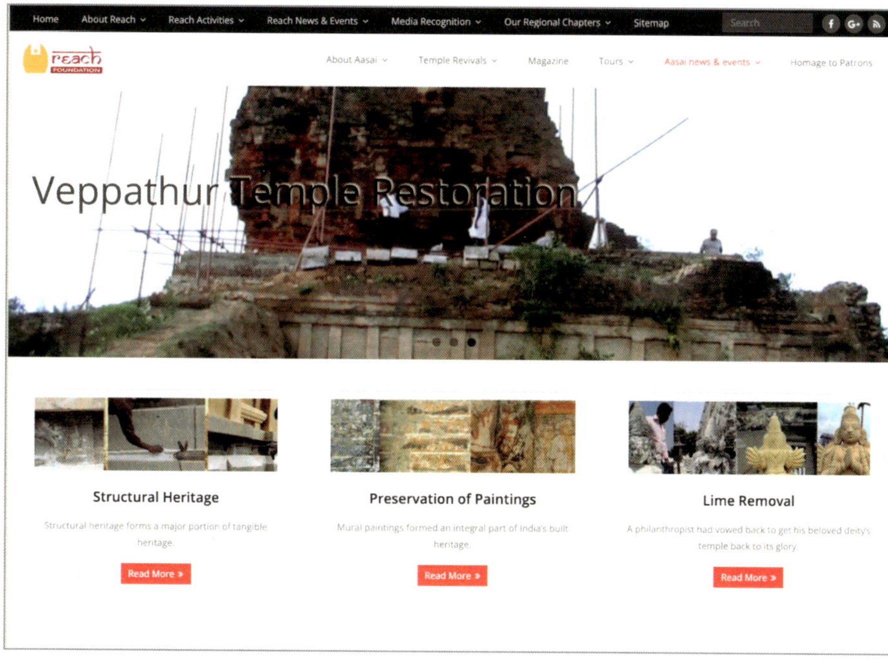

Fig. 13.3. Homepage of the REACH Foundation (http://conserveheritage.org/), with links to pages on the foundation's activities and outreach

Who are these urban volunteers, and why do they invest such great efforts and funds in caring for ruined temples that lie scattered all over the Tamil region? This group of enthusiasts was motivated by the descriptions of the Tamil country in *Ponniyin Selvan*, a famous twentieth-century Tamil novel set in Chola times.[3] The novel paints a vivid picture of a region humming with temples where devout worshippers offer homage to their gods. Wishing to rediscover and preserve the heritage that the book evokes, some young men working in the information technology (IT) industry sought out a group of archaeologists, scholars, and epigraphers who had retired from the Archaeological Survey of India, the country's official custodian of monuments. The elderly specialists understood the historical value of the temples and the techniques appropriate for their restoration; the IT crowd had the drive to sustain their campaign and manage the online presence that is so valuable for publicity, networking, and raising funds. This motley group, which first called itself the Temple Cleaners, grew into the REACH Foundation—an acronym for the Rural Education and Conservation of Heritage Foundation. As the name suggests, the foundation's focus is on heritage sites lying forgotten in small villages in Tamil Nadu (fig. 13.3).

The REACH Foundation's activities seem illustrative of good heritage management practices. The members combine an enthusiasm for small and neglected

Figs. 13.4, 13.5. Kailasanatha Temple, Uthiramerur, Kanchipuram district. View of the vimana prior to (*top*) and after (*bottom*) restoration. Believed to have been built in the 8th century under Pallava rule, this temple was restored by REACH in 2010

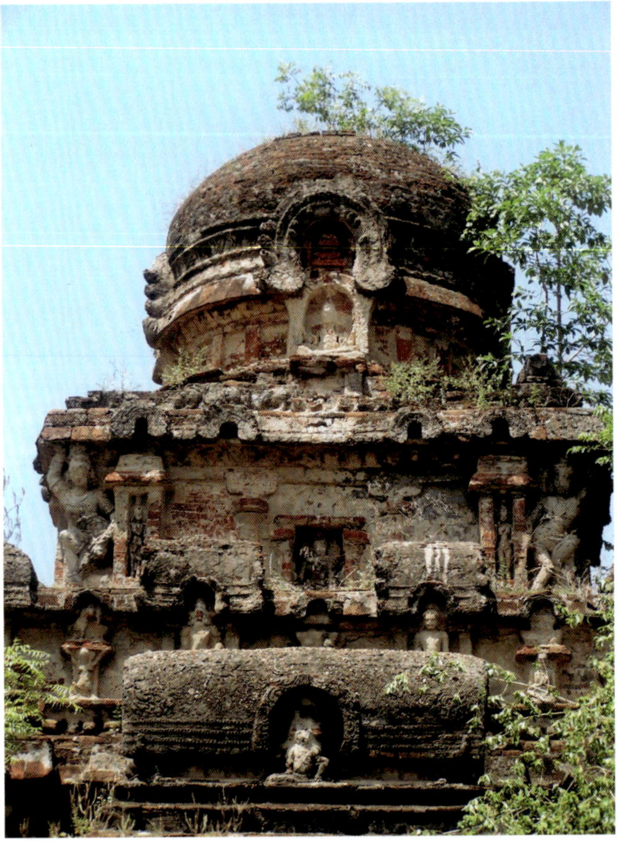

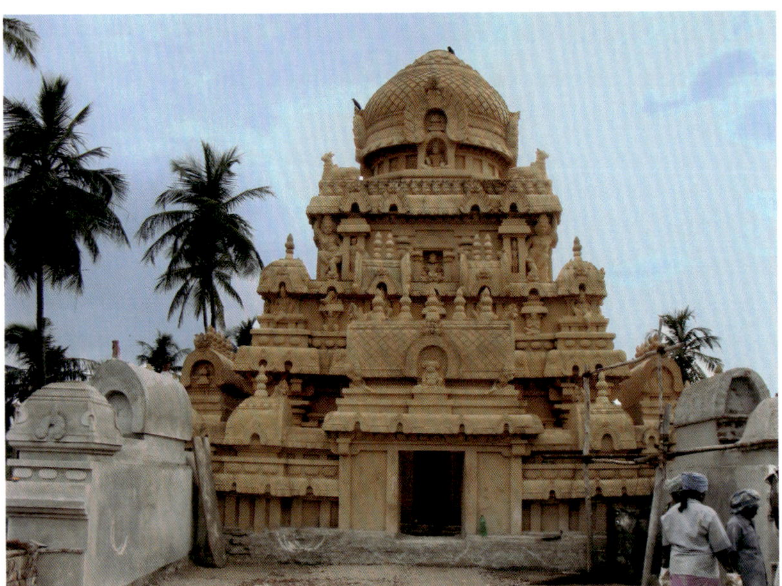

sites, a knowledge of history, and an understanding of the standards of conservation practices (figs. 13.4, 13.5). But REACH differs in some significant ways from established organizations such as the Archaeological Survey of India (ASI) or the Indian National Trust for Art and Cultural Heritage, a prominent non-governmental organization, which are also involved in heritage conservation in India. To understand this difference, let us listen more attentively to the way REACH members describe their work.

ENCHANTMENT

On that first day in Venkadu, when volunteers found that the icon of the god Shiva was still present in the rubble of the shrine, the REACH blogger wrote: "Almost buried, the Shiva Lingam[4] was popping out as if calling us for attention!" The volunteers chanted "Aum Namah Shivaaya" (a mantra in praise of Shiva), and the blogger notes that this "made the bushes get cleared fast."[5]

The blog's language suggests that the god within the shrine willed the REACH volunteers to come and rediscover him; chanting his name made it easier to clear the site because they were doing this in service of Shiva. This kind of animism is seen often in the REACH blog, which presents the deity as the one who activates humans to serve him. When the dry stone of a newly-rediscovered lingam absorbs the oil that is poured on it, it is described as thirsty, eagerly drinking in all that is offered after a centuries-long drought. When a project needs funds and a wealthy philanthropist offers to provide the money, the blog exults that the "Lord himself has sent his devotee" to help them do their work. And when the team comes upon a cache of buried bronzes from the ninth century, they are excited because these are incredibly rare Pallava bronzes that predate the Chola period—but credit for the discovery belongs not to the team that dug them up but to the god who chose to manifest himself to them on that auspicious day.

This is a language of enchantment, where ordinary men and women become tools fulfilling a divine purpose, and their prosaic actions of cleaning, digging, and repairing are accomplished through god's will. In seeking out these temples, gathering their scattered pillars and stones, and reconstructing them, the REACH Foundation's conservation projects are powered by not just an interest in history and heritage but by a devotional attitude. Unsurprisingly, their aim is not just to repair the physical body of the temple. REACH considers a restoration project to be complete only when the temple's icon is reconsecrated so that the divine spirit can return to it, and a local community agrees to tend to the building and conduct worship in it so that the religious life of the building is resumed. Monument conservation is not REACH's goal. Their goal is temple revival.

DECOLONIZING CONSERVATION

In many respects, the goals of the REACH Foundation seem to harmonize with the way the field of heritage conservation is being rethought in the twenty-first century. "Classical" conservation of the nineteenth and twentieth centuries was driven by a concern to maintain the physical integrity of the monument being conserved; authenticity and historical integrity reposed in the body of the building, and international standards of good practice asked the conservator to stabilize what remained of the historical structure and to avoid making additions and alterations, or engaging in forms of repair and reconstruction that would compromise its authenticity. Going forward, all future use of the building, whether for occupation, tourist visitation, or ritual performance, had to be moderated to prevent wear to the building. Here, the material aspect of the building was of paramount importance.

Toward the end of the twentieth century, the paradigm began to shift. The 1994 Nara Document on Authenticity adopted by the UNESCO World Heritage Committee challenged the principles that had been developed in Europe. In Asia, it proposed, "authenticity" lay not in oldness of the physical parts of the structure but in the preservation of traditional skills that allowed historic buildings to be periodically rebuilt.[6] Later, the Okinawa Declaration on Intangible and Tangible Cultural Heritage of 2004 went further when it criticized "conservation measures which give undue weight to material aspects of heritage, without adequate attention to the meaning of associated traditions, rituals, and practices for the community."[7] By shifting the criteria of authenticity from the oldness of the physical structure to the continuity of practices and beliefs in and around it, the Okinawa Declaration made it acceptable to "restore" a monument to the point of rebuilding it anew; and reinstating traditional forms of usage such as worship within it became part of the maintenance of the monument's intangible heritage.

While REACH's approach seems to mesh well with these recent international developments in the heritage field, within India, REACH's activities are, strictly speaking, illegal, for the laws that govern India's heritage regime make a clear separation between the domains of religion and the state. Under Indian heritage law, to restore a monument for worship is a form of illegal occupation. To an outsider this may seem odd: the buildings were meant for worship, are currently ownerless, and exist in India, a country where faith plays a prominent role in public life. As Mark Twain famously said: "India has two million gods and worships them all. In religion, all other countries are paupers; India is the only millionaire."[8] To understand why India's heritage laws developed to exclude religious practices from recurring in abandoned monuments, we need to understand the historical context in which these laws were formed.

REGIMES OF CONTROL FOR INDIA'S MONUMENTS

When colonial authorities began to take an interest in the monuments and artifacts of India, they found the majority of them had been made in service of one of India's many religions. This posed some difficulties. Faith was an important feature of India's social and political life, and perceived insults to religion could light the fuse of an explosive reaction. Even the Great Mutiny of 1857, which had offered the most serious threat to British rule to date, was provoked by rumors that troops would be forced to handle substances forbidden by their religious beliefs. Stung by the mutiny, the British Raj adopted a policy of nonintervention in Indian religious affairs.

Thus, in the latter part of the nineteenth century as the colonial state established the Archaeological Survey of India and tried to bring Indian monuments under its control, it had to take care to avoid hurting religious sensibilities. To this end, the state developed a rule of thumb: if a temple, mosque, or other religious edifice was under active worship, its control would remain with its community, and the government would assist in repairing it only if asked to do so. If, however, the building had fallen out of worship, if no living community of owners or traditional guardians staked a claim to it, and if it was architecturally, artistically, and historically significant enough for the state to feel impelled to extend its care, then the Archaeological Survey of India or the provincial departments of archaeology could notify it as a monument. Once notified, the building became a monument and it entered the secularized domain of archaeology and art. Similarly, if sculptures were discovered during excavations on land owned by a temple, then these were handed over to the temple. If excavated sculptures could be deemed to be ownerless, or were found near a disused temple, they could be transferred to a museum.

Depending on how they were classified as places of worship or monuments, or as icons or works of art, India's buildings and artifacts were divided among two entirely different regimes of value that brought with them different protocols for control and care. This had profound consequences for a site's afterlife. Once a temple had turned into a monument and was placed under the control of archaeological authorities, its care was governed by the conservation policy followed by the Archaeological Survey. "Although there are many ancient buildings whose state of disrepair suggests at first sight a renewal," this 1922 policy states, "it should never be forgotten that their *historical value is gone when their authenticity is destroyed*."[9] For the state's archaeological authorities, authenticity lay in preventing further decay without any attempts at rebuilding what had been lost. Wherever possible, "original" surfaces were to be recovered, to which end layers of colorful paint or limewash were scraped off, revealing the underlying stone. As a result, "conserved" Indian monuments became united by a common vocabulary of partially ruined structures whose surfaces were stripped down to bare stone.[10] This is the reason why temples-turned-monuments in India have all come to wear a certain standardized "look" of age (fig. 13.6).

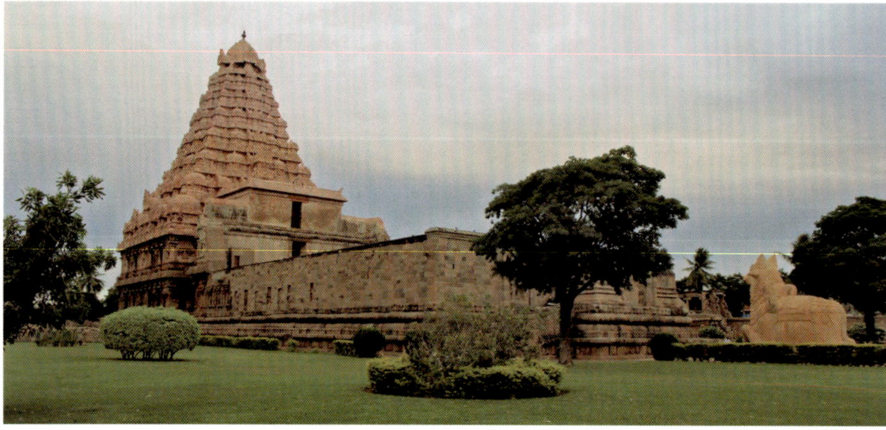

Fig. 13.6. Gangaikondacholapuram Temple, which has been secularized and is under the custody of the Archaeological Survey of India. The carved portion of the exterior wall belongs to the original structure; portions repaired by the ASI are uncarved, making the modern interventions clear

Conservation objectives also regulated the uses to which the temple-turned-monument could be put. The resumption of worship was barred by law at these sites. Guards were posted at monuments to actively prevent prospective worshippers from praying there. As Deborah Sutton tells us, this was necessary because ceremonies of worship were often a community's first step in staking a claim to a property and wresting it away from the state. Having turned the monument into a secular site, the state was invested in keeping it ritual free, not just to retain control over the building, but also "to encourage and enhance a new public gaze." The secular domain of archaeology strove to produce a secular citizenry, united through its interest in the history and aesthetics of architecture. This was colonial modernity's cure for a populace divided within itself into disparate communities of belief.[11]

A functioning temple, on the other hand, looked very different indeed (fig. 13.7). Living temples were free to grow and change with time, adding new structures to accommodate expanding congregations, becoming updated in the style and fashion of the day, acquiring layers of brilliant paint on their sculptures, and adding gold plating to their doorways and temple spires if their donors were generous enough. This continual work of renewal, expansion, and renovation in a living temple is called *jhirnoddhar* (literally "uplifting the old") in Hindi and *tiruppani* ("divine work") in Tamil, and it typically depends upon donations from the devout. Such renovation does not just follow functional needs, but also has an important signaling function: the fact that the temple has attracted enough donations to allow it to repair itself and grow becomes an advertisement of the power and popularity of the

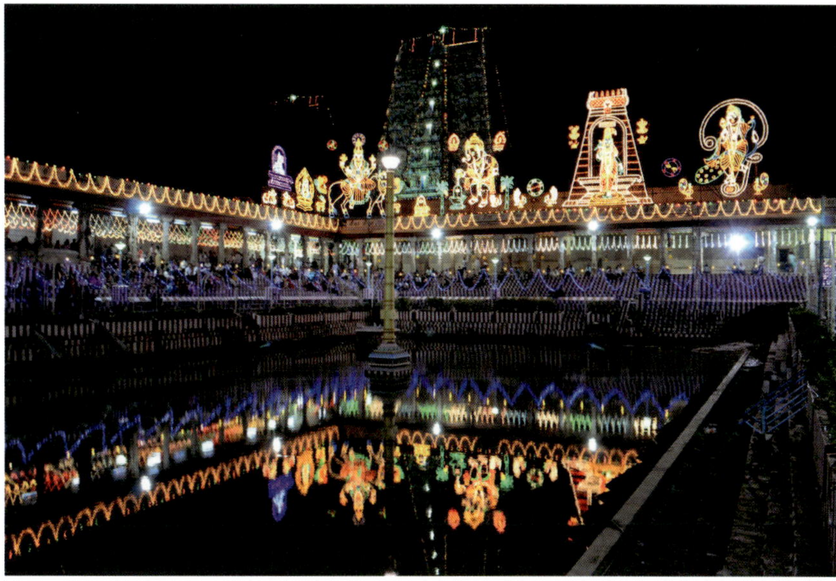

Fig. 13.7. A living temple receives additions and alterations and is updated throughout its life to serve the congregation's needs. Meenakshi temple decorated for the Navarathri festival, 2012

temple, and it offers evidence of the many grateful worshippers who have found an answer to their prayers. The living temple accumulates layers of material and sensory stimuli: gilding, enamel paint, and plaster slathered on the sculpted walls; tin-sheet lean-tos or concrete structures that extend the congregational halls; thronging bazaars that sell flowers, camphor, incense, sacramental food, dresses, and ornaments for worshippers to offer to the gods; chanting priests, bursts of music, crowds of worshippers. All these mark the living temple as an utterly different sensorium from the sedate, stripped-down temples of the "preserved" monumental domain.

REACH'S CODE-SWITCHING

The kind of temple that REACH revives—disused, abandoned, and fallen into disrepair—is the kind of temple that, under current law, should be available for classification as a monument and translation into the secular sphere. But there is such a surfeit of architectural heritage in the region that the ASI and the Tamil Nadu State Archaeological Department have extended their protection only to a few dozen major temples of the reputedly tens of thousands of historic temples in the state.[12] For decades, these lesser temples have failed to attract the attention of the government. By taking the initiative in caring for these neglected temples, REACH is entering into a space left vacant by the archaeological authorities and is able to present itself as the more responsible custodian of cultural heritage.

Since organizations like the REACH Foundation are concerned with temple revival rather than monument conservation, one would expect the shrines revived by them to take on the appearance of other living temples. Instead, we find that the temples restored by REACH bear that very look of age that we associate with archaeological monuments. With their stone surfaces left unpainted, all traces of modern plaster peeled away, and newly carved elements carefully matched to resemble the old, REACH's renewed temples exhibit a tastefully restrained aesthetic reminiscent of ancient monuments protected by the Archaeological Survey.

It is clear that this aesthetic is a consciously chosen one. In their blog posts and in interviews, REACH members speak witheringly of temple custodians who cover the stone temple walls with garish paint or ceramic tiles. They are concerned with reconstructing what appears "historically authentic" in accordance with the protocols followed by the ASI. According to REACH's senior archaeologist, T. Satyamurty,"The aim of conservation should be to make the heritage structure or temple appear old but fresh."[13] While REACH rejects the ASI's prohibition on restoring damaged temples by adding newly carved stones, it does take care to disguise the restorations. Making them look like ancient structures that are in pristine condition, REACH turns the temples into un-ruins.

REACH is not alone in the kind of work it does. It is now one of several initiatives in South India engaged in temple revival, and their number is growing. In Karnataka, the Sri Dharmasthala Manjunatheshwara Dharmothana (SDMD) Trust founded by a wealthy and influential temple has restored more than 250 temples so far.[14] Like REACH, the SDMD Trust also uses the services of retired archaeologists, and its projects, too, aim to produce that same ASI look of age. A journalist covering their work exulted: "While the restoration carried out is of the kind that those who originally built them would have been proud to see, the structures are not just stronger but also true to their original forms. . . . rarely had I seen intervention efforts which didn't look like a terrible cosmetic surgery [whereas in temples restored by the SDMD Trust there were no whitewashed walls, no terrible replicas or sculptures]. The temple seemed as if it had been actually 'restored.'"[15] Here, too, the conservation project strives for an aesthetic of the "authentically" old. To the appreciative viewers, all the contributions of the contemporary agents—archaeologists, donors, engineers masons, sculptors, drivers of earth-moving equipment, unskilled workers—vanish from view, as the temple in its "original form" appears to have magically resurrected itself.

Of course, this "authentic look of age" is a modern confection, born of the chromophobia of nineteenth-century archaeology. Just as we have learned the marble surfaces of Greek and Roman sculpture were once gaudily polychrome, the truly authentic look for a Hindu temple would involve colorful surfaces rather than plain stone. Why do the temple restoration projects of the REACH Foundation and the SDMD Trust share the Archaeological Survey's aesthetic when they do not share its intentions? Does their choice of this "look of age" simply reflect the habitus of the retired archaeologists who direct these projects? Or does it answer to a more broadly distributed middle-class taste? These are possible explanations. But in a paper I coauthored with Saloni Mathur some years ago, we discussed the way in which contemporary religious complexes in India were consciously appropriating the display modes of the museum to exhibit relics or to project sectarian narratives. Through this maneuver, we felt, "the entire epistemological authority established by the museum through its secular avatars, where it declares itself as the teller of truths, was now proving useful for the reconstruction of society along religious lines."[16] When a relic that is believed to testify to a miracle is exhibited not through a ritual showing on feast days but permanently kept in a museum-style vitrine accompanied by a label with tombstone data, the relic is transformed. Instead of being embedded in the realm of faith, the relic is now presented as evidence of the reality of the miracle, which becomes a cold, hard fact.

Something very similar is occurring in these temple restoration projects that choose to (re)make temples in monochrome. By taking on the appearance of ASI-protected monuments, the newly revived temples absorb the reputation and authority of an officially approved and scientifically verified heritage regime. The work these trusts do and the changes they make at the sites are read not as contemporary interventions (which, of course, they are) but as an erasure of all that was wrought by the intervening time, to allow a return to an originary past. In this way, the look of antiquity becomes the look of authenticity.

ARCHAEOLOGY AS REVELATION

The recovery of these temples through an archaeological process, which peels away layers of vegetation, soil, and rubble to reveal what is already present beneath, becomes the process of revealing the hidden truth that has long been buried and forgotten. This truth, buried under the layers of other intrusive communities and faiths, is the primordial presence of Hinduism in this land.[17] Through the restoration of the temples, the land regains its identity. By reviving worship within the temples, each community is reminded of its true and essential nature that has lain buried and forgotten. Once a temple has returned to its originary past, the village in which it is situated can follow it in a journey to its roots.

As described in another REACH blog post, on their way back from one of their trips, a restoration group came upon a *shivalinga* they believed to be quite antique. It was lying in the open, not near any temple, but just adjacent to a school. The REACH volunteers asked the cooks in the school's kitchen to "do at least an *abhishegam* daily (i.e., to anoint it) and offer the food before serving to the children." This would maintain Shiva's presence in the *linga*, and it would also turn the school's midday meal into *prasad*, or sacramental food. The blogger exults: "Even though

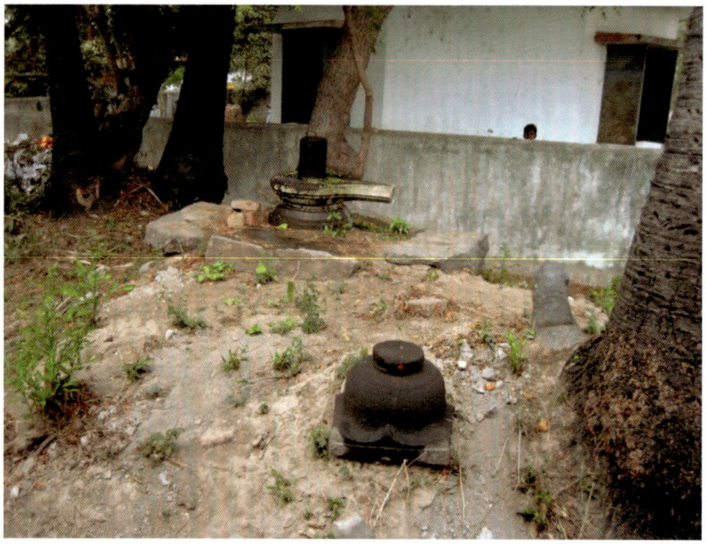

Fig. 13.8. Abandoned *shivalinga* near Arasar Kovil, Pathur, 2010

the (kitchen staff) are converts (Christians) now, they readily agreed to do the *abhishegam* daily and offer food as requested" (fig. 13.8).[18]

The REACH blogger suggests that just as layers of soil and debris must be removed to reveal the temple that lies beneath them, there lies buried within all the people of Tamil Nadu an ancestral memory of being Hindu that can still be discovered under the more recent layers of forgetfulness, or of conversion to another faith. They are restoring not just temples but a community that is being forged through the act of temple repair. What is being effected here is a psychic archaeology alongside a material one.

ALLIANCES WITH THE RIGHT

It is inevitable that there would be a convergence of interests between groups that revive Hindu temples and Hindu right-wing groups. The trope of the temple has always been crucial to the mobilization of Hindutva, or Hindu nationalism, in India. But rather than celebrating the many intact and functioning temples that exist, this discourse has tended to focus on temples that have decayed or have been damaged or destroyed. Indeed, through the second half of the twentieth century, the political project of Hindutva has turned the ruined temple into its key fetish object. The mass-mobilization campaign that propelled the Hindu right-wing party to power in 1998 centered around a vanished temple, believed to have been demolished and now lying under a sixteenth-century mosque built to mark Muslim conquest of a Hindu pilgrimage town. The demolition of that mosque by Hindu "volunteers," subsequent riots, and a bitter contest over the control of the site have left a legacy of violence and division in India, but Hindutva groups now target other mosques at other sites for demolition, to "liberate" the temples that are believed to have stood on the same spots.

In these campaigns, damaged and ruined temples are invoked as the evidence of a thousand years of allegedly oppressive Muslim rule. Upon the image of the broken temple is projected the broken body of the Hindu, wounded and killed by marauding iconoclasts. The ravaged body of the temple is used to rally Hindus to unite to protect their faith. In this discourse, temples must regain their rightful place in the Indian landscape from which they were evacuated. If Muslim property or Muslim persons are removed in the process, the act is not criminal but just, as it is compensating for the depredations of the past.

Today, however, as one follows right-wing social media that celebrates the temple revivals of REACH or the Dharmasthana, one becomes aware of a new enemy on which Hindutva has trained its guns. The marauding Muslim has slipped into being a threat of the past. The new enemy is the godless and secular state.

As right-wing social media users share photographs of neglected or poorly maintained Hindu monuments, they question the competence of the state to care for heritage, asking: "Why is @ASIGoI [the Archaeological Survey of India, Government of India] not preserving these temples? Are funds of @MinOfCultureGoI [Ministry of Culture, Government of India] only for renovating Moghul tombs and mosques? No money for preserving heritage of our Hindu temples?"[19] Posting a short video of a crumbling temple, @hardyatrow asks: "Do we need any more proof that the Govt. has failed to protect our ancient temples? This is a clear indication that non devotees can't maintain temples as they should be maintained" (fig. 13.9).[20] In these

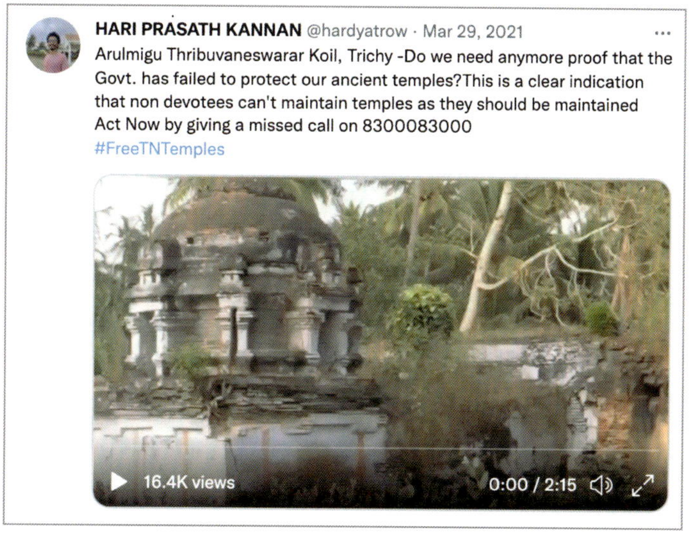

Fig. 13.9. Tweet by @hardyatrow, a Hindutva-supporting Twitter handle, showing a ruined temple as proof of the secular government's incapacity to protect Tamil Nadu's Hindu heritage

circles, REACH's competence in restoring temples becomes an assertion of the irrelevance of the state; Hindutva groups are now equipped to maintain their heritage better than any government organization. Devotionalism, rather than professionalism, becomes the guarantee of commitment to the task: as popular godman Jaggi Vasudev tweets, "Returning temples to the community of devotees is the only way to restore Tamil Temples and preserve Tamil Culture. Only devotees will give their lives to protect and preserve, not uncommitted officials."[21]

Such words and attitudes give a cosmic dimension to the project of conservation, where the forces of good—represented by the Hindu who is capable and devout—must contend with antagonists who are either malignant (the marauding Muslim) or incompetent (the neglectful state). While the talk is of conservation, the images that are insistently shown in these circles focus on ruination, damage, and decay, fueling a sense of past victimhood. Just as the Hindu community must take charge of these temples and restore them, Hindus must take charge of their community and restore its deserved dominance.

CONCLUSION

When I first heard of the REACH foundation, it seemed to be a remarkable experiment in decolonizing heritage practices and bringing conservation-mindedness to communities. But as with many things, the view from up close is rather different from the view from afar. Today, as Hindu majoritarianism has established itself as the main political power in India, and as it extends its grip over India's public spheres, the work of conservation-for-temple-revival is beginning to look less benign than it did ten years ago. Hindutva uses the image of ruined temples to symbolize Hindu victimization that must be avenged; it uses the image of temple restoration to show that its community—fueled by devotion—is more capable than the secular state and is ready to replace it. Instead of a being a tool for social justice, community heritage projects of this kind become tools to exacerbate divisions and exclusions; in this, they show us what happens when policies and approaches that have been developed to protect the interests of disempowered minorities are mobilized by powerful majorities for their own use.

NOTES

1. Gustavo F. Araoz, "Preserving Heritage Places under a New Paradigm," *Journal of Cultural Heritage Management and Sustainable Development* 1, no. 1 (May 27, 2011): 55–60, http://doi.org/10.1108/20441261111129933, cited in Aylin Orbaşli, "Conservation Theory in the Twenty-First Century: Slow Evolution or a Paradigm Shift?," *Journal of Architectural Conservation* 23, no. 3 (September 2, 2017): 157–70, http://doi.org/10.1080/13556207.2017.1368187.

2. This narrative account is based on blog posts by the REACH foundation (discussed below) describing their temple cleaning and conservation work at Venkadu in 2006. An account of the first visit to Venkadu is at "One Day Symposium on Heritage Temples Aug 2007," accessed February 5, 2021, http://conserveheritage.org/index.php/temple-revivals/venkadu/. The second visit is described at "Kundrathur and Venkaadu Visit: Report on Temple Cleaners' Visit to Kundrathur and Venkaadu on 26th March 2006," accessed February 5, 2021, http://conserveheritage.org/index.php/tours/temple-visits/kunrathur-venkadu-visit/.

3. *Ponniyin Selvan* (*The Son of Ponni*) by Kalki Krishnamurthy is widely regarded as the greatest Tamil novel ever written. Serialized in the weekly magazine *Kalki* from 1950 to 1954, it was subsequently published as a novel in five volumes. The book gives a fictionalized account of battles, court intrigues, and affairs of the heart in the time of Rajaraja Chola, who reigned c. 985–1014. For a recent English translation, see Krishnamurthy Kalki and Varaloṭṭi Rengasamy, *Kalki's Ponniyin Selvan: A Historic Novel by Kalki* (Chennai: Kavitha Publications, 2016).

4. A Shivalinga is a cylindrical shaft that is commonly worshipped in temples as an abstract representation of the god Shiva.

5. "Kundrathur and Venkaadu Visit."

6. ICMOS, "The Nara Document on Authenticity," International Council on Monuments and Sites, 1994, http://www.icomos.org/charters/nara-e.pdf.

7. For a summary and assessment of these changing protocols, see Tim Winter, "Beyond Eurocentrism? Heritage Conservation and the Politics of Difference," *International Journal of Heritage Studies* 20, no. 2 (February 17, 2014): 123–37, http://doi.org/10.1080/13527258.2012.736403; and Orbaşli, "Conservation Theory in the Twenty-First Century."

8. Mark Twain, *Following the Equator: A Journey around the World* (Hartford, CT: American Publishing Company, 1901), 2:83.

9. John Marshall, *Conservation Manual: A Handbook for the Use of Archaeological Officers and Others Entrusted with the Care of Ancient Monuments* (Calcutta: Superintendent of Government Printing, India, 1923), 10; italics are original.

10. Indra Sengupta, "A Conservation Code for the Colony: John Marshall's Conservation Manual and Monument Preservation between India and Europe," in *Archaeologizing Heritage? Transcultural Entanglements between Local Social Practices and Global Virtual Realities*, ed. Monica Juneja and Michael S. Falser (Berlin: Springer, 2013), 21–37.

11. Deborah Sutton, "Devotion, Antiquity, and Colonial Custody of the Hindu Temple in British India," *Modern Asian Studies* 47, no. 1 (January 2013): 155, http://doi.org/10.1017/S0026749X11000655.

12. The list of centrally protected monuments in Tamil Nadu is available here: http://www.asichennai.gov.in/monuments_full_list.html. For the list of monuments under the protection of the state department of archaeology, see http://www.tnarch.gov.in/monuments-subnames.

13. Staff Reporter, "Heritage Wardens Symposium in Coimbatore," *REACH Foundation* blog, July 12, 2012, http://reachhistory.blogspot.com/2012/07/.

14. Other organizations involved in similar work include Women's Renaissance Centre Chennai in Tamil Nadu, http://www.wrcchennai.com/; Ugra Narasmiha Charitable Trust in Kerala, http://ugranarasimha.in/; Bharata Punarutthana Trust in Bengaluru, http://reclaimtemples.org/; and Arsha Seva Kendram in Coimbatore, http://arshasevakendram.org/.

15. Harsha Bhat, "This Non-profit Body Which Has Restored Over 200 Heritage Temples Should Be Celebrated," *Swarajya Magazine*, September 3, 2018, http://swarajyamag.com/culture/this-non-profit-body-which-has-restored-over-200-heritage-temples-needs-to-be-celebrated.

16. Saloni Mathur and Kavita Singh, "Reincarnations of the Museum," in *Asian Art History in the Twenty-First Century*, ed. Vishakha N. Desai, Clark Studies in the Visual Arts (Williamstown, MA: Sterling and Francine Clark Art Institute, 2007), 165.

17. This is the position of Hindu majoritarianism, which is not the historically verifiable truth. For instance, Christianity arrived in South India in the 1st century CE; and Buddhism was prevalent in Tamil Nadu before the rise of Hinduism in the 9th century.

18. REACH Foundation, "Arasar Kovil, Edamachi and Kidangarai—Conserve Heritage," *REACH Foundation* blog, accessed March 30, 2021, http://conserveheritage.org/index.php/tours/temple-visits/arasar-kovil-edamachi-kidangarai/.

19. Prashannt, @VAJR, Twitter post, November 6, 2020, http://twitter.com/search?q=%40VAJR%20%40ASIGoI&src=typed_query. I thank Swasti Kumar for drawing my attention to this tweet.

20. Hari Prasath Kanna, @hardyatrow, Twitter post, March 29, 2021, http://twitter.com/hardyatrow/status/1376516151191085062.

21. Sadhguru, @SadhguruJV, Twitter post, March 24, 2021, http://twitter.com/SadhguruJV/status/1374688284194959361.

CONTRIBUTORS

Jennifer Bajorek is associate professor of comparative literature and visual studies at Hampshire College and a research associate of the Faculty of Art, Design, and Architecture at the University of Johannesburg. She writes and does research on literature, art, and photography, with a geographic focus on contemporary Africa and a cultural focus on Francophone worlds. Her research on photography in West Africa includes over a dozen years of collaborations with artists, curators, and museum and heritage professionals in the region and has also been published in book form, in *Unfixed: Photography and Decolonial Imagination in West Africa* (Duke, 2020).

Sven Dupré is director of the Research Institute for History and Art History, and professor of the history of art, science and technology at Utrecht University and at the University of Amsterdam (affiliated with the Conservation & Restoration Program). Previously, he was professor of the history of knowledge at the Freie Universität and director of the research group Art and Knowledge in Premodern Europe at the Max Planck Institute for the History of Science in Berlin. Recent publications include *Histories of Conservation and Art History in Modern Europe* (Routledge, 2022) and *Reconstruction, Replication and Re-enactment in the Humanities and Social Sciences* (Amsterdam University Press, 2020).

Noémie Étienne is professor of art history at the University of Bern and a specialist in the fields of early modern art and material culture, heritage, conservation, and museum studies. Her book *The Restoration of Paintings in Paris, 1750–1815: Practice, Discourse, Materiality* was first published in French in 2012 (Presses Universitaires de Rennes) and subsequently translated by the Getty Conservation Institute in 2017. Her most recent book is *The Art of the Anthropological Diorama* (Les presses du reel, 2020; De Gruyter, 2021), and her current research project is titled "Global Conservation: Histories and Theories."

Annika Svendsen Finne is assistant conservator at Modern Art Conservation and a PhD candidate in art history at the Institute of Fine Arts, New York University. Finne holds an MA and MS in the conservation of historic and artistic works, with a specialty in paintings conservation, from the Institute of Fine Arts. Previously, she worked in the painting conservation department of the Yale University Art Gallery and received additional conservation training at the Museo Nacional del Prado, Kunsthistorisches Museum, and the Museum of Modern Art. She has taught at the Cooper Union School for the Advancement of Art and Science.

Caroline Fowler is the Starr Director of the Research and Academic Program at the Clark Art Institute and teaches in the Graduate Program in the History of Art at Williams College. She is the author of *Drawing and the Senses: An Early Modern History* (Harvey Miller Series in Baroque Art, 2016) and *The Art of Paper: From the Holy Lands to the Americas* (Yale University Press, 2019). She is a specialist in the early modern period, with a focus on the materiality of prints and drawings, philosophies of conservation, the archive and its absences, and the failures and necessities of global art history.

Yukio Lippit is Jeffrey T. Chambers and Andrea Okamura Professor of the History of Art and Architecture at Harvard University. He specializes in Japanese painting. His book *Painting of the Realm: The Kano House of Painters in Seventeenth-Century Japan* (University of Washington Press, 2012) was awarded the Charles Rufus Morey Book Award by the College Art Association and the John Whitney Hall Book Prize by the Association of Asian Studies. Recent publications include *Japanese Zen Buddhism and the Impossible Painting* (Getty, 2017) and *The Artist in Edo* (National Gallery of Art, 2018).

Murad Khan Mumtaz is an assistant professor of Asian art history at Williams College. His book *Faces of God: Images of Devotion in Indo-Muslim Painting* is under contract with Brill. His other publications include essays on the visual and literary reception of the poet-saint Kabir in Muslim South Asia, portraits of saints as aids to meditation in Mughal India, and devotional artworks from early modern Kashmir. Murad examines historical intersections of art, literature, and religious expression in South Asia, with a primary focus on Indo-Muslim patronage. He is also an artist trained in traditional Indian painting techniques.

Brian Michael Murphy is dean of the college and director of the MFA in public action at Bennington College. He is the author of *We the Dead: Preserving Data at the End of the World* (University of North Carolina Press, 2022), and his writings have appeared in *Kenyon Review, Narrative, Kweli, Fairy Tale Review,* and in Italian translation in *Ácoma.* He is a Fulbright Scholar and a recipient of grants from the National Endowment for the Humanities and the Vermont Arts Council. He coedited the *Media-N* special issue "Afterlives of Data" and is managing and nonfiction editor of *Northwest Review.*

Alexander Nagel is Craig Hugh Smyth Professor of Fine Arts at the Institute of Fine Arts, New York University. He teaches courses and writes mostly about late-medieval and early modern European art. His work examines how visual art allows humans to see through time and orient themselves in the world, as well as what happens when models and artifacts of visual art cross temporal and geographical boundaries. Pursuing these interests has engaged him in the history of art history and art conservation, global art studies in postcolonial contexts, the history and theory of anthropology, and histories of humanism and posthumanism.

Alva Noë is a writer and philosopher living in Berkeley, California, and New York. He is the author of *Action in Perception*; *Out of Our Heads: Why You Are Not Your Brain and Other Lessons from the Biology of Consciousness*; *Varieties of Presence*; *Strange Tools: Art and Human Nature*; *Infinite Baseball: Notes from a Philosopher at the Ballpark*; and *Learning To Look: Dispatches from the Art World*. He is a professor of philosophy at the University of California, Berkeley, where he is also a member of the Center for New Media, the Institute for Cognitive and Brain Sciences, and the Program in Critical Theory. He is an Einstein Visiting Fellow at the Free University in Berlin.

Iwatarō Oka is the CEO of Oka Bokkodo Co., Ltd, a conservation studio for National Treasures and Important Cultural Properties in Kyoto, Japan. He received his MA in the history of art in 1996, and in 1997–98 served as a research assistant at the Freer Gallery of Art in the National Museum of Asian Art, Smithsonian Institution. In 2016, he received his PhD from the Kyoto Institute of Technology. In recent years, his research has focused on innovations in the conservation practices for painting and calligraphy, as well as the history of conservation practice.

Fernando Domínguez Rubio is an associate professor of communication at the University of California, San Diego. He holds a PhD in sociology from Cambridge University. He is the author of *Still Life: Ecologies of the Modern Imagination at the Art Museum* (University of Chicago Press, 2020), an ethnography of the Museum of Modern Art, New York, exploring the technologies, climatic infrastructures, and forms of care and labor required to prevent artworks from falling apart. He has written numerous articles on material culture, art, and urban infrastructures. He is also the coeditor of *The Politics of Knowledge* (Routledge, 2012).

Gabriela Siracusano specializes in the material dimension of artistic production from the sixteenth century to the present. She is a scientific researcher at CONICET (National Research Council, Argentina) and director of the Centro MATERIA at the Universidad Nacional de Tres de Febrero (UNTREF). Professor and chair at both UBA and UNTREF, she was a Guggenheim Fellow in 2006–7 and a Getty Scholar in 2016. Siracusano is the author of *El Poder de los Colores* (FCE, 2005; ALAA award 2006), *Pigments and Power in the Andes* (Archetype, 2011), and *La Paleta del Espanto* (Unsamedita, 2011), and coeditor with Agustina R. Romero of *Materia Americana* (Eduntref, 2020).

Kavita Singh is professor at the School of Arts and Aesthetics of Jawaharlal Nehru University, where she teaches courses in the history of Indian painting, particularly the Mughal and Rajput schools, and the history and politics of museums. Singh has published on secularism and religiosity, fraught national identities, and the memorialization of difficult histories as they relate to museums in South Asia and beyond. She has also published essays and monographs on aspects of Mughal and Rajput painting, particularly on style as a signifying system. In 2018, she received the Infosys Prize in Humanities, and she was elected to the American Academy of Arts and Sciences in 2020.

CLARK STUDIES IN THE VISUAL ARTS

The Two Art Histories: The Museum and the University (2002)
Edited by Charles W. Haxthausen
With essays by Dawn Ades, Andreas Beyer, Richard R. Brettell, Stephen Deuchar, Sybille Ebert-Schifferer, Ivan Gaskell, Eckhard Gillen, Richard Kendall, John House, Patricia Mainardi, Griselda Pollock, Mark Rosenthal, Barbara Maria Stafford, Gary Tinterow, William H. Truettner, and Michael F. Zimmermann, and an afterword by Richard Brilliant

Art History, Aesthetics, Visual Studies (2002)
Edited by Michael Ann Holly and Keith Moxey
With essays by David Carrier, Philip Fisher, Hal Foster, Ivan Gaskell, Jonathan Gilmore, Thomas DaCosta Kaufmann, Michael Kelly, Karen Lang, Stephen Melville, Kobena Mercer, Nicholas Mirzoeff, W. J. T. Mitchell, Griselda Pollock, Irene J. Winter, and Janet Wolff

The Art Historian: National Traditions and Institutional Practices (2003)
Edited by Michael F. Zimmermann
With essays by Mieke Bal, Stephen Bann, Horst Bredekamp, H. Perry Chapman, Georges Didi-Huberman, Eric Fernie, Françoise Forster-Hahn, Carlo Ginzburg, Charles W. Haxthausen, Karen Michels, Willibald Sauerländer, Alain Schnapp, and Michael F. Zimmermann

Anthropologies of Art (2005)
Edited by Mariët Westermann
With essays by Hans Belting, Janet Catherine Berlo, Suzanne Preston Blier, Steve Bourget, Sarah Brett-Smith, Shelly Errington, David Freedberg, Anna Grimshaw, Jonathan Hay, Howard Morphy, Ikem Stanley Okoye, Francesco Pellizzi, and Ruth B. Phillips

The Lure of the Object (2006)
Edited by Stephen Melville
With essays by Emily Apter, George Baker, Malcolm Baker, John Brewer, Martha Buskirk, Margaret Iversen, Ewa Lajer-Burcharth, Karen Lang, Mark A. Meadow, Helen Molesworth, Marcia Pointon, Christian Scheidemann, Edward J. Sullivan, and Martha Ward

Compression vs. Expression: Containing and Explaining the World's Art (2006)
Edited by John Onians
With essays by Cao Yiqiang, Wilfried van Damme, Rita Eder, James Elkins, Arlene K. Fleming, Derek Gillman, Jyotindra Jain, Cecilia F. Klein, Yves Le Fur, Dominic Marner, Anitra Nettleton, John Onians, Edmund P. Pillsbury, Michael Rinehart, David Summers, and Georges S. Zouain

Asian Art History in the Twenty-First Century (2007)
Edited by Vishakha N. Desai
With essays by Frederick M. Asher, Melissa Chiu, John Clark, Gao Shiming, Yukio Lippit, Saloni Mathur and Kavita Singh, Kaja M. McGowan, Rana Mitter, Alexandra Munroe, Jerome Silbergeld, Nancy S. Steinhardt, Akira Takagishi, and Gennifer Weisenfeld

Architecture between Spectacle and Use (2008)
Edited by Anthony Vidler
With essays by Mario Carpo, Beatriz Colomina, Mark Dorrian, Kurt W. Forster, Hal Foster, Sarah Williams Goldhagen, Michael Hays, Mark Jarzombek, Felicity D. Scott, Terry Smith, Anthony Vidler, and Mark Wigley

The Meaning of Photography (2008)
Edited by Robin Kelsey and Black Stimson
With essays by Geoffrey Batchen, François Brunet, Mary Ann Doane, José Luis Falconi, Robin Kelsey, Douglas R. Nickel, Blake Stimson, and John Tagg, and additional contributions by Lars Kiel Bertelsen, Anne McCauley, Jorge Ribalta, John Roberts, Eric Rosenberg, Eric C. Shiner, and Bernd Stiegler
Photo essays by Sharon Harper, Lilla LoCurto and Bill Outcault, Fiona Tan, and Akram Zaatari

What Is Research in the Visual Arts? Obsession, Archive, Encounter (2008)
Edited by Michael Ann Holly and Marquard Smith
With essays by Ernst van Alphen, Mieke Bal, Marc Gotlieb, Serge Guilbaut, Michael Ann Holly, Akira Mizuta Lippit, W. J. T. Mitchell, Joanne Morra, Sina Najafi, Alexander Nemerov, Celeste Olalquiaga, Alex Potts, and Reva Wolf

The Migrant's Time: Rethinking Art History and Diaspora (2011)
Edited by Saloni Mathur
With essays by Stanley Abe, Esra Akcan, Iftikhar Dadi, Jennifer González, Ranajit Guha, May Joseph, Miwon Kwon, Kobena Mercer, W. J. T. Mitchell, Aamir R. Mufti, Nikos Papastergiadis, Richard J. Powell, Edward W. Said, and Nora A. Taylor

Fictions of Art History (2013)
Edited by Mark Ledbury
With essays by Paul Barolsky, Thomas Crow, Gloria Kury, Mark Ledbury, Ralph Lieberman, Maria H. Loh, Alexander Nemerov, Joanna Scott, Cole Swensen, Marianna Torgovnick, Caroline Vout, and Marina Warner

Art History in the Wake of the Global Turn (2014)
Edited by Jill H. Casid and Aruna D'Souza
With essays by Esra Akcan, Jill H. Casid, Parul Dave-Mukherji, Aruna D'Souza, Talinn Grigor, Ranjana Khanna, Kobena Mercer, Nicholas Mirzoeff, Steven Nelson, Todd Porterfield, Raqs Media Collective, Kishwar Rizvi, David J. Roxburgh, and Alessandra Russo

Art History and Emergency (2016)
Edited by David Breslin and Darby English
With essays by Caroline Arscott, Manuel J. Borja-Villel, Thomas Crow, Patrick D. Flores, Theaster Gates, Kajri Jain, Anatoli Mikhailov, Mary Miller, Molly Nesbit, Our Literal Speed, and Howard Singerman

Ecologies, Agents, Terrains (2018)
Edited by Christopher P. Heuer and Rebecca Zorach
With essays by Maggie Cao, Jeffrey Jerome Cohen, Matthew Coolidge, Vittoria Di Palma, Robert Felfe, Chelsea Mikael Frazier, Ghana ThinkTank, Christopher P. Heuer, Jessica L. Horton, Sarah Kanouse, Sonya S. Lee, Dylan T. Miner, James Nisbet, Verity Platt, Aurora Tang, Julian Yates, and Rebecca Zorach

This publication was conceived by the Research and Academic Program at the Clark Art Institute. A related conference, titled Conservation I Making I Art I History, was held April 8–9, 2021, at the Clark. For information on programs and publications at the Clark, visit clarkart.edu.

Produced by the Publications Department of the Clark Art Institute, 225 South Street, Williamstown, Massachusetts 01267

Anne Roecklein, *Managing Editor*
Kevin Bicknell, *Editor*
Annie Jun, *Assistant Editor*
David Murphy, *Rights and Image Use Associate*

Copyedited and proofread by Kristin Swan
Design and layout by Roy Brooks, Fold Four, Inc.
Printed by Puritan Capital
Distributed by Yale University Press, New Haven and London, 302 Temple Street, P.O. 902040, New Haven, CT 06520-9040
yalebooks.com/art

Printed and bound in the United States
10 9 8 7 6 5 4 3 2 1

Cover illustration: fig. 8.9 (detail); Title page illustration: fig. 11.3 (detail)

Cataloging-in-Publication Data is available from the Library of Congress.
Library of Congress Control Number: 2022914548
978-1-935998-55-6 (Clark Art Institute)
978-0-300-26694-8 (Yale University Press)

Photography Credits

Permission to reproduce images is provided courtesy of the owners listed in the captions. Additional photography credits are as follows:

Mumtaz, Copy I Repeat: Courtesy of Williams College Museum of Art (fig. 1.1); Creative Commons Public Domain, CCO 1.0 Universal (CCO 1.0) (figs. 1.2, 1.4, 1.5, 1.7, 1.10); photo courtesy of the Metropolitan Museum of Art, photo by Hyla Skopitz (fig. 1.3)

Finne, The Overpaint-ability of Madonnas in 1300s Siena: ArtStor, SCALA, Florence / Art Resource, NY (figs. 2.2–2.4, 2.7)

Lippit, Japanese Painting: Photo by John Tsantes and Neill Greentree (fig. 3.7)

Murphy, The Bettmann Morgue: Getty Images / Bettmann (figs. 7.1, 7.2, 7.4, 7.5); photo by European / FPG / Archive Photos / Hulton Archive / Getty Images (fig. 7.3); AP Images / Carl E. Linde (fig. 7.6)

Siracusano, Minimum Worlds: Museo de Arte Hispanoamericano Isaac Fernández Blanco, Gobierno de la Ciudad Autónoma de Buenos Aires (figs. 8.1, 8.2, 8.4, 8.5, 8.9, 8.10); Centro Materia, UNTREF (fig. 8.3); IIPC-Tarea, UNSAM (figs. 8.6, 8.7); photo by Juan López (fig. 8.8)

Rubio, The Arts of the Same: © Fernando Maquieria, VEGAP, 2017 (fig. 9.1); Attilio Maranzano (fig. 9.2); courtesy of the author (fig. 9.3)

Bajorek, But Who Decided?: Photo by Leslie Rabine, courtesy of Gnilane Ly Faye (fig. 11.1); photo by Ida Mèhomey (fig. 11.3); courtesy of Fatima Fall (fig. 11.4); photo by Caroline Lacey, courtesy of Resolution Photo (figs. 11.5–11.8)

Étienne, Can Conservation Be Decentered?: Photo courtesy of the Museum of Ethnography, Stockholm (figs. 12.1–12.4); photo by Iver Fougner (fig. 12.1); photo by Sanna Törneman (fig. 12.2); photo by Tony Sandin (fig. 12.4); photo by the author (fig. 12.5); REUTERS/Philippe Wojazer (fig. 12.6); photo by Wagner Souza e Silva MAE-USP, Archive Museum der Kulturen Basel (fig. 12.7)

Singh, Conserving Monuments, Reviving Temples: Photo courtesy of J. Chandrasekaran of REACH Foundation (figs. 13.1, 13.2, 13.4, 13.5); screenshot by the author (fig. 13.3); photo by Nandhinikandhasamy, 2016, via Wikimedia Commons, CC4.0 license (fig. 13.6); photo by Rengeshb, available under CC3.0 (fig. 13.7); photo by Rajendran Ganesan (fig. 13.8); http://twitter.com/hardyatrow/status/1376516151191085062?s=20&t=cALo7yP45ZKi2TpQARU8xg (fig. 13.9)